SOUTHERN EXPOSURE

SOUTHERN EXPOSURE
Modern Japanese Literature
from Okinawa

EDITED BY

MICHAEL MOLASKY AND STEVE RABSON

UNIVERSITY OF HAWAI'I PRESS

Honolulu

Library of Congress Cataloging-in-Publication Data

Southern Exposure : modern Japanese literature from Okinawa / edited by Michael
Molasky and Steve Rabson.
p. cm.
Includes bibliographical references.
Contents: A verse from "Translations of old Okinawan poems" (ca. 1922) /
Serei Kunio — My last letter (1927) / Nakamura Kare — Entering the harbor of a
southern island (1931) ; Dead body (1931) / Tsukayama Issui — A conversation (1395) ;
Shell-shocked island (1964) / Yamanokuchi Baku — Dream revelations (1984) /
Takara Ben — Officer Ukuma (1922) / Ikemiyagi Sekiho — Memoirs of a declining
Ryukyuan woman (1932) ; In defense of 'Memoirs of a declining Ryukyuan woman' /
Kushi Fusako — Mr. Saito of heaven building (1938) / Yamanokuchi Baku — Dark
flowers (1955) / Kishaba Jun — Turtleback tombs (1966) / Oshiro Tatsuhiro — Bones
(1973) / Shima Tsuyoshi — The silver motorcycle (1977) / Nakahama Shin — Love letter
from L.A. (1978) / Shimokawa Hiroshi — Love suicide at Kamaara (1984) / Yoshida Sueko
—Will o' the wisp (1985) / Yamanoha Nobuko — Droplets (1997) /
Medoruma Shun — Fortunes by the sea (1998) / Matayoshi Eiki.
ISBN 0-8248-2169-6 (cloth : alk. paper) — ISBN 0-8248-2300-1 (pbk. : alk. paper)
1. Japanese literature—Japan—Okinawa-ken.   2. Japanese literature—20th century.
I. Molasky, Michael, 1956–   II. Rabson, Steve, 1943–

PL886.O542 S68 2000
895.6'08095229—dc21   00–024001

University of Hawai'i Press books are printed on acid-free paper and meet the guidelines
for permanence and durability of the Council on Library Resources.

Printed by The Maple-Vail Book Manufacturing Group
Designed by: Trina Stahl
Cover art: Beach on the border of Camp Schwab in Henoko, Nago City, Okinawa. The sign
reads "U.S. Property" in English and "Tachi-iri kinishi" (No Trespassing) in Japanese.
Photograph by Ishikawa Mao.

For Okamoto Keitoku and Nakahodo Masanori

Contents

FICTION

PREFACE

Compiling a literary anthology invariably entails difficult choices. We have been sorely tempted to include dramatic works, social criticism, and even the lyrics of local folk songs, since all are vital facets of modern Okinawan culture. But time and space constraints have forced us to limit this anthology to fiction and to a small sampling of poetry. We regret being unable to include the work of talented Okinawan writers such as Nagadō Eikichi and Sakiyama Tami, but we hope that this anthology whets the English-language reader's appetite for more literature from Okinawa and encourages other translators to fill in the gaps. We would be particularly gratified if Okinawa's literature begins to find its way into translated collections of Japanese literature. It is with this hope in mind that our anthology is subtitled "Modern Japanese Literature from Okinawa."

For those unfamiliar with the islands, we should note that the name "Okinawa" can refer to the Ryukyu archipelago as a whole or specifically to its main island, where nearly all works of fiction in this anthology are set. Experienced readers of Japanese fiction will not be surprised to find that many of the stories included here use a single English letter to denote place names. Thus one story refers to "K Town" and another to "T— Island." To first-time readers this may seem awkward at first, but it is common practice in twentieth-century Japanese literature, and in any case, translators are left few alternatives but to retain the cryptic reference. All Japanese personal names appear in Japanese order (surname first) throughout this book. A macron placed over an "o" or "u" in a Japanese word indicates a long vowel, but we have omitted macrons over the common place names "Tokyo" and "Ryukyu" except when they appear in a Japanese phrase or book title. We must also note that two translations included in this anthology were previously published in the following journals: Norma Field's translation of Takara Ben's poem, "Dream Revelations," first appeared in *Positions* (vol. 1, no. 3); Michael Molasky's translation of Medoruma Shun's "Droplets" was first published in *Southwest Review* (vol. 83, no. 4, Winter 1998).

We are delighted that the University of Hawai'i Press agreed to publish this anthology, and our thanks go to our editor, Sharon Yamamoto, who supported this project from the outset, and to Susan Biggs Corrado for her astute copyediting. We are also grateful to the two anonymous outside readers who offered valuable suggestions for improving the manuscript. In Okinawa, Professors Komesu Okifumi and Yamazato Katsunori, both of the University of the Ryukyus, offered advice on select translations, and the authors Ōshiro Tatsuhiro and Medoruma Shun met with us to answer questions we had in translating their work. We wish to express our gratitude to all of the writers (or their families) who permitted us to include their work in this anthology. Special thanks must go to Professor Higa Minoru, who encouraged us to undertake this project. Our mentors in Okinawa, Professors Okamoto Keitoku and Nakahodo Masanori of the University of the Ryukyus, have been extraordinarily generous with their time and with their immense knowledge of modern Okinawan literature. It is to them that we dedicate this book.

INTRODUCTION

MICHAEL MOLASKY AND STEVE RABSON

IN 1996 AND 1997, writers from Okinawa won the Akutagawa Prize, Japan's most prestigious award for fiction. Matayoshi Eiki, a veteran author in his own right, became the first Okinawan to receive the award in twenty-five years with his 1996 novella, *Pig's Revenge*.[1] At the time, jaded critics observed that the competition had grown so weak in recent decades as to render the semi-annual literary prize practically meaningless. Besides, they added, Okinawa had been in the headlines daily for opposing the Japanese government over its support for keeping American military bases on their islands, so it should come as no surprise that the award went to an Okinawan writer. On top of that, the Akutagawa Prize had just been given to a writer of Korean descent, and it was obvious that Japanese "minority literature" was a hot commodity. So why all the fuss, these critics asked.

Even less cynical observers agree that for the past two decades, some of Japan's most creative artists have devoted themselves to producing *manga* and *anime* rather than fiction or poetry. A few have even argued that contemporary Japanese fiction has increasingly come to resemble these popular comic books and animated movies and that today's authors have turned their backs on their great literary predecessors. Where, they ask, are the Japanese novelists today who promise to become the next Dostoyevsky or Proust, Soseki or Tanizaki?

Yet when a virtually unknown Okinawan writer named Medoruma Shun (who happens to be an avid reader of Dostoyevsky) was awarded the Akutagawa Prize in August 1997 for his story, "Droplets," even the harshest critics were given pause. Okinawa's entire population amounts to a mere 1 percent of Japan's, and practically all of its active writers live in the remote island prefecture, far from Tokyo's literary scene. Few Okinawan authors support themselves solely through writing; most have full-time jobs—including Medoruma (a high school teacher)—which limits the amount of time they can devote to their literature. These conditions, and the propensity of literary award committees to avoid similarly "unusual" candidates two years in a row, made a second Okinawan writer an unlikely bet for the 1997 prize. Thus when Medoruma was selected with near unanimous acclaim, the critics suddenly stopped debating the politics of the committee's decision and instead began discussing the story itself. Critics also asked why Okinawa seemed to provide such fertile soil for aspiring writers while, in many of their minds, literature in mainland Japan was languishing.[2]

Southern Exposure offers English-language readers the chance to draw their own conclusions about the work of Medoruma, Matayoshi, and other Okinawan writers. Clearly, literary awards are not always the most reliable indicators of a work's "value" (however one chooses to define it), nor can they safely predict a work's potential staying power. And although the entire prefecture seems to rejoice whenever an Okinawan writer wins a major literary prize, the authors themselves are well aware that fame in Japan is often short-lived (especially with the plethora of literary awards being handed out these days) and that they must continue to walk a fine line if they are to retain their local readership while being accessible to mainland Japanese. For these reasons, we have included works by comparatively unknown local writers as well as by critically acclaimed Okinawans—such as Yamanokuchi Baku, Ōshiro Tatsuhiro, Matayoshi Eiki, and Medoruma Shun—who regularly publish in mainstream Japanese literary forums. We have also tried to select works that are representative of their respective eras yet accessible to English-language readers with a limited knowledge of Okinawa.

Of course, readers will benefit from some familiarity with Okinawa—its literary and cultural traditions, its history and landscape—hence this introduction, which is divided into two parts. Below, we offer a brief overview of Okinawa's modern literary history, focusing on its relation to mainland Japanese literature and on the particular linguistic challenges facing Okinawan writers. This section is followed by a broader discussion of Okinawan history and culture. The anthology itself is arranged chronologically by genre. It begins with a small sampling of poetry, mostly from the 1920s and 1930s, when it was poets such as Yamanokuchi Baku (and not writers of fiction) who were making the biggest splash in Japanese literary circles. Yet our emphasis is on fiction, especially that published after Okinawa's reversion to Japanese prefectural status in 1972, for this "post-reversion era" has enjoyed an efflorescence of cultural activity that continues unabated today, in both literature and the performing arts.

OKINAWA'S best-known cultural export during the past quarter century has been the hybrid musical tradition known as "Okinawan rock." Created largely by musicians who cut their teeth playing hard rock for G.I.s in Okinawa's base towns, this music evolved and gradually broadened its appeal by adapting instruments, melodic patterns, and costumes from the region's vibrant folk music tradition. As one of Japan's minority groups, Okinawans have pioneered the nation's "ethno-pop" music scene (although it must be added that many Japanese, including Okinawans, are reluctant to apply the term "minority group" to their own society). In drama as well, Okinawan troupes have gained popularity in recent years as they began performing in cities throughout Japan. Often adorned in traditional regional garb and mixing local dialects with standard Japanese, several theater groups have succeeded in amalgamating their distinctive folk culture and its comic traditions into an accessible art form that seems at once exotic and familiar to Japanese audiences.

Compared with the performing arts, Okinawan literature has enjoyed less commercial success in Japan's cultural marketplace. Of course, few mainland Japanese writers of what is considered "serious literature" *(junbungaku)* manage to survive on book sales alone. Most take on other writing jobs to supplement their income, publishing essays and criticism in newspapers and magazines, thereby keeping their names in the public eye. Okinawan writers, on the other hand, have largely eschewed this approach, in part because they simply do not have the name value of mainland writers, but also because it is difficult to sustain the requisite connections with Tokyo's literary world when one lives so far away.[3] Isolation may have its virtues, however, and as we hope this anthology shows, Okinawa has fostered an unabashedly "regional" literature capable of appealing well beyond its narrow borders. Rooted in a lush, semi-tropical landscape and forged by the history of Japan's prewar subjugation of the islands, by the devastating war that ensued, and by the prolonged postwar U.S. occupation and its ongoing military presence, Okinawans today are writing the kind of ambitious literature that seems increasingly rare in mainland Japan. Okinawan literature maintains an intense engagement with nature, society, and history equaled by few Japanese writers since Nakagami Kenji (1946–1992) made his debut in the 1970s. And it must not be forgotten that Nakagami's idiosyncratic literary world was partially a product of his own background as an outcaste *burakumin*.

From Japan's 1879 annexation of the Ryukyu Islands until the end of the Pacific War, Okinawans were treated as second-class citizens and, like the *burakumin*, tended to suffer from a profound sense of inferiority toward "mainstream Japanese." Many Okinawans, especially those who aspired to the elite class or who worked in mainland Japan, struggled to assimilate Japanese ways of life—often with little success and at great emotional cost. If the Battle of Okinawa and ensuing American military occupation are the central themes of the region's postwar literature, then the struggle over Okinawa's cultural identity appears to be the predominant issue in prewar literature. This struggle is described in several works featured in this anthology: Ikemiyagi Sekihō's "Officer Ukuma" (1922), Kushi Fusako's "Memoirs of a Declining Ryukyuan Woman" (1932), and Yamanokuchi Baku's 1935 poem, "A Conversation," and his 1938 story, "Mr. Saitō of Heaven Building" (although in the latter work, the character who tries to "pass" as Japanese is actually Korean).

Yet not every prewar Okinawan writer was so concerned with questions of identity. For example, at roughly the same time as the above works were published, a group of poets, including two featured here—Nakamura Kare and Tsukayama Issui—began pursuing other themes and experimenting with modes of expression closely identified in Japan with literary modernism. Both men spent time in Tokyo and were affiliated with the coterie of prominent Japanese poets: Nakamura with Kitahara Hakushū and Tsukayama with Satō Sōnosuke. Although Nakamura and Tsukayama never achieved the popularity or widespread critical acclaim of Yamanokuchi Baku, they did succeed in creating memorable works that attest to the variety and vitality of Okinawan poetry in the prewar years.[4]

We begin our anthology with the 1920s because this is when a range of discernibly "modern" (but not necessarily modernist) Okinawan writers first emerged.[5] As with their mainland Japanese counterparts, Okinawan writers published comparatively little literature of interest from the late 1930s until the end of the Pacific War. In the early postwar years, however, while a young generation of Japanese writers such as Ōoka Shōhei, Noma Hiroshi, Shiina Rinzō, and Ishikawa Jun were bringing forth challenging new works, living conditions in Okinawa were so desperate that few residents had the leisure to write. The first dynamic period in postwar Okinawan literature did not arrive until the mid-1950s with the appearance of the radical student magazine, *Ryūdai bungaku* (University of the Ryukyus literature). Begun by students at the University of the Ryukyus as a forum for publishing their own fiction and poetry, the magazine quickly emerged as a hotbed for critical debates about the "proper" role of literature in a society undergoing foreign military occupation. Philosophically, the students were inspired by the "socialist realism" of Tokyo critics such as Odagiri Hideo and Sasaki Kiichi, who were affiliated with the leftist literary journals *Kindai bungaku* (Modern literature) and *Shin Nihon bungaku* (New Japanese literature). The student editors of *Ryūdai bungaku* insisted that literature should address contemporary political and social conditions in Okinawa, and they published not only literary works excoriating the American occupiers, but theoretical treatises equally critical of local writers prominent at that time.[6] Their take-no-prisoners assault on older Okinawan writers led to heated public discussions of literary theory, politics, and history. But as a forum for fiction and poetry, *Ryūdai bungaku* published relatively few works that continue to be read today. We have included Kishaba Jun's 1955 story, "Dark Flowers," as an example of the fiction published in this student magazine.[7] "Dark Flowers" was reprinted the following year in the national circulation monthly *Shin Nihon bungaku,* a leftist literary magazine based in Tokyo that had served as an inspiration for many of *Ryūdai bungaku*'s early contributors.

Ryūdai bungaku earned a place in postwar Okinawan literary history not only for the lively debates it spawned, but also because two of its editors, Arakawa Akira and Kawamitsu Shin'ichi, went on to become powerful journalists in Okinawa. Both men worked at *The Okinawa Times,* where they eventually rose to the positions of president and vice president, respectively. Arakawa and Kawamitsu also emerged as influential figures in the region's cultural life, for in addition to their work at the newspaper, each continued to write poetry and criticism, and in 1966 they founded *Shin Okinawa bungaku* (New Okinawan literature), a magazine that, unlike *Ryūdai bungaku*—which was narrow in its political and aesthetic sympathies—became Okinawa's preeminent forum for publishing a wide range of literature and criticism.[8] Two of the stories published in this anthology, Ōshiro Tatsuhiro's "Turtleback Tombs" (1966) and Yoshida Sueko's "Love Suicide at Kamaara" (1984), first appeared in *Shin Okinawa bungaku,* as did Ōshiro's prize-winning novella, *Cocktail Party.* Besides publishing regional literature and critical debates, the magazine featured interviews and essays by prominent mainland writers and intellectuals such as Ōe Kenzaburō, Irokawa Daikichi, and Yasuoka Shōtarō, as well as articles by foreign scholars of Okinawan culture.[9] By the 1990s, however, *Shin Okinawa bungaku*'s influence had begun to wane, and the final issue was published in 1993. Okinawa's reversion to Japan had brought many changes in the economic, social, and cultural spheres, so perhaps it was inevitable that a magazine so closely associated with earlier, more tumultuous times would give way as a new generation of writers emerged.[10]

This new generation included not only men such as Matayoshi Eiki and Medoruma Shun, mentioned earlier, but also several promising women writers, each of whom pursued different issues and developed her own narrative approach, thereby bringing welcome variety to Okinawa's literary landscape.[11] Few women had been active in Okinawan letters until the 1980s, when Sakiyama Tami, Nakawaka Naoko, Yamanoha Nobuko, and Yoshida Sueko began publishing stories that garnered acclaim by local critics. At present, none of these women writers has achieved a large readership outside Okinawa (they publish mainly in regional literary forums), but this may have more to do with the publishing industry than with the potential appeal of their work. In any case, readers of this anthology need only compare Yamanoha's "Will o' the Wisp" (1985) with Yoshida's "Love Suicide at Kamaara" (published the previous year) to appreciate the diversity of recent women's literature in Okinawa.

Looking back at the past eighty years of Okinawa's literature, one could claim, with only slight overstatement, that whereas the region's prewar writers were predominantly concerned with questions of Okinawan identity vis-à-vis mainland Japan, its postwar writers have often explored the same question, albeit refracted through the experience of war and American occupation. This is not to imply that modern Okinawan literature merely amounts to the practice of collective navel gazing; on the contrary, it is a tradition seriously engaged with the outside world, be it that of the natural environment or the forces of history. But even when the question of identity is not the focus of a given work, it invariably imposes itself on the writer, since Okinawa's physical topography, social customs, historical experience, and—of most immediate concern to writers of literature—its dialects (or languages) differ so sharply from those elsewhere in Japan that the problem of "Okinawan difference" is inescapable.

Admittedly, the extent of this difference is bound to diminish as a new generation of Okinawan writers emerges—writers who speak only standard Japanese, who experienced neither the war nor the ensuing American occupation, and who grew up with regular access to Japan's mass media and its big cities. But the writers represented in this volume have all faced the quandary of how culturally particularistic to make their literature. On the one hand, any work laden with unexplained references to Okinawa's landscape, religious practices, or historical events, not to mention any work written with long passages in regional dialect, risks alienating mainland Japanese readers. On the other hand, writers who appear too conscious of their mainland readers (as manifested in self-exoticization or didacticism) risk alienating their Okinawan readers. Nothing better crystallizes this dilemma than the "dialect problem" *(hōgen mondai)*. But before considering the use of Okinawan dialect in literary texts, it helps to be familiar with some basic linguistic insights into the nature of dialects.

Linguists remind us that the difference between a "language" and a "dialect" is often more of a political issue than a purely linguistic one.[12] "A language is merely a dialect with a national flag" is one way linguists have encapsulated this distinction; another is to describe a language as "a dialect with an army." For example, one could argue that we routinely refer to French, Italian, Portuguese, and Spanish as distinct languages primarily because they are the dominant languages within those separate political entities known (in English) as France, Italy, Portugal, and Spain. Yet many of the "dialects" spoken within China, India, Japan, and the nations of Africa exhibit greater linguistic variation (morphological, phonological, etc.) from one another than do these Romance languages. Among the Japanese "dialects," those of the Ryukyu Islands and of the indigenous Ainu of northern Japan differ most widely from modern, "standard" Japanese and could (if one ignored political and ideological reasons) justifiably be considered full-fledged languages. In fact, the dialects of the Ryukyus are, on average, less intelligible to Japanese speakers than are, say, Parisian French to monolingual speakers of Italian, and Portuguese to speakers of Spanish.[13] Further complicating the dialect problem, the Ryukyu Islands contain several languages/dialects that are unintelligible even to most Okinawans. Despite compelling reasons to refer to these as "Okinawan languages," to conform with standard practice (and to abide by political realities), we have referred to them in the conventional way, as "dialects," throughout this book.

Whether and how to employ dialect in a literary text remains a vexing question for Okinawan writers, since any choice carries with it serious ideological and financial implications. Should the entire text be written in dialect? If so, depending on how it is written, it might well be incomprehensible to over 99 percent of Japan's populace. And depending on which Ryukyuan dialect is used (for example, that of Miyako Island or Yonaguni Island), the text could elude even most Okinawan readers, thereby further reducing the potential audience.

Should dialect be restricted to passages consisting only of dialogue? Should it be glossed or written in *kanji* (Chinese characters) to make it more accessible? Is it acceptable to create a modified dialect—thereby sacrificing authenticity—in order to reduce the need for glosses?[14] These are only a few of the questions that regularly confront Okinawan writers. Nearly all of these writers today either eschew the use of dialect altogether or restrict it to select passages in their texts, which they gloss or modify to make accessible to the average Japanese reader.[15] Among those works represented in this anthology, several employ dialect: "Shell-shocked Island" (1964), "Turtleback Tombs,"[16] "Dream Revelations" (1984), and "Droplets" make the most explicit use of dialect, although none of these works is written primarily in dialect, and each is written so as to be accessible to readers of standard Japanese.

The use of dialect in literary texts also poses a quandary for translators. In this anthology, rather than requiring all translators to adopt the same approach to dialect, each individual has adopted an approach he or she felt best served the work at hand. As a result, the anthology presents many different ways of handling dialect in Okinawan texts:

1. render the dialect into standard English with little or no textual indication that dialect is used;
2. romanize rather than translate the words or phrases that appear in dialect and then define them using footnotes ("Shell-shocked Island," "Dream Revelations");
3. do the same without defining or translating the words (an approach used for select proper nouns in "Droplets" and "Fortunes by the Sea" [1998]);
4. italicize the word in dialect and offer an explanation in the text as unobtrusively as possible (many of our translators have selectively adopted this approach);
5. translate those passages appearing in dialect into an English-language dialect ("Droplets").[17]

Every option invariably entails a compromise, although the fifth may be the riskiest, since any given dialect carries with it such cultural and regional specificity that it threatens to defy translation into the dialect of another language.

Yet with certain texts there remain compelling reasons for trying to create an approximation of the dialect in translation. For example, in "Droplets," Medoruma Shun sparingly uses the dialect of the Motobu Peninsula in the northern part of Okinawa Island, not only to underscore the linguistic particularity of the setting, but also to subtly distinguish among individual characters in terms of social class. Thus in this text, gradations in dialect use—from a thoroughly "countrified" nonstandard dialect to standard Tokyo Japanese—establish critical differences among the story's characters. To cite only a few examples, the main character's wife, Ushi (which means cow and was once a common name given to girls in rural Okinawa), grew up working in the fields and peddling fish. We can assume that she never went beyond elementary school and has never left Okinawa. In short, she is portrayed as an uneducated woman who, if speaking American English, would more likely use "I ain't" than "I'm not." (To his credit, however, the author neither patronizes nor idealizes her.) In Medoruma's text, nearly all of Ushi's first-person thoughts and utterances appear in dialect, sometimes unglossed so as to retain its ring of authenticity. In contrast, Ushi's husband, Tokushō, attended an elite prewar high school and, although he is described as being uncomfortable speaking publicly in standard Japanese, this is the language in which his speech and thoughts are conveyed throughout most of the text. And the young doctor featured in the story, although Okinawan as well, speaks only in standard Japanese. After conferring with the author, the translator of "Droplets" tried to retain these differences by rendering select passages of dialect into a nonstandard American English based loosely on the speech patterns of Appalachia. Of course, whether this particular translation succeeds is for each reader to decide. But we believe that an English anthology of Japanese literature from Okinawa best serves its readers by offering a range of approaches to the translation of local dialect, thereby underscoring "the dialect problem" itself as well as the different textual strategies Okinawan writers have adopted for coping with it.

THE above discussion is intended to help readers situate Okinawa's modern literature in relation to mainstream Japanese literary history. The following introduction to the region's landscape, history, and culture should further enhance the reader's understanding of the literature contained in this anthology.

First-time visitors to Okinawa expecting to find a society utterly different from that of mainland Japan might be surprised at the many superficial resemblances between the two. They will notice the same signs in Japanese, the same ubiquitous emblems for Japanese corporations, the same department stores, fast food chains, and travel agencies as are found elsewhere in Japan. Yen is used for purchases, and Tokyo (standard) Japanese is spoken in the shops. Visitors can enjoy sushi, tempura, and *sake* in restaurants and sing the latest hits from Tokyo in *karaoke* bars. These songs are also on the radio, and mainland news, variety shows, and soap operas appear on nationwide network television.

Yet if Okinawa's social landscape has come to resemble that of Japan's main islands, its natural landscape remains distinctive—in spite of the environmental depredations caused by local development, Japanese resorts, and American military bases. Okinawa's semi-tropical climate brings warmer weather, except during summer, and is home to sugarcane, banyan trees, hibiscus flowers, and other plant life that strike mainland Japanese as exotic. Even the cherry blossoms bloom months earlier in Okinawa than on the mainland and burst forth in robust pinks instead of delicate whites. But the most distinctive facet of Okinawa's semi-tropical landscape is the sea, which glitters in brilliant sapphire blues and emerald greens beneath the puffy white clouds that hover just above its surface. These spectacular colors, produced by coral, are found nowhere in Japan except in the Ryukyu Islands, a name chosen by ancient Chinese meaning "circle of jewels." One story in this anthology, Yamanoha Nobuko's "Will o' the Wisp," offers a haunting yet voluptuous rendering of this underwater world of coral reefs.

Along with the striking natural scenery, first-time visitors cannot help but notice noisy low-flying aircraft, the camouflage-colored truck convoys, and the vast, sprawling bases among some forty U.S. military installations that occupy one-fifth of Okinawa Island, the largest and most populous in the Ryukyus. Approximately 30,000 troops and nearly an equal number of American dependents and civilian employees reside among the 1.2 million Okinawans. Unlike the mainland, where comparatively few American bases are distributed over an 800-mile stretch, Okinawa Island, only 67 miles long and comprising 0.6 percent of the nation's land, bears 75 percent of the total U.S. military presence in Japan.[18]

Throughout the islands, even on land adjacent to the bases, are elaborate stone tombs shaped like small houses, many with turtleback-style roofs not found in mainland Japan. And unlike elsewhere in Japan, small statues of guardian deities resembling miniature lions (known as *shiisaa*) are found perched on many buildings and homes. Family names on shop signs in Okinawa are different from mainland Japanese surnames. Restaurants everywhere serve Okinawan noodles, fruits, and vegetables not readily available elsewhere in Japan, as well as various cuts of pork in dishes resembling Chinese cuisine. As for liquid refreshment, men and women of all ages often prefer *awamori*, the local rice brandy, to mainland *sake* or imported liquors.

Newcomers will hear, especially among those middle-aged and older, either standard Japanese spoken with a strong local accent or, as explained above, a separate dialect that is related linguistically to Japanese but remains incomprehensible to mainlanders. Also often heard are Okinawan songs with *sanshin* accompaniment. The Okinawan version of this banjo-like instrument resembles its mainland counterpart, the samisen, in that both have three strings and a long, fretless neck, but the *sanshin* (also called the *jabisen*) is made from snakeskin and is plucked with a small finger pick, while the samisen is traditionally made from cat skin and played with a large plectrum. Okinawan folk music, known locally as *shima-uta* (island songs), is heard not only in *karaoke* bars, but also on radio, on television, and often from open windows in residential districts. More than anywhere else in Japan, performances of local folk music abound in Okinawa, and as with linguistic dialects, musical styles vary from one island group to the next within the Ryukyu archipelago.

Physiological differences between Okinawans and mainland Japanese are often apparent as well, raising the issues of migration and early Ryukyuan history, for the slightly darker complexions and rounder features of many Okinawans are a result of migrations to the Ryukyu Islands from ancient times. Early immigrants from East and Northeast Asia populated both the Ryukyus and what is now mainland Japan, but many of the people from Southeast Asia and the Pacific Islands, who braved the long voyage northward, settled in what is now Okinawa. Besides navigational skills, these immigrants brought with them expertise in farming, fisheries, and dwelling construction. People from what is now Japan are believed to have introduced such iron implements as metal pots, agricultural tools, and weapons into the Ryukyu Islands. Early political organization in the Ryukyus centered around regional lords called *aji* (*anji* in standard Japanese), with *nuru* *(noro)* priestesses in charge of ritual observances and other spiritual matters. Centuries of rivalries, wars, and changing alliances among the *aji* finally led, in the twelfth century, to a consolidation into three separate kingdoms—Nanzan (South), Chūzan (Central), and Hokuzan (North).

In 1372, emissaries arrived from the Ming Court and mildly pressured King Satto of Chūzan to begin a tributary relationship with China like that of other nations in East Asia where aspects of Chinese politics and culture were widely imitated and adapted. In Okinawa, too, Chinese influences in such spheres as political organization, court ritual, religion, architecture, and diet have been profound, with many still discernible today. After King Shō Hashi of Chūzan, the strongest of the three regions, established a unified Ryukyu kingdom under his authority in 1429, a new palace was built in the Chinese style at the capital of Shuri to accommodate elaborate court ceremonies newly borrowed, with some modifications, from China.[19]

For much of the next two centuries the kingdom enjoyed relative prosperity based in large part on a flourishing import-export trade with China, Japan, Korea, and Southeast Asia. This trade was made possible by a highly developed merchant marine that also shipped cargo between countries during what is often called the Golden Age of the Ryukyu kingdom.[20] In addition, it was a time of cultural efflorescence,

when new parks, pavilions, and temples were built, and artisans produced distinctive lacquerware and jewelry as well as some of the
world's finest textiles. During this period an indigenous literary tradition was established with the adoption of the Japanese *kana* syllabary
for general use.[21] Between 1532 and 1623, the court at Shuri sponsored
compilation of the *Omoro sōshi*, an anthology of ancient songs and
ryūka poetry still admired and studied today as Okinawa's most important work of classical literature. Okinawa's *ryūka* usually follows the
four-line, thirty-syllable pattern of 8-8-8-6, while mainland *waka* is
usually 5-7-5-7-7.[22] Composed between the twelfth and sixteenth centuries, selections in the *Omoro sōshi* include religious chants, narratives
of legends, ceremonial odes, and poetry on everyday life. The persona
of the poem below is a crewmember on a trading ship far from home.

> *Straight southern wind!*
> *When the southern wind whispers,*
> *Let the* Suzunari *bring back*
> *The trade goods from China and*
> *the South Seas* [*to our king*].[23]

At the end of the sixteenth century, Japan's domination in the
Ryukyus began. Trouble started in 1590, when King Shō Nei declined
to provide troops and matériel for an invasion of China planned by
Toyotomi Hideyoshi, who had emerged as military overlord of Japan
toward the end of a long period of civil wars. As pressure on Shō Nei
mounted, the king belatedly sent supplies of food, but the invasion
bogged down in Korea, where Hideyoshi died in 1598. Two years later,
Tokugawa Ieyasu prevailed in the decisive battle at Sekigahara to
become Japan's new military overlord, or shogun. As part of an agreement that consolidated Tokugawa power throughout the country, he
bestowed the title Lord of the Twelve Southern Islands on Shimazu
Iehisa, daimyo of the Satsuma domain in southernmost Kyushu. Iehisa
quickly ordered Shō Nei to accept Satsuma authority over the Ryukyus,
but the king again refused to submit. This time, however, the daimyo
sent three thousand samurai in a fleet of two hundred ships to "pun-
ish" the kingdom.[24] Having maintained a defense force sufficient to

deal with pirates from abroad and rebellions in the outer islands, the kingdom repulsed the initial attack by sea. But overland routes to Shuri lacked adequate defenses, so Satsuma's ground forces advanced rapidly to within easy cannon range of the palace, and the battle was over.

Thus began a 270-year period of divided loyalties. Although Ryukyuans resisted early efforts by the Satsuma daimyo to divert profits from the kingdom's declining trade with China, by the late seventeenth century merchants from Satsuma and Ryukyu began to cooperate and profit mutually from this trade, now revived under the Satsuma daimyo's supervision. Japanese influences in Ryukyu from earlier times included books, words, and songs in the Japanese language. At first Satsuma encouraged the study of Japanese language and culture as part of the curriculum for the kingdom's elite. Furthermore, some people wore Japanese clothing and hairstyles. But in order to maintain trade with China, Satsuma ordered Ryukyuans to conceal from visiting Chinese all Japanese political and cultural manifestations, since China did not recognize Japan as a tributary state. Thus in the mid-seventeenth century Satsuma began to encourage Chinese cultural influences, reflected in revised court rituals, new temple construction, and the revival of Kume, the village where Chinese immigrants and their descendants had traditionally resided and which also had been a center for the study of China. Once a flourishing community, Kume had fallen on hard times; and it again suffered during the later period described in Ikemiyagi Sekiho's story, "Officer Ukuma."

Aside from the benefits of Ryukyu's overseas trade, Satsuma leaders were able to use their domain's relationship with a "foreign kingdom" to enhance their prestige within Japan. The daimyo led periodic processions of Ryukyuans—who were again instructed not to dress or behave in a manner that would betray Japanese influences—through Japan to Edo (Tokyo). Observers along the route reportedly were fascinated, especially with dances the Ryukyuans performed; and Satsuma's relationship with the kingdom led to a promotion for its daimyo by the Edo shogunate, which, in turn, made use of the Satsuma-Ryukyu-China connection in their own difficult dealings with China.[25]

Yet despite Satsuma's manipulative, restrictive, and sometimes contradictory policies, relations between Ryukyu and Japan during this period were by no means as hostile as they are sometimes portrayed. Although travel back and forth was limited mostly to official business, mutual influences were evident, especially in culture and the arts. Popular music and dance from Edo and Osaka had already caught on in the Ryukyus from the time when travel was freer, and local songs, in turn, had become popular in Japan, as Okinawan music is today. The traditional *kumi-odori* theater borrowed aspects of Japan's Nō and Kabuki drama, while Japanese theater adopted costumes, dances, and music from the Ryukyus. Naha, Okinawa's capital and its largest city today, was known in Japan as a center of fashion, the arts, good food, and entertainment.[26] Its licensed quarter of Tsuji, also described in "Officer Ukuma," was a subject for Japanese poetry and prose, and for some of the most famous *ryūka* poems. In her best-known work, Yoshiya Tsuru (1650–1668) laments the fate of a woman sold into prostitution there.

> *Oh, you hateful bridge of Hija!*
> *Were you built by heartless people*
> *Merely to hurry me across*
> *On to that curst quarter?*[27]

As in Japanese literature generally, the oppressive plight of the prostitute has been a recurring motif in Okinawan literature to the present day and is portrayed in Yoshida Sueko's "Love Suicide at Kamaara." In Okinawa, however, prostitution often has been depicted in the context of oppression from the outside—from mainland Japan as well as from the United States since 1945.

In the 1870s, two and a half centuries of Satsuma interference finally came to an end after the Meiji Restoration of 1868 led to the establishment of Japan's modern state. But far from restoring the kingdom's independence, the new government moved steadily to consolidate its domination by deposing the king and absorbing Ryukyu into the Japanese polity as Okinawa Prefecture in 1879. This policy, euphemistically called the "Ryukyu Disposition" (*Ryūkyū shobun),* was carried out despite local protests and a major dispute with the government of China, which still claimed suzereignty over the Ryukyu Islands based on the 1372 agreement with King Satto. Within Okinawa itself a faction favoring continued ties with China retained some influence until Japan won the Sino-Japanese War of 1894–1895.

Yet by the 1890s, pressure was increasing from inside and outside Okinawa for a more thorough policy of assimilation to Japan, one that was not only institutional, but cultural and ideological as well. Unlike the Satsuma daimyo, who had ordered Ryukyu to maintain an appearance of independence, the Japanese government now demanded unqualified acceptance of its political control and emperor-centered ideology. The government also called for the abolishment of such traditional customs as tattooing the backs of women's hands and consulting female shamans (yuta), whose advice is, nevertheless, still sought today. The stigma of tattoos is noted in "A Conversation" and in "Memoirs of a Declining Ryukyuan Woman"; and the figure of the shaman appears in several stories, including Nakahara Shin's "The Silver Motorcycle" (1977), Medoruma Shun's "Droplets," and Matayoshi Eiki's "Fortunes by the Sea." Pressure to assimilate emanated not only from the government in Tokyo, which forcibly replaced local officials with mainland personnel, but from Okinawa itself, where a growing number of people came to believe, especially after Japan's unexpected victory in the Sino-Japanese War, that affiliation with this rising nation offered their best hope for the future. Thus it was Okinawans themselves who initiated such policies as the mandatory use of standard (i.e., Tokyo) Japanese language in the schools and such trends as wearing the dress and hairstyles of mainland Japanese, as some people had done earlier in the days of the Ryukyu kingdom.[28]

Unfortunately, such ostensible shows of admiration were not always reciprocated. Among the Tokyo government's initial appointees to Okinawa were administrators well informed about and responsive to the urgent needs of Japan's newest and poorest prefecture. Uesugi Shigenori, Okinawa's second governor, toured the countryside and vigorously advocated programs for improving the lives of local residents. But his carefully crafted proposals for streamlining local government and using the estimated savings to improve education and promote industry were consistently rejected in Tokyo, even though they would have required no additional taxes on Okinawans or spending from the national treasury. Although the Meiji government claimed that the prefecture was an integral part of the nation, Okinawa received less government investment and paid higher taxes proportionately than other localities. As Gregory Smits writes, "Japanese actions within the new prefecture . . . indicate a de facto status more like a colony or conquered territory than an integral part of the motherland."[29] Later, the quality of central government appointees declined sharply, especially in the lower ranks of bureaucrats and police. Officials, who had supposedly been entrusted with the welfare of local residents, often resented their assignment to a "remote" post and treated Okinawans with disdain as "country cousins," causing fear and feelings of inferiority.[30] During this time, prejudice against Okinawans—as an ethnic group with a culture different in many ways from other regions of Japan—became widespread and enduring. Okinawans grew especially wary of the police force, comprised of many men from the new Kagoshima Prefecture, which had replaced most of the old Satsuma domain. Police mistreatment of Okinawans is depicted in "Officer Ukuma," as is the prejudice that even Okinawan members of the force suffered at the hands of officers from the mainland. "Officer Ukuma" and other stories from the 1920s and 1930s (e.g., "Memoirs of a Declining Ryukyuan Woman") suggest that elite Okinawans were especially apt to internalize the prejudices of mainland Japanese, only to find themselves alienated from relatives and neighbors, yet not fully accepted by those Japanese whose approval they so anxiously sought. This is a common predicament in colonial situations throughout the world, and Okinawa's relationship with mainland Japan (regardless of whether it should strictly be described as "colonial") fostered similar social problems.

The early decades of the twentieth century saw large numbers of Okinawans moving to mainland Japan for schooling and jobs, especially in Osaka, Tokyo, and other cities that offered opportunities unavailable in their own impoverished prefecture. On the mainland, too, Okinawans encountered prejudice as well as outright discrimination: signs that explicitly barred Okinawans, Koreans, and Chinese hindered them from finding lodging and employment. To avoid this and more subtle forms of prejudice, some Okinawans tried to conceal their origins and "pass" as mainland Japanese. The painful dilemma of one man who kept the secret of his birthplace even from his own wife and daughter is portrayed in "Memoirs of a Declining Ryukyuan Woman." In "Mr. Saitō of Heaven Building," Yamanokuchi Baku describes the misconceptions and stereotyping encountered by certain "minority" groups in Japan. The main character is a Korean who has taken the Japanese name Saitō as part of an unsuccessful effort to conceal his birthplace. Yamanokuchi Baku directly addresses the issue from an Okinawan perspective in his poem, "A Conversation."

Yet as in the previous era of cultural interaction, the treatment of Okinawans on the mainland was by no means unremittingly hostile. A number of writers found critical acclaim and a market for their work. As noted earlier, poets in particular were welcomed into mainland literary circles and had their poetry printed by prominent magazines and book publishers.[31] In their poems and stories, writers from Okinawa not only described their homeland, but also offered illuminating perspectives on life in mainland Japan. Among Okinawa's poets, Yamanokuchi Baku remains the most popular and critically acclaimed both inside and outside the prefecture, and we have included several of his short works—prose as well as poetry—in this anthology.

Meanwhile, during the 1920s and 1930s, economic conditions worsened in Okinawa as prices dropped sharply for the island's sugar crop and as Japan slid into the worldwide depression. In a prefecture paying the highest taxes while receiving the fewest social services, pressures to emigrate mounted even as discriminatory laws against Asian immigrants came into force in the United States and other countries. The desperate conditions in Okinawa during this period are portrayed through the destitution and disintegration of one family in "Memoirs of a Declining Ryukyuan Woman."

With Japan's invasion of Manchuria in 1931, the nation became embroiled in a catastrophic war that would drag on for fifteen years. Many Okinawan civilians were sent to Taiwan, Saipan, and other Japanese-occupied territories to help increase production for the expanding empire; most who remained in Okinawa were besieged by some of the most brutal fighting of the war. On October 10, 1944,

Allied planes conducted a massive air raid on Naha, destroying 90 percent of the city and leaving 12,000 buildings in ruins and 50,000 residents homeless. Less than six months later, a small contingent of American forces landed on the Kerama Islands, located just west of Naha, and on April 1, 1945, 20,000 American troops came ashore on the central part of Okinawa Island.[32] Thus began the deadliest battle of the Pacific War and the only land battle waged within Japan's national borders.[33]

The fighting on Okinawa lasted nearly three months and claimed the lives of approximately 230,000 people, including over 12,000 Americans and 147,000 Okinawans, most of whom were women, children, and the elderly. The number killed represents roughly one-fourth of the island's prewar population. It is hard to exaggerate the intensity of the fighting or the devastation wrought on both Okinawa's landscape and its people. By 1945, the Japanese military had conscripted nearly all Okinawans over fourteen years of age for some form of battlefield service. Among those called to serve were the famous *Himeyuri-tai* (literally, Princess Lily Corps), which consisted of high school girls serving as battlefield nurses. Indoctrinated by an ideology that encouraged suicide rather than surrender and that led them to believe they would be raped if captured, many of these student nurses killed themselves by jumping off cliffs or huddling around a hand grenade and pulling the pin. Their tragic deaths have come to embody, in Japan's popular imagination, the Battle of Okinawa as well as the suffering that war inevitably entails. During the past half century, the *Himeyuri-tai* has been memorialized through books and several feature films, the most successful of which indulge in a mixture of sentimentality and eroticism that Japanese audiences seem to find irresistible.[34] Himeyuri Memorial Park, containing a museum and a shrine to these young victims, remains among Okinawa's most visited sites—although the busloads of tourists from Japan's main islands also patronize the nearby stands where local merchants, with no apparent sense of irony, hawk American military surplus goods as souvenirs. The figure of the *himeyuri* nurse appears in Medoruma Shun's "Droplets," but the author uses this image less to tug on his readers' heartstrings than to explore how Okinawans themselves have repressed, transformed, and capitalized on their war memories.

In addition to the overwhelming human losses, the Battle of Okinawa caused irreparable material damage to the region's unique cultural heritage. Nothing more vividly symbolizes this cultural loss than the destruction of Shuri Castle, the center of the former Ryukyu kingdom and Okinawa's most tangible link to its past. The Japanese army command on Okinawa had established the castle as their headquarters, and in April 1945, American battleships began pounding the thick stone walls with thousands of tons of artillery. After four days the castle walls finally gave way under a bombardment called the "Typhoon of Steel," the phrase that was later applied to the Battle of Okinawa as a whole. Many Okinawans see the appropriation of Shuri Castle by the Japanese army and its subsequent destruction by the American forces as symbolizing a recurrent theme in Ryukyuan history—namely, that of Okinawans trapped between two outside powers, as pawns sacrificed in a larger conflict.

The novelist and playwright Ōshiro Tatsuhiro was among the first to challenge this "victim-centered" view of history in his 1966 novella, *Cocktail Party*. The story implies that before Okinawans can rightfully establish a claim to victimhood, they first must confront their own complicity with Japan's wartime imperialism. As a tale about an Okinawan girl raped by an American soldier, *Cocktail Party* also eerily anticipates the notorious September 1995 rape incident that triggered massive protests throughout Okinawa against America's ongoing military presence.[35] Despite the contemporary acclaim accorded *Cocktail Party* (it was the first work by an Okinawan writer to be awarded the Akutagawa Prize), Ōshiro himself always considered his "Turtleback Tombs" to be more successful as literature. Turtleback tombs are found nowhere in Japan except the Ryukyu Islands, where they are scattered across the landscape and built into the ground to form cave-like structures resembling tortoiseshells. The family portrayed in Ōshiro's story is forced to seek shelter in their ancestral tomb from the devastating American naval bombardment of the island. They struggle to find solace during the crisis in their traditional extended family and in a local religion that stresses, in its beliefs and rituals, a family's continuity over the generations. The tombs were a common refuge for Okinawans fleeing the fighting, and on a symbolic level they resemble Shuri Castle, since both represent links to the Ryukyuan past, to a sacred space and time violated by the incursion of war and foreign powers.

As American forces gained control over the central part of the island in April 1945, the fighting moved south, and tens of thousands of fleeing civilians unable to find refuge were killed in the crossfire. Many of those hiding in the caves and tombs died at their own hands or at those of relatives. At least seven hundred Okinawans chose suicide over surrender and capture by the enemy.[36] In Okinawa, as elsewhere in Japan, women expected to be raped and then killed by the American soldiers. Deciding that death was less humiliating than surrender, some resorted to acts of utter desperation, killing their children and then taking their own lives. Other civilians were killed by Japanese soldiers, not only in accidental "friendly fire," but intentionally as well. Some Japanese soldiers, seeking shelter from enemy fire, forced Okinawans out of caves and ancestral tombs; others who took refuge inside with Okinawan families reportedly killed crying babies so as to conceal their own whereabouts. Soldiers also shot Okinawans speaking in regional dialect as suspected spies. And as defeat became inevitable, the soldiers even lined up Okinawan civilians and shot them out of sheer frustration. The killing of infants by mainland soldiers is described in Shima Tsuyoshi's 1973 story, "Bones." As its title suggests, this work, like so many postwar Okinawan stories, explores buried memories of the war and the dead spirits who continue to evoke them.

Of course, the American military also contributed to Okinawa's civilian death toll. The 1944 air raid on Naha and the spring 1945 U.S. naval bombardment killed combatant and noncombatant alike. In battle, American soldiers who discovered people hiding in caves or tombs would order them outside, and those who refused were sometimes killed with flamethrowers or with grenades tossed into their hiding place, even when civilians were suspected to be inside.

Yet Okinawans who did surrender were often surprised at the comparatively humane treatment they received from the American enemy. Nearly everyone on the main island of Okinawa in the spring and summer of 1945 was placed in American internment camps. On June 23, 1945, Japanese army commander Ushijima Mitsuru committed suicide, and military resistance to the Allied Forces in Okinawa largely ceased; since then, June 23 has come to commemorate the war's end for many Okinawans, as obliquely noted in "Bones" and "Droplets." By this time, roughly one thousand civilians and soldiers were being placed into the camps each day, with separate facilities established for combatants and noncombatants. Life in the camps was by no means easy, but the Americans provided desperately needed food, clothing, shelter, and medical treatment. Suddenly, it seemed, the enemy became the savior, and Okinawan civilians whose provisions had been usurped by Japanese soldiers during the battle sometimes remark that the Americans were more friendly than their own countrymen from the mainland.

After struggling for decades to gain recognition as full-fledged Japanese citizens, and after having served bravely in battle only to see their loyalty disparaged by the very forces for which they fought, at war's end many Okinawans felt betrayed by Japan. In accordance with the Nimitz Proclamation, their islands were severed from Japan and placed under American occupation, which continued until Okinawa's reversion to Japanese prefectural status on May 15, 1972.[37]

Not surprisingly, the war looms large in contemporary Okinawan literature, as does the ensuing twenty-seven-year American occupation. Yet the end of the war and the beginning of the occupation are less easily distinguished in Okinawa than in Japan's main islands. For most Japanese, August 15 clearly marks the war's end and the beginning of the postwar era, but for those Okinawans placed in internment camps months before Japan surrendered to the Allies, the war and occupation overlapped. Thus Okinawans' understanding of both differs significantly from that of most Japanese. After all, the occupation forces did not arrive in mainland Japan until nearly two weeks after the nation had surrendered, and few Japanese who spent the war years at home even encountered an American soldier until that time. Brimming with confidence, optimism, and that uniquely American blend of innocence and arrogance, the occupiers were surprisingly friendly to Japan's occupied populace, according to most accounts.

In contrast, residents of Okinawa in the spring of 1945 first encountered American soldiers not as a relaxed occupation force entering a defeated nation, but as the enemy still engaged in the frenzy of battle. This is not to ignore the hundreds of thousands of mainland Japanese killed by American aerial bombings, which targeted nearly every city in the nation, nor to forget the atomic horrors of Hiroshima and Nagasaki. But while death is the great equalizer, from the perspective of the war's survivors—especially noncombatants—there remains an irreducible difference between an invisible enemy dropping bombs from the sky and a live, foreign soldier pointing a gun at one's face. In Okinawa, it was these same soldiers who ushered in the postwar era, both as material benefactors and military occupiers, and this made for a particularly ambivalent relationship with the American forces.

Okinawans desperately relied on the occupiers for the first few years after the war. No currency was even in place until May 1946, and the Americans supplied nearly all daily necessities.[38] On the Japanese mainland, contact between the occupiers and the occupied was usually limited to public places; Okinawans, however, literally lived with the occupiers until their release from the internment camps. These camps offered a crash course in American military culture, introducing Okinawans to Spam, biscuits, and other delicacies contained in "K-rations." Those needing clothes were provided with HBTs—"herringbone twill" military jackets. Smokers savored Lucky Strikes, and children chomped on chewing gum. Although provisions were not always sufficient, they did prevent widespread famine and disease among the destitute populace.

It was not until March 1947 that Okinawans were permitted to move freely about their island. In mainland Japan, while a new constitution was promulgated and a host of democratic reforms were being enacted, many Okinawans continued to live in internment camps under a state of martial law. It is true that the American occupiers of Okinawa, like their counterparts on Japan's main islands, often showed unexpected generosity and goodwill toward their occupied subjects, but they were poorly organized, staffed, and funded compared with Gen. Douglas MacArthur's administration in Tokyo. Moreover, the occupation of mainland Japan was understood to be a temporary affair, whereas by 1948 the United States intended to keep the Ryukyus as a permanent American military bastion in East Asia.[39] The San Francisco Peace Treaty, signed in 1951 and taking effect in April 1952, formalized this intention by ending the American occupation of Japan's main islands while ceding most of the Ryukyu Islands to the United States. The day the treaty was signed is referred to in Okinawa as the "Day of Shame," for it seemed as if Japan's independence had been obtained in exchange for Okinawa's continued subordination to the United States.

With the Communists' assumption of power in China in 1949 and the outbreak of the Korean War the following year, the United States rushed to expand its military facilities in Okinawa during the early 1950s. This brought a welcome infusion of cash and jobs but did little to spark development of a diversified local economy. The base expansion program also entailed taking land from unwilling owners—sometimes at gunpoint. By the mid-1950s, struggles over expropriated land culminated in island-wide protests that forced the U.S. government to abandon a policy of lump-sum payments for land and, instead, to make regular payments under a system of mandatory "leases." This system is continued by the Japanese government today and has been at the center of recent protests and lawsuits.[40] The forced expropriation of land is mentioned in Kishaba Jun's "Dark Flowers"; and Matayoshi Eiki's "Fortunes by the Sea," set roughly forty years later, shows the long-term impact on Okinawans who have become complacent landlords to the U.S. military.

The 1950s protesters consisted of a broad coalition of farmers, students, teachers, and labor activists, and the movement's organizers included a group of students from the University of the Ryukyus, which, ironically, had been established by the American authorities only a few years earlier to foster goodwill and democracy. Among the student organizers were the editors of the university's radical literary magazine, *Ryūdai bungaku*, mentioned earlier. The magazine had already attracted the attention of American censors for its unflinching criticism of the occupation, and in 1956, Arakawa Akira (who by that time was already working for *The Okinawa Times*) published a five-part poem titled "The Colored Race" in *Ryūdai bungaku*. This bellicose protest poem calls on African American soldiers to join with the occupied

Okinawans as fellow members of "the colored race" and to rise up and destroy the white-dominated society that suppressed them both.[41] The editors of *Ryūdai bungaku*, in an effort to circumvent censorship by American occupation authorities, released this issue without submitting it for the requisite prepublication clearance.[42] In response, occupation censors cracked down on the magazine: they recalled all copies previously distributed, banned publication of *Ryūdai bungaku* for six months, and, with the cooperation of the university administration, expelled four of the editors who had been especially active in the protest movement. This effectively shut down the magazine for a full year.

The mid-1950s were lively times for political activists in Okinawa, many of whom were aspiring literati as well, but in the end they failed to obtain significant concessions from the occupiers—or, it must be repeated, to produce much literature still read today. In the realm of fiction, most critics agree that modern Okinawan literature did not come into its own until a decade later with the publication of Ōshiro Tatsuhiro's "Turtleback Tombs" and *Cocktail Party*. By this time, the United States was relying heavily on its Okinawan bases as it became more embroiled in the Vietnam War, and a burgeoning movement advocating Okinawa's reversion to Japan again created a tense political environment on the islands.[43] It was during these tumultuous times that the region's most influential postwar literary magazine, *Shin Okinawa bungaku*, was launched by poet, critic, and journalist Arakawa Akira, together with his cohort Kawamitsu Shin'ichi and other writer-activists from *Ryūdai bungaku*. For the next two decades, *Shin Okinawa bungaku* served as the region's leading literary forum for both new and established writers.[44]

During the height of the Vietnam War, American dollars were pouring into Okinawa's base towns, and today former bar owners wax nostalgic over those evenings when G.I.s, on leave from Vietnam, would strut into the bar, buy drinks for everyone, and spend so much cash that it had to be stuffed into buckets on the floor. These young men, uncertain if they would again return from Vietnam alive, often were desperate in their pursuit of "R&R" (rest and recuperation). Their dollars not only filled the coffers of bars and souvenir shops in base towns such as Koza, Kin, and Henoko, they also lined the pockets of

Okinawa's many prostitutes and G.I. mistresses. Many stories about this period explore the lives of women who worked in G.I. bars and brothels. Yoshida Sueko's "Love Suicide at Kamaara" adopts the unusual viewpoint of an aging Okinawan prostitute during the Vietnam War who desperately seeks solace in the youthful body of an American deserter. Other works, such as Shimokawa Hiroshi's "Love Letter from L.A." (1978), examine the lonely lives of Okinawan women separated from their American husbands.[45]

Throughout the twenty-seven-year American occupation, the vast majority of Okinawans wanted to reclaim their status as Japanese citizens. The "reversion movement" gained momentum as resistance to the Vietnam War grew in both Okinawa and mainland Japan, and in 1969, Prime Minister Satō Eisaku and President Richard Nixon agreed to restore Okinawa's prefectural status, although the conditions underlying this agreement elicited intense debate. A small group of intellectuals and a few advocates of Ryukyuan independence objected to the very terms of this debate, arguing that the expression "reversion to the ancestral land" *(sokoku fukki)* assumes that Japan had a legitimate historical claim to the Ryukyus, when in fact the islands had been a distinct political and cultural entity until the Meiji government abolished the Ryukyu kingdom and annexed it in 1879. The reversion accord remains a contentious issue today, since America's military bases in Japan remain disproportionately concentrated in Okinawa, and most of the prefecture's recent political struggles can be traced to the reversion accord or to the American land seizures of the 1950s.

Reversion did bring greater economic and political opportunity to Okinawa, and most residents were elated to be able to use yen instead of dollars, to drive on paved roads, and to work in the new jobs created by Japanese investment in the islands. During much of the occupation, Okinawans wishing to travel to the mainland needed passports specially issued by the occupation authorities; now, they could travel freely and could obtain Japanese passports for trips abroad. Yet reversion brought problems as well, when mainland corporations overwhelmed local businesses, devastated areas of the landscape, and destroyed local artifacts with such construction projects as the resort hotel described in Shima Tsuyoshi's "Bones."

Despite Okinawa's integration into the Japanese economy in the decades following reversion, today among Japan's forty-seven prefectures, Okinawa has the nation's lowest per capita income (70 percent of the national average) and the highest unemployment rate, which consistently hovers at nearly twice the national average. The prefecture also ranks at the bottom in the percentage of students who go on to junior college or university. Okinawa is consistently near the top in divorce rates and in the percentage of single-parent households.[46] In spite of these social woes, Okinawans generally live longer than mainland Japanese—and Japan boasts one of the world's highest longevity rates. It is unclear whether Okinawan longevity should be attributed primarily to genetics, diet, climate, or to the comparatively relaxed pace of life. But as the above account suggests, Okinawa remains in many ways different from the rest of Japan, both in terms of the problems that plague the region and in its distinct culture. We hope the pages that follow attest to the vitality of this culture.

NOTES

1. The Japanese title is *Buta no mukui* (Tokyo: Bungei shunjū, 1996). The first Okinawan writer to receive the Akutagawa Prize was Ōshiro Tatsuhiro for his 1967 novella, *Cocktail Party* (Kakuteru paatii); the second was Higashi Mineo for his 1971 novella, *Child of Okinawa* (Okinawa no shōnen). An English translation of both works can be found in Steve Rabson, trans., *Okinawa: Two Postwar Novellas* (Berkeley: Institute of East Asian Studies, 1989; reprinted 1996). Both Japanese texts are contained in Okinawa bungaku zenshū henshū iinkai, eds., *Okinawa bungaku zenshū*, vol. 7 (Tokyo: Kokusho kankōkai, 1990).

2. For some representative critical commentary, see the remarks by the Akutagawa Prize Selection Committee (Akutagawa-shō senkō iinkai) in *Bungei shunjū* 75(11) (September 1997):426–431. "Droplets" (Suiteki) can be found in this magazine on 432–450. It was also published with two

other stories by the author in Medoruma Shun, *Suiteki* (Tokyo: Bungei shunjū, 1997).

3. Even today, the vast majority of prominent Japanese writers live within commuting distance of Tokyo, although one mainland writer, Ikezawa Natsuki, has settled in Okinawa.

4. On Nakamura Kare, Tsukayama Issui, and other Okinawan poets during this era, see Nakahodo Masanori, *Okinawa no bungaku: 1927–1945* (Naha: Okinawa taimususha, 1991); see also Nakahodo's essay, "Okinawa kindai shishi gaisetsu: Meiji, Taishō Shōwa senzenki," in Okinawa bungaku zenshū henshū iinkai, eds., *Okinawa bungaku zenshū*, vol. 1 (Tokyo: Kokusho kankōkai, 1991), 363–378.

5. It is always difficult to pinpoint the emergence of a "modern literature." The categories related to modernity ("the modern," "modernism," "post-modernism," etc.) are themselves notoriously elusive, and the challenge of defining them in the context of Okinawan literature is exacerbated because notions of modernity in Okinawa were heavily mediated by cultural developments in mainland Japan, which in turn resulted from Japanese attempts to interpret and domesticate a wide range of European cultural movements (which were, in turn, responding to their respective traditions). Not surprisingly, modernity has been closely associated with "the West" in Japanese cultural histories, such that "modernization" is often tacitly equated with "Westernization" from roughly the 1880s through the 1930s. In Okinawa, where the "modern" was mediated through contemporary Japanese urban culture, it was as much a case of "Japanization" as of "Westernization"–although neither term does justice to these complex processes of change. Thus characteristics widely associated with the emergence of modern literature in Japan emerge several decades later in Okinawa. These characteristics include, in Karatani Kōjin's formulation, "the discovery of interiority" and of "landscape." Also included are qualities widely associated with literary modernism in Europe and the United States, such as a profound sense of disjunction with the recent past, a heightened awareness of the materiality of language, and writers' attempts to represent self-consciousness in its full immediacy. Yet for Okinawans, the newly discovered "subject" or "individual," which so preoccupied Japanese writers such as Natsume Sōseki, evoked a different anxiety: they were concerned less with the impact of an omnipotent "West" on the Japanese "self" than with mainland Japan's colonial domination of Okinawa and its deleterious impact on the region's people and culture.

For two different approaches to the problem of modernity and Japanese literature, see Karatani Kōjin, *Origins of Modern Japanese Literature*, trans. ed. by Brett de Bary (Durham, N.C.: Duke University Press, 1993); and Dennis Washburn, *The Dilemma of the Modern in Japanese Fiction* (New Haven, Conn.: Yale University Press, 1995). On Okinawan literature and modernity, see Okamoto Keitoku, Okinawa bungaku no chihei (Tokyo: San'ichi shobō, 1981), 7–27. On the subject in Meiji literature, see James Fujii, *Complicit Fictions: The Subject in the Modern Japanese Prose Narrative* (Berkeley: University of California Press, 1992). On the many permutations of literary modernism in Europe and the Americas, see Peter Nichols, *Modernisms: A Literary Guide* (Berkeley: University of California Press, 1995).

6. Okamoto Keitoku, *Gendai Okinawa no bungaku to shisō* (Naha: Okinawa Taimususha, 1981), 115–116.

7. The most detailed study of *Ryūdai bungaku* is Kano Masanao, *Sengo Okinawa no shisōzō* (Tokyo: Asahi shinbunsha, 1987), 113–160. Also see Ōe Kenzaburō, *Okinawa keiken: Ōe Kenzaburō dōjidai ronshū* (Tokyo: Iwanami shoten, 1981), 374–377; Okamoto, *Gendai Okinawa no bungaku to shisō*, 113–126; and Okamoto, *Okinawa bungaku no chihei*, 57–61. Okamoto was an editor and writer for the magazine while a student at the University of the Ryukyus. In English, see Michael Molasky, *The American Occupation of Japan and Okinawa: Literature and Memory* (London: Routledge, 1999), 93–102. This section also contains a partial translation and analysis of Arakawa Akira's incendiary protest poem, "The Colored Race" (Yūshoku jinshu shō—sono ichi), which was published in *Ryūdai bungaku* one year after "Dark Flowers."

8. Other local forums for publishing literature include the literary magazine *Aoi umi* (Blue sea) and the two regional newspapers, *Ryūkyū shinpō* and *Okinawa Taimusu* (The Okinawa Times). The *Ryūkyū shinpō* held an annual short-story contest that encouraged fledgling writers to submit their work; the prize-winning stories from 1973–1993 are published in Ryūkyū shinpōsha, eds., *Okinawa tanpen shōsetsushū* (Naha: Ryūkyū shinpōsha, 1993). Both newspapers also have a publishing arm that concentrates on Okinawan social and cultural issues, and many of the region's leading intellectuals (including Ōshiro Tatsuhiro and Takara Ben, both featured in this anthology) have published books with these presses.

9. For an overview of the history of *Shin Okinawa bungaku*, see the spring

1993 special issue, which looks back on the magazine's past and includes a helpful author index of everyone who published in its pages.

10. *The Okinawa Times*, which supported *Shin Okinawa bungaku*, now publishes an annual literary magazine, *Okinawa bungei nenkan* (Yearbook of Okinawan literature), and the *Ryūkyū shinpō* continues to offer its annual short-story prize. New local forums for publishing literature and criticism exist as well, most notably the glossy, hip magazine, *Edge* (title appears in English), and *Keeshi kaji*, a quarterly magazine of thought and criticism organized by literature scholar Okamoto Keitoku and historian/social activist Arasaki Moriteru. The latter magazine continues the activist legacy of *Shin Okinawa bungaku*. The title is Okinawan dialect for *"kaeshi kaze"* (returning winds or reverse winds). The magazine's subtitle elucidates the meaning: *Jōkyō ni "keeshi kaji" o* (Bring reverse winds to blow on the [social and political] situation). *"Jōkyō,"* or "situation," is a word that immediately links the magazine and its editors to the thought of the 1960s and Japan's New Left. In contrast, *Edge* is associated with a more recent oppositional consciousness, one that appeals to a younger, less elite readership.

11. Strictly speaking, Okinawan critics would not view all of these writers as being of the same generation, since Yamanoha was born in 1941 and Medoruma in 1960. Nor does date of birth alone separate these writers, since Matayoshi began publishing during the Vietnam War, whereas most of the others did not begin to establish a reputation until nearly a decade later. Nevertheless, all of them should be distinguished from the previous generation(s) of postwar writers such as Kishaba Jun and Ōshiro Tatsuhiro. Okamoto Keitoku—who was himself a contributor to *Ryūdai bungaku* during his student days—views this new generation as being less constrained by their immediate social and political conditions than were their predecessors. This is not to suggest that these writers are oblivious to the ongoing relevance of war or occupation in Okinawan life (see Yoshida's "Love Suicide at Kamaara" and Medoruma's "Droplets" for compelling evidence to the contrary). Okamoto is simply claiming that these historical events do not circumscribe the younger writers' imagined worlds in the way they often did with the previous generation. This is especially apparent in the narrative modes (fantasy, magical realism, etc.) with which many of the young writers have experimented. Okamoto Keitoku, "'Okinawa henkan' go no bungaku tenbō," in Okinawa bungaku

zenshū henshū iinkai, eds., *Okinawa bungaku zenshū*, vol. 9 (Tokyo: Kokusho kankōkai, 1990), 414–415.

12. For a useful overview of issues related to language and identity, including dialects, see John Edwards, *Language, Society and Identity* (London: Basil Blackwell, 1985). Edwards discusses the language/dialect issue on 19–22.

13. Consider Okinawan director Takamine Gō's 1989 award-winning film, *Untamagiru*, which uses Okinawan dialect for both spoken narration and dialogue: when shown in mainland Japan, the entire film appeared with Japanese subtitles to make it intelligible. Linguistically, in other words, it was treated there as a foreign-language film. *Untamagiru* won the Caligari Film Award at the 1990 Berlin Film Festival. Admittedly, if one distinguishes a language from a dialect using the criterion of "mutual unintelligibility," then no dialect spoken within Japan's national boundaries today could be considered a full-fledged language, since standard Japanese is understood everywhere.

14. In his novella, *Child of Okinawa* (Okinawa no shōnen), Higashi Mineo is said to have created, with great skill, a modified dialect that rang true to local residents while being accessible to non-Okinawan readers.

15. The inherent flexibility of Japanese orthography allows writers several alternatives for recording passages in dialect. They can freely choose whether to write a word in *kanji*, thereby conveying its approximate meaning while representing the regional pronunciation through an adjacent gloss printed in a smaller font using the *hiragana* or *katakana* syllabaries. Conversely, to use one of the two syllabaries and gloss the word with *kanji* lends primacy to the spoken dialect, requiring mainland readers to rely on the adjacent gloss for semantic information. The use of English letters is another option available for rendering spoken dialect into the written word. Any of these choices carries ideological implications: not only is primacy generally associated with whatever is featured in the main text (as opposed to the adjacent gloss), but use of *katakana* (which is often used to write loanwords from European languages) or of English letters can underscore the dialect's difference from "standard" Japanese—unless, of course, the author wishes to appropriate the cultural center and relegate the standard language of Tokyo to the margins by writing it in *katakana* or English letters.

16. Ōshiro subtitled this story "An Experimental Account in Local Dialect" (Jikken hōgen o motsu aru fudoki).

17. Another option, which none of the translators in this volume has adopted, is to render the dialect into standard English, using italics to highlight all passages that appear in dialect in the original text.

18. For statistics and a concise overview of the U.S. bases in Okinawa, see Nagamoto Tomohiro, "Okinawa, kichi mondai no rekishi to genzai," in Ishikawa Mao, Kuniyoshi Kazuo, and Nagamoto Tomohiro, *Kore ga Okinawa no beigun da* (Tokyo: Kōbunken, 1995), 193–220. Okinawa Prefecture also publishes data, in both English and Japanese, related to U.S. bases, crimes, and accidents involving American military personnel and their dependents.

19. George H. Kerr, *Okinawa: The History of an Island People*, 2d ed. (Rutland, Vt.: Charles E. Tuttle, 1984), 109.

20. Steve Rabson, "Meiji Assimilation Policy in Okinawa: Promotion, Resistance, and 'Reconstruction,'" in Helen Hardacre and Adam L. Kern, eds., *New Directions in the Study of Meiji Japan* (New York: Brill, 1997), 638.

21. Kerr, *Okinawa*, 108–112.

22. In the original texts, neither *ryūka* nor *waka* is regularly broken into separate lines, as is common in English translation. And while we have used the common but less precise term "syllable," technically speaking, these units should be referred to as "mora," so as to distinguish between long and short vowels that are critical in both standard Japanese and Ryukyuan dialects.

23. Translated by Sakihara Mitsugu in his book, *A Brief History of Early Okinawa Based on the Omoro Sōshi* (Tokyo: Honpō Shoseki Press, 1987), 182.

24. Rabson, "Meiji Assimilation Policy in Okinawa," 639.

25. Gregory Smits, *Visions of Ryukyu: Identity and Early-Modern Ideology in Thought and Politics* (Honolulu: University of Hawai'i Press, 1999), 27–31.

26. Rabson, "Meiji Assimilation Policy in Okinawa," 640.

27. Translated by Taira Buntarō [printed as "Bntaro"], *My Favorite Okinawan Poems* (Tokyo: Hokuseidō, 1969), 49.

28. On Okinawan struggles with assimilation, see Tomiyama Ichirō, *Kindai Nihon shakai to "Okinawajin"* (Tokyo: Nihon keizai hyōronsha, 1990). Also, Alan Christy, "The Making of Imperial Subjects in Okinawa," *Positions* 1(3) (Winter 1993):607–639.

29. Smits, *Visions of Ryukyu*, 46.

30. Kerr, *Okinawa*, 398; Rabson, "Meiji Assimilation Policy in Okinawa," 641.

31. Okamoto, *Okinawa bungaku no chihei*, 7–27.

32. Statistics are taken from Okinawa-ken, eds., *Okinawa: Kunan no gendaishi* (Tokyo: Iwanami dōjidai raiburarii no. 275, 1996), 20–21. For a detailed account of the Battle of Okinawa in English, see George Feifer, *Tennozan: The Battle of Okinawa and the Atomic Bomb* (New York: Ticknor and Fields, 1994).

33. Okinawa's ambiguous historical relationship to Japan renders the category "national borders" itself problematic. Technically, however, between 1879 and 1945 Okinawa was a Japanese prefecture and not a colony.

34. For a fictional account of the Princess Lily Nurse Corps in English, see Jo Nobuko Martin, *A Princess Lily of the Ryukyus* (Tokyo: Shin Nippon kyōiku tosho, 1984). A graphic firsthand account can be found in Haruko Taya Cook and Theodore F. Cook, eds., *Japan at War* (New York: The Free Press, 1992), 354–363. For a critical study, see Linda Angst, *In a Dark Time: Community, Memory and the Discursive Construction of Gendered Selves in Post War Okinawa*, Ph.D. dissertation, Yale University, 2000.

35. For a detailed study of *Cocktail Party* and other literary accounts of the American occupation years, see Molasky, *American Occupation of Japan and Okinawa*.

36. Ōta Masahide, "The U.S. Occupation of Okinawa and Postwar Reforms in Japan Proper," in Robert E. Ward and Yoshikazu Sakamoto, eds., *Democratizing Japan* (Honolulu: University of Hawai'i Press, 1987), 290. On group suicides, see Ishihara Masaie, *Shōgen Okinawa-sen: Senjō no kōkei* (Tokyo: Aoki shoten, 1984); and Shimojima Tetsurō, *Okinawa: Chibichirigama no "shūdan jiketsu"* (Tokyo: Iwanami bukkuretto no. 246, 1992).

37. Ōta, "U.S. Occupation of Okinawa and Postwar Reforms in Japan Proper," 288–290.

38. Miyagi Etsujirō, *Okinawa senryō no 27-nenkan: Amerika gunsei to bunka no henyō* (Tokyo: Iwanami bukkuretto no. 268, Iwanami shoten, 1992),

11–17. On the complicated history of currency on postwar Okinawa, see Makino Hirotaka, *Sengo Okinawa no tsūka* (Naha: Hirugi-sha, 1987).

39. Ōta, "U.S. Occupation of Okinawa and Postwar Reforms in Japan Proper," 291.

40. Office of Historiography, Department of Archives Administration, Okinawa Prefectural Culture Promotion Foundation, eds., *Okinawa-ken shi bijuaru ban (sengo 1): Bulldozers and Bayonets* (Naha: Okinawa Prefectural Board of Education, 1998), 50. This is an informative bilingual source on the land confiscation issue, replete with photographs and contemporary newspaper articles. Also on land confiscation and local protests, see Arasaki Moriteru, *Sengo Okinawashi* (Tokyo: Nihon hyōronsha, 1976).

41. For an analysis and partial translation of "The Colored Race," see Molasky, *American Occupation of Japan and Okinawa*, chapter 3.

42. Censorship clearance entailed submitting each issue to university authorities as well as to the censorship section of the U.S. Civil Administration of the Ryukyu Islands (USCAR), the occupation administration, in advance of publication. On the censorship of *Ryūdai bungaku*, see Kano, *Sengo Okinawa no shisō-zō*, 135; Ōe, *Okinawa keiken*, 32–33. Kano's meticulous study of *Ryūdai bungaku* includes a chart that lists the editors for each issue, giving their real names when pseudonyms are used. See Kano, 115–117.

43. Thomas R. H. Havens, *Fire across the Sea: The Vietnam War and Japan, 1965–1975* (Princeton, N.J.: Princeton University Press, 1987), chapter 7.

44. See the magazine's final issue, *Shin Okinawa bungaku* (Spring 1993), for a review of the magazine's history, together with a cumulative index listing all works, essays, and contributors.

45. Another such story is Nagadō Eikichi's "Paper Airplane from the Empire State Building" (Empaia suteeto biru no kami-hikōki) (Tokyo: Shinchō-sha, 1994). For a summary of this and other works by Nagadō, see the epilogue in Molasky, *American Occupation of Japan and Okinawa*.

46. The May 30, 1998, edition of *Ryūkyū shinpō* lists the prefectural unemployment rate as 7.8 percent for April 1998. A 1997 report issued by the Japanese Ministry of Education notes that only 23.5 percent of Okinawan high school graduates enter college or junior college, the lowest percentage of all Japanese prefectures. The national average is 37.6 percent. See

Monbushō, eds., *Gakkō kihon chōsa hōkokusho* (1997). In 1993, Okinawa Prefecture's live birth rate was 13.8 per 1,000—more than 3 births per 1,000 above the next highest prefecture. Okinawa's divorce rate for that year was 2.18 per 1,000. The national average was 1.52; Osaka had the second-highest divorce rate at 1.96, and Hokkaido was third at 1.94. See Statistics Bureau of the Management and Coordination Agency, eds., Japan Statistical Yearbook 1996 (based on data compiled by the Ministry of Health and Welfare).

POETRY

SEREI KUNIO (1897–1950)

Serei is considered among the most talented Okinawan poets of the Taishō era (1912–1926). He published not only his own books of poetry, but contributed poems to mainland magazines such as Gendai shika *(Modern poetry). In the early 1920s, he began translating classical Okinawan poems known as "ryūka" (see the introduction) into modern Japanese. This entailed translating Ryukyuan dialect into standard Japanese and rendering its classical grammar into a modern poetic language (although many verses retain premodern inflections). Together, they were simply titled "Translations of Old Okinawan Poems" (Ryūka yaku) and, although unpublished until much later, are thought to have been completed in 1922.*

The verse below is an English translation of Serei's Japanese translation of an early eighteenth-century ryūka. *His translation abandons the poem's traditional prosodic structure, although it includes a few elements of classical Japanese grammar. The original poem, written by a woman, decries the official prohibition at that time against romantic liaisons.*

A Verse from "Translations of Old Okinawan Poems"

Serei Kunio

To restrain my secret love for you
Does the signpost stand tall?
No, it ought not be so.
The edict of interdiction under a pine tree in Onna.

Translated by Hosea Hirata

NAKAMURA KARE (1905–1951)

An enigmatic figure, Nakamura went to Tokyo in the 1920s, where he was briefly affiliated with the prominent poet Kitahara Hakushū and his magazine, Kindai fūkei *(Modern scene). Many of Nakamura's poems appeared in this magazine in 1927 and 1928, including "My Last Letter" (Saigo no tegami), which was published in September 1928. It turned out to be Nakamura's last poem to appear in* Kindai fūkei. *Nakamura continued to publish in small poetry magazines for a few years, but then he disappeared from public view. Despite his evident talent and originality, Nakamura never published his own volume of poetry and today remains unknown by all but a handful of specialists.*

My Last Letter

Nakamura Kare

I'll turn into a piece of ice, and
At one o'clock P.M.
Vanish in the middle of the village square.

I'll hide inside that German-made alarm clock you gave me.
So, climb to the top of the lighthouse
And throw it as far out to sea as you can.

I wonder if
          There are any cute, little fish
Way out in the middle of the Pacific.
I want them to devour me, so
I'll turn into a pea and plunge in.

Hey, Set-chan:
Because you won't listen to me,
I'm really going to do one of these three things.
Be well. Sayonara.

Translated by Michael Molasky

Tsukayama Issui (1905–1981)

As with many of his contemporaries, Tsukayama left Okinawa for Tokyo. There, he joined Satō Sōnosuke's poetry circle, which produced the magazine Shi no ie *(House of poetry). Tsukayama published regularly in this and other magazines during the early 1930s, experimenting with various forms of modernism. "Entering the Harbor of a Southern Island" (Nantō nyūkō) and "Dead Body" (Shitai) appeared in his 1931 collection of poems,* The Inorganic Public Square *(Mukibutsu hiroba). He never published another book, however, and today he has been largely forgotten by readers of poetry in Okinawa as well as in mainland Japan.*

Entering the Harbor of a Southern Island

Tsukayama Issui

indigo island
smoke rising
red roofs
vegetation
clouds
    above the flowers
        beneath the leaves
blue parasol
winds from the dunes
sea birds flock
    around the flags atop shipmasts
the town
and here, on our boat,
the crew moves about the deck
    in light summer clothes
passengers line the rail
and chat about the harbor

Translated by Michael Molasky

Dead Body

Tsukayama Issui

A corpse washed ashore.
Its skin peeling off under the sun.
Yes, the August Lady is a dead body.
Rays of light coil round and round a parasol.
Within it, the heat is getting horny.
This dead body making out with the heat, I step over.

Translated by Hosea Hirata

Yamanokuchi Baku (1903–1963)

"Yamanokuchi Baku" is the pen name of Yamaguchi Jūsaburō. Referred to fondly as "Baku" by readers and critics, he is Okinawa's best-known poet. Born in Naha, he began publishing poetry in newspapers as a teenager, and in 1922 he moved to Tokyo, where he lived most of his life. By the late 1930s, he had published two collections of poetry and several stories in respected Japanese literary magazines. Known for his deceptively simple, colloquial style and wry humor, many of his works draw on his experiences as an impoverished poet eking out a living in Tokyo on odd jobs and borrowed funds. Some poems and stories describe the experience of Okinawans or other minorities living in mainland Japan; others depict Okinawa itself, especially later poems such as "Shell-shocked Island" (Tama o abita shima), published in 1964. Today, Baku is commemorated with the Yamanokuchi Baku Prize, which is awarded annually to a promising poet.

The prose passage below is from The Days of My Youth *(Seinen jidai), published in 1963, and introduces the 1935 poem, "A Conversation" (Kaiwa).*

45

FROM *THE DAYS OF MY YOUTH*

YAMANOKUCHI BAKU

IN THE COFFEE shop where I used to hang out, one of the regular customers showed up one day after a long absence, his face deeply tanned. He announced in a loud voice to the woman who ran the shop and her daughter that he had been on a business trip to Okinawa. I'd been talking to some other people at the time, but, being from Okinawa, I was slightly irritated to hear him mention it. Most Okinawans of my generation feel uncomfortable at such times. Still, I could not suppress a certain interest in this man's impressions of Okinawa. But hearing him talk about how he was invited to the home of a "chieftain," how he drank *awamori* from a soup bowl, and how "the natives" do this and that, I felt as though he was conjuring up visions of a place I'd never seen. Although aware that this was simply a tourist's amusement, I was saddened, not only because I am Okinawan, but also because the manager's daughter was listening wide-eyed to this man's every word. I had been planning for some time to graduate from my lumpen life-style, and my relationship with this girl had progressed to the point where I was intending to ask her to marry me. I couldn't help wondering what she would think if she knew I was Okinawan. Sitting in a booth of that coffee shop, I concentrated all my energy on writing this poem.

A CONVERSATION

YAMANOKUCHI BAKU

"Where are you from," she asked.
I thought about where I was from and lit a cigarette.
That place colored by associations with tattoos, the *jabisen*,
and ways as strange as ornamental designs.
"Very far away," I answered.
"In what direction," she asked.
That place of gloomy customs near the southern tip of the
      Japanese
archipelago where women carry piglets on their heads and
      people walk
barefoot. Was this where I was from?
"South," I answered.
"Where in the south," she asked.
In the south, that zone of indigo seas where it's always
      summer and dragon
orchids, sultan umbrellas, octopus pines, and papayas all
      nestle together
under the bright sunlight. That place shrouded in miscon-
      ceptions
where, it is said, the people aren't Japanese and can't under-
      stand the
Japanese language.
"The subtropics," I answered.
"Oh, the subtropics!" she said.

Yes, my dear, can't you see "the subtropics" right here before
    your eyes?
Like me, the people there are Japanese, speak Japanese, and
    were born
in the subtropics. But, viewed through popular stereotypes,
    that place I am from
has become a synonym for chieftains, natives, karate, and
    awamori.
"Somewhere near the equator," I said.

TRANSLATED BY STEVE RABSON

Shell-shocked Island

Yamanokuchi Baku

The moment I set foot on the island soil
and greeted them *Ganjuy*[1]
Very well, thank you
the island people replied in Japanese
My nostalgia at a bit of a loss
I muttered
　　Uchi nahguchi madhin muru
　　Ikusani sattaru basui[2]
to which the island people feigned a smile
but remarked how well I spoke the Okinawa dialect

Translated by Rie Takagi

---

1. How have you been?
2. Was even your dialect destroyed by the war?

Takara Ben (1949–)

"Takara Ben" is the pen name of Takamine Chōsei. Born 1949 in Tamagusuku, he received a B.S. in chemistry from Shizuoka University and also attended graduate school in the Philippines. For many years Takara taught chemistry at Futenma High School and now is educational advisor for the prefectural Office of Education. He maintains an energetic schedule that combines political activism with the writing of poetry and social criticism. His first poetry collection was published in 1979. Since then, he has published several books of poetry and criticism and is the recipient of numerous Okinawan literary awards.

In recent years Takara has forged alliances with Ainu activists in Hokkaidō to explore issues shared by Japan's "indigenous" populations. He has also been an outspoken proponent of Ryukyuan independence. Takara insists on referring to his homeland as "Ryukyu" to emphasize its cultural distinctiveness from mainland Japan and to underscore the region's historical ties to China and Southeast Asia. Published in 1984, "Dream Revelations" (Yume no mokuji) reveals Takara's interest in traditional Ryukyuan cosmology and its resonance in contemporary Okinawa.

Dream Revelations

Takara Ben

—the postwar
could only have existed
in the forms in which it was lived
by those who lived it out
in their separate ways—

someone is murmuring
it must have been
    a dream

In the sacred grove of Hamagawa
in the shadow of the rocks on the shore,
    their hair dyed red,
    lipstick moist
two island girls
white arms bared to the pit
    waited,
staring into the distant
bluegreen channels of *nirai kanai*[1]
for the black-skinned, white-skinned G.I.s
    who would come

---

1. The other world in Ryukyuan cosmology. Pictured often as the home of beneficent deities, it is also the dwelling place of malevolent spirits. *Nirai kanai* is commonly located beyond the ocean horizon, as it is here, but some regional sources imagine it on the ocean floor or even underground.

Eke hai[2]
that dream last night
O dream of midnight
        dreams
leave no trace
        dreams
vanish in thin air, still
in the ocean bottom of the dream,
his heart shattered,
the long shadow of a boy
        chasing

Typhoon Jane[3] sent everything flying
        the sand flew
        the leaves on trees shredded
        the island bananas split
        the red tiles flew

Even the lamplight is out
on the third morning when
        in the morning glow
collapsed thatched roofs appear
        and parched by ocean winds
the bottomless mouth of a lagoon
        gapes,
face of the village looming up

As far as the eye can see
mowed down sugar canes
        at ocean's edge

---

2. Exclamations. This and subsequent italicized passages are taken from poem 79,
vol. 12 of the *Omoro sōshi,* a collection of lyrics from the various Ryukyu Islands compiled in the sixteenth and seventeenth centuries by order of the monarchy (centered
in Shuri, on Okinawa Island).
3. The American occupation extended to the naming of typhoons.

over frothing coral forests
waves break
above black rotted sweet potato fields
only blue sky
soaring clear
and one giant swirling green eye
peering down

Somewhere
the wind still groans
In the depths of the pupil of the boy
staring back at the eye
the sun burned,
a nameless migrant butterfly
danced, swaying:
mandala of a southern land
O butterfly

You who were born in Kishaba
O girl from Kishaba
Eke hai
that dream last night
in that dream of midnight
hidden behind the rocks
the boy
was stealing glimpses
of the two island girls
One girl he ran into
all the time
on the alley by the inn
in the hills of ancient chronicles[4]
till last year
her school uniform was blinding white

---

4. Where the founding deities, a male and female couple, may have first alighted; the site of an American officers' club after the war.

her breasts bounced beneath buttons
        ready to pop

In the village house
father, with ailing lungs
        slept
sweating out a high-noon dream
        the shelling's gouged out
        my shoulders and my eyes
        my ears hurt
he groaned

Uncle Sasuke
who works at the village office
came to visit,
stood at attention
and saluted;
"How is your father?
I pray for the good fortune
of my comrade-in-arms"
he said.
When he heard this,
tears began to roll
        off the boy's face

Mother watched me
        weeping
tubful of fish and squid
        for peddling
on her head
her feet bare,
        my mother
        of young summer[5]

_____

5. A fixed phrase in traditional verse referring to the earliest part of summer, when
the heads of rice appear.

54

in the folds of her abaca cloth collar
down the valley between her breasts
flowed the glistening sweat
        of a mermaid

Each time a big wave
gouges out the white beach
the base of caverns
crushed by bulldozer
is exposed
I chip the rock
and take away a sliver
from the shores of dream
to spin the threads
        of memory

Mornings come around
to a temporary dwelling
        in the city
Where will I find
the pebble I brought back
Ah, to hold that girl,
to dream that girl

On mornings when I'm struck
        by dream revelations
I break off a sunflower
in the noonday garden
and begin walking
beyond the village where
        without a word
I've left behind
aging father and mother

TRANSLATED BY NORMA FIELD

FICTION

Ikemiyagi Sekihō (1893–1951)

Although it is never named, the main setting for "Officer Ukuma" (Ukuma junsa) is almost certainly the Kume section of Naha, home of early Chinese immigrants to Okinawa and their descendants, and also the author's birthplace. After studying at Waseda University in Tokyo, Ikemiyagi returned to Okinawa in 1916, working as a newspaper reporter and a Japanese-language teacher in public school. Besides fiction written mostly in the 1920s, he published a collection of Okinawan historical tales in 1931. "Officer Ukuma" was selected from competitive submissions in 1922 for its first publication in the mainland literary magazine Kaihō. *The Tsuji "pleasure quarter," the other locale described in this story, has been the setting for numerous poems and stories in Okinawa since the seventeenth century (see the introduction).*

Officer Ukuma

———◦◦◦◦———

Ikemiyagi Sekihō

On the outskirts of Naha, the capital city of Ryukyu, is a certain village I'll refer to as "X." Its residents are of Chinese descent, and most of them—no, I should say nearly all—are poor and do menial work. Frog catchers go out to the rice fields to hunt for frogs, which they skin and take to market. Frogs are considered a delicacy by people in Naha and in the nearby town of Shuri. There are also fishermen and weavers among the villagers. Their work is humble, and people in other parts of Naha look down on them as "those X'ers," but they enjoy a simple, communal life with few worries.

Their village is thickly shaded by towering subtropical trees—banyan, *deigo*, and *fukugi*. Low bamboo hedges encircle each shabby house made from thatched miscanthus reeds. In the morning the village men walk to the rice fields carrying fishing poles and nets, while the women spread straw mats under the cool shade of the trees and weave hats and sandals, singing the mournful melodies of Ryukyuan folk songs. In the evening, after the men come home from the fields, their wives and daughters go to market to sell the freshly caught frogs and carp. With the little money they make, they buy fish and one square wooden container each of *awamori*, then return holding lighted torches so they won't be bitten by poisonous *habu* snakes. At home they are greeted happily by the men who, after finishing the meager evening meal, stretch out, quietly sipping *awamori*. So accustomed are the villagers to this life that they never find it sad. Though poor, they pool their money so that in bad times they can help each other out. And in this southern clime, no day, even in winter, is too hard to bear. They live simply and in peace.

But when one of their own, Ukuma Hyaaku, attained the highly respected position of policeman, it was not only an honor for the Ukuma family, but for the entire village. For these Chinese descendants, who barely eked out a living with their menial labor, becoming a government official was no small feat. Indeed, it was close to a miracle.

When word had spread of Ukuma Hyaaku's ambition to be a policeman, all the villagers rejoiced as though his good fortune would be their own, and everyone prayed fervently for his success. The young man's father excused him from his daily chores to encourage him in his studies, and his mother engaged a shaman, traveling with her to many sacred sites to pray that Hyaaku would pass the qualifying examination. The day before the exam, Hyaaku's mother took him to the family's ancestral tomb, where she recited a lengthy prayer.

The hopes of Hyaaku, his family, and the village were realized when he passed the examination with flying colors. It was considered a triumph for all, and everyone took half a day off from work for a banquet celebrating Hyaaku's success. The village men gathered on the shaded lawn in front of Hyaaku's home, where they passed away the afternoon drinking *awamori* and plucking the three-stringed *jabisen*, while nearby the youngsters played at imitating actors in Ryukyuan dance dramas.

It had been May in the early 1920s, a time of year when one didn't feel cold even wearing an abaca-cloth kimono. Red *deigo* flowers were just beginning to bloom, and white lilies were opening here and there in the grass of shady groves. Absorbing the fierce southern sunlight, hibiscus flamed brightly among the hedges.

The village men, stripped to their waists, sang, danced, and played the *jabisen* while the women gathered around to watch with obvious pleasure. Our Ukuma Hyaaku looked odd amid all this noisy merrymaking as he sat in a chair someone had brought out for him, like some victorious general, wearing a uniform and cap and carrying a glistening sword. The women stared with admiration and awe at his strangely imposing figure.

The banquet went on this way until dawn, with music and boisterous laughter echoing through the forest on what would ordinarily have been a quiet night in the village.

After he finished his training, Officer Ukuma started working alternate days at the main police station, where he'd been assigned because of his high marks. He spent every other day at home reading books, and his family was proud to see him leave and come back from the station wearing his cap and uniform. When told by visitors from time to time that their son had been seen walking somewhere in his uniform, his family could scarcely contain their delight. And the visitors, too, spoke joyfully, as if seeing him had been some special event, and a few said they hoped their own sons would become policemen someday.

On the twenty-fifth of the month, Hyaaku left for home with his wages in his pocket. His heartbeat had quickened with joy when he held this money for the first time, and now he fingered the thick envelope tucked inside his right pocket as he walked along briskly. Arriving at home, he barely managed to calm his excitement, then went into the living room and tried to look nonchalant as he took out the envelope and handed it to his mother.

"Well, now!" His mother spoke happily as she took the envelope and examined its contents. "Twenty-three yen," she said after counting the bills. "It's not much." Though she'd already heard that this was all his salary would be, she seemed surprised when she actually saw the money.

The next two or three months went by peacefully, but Hyaaku's family began to feel that he was growing distant from them. He rarely spent time with other young people in the village anymore, and they seemed to lose interest in him as well. He thought only about how he might succeed as a policeman and how he could use his present position as a stepping-stone to something higher.

Hyaaku grew more and more short-tempered. Whenever he came home he complained, "This house is dirty. It's filthy!" And, blaming his sister, he bawled her out constantly. After his fellow officers dropped by one day, he got even more upset about the house. Hyaaku's mother cried at the sight of him railing at his sister and wondered what had caused her good-natured son to change so drastically.

But things only got worse, and Hyaaku began meddling in the lives of his fellow villagers. One day during a local festival he stood up in front of the crowd gathered in the village square and, looking as if he'd been waiting for just such an opportunity, began to speak. At first the villagers thought Hyaaku would be announcing good news of some benefit for them. Since Hyaaku was a policeman and a fellow villager, they expected to hear that, through him, the city government would be making improvements in their living conditions. They imagined he would say something about lower taxes, road repairs, or perhaps free medical care. What Hyaaku told them, however, completely betrayed their expectations.

"From now on the sewers must be cleaned thoroughly every day. When it's hot in the summer, many of you go around without clothes. This is a crime punishable by law, so if a policeman sees you, expect to be fined. I'm a policeman, too, and from now on I won't let you get away with anything just because you say you're from this village. We public officials value nothing more than impartiality. So we can't look the other way even if a member of our own families or a relative does something wrong or vulgar."

He went on to chastise them for things that, until now, they had done without a second thought. "Furthermore," he said, "drinking until late at night and singing is forbidden. You must drink less, work harder, and save your money, so you can get more respectable jobs."

Hyaaku continued this loud and heated harangue while the villagers stared at him, looking very uncomfortable. They could not bear the thought that Hyaaku now saw himself in a position different from their own. So when the festival ceremonies ended and the drinking and merrymaking began, not one person offered him a cup of *awamori*.

During those days Hyaaku's fellow officers often visited him at home. He would offer his guests *awamori*, and some of them stayed on from afternoon late into the night, drinking and raising a ruckus. These tough, brawny young men were loud and rude. Unlike the local people, they didn't play the *jabisen* or sing Ryukyuan folk songs, but would bang on their plates and bowls, singing incomprehensible songs from Kagoshima and reciting Chinese verse. Occasionally one of them would stand up all of a sudden, brandishing a stick, and do a sword dance. Their wild behavior frightened Hyaaku's quiet family, who did not even want these men in their house. They were especially upset at Hyaaku for joining in their carousing.

From olden times these villagers had instinctively feared the police. Nevertheless, at first they rejoiced when Hyaaku became a policeman. But now they were worried about his dramatic change in attitude; and on top of that, the other policemen's frequent comings and goings from Hyaaku's house also made them uneasy. These officers, staggering through the streets on their way home, would shout insults at the villagers who wore few clothes when they worked. As such things occurred more often, the villagers began to curse the very presence of Hyaaku's house in their midst, which they only rarely visited.

Gradually, even Hyaaku himself began to sense the changed attitude of those around him. At home he was always irritated. And the cold looks of villagers he encountered on the street made him hostile. It angered him that he was now the village outcast, and to make matters worse, he discovered that his fellow officers were making fun of him because he came from this village. When he overheard them call him "that X'er," he could feel his face grow hot. Hyaaku was so ashamed of his birthplace, where he still lived, that he talked to his family about moving, but they could not agree. Nothing hurt them more than the thought of leaving this village—not only because they had grown so used it, but also because moving was sure to make them even poorer.

Thus Hyaaku could find no relief from the hostility he felt toward the village, and he grew increasingly lonely. Among his fellow officers he could not find a single true friend. Since most of them were from other prefectures—Kagoshima, Saga, and Miyazaki—their lives and feelings differed sharply from his own. Although he could join them for drinking and merrymaking, he was unable to speak with them from the heart. Even when they talked at the police station, he sometimes found himself murmuring, "They are strangers." And he sensed that they also viewed him as an outsider. Yet even though Hyaaku's feelings of isolation were becoming unbearable, his fellow officers continued visiting his house to drink and were every bit as rambunctious as before.

Summer that year was very hot, and there was a long drought. Every day dazzling sunlight filled the clear, bright Ryukyuan sky. The sultry scent of earth and weeds wafted up into the parched air as the powerful sunlight reflected off Naha's red-tiled roofs and bore down on people's eyes and skin. The grass that grew above the high stone walls around houses became withered and crackling dry. One moment a lizard with gleaming silver skin could be seen dashing out from a wall only to hide itself again seconds later inside a crack in the stones. In the afternoon hours, the sun made the road seem like a desert, filling the air with its silent, piercing rays.

Sometimes a waft of clouds would appear in one portion of the sky like shimmering layers of mica, and people thought how wonderful it would be if the clouds turned to rain. In the late afternoon, the setting sun would blaze through the layered clouds, and when the villagers saw its rays shining on the green hills and forests, they would hope for rain the next day. The dream-like voices of children singing echoed in the quiet sky that glowed as the sun set.

> The fabled monkey's home has burned.
> To fix it let's buy a bit of birdlime.

The children would sing this song happily, though they didn't understand the words, at any hour of the evening. But when the sun finally set, the layers of clouds vanished and the sky seemed to envelop the earth with throngs of stars glowing brightly like sweeping grains of silver dust.

As the days and nights dragged on this way, Hyaaku seemed to wilt like the withered grasses and trees, growing utterly downcast. He could find no relief even in his work, and life had become unbearably dreary.

One night, when he was fed up with these doldrums, a fellow officer from Kagoshima invited him to go for a walk along the seashore. Even those who had lived here long admired the beautiful evening hues on the beaches of this coral island. The reef looked like it had been whittled down here and there, and in some places the tide had gnawed out deep, dark hollows. The wave crests surging toward the beach would seem about to melt away, then reemerge, ashen and white, beneath the pale blue moonlight. Sorrowful melodies came flowing like a mountain stream from the hills or the shore where prostitutes sang love songs. Their alluring voices seemed to beckon Hyaaku as cool breezes wafting off the ocean danced over his skin. Near where he sat, from time to time, he could see in the moonlight the fair-skinned face of a prostitute dressed in a thin *tonpyan* kimono as she swam by expressionlessly. On his way back that night, invited by his fellow officer, Hyaaku went for the first time to Tsuji, Naha's renowned brothel district.

Facing its streets were long rows of two-story houses surrounded by high stone walls. From inside drifted the plucked notes of *jabisen*, the echo of drums, and the high-pitched voices of young women. Hyaaku's friend entered through the roofed gate at a certain house, knocked on the door, and gave a signal. At length a girl's voice asked, "Who is it?" and the door opened. The girl, seeing Hyaaku's friend, smiled broadly. "Come in," she said, and the two men were led to a six-mat guestroom. Inside was an alcove decorated with a scroll of Chinese poetry, and a black lacquered koto lay nearby. In front of one wall sat a long lacquer chest, its brass fittings gleaming brightly. The cupboard beside it also seemed very new, its varnish still fragrant. Across the room stood a large folding screen on which was painted a *deigo* tree with a white parrot perched on one of the branches that bloomed in a profusion of red blossoms.

To Hyaaku it all looked beautiful and exotic. After a time some women came in carrying liquor and food on red lacquer trays. While the two men drank, the women played the *jabisen* and sang. Presently a geisha, who seemed to be about fourteen or fifteen, appeared wearing a flashy red-patterned kimono and performed dances grasping a halberd and waving a fan.

At first Hyaaku was shy, but as the *awamori* began to take effect, even he eased into a rare, rollicking mood. At last he was telling jokes that had the women laughing and was beating with surprising facility on some drums in the room.

That night Hyaaku bought a woman for the first time. The girl he was matched with, a prostitute called Little Kamarū, seemed scarcely out of puberty—probably seventeen or so—with a round, doll-like face.

Something in her sweet, childlike manner captivated him. When the party ended and they went together to her room at the rear of the house, Hyaaku sobered up all at once and felt strangely uneasy. He leaned against the wooden tray around the hibachi while she hung the blue mosquito netting and pretended not to notice her changing out of her kimono. But as she disrobed he caught a glimpse of her white shoulders, and the sight of her long arms moving gracefully caused his eyelids to tremble.

The girl, now dressed only in a thin nightgown, entered the mosquito netting, fastened down on three sides, and slipped over beside Hyaaku. Silently, he poured water from a clay pot into a teacup and drank it. The girl picked up a round fan but made no effort to fan herself as she leaned over beside him against the charcoal brazier and stared down at the white ashes inside. Every now and then Hyaaku could hear her breathing deeply.

THE next morning Hyaaku found himself sleeping next to the girl under the blue mosquito netting. Though mildly surprised and embarrassed, he was secretly delighted. But when she awoke, the girl seemed to be in a very bad mood. Later she saw him out to the front gate. "Please come again tomorrow," she said. Hearing this, Hyaaku imagined he might be followed and left hurriedly, returning home on a road few people traveled. That day, when he faced his family, he felt awful. No matter how much he told himself that what had happened last night was of no consequence, he continued to feel he had done something terrible.

Hyaaku vowed he would never stay in Tsuji again. His fellow officer had invited him that first time and arranged for the girl. But Hyaaku had not paid her and thought he'd better go back just to give her the money. So on the evening he received his salary, Hyaaku went alone to her house. He said little after entering her room and remained standing as he downed two or three cups of the Chinese tea Ryukyuans like to drink. Then, very awkwardly, he took out a five-yen note from his wallet and handed it to the girl, but she refused to take the money. And, thinking he wanted to leave, she asked him to stay. Just then another girl, her companion, came into the room. "Please stay and visit a while," she also urged him. So that night, too, he drank *awamori* and slept in Kamarū's room.

The next day, when Hyaaku returned home, he gave his mother the remaining eighteen yen from his salary and told her he had deposited five yen in his postal savings account. Then he explained in great detail how the postal savings system worked. His mother nodded silently.

Without planning to, Hyaaku visited the girl's place two or three times after that, and the more he saw her the more something about her attracted him. He wasn't sure if it was her soft, beautiful body, her kind, gentle demeanor, or the glittering, gay surroundings in which she lived. But he felt drawn to her like a magnet.

This girl, Kamarū, was the daughter of a family who had once owned many acres of farmland in the countryside. But after her father died, her none-too-bright older brother had been deceived by swindlers and lost the family fortune. After squandering all of their property, he fell deeply in debt, and to repay the family's losses, his sister was sold into prostitution. The intimacy with which she confided this to Hyaaku, so different from her attitude toward him on their first meeting, caused him to feel even more drawn to her.

The relentless drought that year brought bad times for everyone. In the pleasure quarters, all the houses lost customers. Only two or three regulars showed up at Kamarū's place, and even their visits became more infrequent. No matter what time Hyaaku went to visit Kamarū, he always found her waiting impatiently for him. And the more she showed her feelings for him, the more his feelings for her deepened, and he no longer tried to control them.

When Hyaaku went to see Kamarū on the evening of his next pay-day, he boldly handed her two ten-yen bills.

"You'll be in trouble if you give me this much. One is enough," she said, returning the other bill to him.

"Take it," he insisted, handing it back to her. "I should give you more. Next time I will."

When Hyaaku went home the next day, he told his mother he had loaned his month's salary to a fellow officer in a financial emergency who would pay it back the following month. Even as he spoke, he could feel his face growing hot and his voice trembling. His mother looked at him suspiciously but said nothing.

On the afternoon of September 27 a cold wind began to blow. Hyaaku was working at the police station and had just started wondering if it was going to rain when a typhoon warning arrived from the weather bureau. "Violent winds expected locally. Caution advised in coastal areas." A low-pressure system had formed in the ocean 160 knots southeast of Ishigaki Island and was said to be moving in a northwesterly direction toward Okinawa.

By evening the storm was raging. The thick branches of the huge trees in front of the police station swayed in the wind. Baby sparrows, lost and confused, flew in circles, beating their wings. Yellow dragonflies, swept this way and that by the gale, swarmed around the mulberry trees. And in the sky far above the town could be heard the shrieking cries of seagulls seeking refuge.

That night Hyaaku changed at the station from his uniform into his street clothes, then went to Kamarū's place. Her house was filled with fear as the girls waited anxiously for the violent wind and rain. To avoid having things blown and tossed about, Hyaaku helped the girls put everything inside the house. The sun had just set when the storm brought torrents of rain. As the doors of the house began rattling, the walls and beams trembled. After a time, the electricity went out, and candles were lit. Kamarū's face looked pale in the candlelight flickering through the gloom. When the doors started shaking violently, she hurried over next to Hyaaku, crying, "I wonder if we're safe here!" Outside, the gale howled and sent tiles flying off the roof to crash shattering against the stone wall in front of the house.

The violent storm continued for three days and three nights. Skipping a day of work, Hyaaku spent all of those nights with Kamarū. Amid the sounds of roaring wind and rain, they looked into each other's eyes and talked of many things, their mutual attachment growing stronger than ever. By now they could not bear the thought of being apart, even for a single day. Hyaaku proposed they live together but knew this was impossible, since he had no income other than his twenty-three-yen monthly salary. *How I wish I had money!* he thought, and understood for the first time why a man would commit a crime for a woman. He realized that *right now, if the opportunity came, even I . . .* and was frightened by his own thoughts.

On the fourth day the wind and rain stopped, so Hyaaku left Kamarū's place around noon but didn't feel like going home. Instead, he walked aimlessly through a cemetery behind the pleasure quarters. Here and there on the wide hillcrest sat Ryukyuan-style tombs carved from sheets of rock lacquered white, making them look like stone huts. With the rain gone, the sky was clear, but in this deserted field of graves Hyaaku felt lonely.

With no destination in mind, he wandered among the graves, passing in front of a gabled tomb, when the shadow of something moving inside caught his eye. Peering in, Hyaaku saw it was a man. He rushed inside all at once and dragged him out. In that moment Hyaaku's languid mood vanished, and he became the consummate policeman

"Sir, I have not done anything wrong. I am just hiding here," the man said. Hyaaku forcibly searched the man's clothing and found one yen and fifty sen tucked into his waistband. He assumed the man had stolen the money. Though Hyaaku repeatedly asked the man his name and address, he wouldn't say a thing. "I will not do anything bad, sir," he said, as Hyaaku dragged him off to the police station for questioning. Hyaaku was filled with pride at having arrested his first criminal. He shoved the man roughly into the interrogation room, as if he'd been some stray dog, then went to give his report to the police inspector. Warm sweat dripped from Hyaaku's forehead onto his cheeks.

When the inspector heard Hyaaku's report, he smiled. "Well, now, this is your first real achievement. Good work. Hey, Chief Watanabe," he called, and ordered the patrol chief to interrogate the suspect. Officer Ukuma stood nearby and listened to the questioning. He admired the skill with which the chief conducted his interrogation, thinking how great it would be if the suspect really turned out to have committed a theft. On the other hand, if he hadn't, Hyaaku realized it would make him look inept, and waves of anxiety began rolling over him. But as the questioning progressed, it became clear that the man had indeed stolen the money, and eventually he confessed.

"I was a wealthy son in a certain town but got into business over my head, lost everything, and had to sell our rice fields and farm land.

So you see, originally, I wasn't poor or a thief. Then, on top of my family's financial ruin, we had one poor crop after another, and it got so hard for us to make a living that I came to Naha on my way to Daitō Island. I was going there to find work as a migrant laborer but failed the physical because of some infectious disease and couldn't go." (Hyaaku thought it was probably tuberculosis, since even as he spoke, the man coughed frequently.)

"At that point all I could do was look for work in Naha, but before I could find some, I spent all the money I had and got thrown out of my rented room. I was walking around town when the storm hit, so I searched for shelter and found that open tomb. Staying inside there I was afraid I would starve. Fortunately, the rain let up this morning, so I left the tomb and headed for town. I went into a liquor store to ask for some water and saw some bills lying on top of a wine barrel. Before I knew what I was doing, I grabbed them. Then I got scared holding that money in my hand, and without looking back, I ran away again to the open tomb. So you see, originally, I was no thief. My younger sister has done quite well as a prostitute in Tsuji. If only I'd gone to her place I could have found a way out of my troubles, but with the awful state of my clothes I was afraid of what she'd think. Please forgive me. I'll never do anything like this again."

As the man told his story in a heavy Ryukyuan country accent, his voice gradually started to waver, and by the time he'd finished, tears were streaming down his cheeks. "Sir, please forgive me. Please." He bowed so low his head touched the floor.

Seeing this, the chief laughed loudly, obviously proud of his successful interrogation. "How about that, Officer Ukuma. It's just as you suspected. A true crime! Ha, ha, ha."

But Officer Ukuma was unable to laugh, and a lump of fear filled his chest and threatened to cut off his breathing.

"Well, what's your name?" the chief demanded.

The man did not answer, and now Officer Ukuma's face revealed the unbearable tension he felt as he stared at him. It might have been his imagination, but the man's face seemed to resemble that of Kamarū, who he had left only a short time earlier.

Pressed relentlessly by the chief, the man finally spoke. "I'm Gima Tarū."

Now panic seized Officer Ukuma.

After revealing his name, the man took a deep breath and told the chief his age as well as the name, age, and address of his younger sister. Then, again he pleaded for forgiveness.

Officer Ukuma's hunch had been correct, and this man was none other than Kamarū's older brother. Painfully regretting his arrest, he raged and cursed at himself for having been so proud of dragging this man into the station only a short time ago. Now the chief turned toward him. "Hey, Officer Ukuma," he said, "since we have to question his younger sister as a witness, you go to her place and bring her in."

Officer Ukuma felt all the blood in his body rush to his head. For a time he could only stare blankly at the chief. Then his eyes began smoldering with the fear and rage of a wild beast fallen into a trap.

TRANSLATED BY DAVINDER BHOWMIK

Kushi Fusako (1903–1986)

*Kushi Fusako was born in the former Ryukyu kingdom's capital of Shuri
to a family of noble lineage whose fortunes declined rapidly after the
Meiji Restoration and the failure of their sugar sales company. Kushi
moved several times during her childhood, transferring schools often. She
graduated from Okinawa Prefectural High School in 1920 and then
taught for a time at an elementary school in Yomitan, but she moved to
Tokyo in order to pursue a writing career.*

When the monthly women's magazine Fujin kōron *(Women's forum)
first published "Memoirs of a Declining Ryukyuan Woman" in June
1932, Kushi was hailed by critics as a promising literary talent. However, the story drew strong condemnation from the leaders of Okinawa
prefectural and student associations on the mainland for its depiction of
an Okinawan businessman living in Tokyo who, seeking to escape prejudice, concealed his origins even from his wife and daughter. In the following month's issue of* Fujin kōron, *Kushi published an eloquent defense
of her story (translated after the story below). The published rebuttal
adroitly exposes the claims of her detractors, showing how they have
become abettors of the very prejudice they decry. Yet this bitter experience
led Kushi to stop writing for publication and to avoid public attention for
the rest of her life.*

*The cities identified in this story by the letters "S" and "N" are almost
surely Shuri (Kushi's birthplace) and Naha (Okinawa's capital).*

Memoirs of a Declining Ryukyuan Woman

Kushi Fusako

I was visiting a friend who had just returned from a family funeral on our home island. I expected to hear from her about my mother but was afraid of what she might say. It was hard for me to imagine my mother surviving this winter with her failing health, and I listened to my friend, feeling as if I had walked out onto thin ice. But she spoke only of my mother's unflagging endurance, and I could detect no sign of concealment on her face, which looked as if it had been freshly swept by the salt sea breeze of our island. Then, sighing deeply, she began to talk about the state of total exhaustion in Ryukyu.

"It's pitch-black at night in S City. I heard that all the rich folks there want desperately to move to N to avoid high taxes. The stone hedges in front of the houses are all crumbling now, and most of the yards inside have been turned into farm fields. Can you believe that S is still Ryukyu's second largest city? To make matters worse, emigration abroad has been banned. People can barely make a living these days by going to work on the mainland."

"I know."

For a time we forgot everything else as we talked of our homeland. My friend, looking worried, explained how she wanted to bring her mother up to Tokyo and help her start a business selling Oshima *tsumugi* cloth.

"The problem is her tattoo."

Tattoos have caused suffering in almost every Ryukyuan family. Even if a woman can save enough money to send several sons to higher school, she is destined to be left behind in her hometown until she

73

dies, thanks to those tattoos on the back of her hands. In the worst cases, mothers have died without ever knowing the names of their grandchildren. The more their sons succeed, the more strictly the mothers have to be confined to their "homes," where they are given a tiny bit of freedom and supported by whatever petty allowance their sons care to provide. Of course, there have been a few exceptions.

Ryukyuan intellectuals are not nearly so bold as those Koreans or Taiwanese who live in mainland Japan. While they openly maintain their customs and manners, we tend to form hidden clusters, like mushrooms, even in this vast metropolis of Tokyo. Though individuals, we can't help but share the loneliness of being Ryukyuan, a loneliness that echoes in our hearts like the sound of the *sanshin*. Yet we never speak of this plaintive sound. If one of us broaches the subject, we avert our eyes, coldly, like two cripples passing on the sidewalk.

We are a people in desperate need of some rapid awakening, but only live from day to day mired in vacillation and pretense, blinded by the deep-rooted mentality of petite bourgeoisie. We always seem to be at the tail end of history, dragged along roads already ruined by others.

Now other dark thoughts filled my mind as I walked along beside the bergamot orange hedges on the way home from my friend's place. I remembered that I was supposed to meet my uncle at a certain train station. He was another of our people who could not reveal the truth about himself for all the twenty years he had lived in the middle of Tokyo. He managed several branches of a company, supervised university and technical school graduates, and lived in a spacious apartment with a bossy wife and a daughter in her prime who was soon to be married. Yet he had never disclosed the slightest hint to any of them that he was Ryukyuan.

Before I knew it, the faded green train had carried me to X Station, where I went to meet him, as usual, in the third-class waiting room, covering my face with a shawl. Only a few hours remained before New Year's Eve, and there was a tension in the room that reminded me of a tightly wound spring. Everyone looked nervous. Only the young women, with their hair done up for the occasion in traditional Japanese style, basked in the calm afternoon sunlight and seemed to glow in anticipation. Watching them, I felt like some alien creature, constantly scratching my dandruff-filled hair. My body and spirit had all the vitality of a dead cat.

In one corner of the waiting room, a man in an old padded kimono, dirty and worn, was being interrogated by a policeman. The only reason seemed to be that he'd been lying on the floor. Why are the poor always the first to be regarded as criminals? Though this seemed to be someone else's problem, for some reason it disturbed me almost more than I could bear.

"Hello."

All at once I noticed my uncle standing in front of me. Without returning my silent bow, he sat down next to me, clenching a cigar between his teeth. Our awkward conversation lasted about two minutes.

"I've just been too busy," he said brusquely in what sounded like an excuse. "Please send this as usual." He took a ten-yen bill out of his wallet and put it down beside me.

"Certainly." My answer was also curt, as usual.

Our talks always ended quickly.

I gazed after him until his bulky figure had crossed the station square and was swallowed up in the crowd. It occurred to me that his body blended in well with the city buildings and with his large office desk, which was piled high with business letters. It was an even more perfect match, I thought, than the plum trees and bush warblers often portrayed together in traditional Japanese paintings. He was typical of that corporate breed of men who look as if they were born for these surroundings. Watching his back as he moved away, I felt only a machine-like precision, power, and coldness. The last fading rays of sunset that hovered over the layers of buildings seemed to reflect the gloom in my heart.

Though I had never met his wife or daughter, from what my uncle said, I had a general picture of how he lived. Of course, I do not know his home address. I once visited his office after finding that address in the telephone directory, but he had politely forbidden me to come again. This didn't really bother me, though, since I had no intention of relying on him for anything.

At home he kept three maids, an elderly handyman, and a piano. This is the story of how he started sending three yen every month to his stepmother at his other "home."

ONE day five years ago he suddenly returned to Ryukyu. Thirty years had passed since he disappeared, shortly after being discharged from the army somewhere in Kyushu, and people even suspected he had died.

Apparently, he thought my family was still prospering. After giving our name to a ricksha man, he looked all over town for our house and finally arrived that evening at our wretched little shop, which sat behind a mailbox in a yard barely ten feet square. My mother bowed down almost to the ground, all in a fluster because she had mistaken this arrogant-looking man in a Western suit for the tax collector who always scolded her for the way she kept accounts on items like cigarettes and salt.

My uncle's own family and relatives, too, had all fallen on hard times. The mistress who had become his father's wife was reduced to wearing patched kimonos and lived with his grandmother, now hard of hearing, in a house with no floor padding under the tatami mats. His grandmother had come to resemble a child fearful of strangers as she sat facing the wall all day long silently spinning jute yarn. His father's wife, whose hair had turned white on top, eked out a living doing errands and washing clothes.

Despite her circumstances, this woman seemed to be the picture of trust and devotion, maybe in part because his father had so cherished her when he was young. Yet his affection waned after a few years, and his later profligacy threw her into the depths of despair. It wasn't long before he lost his head over some woman from the demimonde and, drawn by lust and her modest fortune, brought her into the house. Now his wife again fell to the status of maidservant. She slept curled up on the kitchen floor and did all the housework, washing everyone's clothes by hand and cooking for all of them. Yet she suppressed the urge to complain, never protesting to anyone. This was probably why she always looked as if she had just been crying.

It was during this time that my uncle's younger brother suddenly died, and the young, widowed wife and their three-year-old boy were added to the impoverished household. His father's wife, unbearably lonely, welcomed these new family members. And, while the widow weaved, the wife kept busy doing errands for people and cooking meals as before, along with baby-sitting for her grandson-in-law. Meanwhile, her estranged husband tried to make money in the fortune-telling business, but he failed miserably and soon returned to a life of dissipation with his mistress.

Poverty constantly threatened this complicated family. The mistress' meager savings were soon exhausted, and harsh reality was forced upon these two middle-aged voluptuaries. Then one morning, people were astonished to learn that the young widow had run away. And, less than half a year later, the wayward husband was confined to bed with tuberculosis. Now they were truly destitute.

After a time, the mistress also ran away, leaving in this ravaged family only a small boy, a tuberculosis patient, the patient's senile mother, nearing ninety, and the wife, who was also entering old age. Though she worked to the very limits of her strength, it was like sprinkling drops of water on parched soil. With that tearful expression on her face, she made the rounds of every relative she knew, begging for help, but found them all in similar straits. Occasionally, they would give her twenty or thirty sen, which she spent on sweets for the boy or medicine for her husband, never thinking of herself. All her clothes were threadbare hand-me-downs from relatives, and the hems and sleeves would soon be drooping like rags until a sympathetic family member gave her another piece of cast-off clothing. Having lost all pride, she received anything they gave her with a childlike delight that had, pitifully, become second nature by now.

She boiled foreign-grown rice into gruel for her mother-in-law, her sick husband, and the boy; but for herself she cooked only a few sweet potatoes that would comprise her meals over the next five or six days.

She carried the boy on her back wherever she went. When he cried for a piece of brown sugar, pressing his head against her back, she felt her heart would break. "Poor thing. Please don't cry," she would say in her faltering voice, trying to comfort him, but she only ended up bursting into tears herself. It hurt her even more to think that he had given up on real sweets and just asked for brown sugar. Yet only during the days she spent with the boy did her face, which always had that tearful look, recover the tiny trace of a smile.

It was on one of those days that her husband finally died, leaving them nothing. Fate is like a rolling stone, and only God knows where it will stop. With her husband's death, at least she felt relieved of the burden to support him. But now the boy, who, though not related to her by blood, had become her only hope in life, came down with acute intestinal fever, and her world was plunged into total darkness. Like a woman gone mad, she wandered from doctor to doctor; then, having lost her powers of reason, she went on to try any superstitious remedy anyone suggested. She even began feeding this seriously ill child huge portions of candy, hoping to make up for his past malnutrition. Yet no one could stop her from following this blind impulse, for she couldn't bear the thought of allowing him to die without eating the sweets he loved.

In the end, his death left her insane with grief. She would gaze into space like an idiot for hours at a time and walk the streets with lowered eyes, the strands of her disheveled chignon dangling down her back. The little band of music makers that marched through town one day each week to advertise the movies had once brought the boy bounding out into the dusty street, but now it came only as a dreadful reminder of him, driving her again to bitter weeping. The tearful expression on her face grew even more sorrowful, and she seemed to be struggling constantly against the lure of death.

Yet there was one person who had been utterly indifferent to all these misfortunes: my uncle's grandmother. She appeared to accept the deaths of her own son and grandson with equanimity and even grinned when her great-grandson died. The only noticeable change in her was such an enormous increase in her appetite that she would ask for breakfast again four or five minutes after finishing it.

This was the state of my uncle's "home" when he returned after his long absence.

SINCE my uncle hated to stay in his own house, he lodged with my family. Our home consisted only of the dilapidated store, that ten-foot yard, and a small room of six tatami mats. We could let him use the room, though, because I had gone to live in the countryside, where I worked as an elementary school teacher.

When my mother took him around to the relatives announcing his return, he was welcomed everywhere with stained, sagging tatami and chipped teacups. Each family's conversation, gloomy as the rainy season, was all about the troubles that weighed down on them. The stone hedges were crumbling, the weeds were growing, and there were too many old people in the family. Yet instead of sympathy for the miserable state of his homeland, my uncle seemed to feel only disgust. And, after less than three weeks, he abandoned it again without telling anyone that he was leaving or where he was going.

"I've already transferred my family register to X Prefecture on the mainland," he explained to someone just before he left. "In fact, nobody in Tokyo knows I'm from Ryukyu. I do a good business with prestigious companies and have lots of university graduates working for me. You have to understand that if people found out I was Ryukyuan, it would cause me all kinds of trouble. To be honest, I even lied to my wife, telling her I was going to visit Beppu City in Kyushu."

At first his relatives had been captivated by his success in life and eagerly sought his company, only to have him reject them, refusing in his disgust even to let them see him off at the pier. He'd acted as if he wanted only to slice off these creatures that clung to him like octopus legs and get away as fast as he could.

I had known neither of his return nor of his departure until I heard my mother complaining about him. Yet I could truly sympathize with my uncle, who had only finished elementary school and was struggling to keep up this pretense to protect the business he had built with his sweat and blood. As I sat in the dirty, horse-drawn wagon, which bounced and jolted me on the ride back from my mother's house to the village where I worked, I could not help reflecting on the decline of our isolated homeland, Ryukyu.

The scenery all around me at dusk evoked poignantly the essence of these islands: sweet-potato vines trailing on the craggy soil, groves of lanky sugarcane plants, rows of red pine trees, clusters of fern palms, banyan trees with their aerial roots hanging down in thick strands like an old man's beard, and the sun setting radiantly in a shimmer of deep red behind the ridge of hills. It all flowed deep into my heart like the tide that rises to fill the bay.

The sounds of the horse trotting in choppy rhythms along the road and the coachman singing in a low, wailing voice seemed perfectly suited to our homeland's decline, as did the coachman's song in Ryukyuan dialect.

Who are you blaming
with your cries, oh plover?
My heart weeps, too,
when I hear your sad song.
The moon in the sky
is the same old moon as before.
What has changed
are the hearts of men and women.

With its sorrowful strains so common in Ryukyuan lyrics, the song reminded me of a poem by Karl Busse. Even our songs that aren't sad often have rhythmic chants of nonsense syllables and melodies of passionate abandon like those heard in American jazz.

Such music was probably born of the smoldering emotions in a people oppressed for hundreds of years. Yet I loved this scenery at sunset and yearned for something in myself to compare with its declining beauty.

TRANSLATED BY KIMIKO MIYAGI

In Defense of "Memoirs of a Declining Ryukyuan Woman"

Kushi Fusako

The current and former presidents of the Okinawa Student Association visited the other day to denounce me for what I wrote in the June issue of *Fujin kōron* and to demand an apology. I am taking this opportunity to publish a defense.

First of all, these two men insisted that I stop writing because they found my revealing portrayal of our homeland extremely embarrassing. In addition, they ordered me to apologize for my depiction of one character in the story, my uncle, so that readers would not get the mistaken impression that all Okinawan men are like him. Yet in this story I wrote neither anything distorted about my uncle nor any suggestion that all successful Okinawans are like him. So I regret that I can find no suitable words of apology to satisfy these men.

Listening to them, I sensed that they were particularly upset by one phrase I used in the story: "the Okinawan people." It annoyed them, they said, to have Okinawans put in the same category as "the Ainu people" or "the Korean people," minorities with which this word is often associated in Japan. Yet are we not living in modern times? I have no sympathy for their efforts to construct racial hierarchies of Ainu, Korean, and so-called "pure Japanese," or for their desire to feel some kind of superiority by placing themselves in the "highest" category. (I know, of course, that their views are not shared by everyone.)

Their outraged claims that what I wrote "demeans" and "discriminates against" Okinawans reveals, paradoxically, their own racial prejudice toward Ainu and Koreans. I don't care whether Okinawans are identified with Ainu or with "pure Japanese" because I firmly believe that, despite superficial differences resulting from environmental conditions, we are all Asians and equal as human beings. It was in this sense that I used the word "people," and certainly not to insult the Okinawan people of whom I myself am one.

I cannot deny that I have also felt the loneliness of being Okinawan as described in this story and that, in the past, I have struggled to hide my identity. However, I now realize the futility of this effort, for the constant fear of exposure leads only to the loss of dignity and to the weakening of one's spirit. I believe that we no longer need to demean ourselves by pandering to those who are ignorant about us. Truth is our only alternative, no matter how desperately we might wish to conceal it. (At this point, I planned to give some examples of our traditional folk practices from recent publications but will refrain because I would only be denounced again for revealing too much about Okinawan customs.)

These men told me of their painstaking efforts to camouflage the manners and customs of our islands from outsiders and of their vigorous exhortations for our people to reform. Yet I do not believe that our customs that differ from those on the mainland should necessarily be despised and discarded. Since such practices have deep roots in our culture, our natural environment, and especially our economic circumstances, obviously our ancestors were not so narrow-minded as these college men of today.

The representatives of the Student Association claim that my writing damages Okinawans' prospects for jobs and marriage on the mainland, but isn't it really their own servile attitude that is damaging our prospects? In this modern age even most capitalists are well aware of the evils wrought by discrimination. These men should aim their protests at those capitalists who still discriminate against Okinawans instead of trying so hard to silence a voice from the heart of one uneducated woman.

Like mainlanders, Okinawans serve in the military and perform their other duties as citizens. So why must Okinawan men hide their origins when they marry mainland women, which prevents them from ever visiting their families again? Or why don't successful Okinawan men marry Okinawan women, who are ready to be their devoted wives, instead of chasing after mainland women who would never accept an Okinawan husband?

I want my readers to understand that I never intended to write ill of my homeland; I only wished to show the pure heart of Ryukyuans, who remain largely untainted by modern culture. I was shocked to learn that my story, written so candidly, has disturbed men who have attained such high social status. I do apologize for their hurt feelings. I can well imagine how angry they are at me, an Okinawan woman with no higher education. It is the rule in Okinawa that only men with power are supposed to express their opinions, while people without power and formal education have no alternative but to follow behind them. As long as those with power control us, we who are powerless have no hope of salvation.

I also ask readers to note that all times and places in my story have been changed to avoid embarrassing anyone who might be regarded as a model for its characters.

TRANSLATED BY KIMIKO MIYAGI

Yamanokuchi Baku (1903–1963)

"Yamanokuchi Baku" is the pen name of Yamaguchi Jūsaburō. Referred to fondly as "Baku" by readers and critics, he is Okinawa's best-known poet. Born in Naha, he began publishing poetry in newspapers as a teenager, and in 1922 he moved to Tokyo, where he lived most of his life. By the late 1930s, he had published two collections of poetry and several stories in respected Japanese literary magazines. Known for his deceptively simple, colloquial style and wry humor, many of his works draw on his experiences as an impoverished poet eking out a living in Tokyo on odd jobs and borrowed funds. Some poems and stories describe the experience of Okinawans or other minorities living in mainland Japan; others depict Okinawa itself, especially later poems such as "Shell-shocked Island" (Tama o abita shima), published in 1964. Today, Baku is commemorated with the Yamanokuchi Baku Prize, which is awarded annually to a promising poet.

"Mr. Saitō of Heaven Building" (Tengoku-biru no Saitō-san) was published in 1938.

Mr. Saitō of Heaven Building

Yamanokuchi Baku

HIRATSUKA, A FRIEND from when I worked in the shipping department at Tōkaidō Booksellers, told me that my request was most unbecoming for a poet. Nevertheless, he handed me one of his business cards. On it he'd written, "I introduce to you Mr. Yamanokuchi Baku, a poet." Since this was meant to be a job reference, the word "poet" may have been irrelevant. Anyway, with card in hand, I headed across the river for Heaven Building.

The building, right next to the railway station, was a shabby, four-story walk-up with a dim, dirty hallway and no sign of people. I climbed the stairs to the second floor, careful to quiet the noise from my wooden clogs. To the left of the stairway at the end of the corridor I saw the sign on the office door:

CENTER FOR THE PROMOTION OF EASTERN MEDICINE

When I knocked, a pale young man opened the door. I handed him the business card Hiratsuka had given me, and moments later I was met by a short, stocky man in a white lab coat. I was astonished when I recognized him. It had been some time since Hiratsuka and I had been to the employees' cafeteria at Tokyo Station, but at some point this old man who used to work there had evidently started working here, so we knew each other, at least by sight. He led me inside and introduced me to the manager.

The manager had furrowed eyebrows and a pale, wide forehead, and the back of his head was unusually flat. He seemed rather tight-lipped and was dressed in kimono with a formal *hakama* gown. This was my first meeting with Mr. Saitō. He asked what I'd been doing recently, and when I said I was a poet, he nodded, explaining that he, too, had written poetry some time ago. But "affa all," he said with a slight mispronunciation, in this age of capitalism, making a living had to come first, so poetry was now just a hobby.

Mr. Saitō's company sold moxa-burning home-remedy kits for treating various bodily ailments. Every two weeks a new group of students was recruited for classes in anatomy, hygiene, and moxa application. Then, before graduation, each student was sold one of the treatment kits.

It was a clever setup because the center did not issue business permits to the students until they purchased a kit. Actually, they came for training in order to obtain a permit, and those who could not afford the kit would claim they had earned a permit simply by completing the course. But the real purpose of the business was to sell kits, not issue permits. So Mr. Saitō would argue that nobody is qualified to practice without a kit, adding that one could hardly practice with only a permit. At this point the students would give in, persuaded to buy a kit.

In fact, unlike physicians, practitioners of what was officially called "therapeutics" needed no formal certification under local laws to open a clinic and practice, using these kits. Yet for some strange reason, most students were convinced that they needed the certification, not the kit, in order to start their practice. Naturally, as amateurs, they were unfamiliar with local laws. The ad Mr. Saitō ran was especially clever, offering the chance to "Start a modern business. No exam required!" This gave the impression that, normally, an exam was required but that, after training at the center, a person could open a business without taking one. So by the time the people who were sucked in finally realized that they could have started a practice without completing the course or buying a kit, not only would they already have graduated, but would have purchased a kit as well.

I was hired to handle the job of office correspondence. The kind of treatment kits sold at the center had become quite popular, and more and more people were practicing "therapeutics." Every day dozens of inquiries arrived from around the country. People wrote saying they had a kit but wanted a permit to start practicing; offering to purchase a kit in exchange for a permit; promising to buy a kit as soon as they made enough money but wanting the permit first; asking if there was some way they could obtain just the permit; asking if they could begin their practice as soon as they purchased a kit; asking if we would accept monthly installments because they were short of cash; complaining that the price was too high and requesting a discount; wanting to know what the wholesale price was; and asking whether mere grade school graduates could start a practice if they purchased a kit. These letters were my customers, and I conducted business with them following Mr. Saitō's methods.

Contrary to what many people think, I have a jovial side that showed, for example, in my days as a heater installer. While my co-workers at a site shouted their rhythmic work chants, I would make them laugh by adding syncopated syllables on the offbeats. Even during my shipping days at Tōkaidō, I was constantly joking as we roped and packed. So when I came to Mr. Saitō's office, it was easy for me to get to know everyone right away.

In those days Mr. Saitō was a man of few words and always received his customers sitting up perfectly straight in his chair.

One day a man came to register for a class and, after completing the forms, invited Mr. Saitō out for dinner. The man was most grateful, he said, to Mr. Saitō for the opportunity to train at the center. But Mr. Saitō only frowned and clammed up, looking very upset. The customer repeatedly pleaded with him to come along, but Mr. Saitō continued to refuse, saying he didn't need to eat. By this time, the man had taken things too far to withdraw his invitation and looked terribly embarrassed. I could see that further rejection was sure to devastate him and couldn't help sympathizing. So I cleared my throat, momentarily attracting Mr. Saitō's attention, then gestured for him to go along. Whereupon he rose to his feet all at once like a robot, marched toward the door, and said, as if to encourage his seated customer, "Forgive me, then, if I accept your kind invitation."

Through a series of such incidents I gradually came to know Mr. Saitō. And during this time he seemed to become more relaxed with me. He always talked strictly business with the class instructors and other office workers, furrowing his brow, but with me he became more outgoing, even gossiping occasionally about women in the neighborhood.

The one thing Mr. Saitō hated most was when the topic of conversation turned to his birthplace. At such times his face revealed how he struggled with his origins.

When he wasn't around, the office workers and visiting vendors would invariably start talking about him, debating his birthplace. Mr. Saitō never revealed it. Whenever the subject came up, he always said he was from Kyushu, no matter who asked. And the employees would gather often to gossip about it.

They said that someone from Kyushu wouldn't mispronounce a simple Japanese word like *geta*, for sandals, as *"keta"* and concluded that Saitō wasn't his real name. Why in the world doesn't he simply say where he's from, they would ask, as if there were some mysterious reason for his reluctance. Just around the time they began to taunt him about it to his face, a tragic incident occurred.

One day a box salesman visiting the office asked Mr. Saitō if he was really from Kyushu. When Mr. Saitō replied that he was, the man asked which part. When Mr. Saitō said Fukuoka Prefecture, the man wanted to know which county. When Mr. Saitō answered, the man asked which village. Mr. Saitō gave its name, but now the salesman turned suddenly belligerent, claiming he was from that same village and demanding to know what section Mr. Saitō had lived in.

Even then, Mr. Saitō didn't reveal where he was from, saying only that he had left his birthplace as a small child, too young to remember anything about it.

Many, many times I witnessed Mr. Saitō in this predicament.

Anyway, I doubt that box salesman was really from Kyushu. Besides, who the hell were these office workers to waste time gossiping with a salesman when they were supposed to be working hard for Mr. Saitō? It pained me just to look at them. In fact, they all knew very well that Mr. Saitō was from Korea by the way he mispronounced those words like *geta,* for sandals, as *"keta"* and *gakkō,* for school, as *"kakkō."* So why did they want to make him talk about it?

For all my thirty years of life my homeland has been Ryukyu. But living in Tokyo as a man from Ryukyu for the past sixteen years, I've run into people wherever I go who think like that box salesman. They stare at me strangely—as if I'm not even human. And in those stares I can hear their questions. Is Ryukyu in Okinawa Prefecture? Do the people there eat rice? Do they speak Japanese?

Of course, there are countries like England, Germany, and France where Japanese is not the native language. And there are people who don't eat rice as a staple food. So such questions might not seem strange. But for me, as a Ryukyuan, they grated on my nerves.

One day it was raining.

I'd been leaning against the office window watching the traffic of umbrellas passing below when the office boy called me. I turned and saw him bringing an umbrella over to show me. On the handle of this Western-style umbrella was a signature boldly penned in Roman letters. Mr. Saitō's acute self-consciousness seemed to be revealed in the spelling of his name as "Saidō."

As time passed, Mr. Saitō switched ever so gradually from wearing kimonos to suits. He also seemed to grow less self-conscious, and the signature on his umbrella, though still in Roman letters, became "Saitō." Now, when invited out for dinner, he would leave the office cheerfully. A quiet coffee shop opened in the neighborhood where he began meeting with clients and vendors. When he came over to watch me pack, he complimented me that "affa all, packing should be done by an expert." And, although other employees' half-day absences seemed not to bother him in the least, he got agitated whenever I wasn't around. He would ask repeatedly where I'd gone or mumble to himself that I must be out for coffee again. Sometimes he even sent the office boy to look for me.

One day, just as I was coming out of the bathroom, I ran into the office boy. He hurriedly grabbed my hand and pulled me toward the manager's desk, explaining that Mr. Saitō had been grumbling again because I was out of the office. I asked Mr. Saitō if he had called me. At first he opened his mouth and tried to speak, but then closed it and swallowed hard.

"Yes, I did, Baku-san," he said finally. "How can you get any work done drinking coffee all day long?"

I asked if he thought there was coffee in the bathroom. He conceded there wasn't but said he'd been told by the girl at the coffee shop that I went there at least once a day. Of course, it was only after Mr. Saitō had given me permission and fifteen sen for lunch money that I'd started going out for coffee. Still, Mr. Saitō grumbled on about my being away from the office. But soon his conversation turned to the coffee shop, revealing that he was spending a lot of time there himself. In fact, he became rather obsessed with the subject, complaining that everyone only went there to ogle the waitress, including me. In the meantime, he seemed unconcerned that the office boy, after bringing me in, had immediately disappeared from the office.

During this time the business was booming.

Mr. Saitō often sat in front of the safe making plans for new ventures. Before long, "The School of Eastern Medical Practice" was completed with the remodeling of the large hall across from the office into a classroom. The school began to attract more and brighter students, ranging from graduates of pharmacy colleges and private universities to dentists, teachers at women's high schools, and graduates of middle schools. The youngest pupils were around sixteen or seventeen, but most were retirees.

With this steadily growing enterprise, Mr. Saitō became busier and livelier. And, as increasing numbers of salesmen visited the office, he found himself having to explain more and more that his homeland was Kyushu. By now he'd even won the confidence of the landlord, who made him the new building superintendent.

Most of the students at the School of Eastern Medical Practice had made their way there after being threatened repeatedly with the loss of their jobs, or they were worn out by the drudgery of unemployment. Sacrificing their pensions, taking out loans, or withdrawing their savings to pay the tuition, they came there to realize a dream—the dream of becoming self-employed medical practitioners who, after graduating from this school, would never have to look for a job again.

Incorporating this dream into his business strategy was another of Mr. Saitō's talents. If customers complained that their monthly tuition was too high or that the courses were too long, he would immediately feed them the dream.

"You say the tuition is too high, the term is too long. But if you consider it as an investment in yourself, the amount is very small. You might hope to work at a company for life, but once you're fired, there's nothing you can do. But as a medical practitioner, you've got it made! No one can fire you if you work for yourself. Think of it that way, and it's a real bargain."

But it was not as if all graduates could immediately become medical practitioners. To treat patients using "therapeutics," they could simply borrow the money to buy a kit and begin. However, to work as medical practitioners, they needed proper qualifications. And the fact that the School of Eastern Medical Practice could not award graduates with a certificate for medical practice was a key in its marketing strategy. Medical certification was not something that could be bought, but obtained only by passing a rigorous qualifying examination. The school was intended to attract students studying for this exam, but whether graduates actually passed was not its responsibility. Some who failed would repeat the course, only to fail again. And even if they took the class a third time, they still might not pass. Finally, the school would urge them to buy a kit.

Sake was served at the school's graduation ceremonies. It was a lavish display of gratitude from the students for their instructors, who were easy to recognize with their mustaches or beards. Everyone would get thoroughly intoxicated, and singing soon echoed through the rooms as female students and their bearded instructors revealed their hidden musical talents.

The school continued to grow, enhancing not only Mr. Saitō's confidence in his business skills, but also his ambitions and desires. Hiring a doctor, Mr. Saitō opened a clinic that he managed separately from the school. And soon he was conspicuously absent from the office several days a week. He grumbled that although everything had gotten busier, he had only one body and couldn't possibly spend the whole day at the school, the office, *and* the clinic. These absences were soon followed by another pattern. From time to time Mr. Saitō's wife would show up at the office. Originally from one of Tokyo's neighboring prefectures, she had tiny deep-set eyes, a skinny, smallish frame, and a speaking voice that carried a metallic ring. No one bothered to ask about her homeland, but they were all amused by the age difference between her and Mr. Saitō, who was four or five years younger. This shorter-than-average, older woman posed a sharp contrast to Mr. Saitō, a tall gentleman with handsome features.

The first few times Mr. Saitō's wife came, she would see that her husband was out of the office and just sit in a corner until he returned. Then they would go home together. Seeing this, the office boy remarked to me how much Mr. Saitō's wife must adore him. However, when she began to question me about where her husband had gone, what time he said he'd be back, and when the office closed, I became quite wary of her. In the beginning, Mr. Saitō had informed us of his destinations. He would say that he was going to the clinic but would return shortly, or that he could be contacted at the building superintendent's office, or that he was going to the local government office on school business. But before long, he stopped telling us where he was off to or when he'd be back, saying simply, "I'm going out for a while."

I once mentioned to Mr. Saitō that it was awkward for people in the office, not knowing his whereabouts when his wife asked. He told me we should just make up an answer and ignore her. I tried my best to do this, but there was one time when I failed miserably. That evening, when Mrs. Saitō came to the office, my excuse was that Mr. Saitō had gone to the clinic. She asked what time he'd left the office, but when I said around three, she was obviously disturbed. She'd already visited the office around three, she said, but was told then by the office boy that Mr. Saitō had left around two. She then asked where I'd been at the time, and I remembered seeing the hands on the clock at the coffee shop pointing to 5:00. The truth was that when Mr. Saitō left the office, I'd shut myself up in an empty room to work on my poetry, then went out for coffee. She must have walked into the office just as I'd returned from the coffee shop. I knew I'd been sloughing off work from around two until five, but Mr. Saitō was partly to blame for not returning punctually to the office. In any case, Mrs. Saitō was a clever woman, and she'd already dropped in at the clinic before coming to the office the second time. To make matters worse, she'd been told at the clinic that no one had seen Mr. Saitō all day.

Mr. Saitō's recent whereabouts remained a mystery until one day, after his usual departure, a highly plausible rumor began spreading through the office. One of the employees came in saying he'd discovered that Mr. Saitō had found himself "one of these," raising his little finger to indicate a female friend. He remarked how worldly Mr. Saitō had become and even compared his frequent absences to my trips out for coffee. Of course, I wasn't going out to meet a "little finger."

After that, whenever Mr. Saitō returned to the office, we were sure he'd been to his "little finger's" place. He would stand next to his chair for a while with a blank expression on his face. Then he would come over to sit beside me and ask if "she" had been there that day. Though I knew very well that he was referring to his wife, I couldn't always suppress a mischievous reflex and would ask, "To whom are you referring?" At first Mr. Saitō would pretend he hadn't heard me, but, stroking his chin, he would eventually rephrase the question, asking politely if his wife had come to the office that day. It was then that Mr. Saitō's face turned sheepish, just like a child's.

And yet, even at these times, I felt there was an unacknowledged rapport flowing between Mr. Saitō and me. Though barely detectable, it might have been called—if I may flatter myself—a mutual trust between human beings. And perhaps we shared it because, on a certain level, I could empathize with him.

For one thing, I never encroached upon the ethnic consciousness that welled up inside Mr. Saitō. Only once did I broach the subject, to assuage his anxiety over unpronounceable syllables, which was revealed in the signature on his umbrella handle. I believe this helped to lighten his tragedy. I jokingly mimicked the gestures of people who came to see him and even felt like praying for him whenever he said he was going out for a while. And, of course, I was the one who protected him from his wife by making up excuses and straining mightily so that my face wouldn't reveal that he had gone to see his "little finger."

Who else could possibly have been so friendly with him? Mr. Saitō must have recognized in me some quality he was looking for. Yet he often said he hated poets, complaining how a poet can skip his lunch but never miss a day at the coffee shop; how a poet can wear summer clothes even in the middle of winter; how a poet's mind, even in the office, seems to wander off to his poetry. As the two of us grew closer, the more he shunned the poet. It was, therefore, the poet he decried, not me. I wasn't the sort of poet to go storming around the office disturbing other people's work, but Mr. Saitō always acted as if he wanted to purge the poet in me, and then lead the nonpoet into a closer friendship with him.

One day Mr. Saitō came to tell me he was worried about the poet and to ask for my advice. His question, as usual, concerned the poet, and he asked which I would rather give up, work or poetry. He talked as though I were a child with a toy, then defended his attitude by telling me, "I'm not saying this for my sake, Baku-san, but for yours!"

Of course, he was saying it for his own sake, too, though the poet understood this better than I did. Feeling somewhat relieved, I decided to give up being a poet for a while. At this point Mr. Saitō took a sheet of paper out of his jacket pocket and said that if I truly intended to give up being a poet, I should read and sign it. Then he handed me the paper.

Oath
- I will quit altogether being a poet.
- I will cut my hair.
- I will stop going to the coffee shop for the time being.
- I will not leave my seat unless my work requires it.
- I will devote myself to the practice of Eastern medicine.

I signed, and the poet was now locked up in a cage tucked away in Mr. Saitō's desk drawer. However, Mr. Saitō continued, as before, to leave the office "for a while," and this "for a while" always turned out to be a long time. Whenever he was away, I released the poet from his cage, immersing myself in poetry and coffee. Mr. Saitō's wife, too, continued to show up at the office and ask where her husband had gone.

Eventually, ownership changed hands at the School of Eastern Medical Practice, and it disappeared from the second floor of Heaven Building. The clinic doctor, who spent most of his time drifting from one dance hall to another, had allowed his handsome features to destroy him and drive him out of Tokyo. After that, the clinic closed, and even the medical-kit business was turned over to someone else. I, too, wandered from job to job. But Mr. Saitō stayed all alone in the superintendent's office at Heaven Building and seemed to be planning a comeback, ready to try something new.

Then one day I visited Mr. Saitō's home. I had recently quit working on a Sumida River barge and was taking odd jobs for a plumber and a sewage disposal service. It must have been around 8:00 in the evening.

Mrs. Saitō looked worn down with worries as she sat holding a cigarette between two fingers. Mr. Saitō, standing nearby with no shirt on, did not make his usual impression as a gentleman that night. It had been some time since I'd seen them, and after I sat down, Mr. Saitō began glancing back and forth at me and his wife. I felt a disturbing tension between them but couldn't just get up and leave. Looking at Mr. Saitō's bare chest and then at his wife's hollowed eyes, I regretted my unfortunate entrance into this situation. "It's been a long time," I finally said, and his wife's thin lips suddenly started to quiver.

"Baku-san, you must have known all about it," she said. "He's been keeping a mistress."

"Well . . ." I was still fumbling for an answer when she suddenly retorted.

"What do you mean, 'well'?" You were in that office every day for years, so there's no way you couldn't have known about it. You may try to play dumb, Baku-san, but there's no way you couldn't have known."

I was indeed playing dumb but hadn't been able to bring myself to answer her before with something like, "Oh, no, not really. A mistress?"

Anyway, there was nothing she didn't already know, and she just dumped it all out in front of us without a hint of concern for her husband, starting with how the mistress had a baby boy.

At first he'd kept the mistress in Tokyo's Ushigome neighborhood, but after Mrs. Saitō found out, he'd supposedly severed all ties and sent her back to her hometown for good. His wife complained to me how she had no children of her own while the mistress had a boy, and how Mr. Saitō had spent all their money on the mistress so that, even if she wanted to divorce him, there was no way she could live on her own. On top of that, when Mrs. Saitō had hired a detective to check in the mistress' hometown, it turned out that she'd only stayed there four or five days and was now back in the Kojimachi area of Tokyo. Mrs. Saitō had begged her husband to let her meet this mistress just once, but he continued to insist that she was no longer in Tokyo.

The next day I went to visit Mr. Saitō in the superintendent's office at Heaven Building, since I hadn't been able to do what I'd intended the night before at his home. I recognized the two or three visitors sitting in his office.

Along the bridge of Mr. Saitō's nose ran a long, rust-colored streak. This could only have been the conclusion of last night's argument. Pointing at his face, I asked him about it.

Mr. Saitō said he'd fallen off a ladder, but after his visitors left, he took both hands out of his pants pockets and showed them to me.

When I said that those sores, too, must have come from falling off the ladder, he laughed like a baby.

"She found out," he told me.

I haven't seen Mr. Saitō in quite a while, but his words still ring in my ears, reminding me that in Heaven Building that other homeland has yet to be "found out."

TRANSLATED BY RIE TAKAGI

KISHABA JUN (1934-)

Kishaba Jun, whose real name is Kishaba Chōjun, was born in Naha. "Dark Flowers" (Kurai hana) appeared in a 1955 issue of Ryūdai bungaku *(University of the Ryukyus literature), an activist student literary magazine. The following year the story was reprinted in* Shin Nihon bungaku, *a national circulation monthly also known for its political radicalism.*

Set during the Korean War (1950–1953), "Dark Flowers" shows how American racial prejudices were adopted by Okinawans during the U.S. occupation. It takes place at least two years after President Truman ordered the U.S. armed forces to desegregate in 1948. The military dragged its feet on desegregation, however, maintaining virtually all-black units as late as the Korean War. In Okinawa, discrimination among Americans, though now theoretically illegal, was still conspicuous on and off base. For African American soldiers, it meant slower promotions, menial military jobs, and even separate, shabbier bars in the G.I. "amusement areas" of towns near the larger bases.

The Korean War led to rapid economic expansion in both mainland Japan and Okinawa, but in Okinawa the benefits were more closely linked to military bases and the surrounding towns. Sudden proliferations of prostitution and other "entertainment" enterprises were among the resulting economic distortions of this "boom." The U.S. base expansion policy also brought devastating losses and hardships to many Okinawans. Depicted in this story are the U.S. government seizures—often at gunpoint and amid mass arrests—of privately owned farmlands on which the military built or expanded its bases (see the introduction). Since money is central to the story, it is helpful to know that before 1958, occupation authorities in Okinawa issued a "B-yen" currency that was not usable in Japan. Then, in September of that year, American authorities switched Okinawa's currency to U.S. dollars, which remained the official medium of exchange until the occupation finally ended in 1972. With Okinawa's reversion to Japan, U.S. dollars were converted to Japanese yen, which again became the local currency for the first time since 1945. Yet even today in some areas around U.S. military bases, businesses such as taxis and bars will accept dollars for payment. And there are still bars and restaurants that print menus only in English and list prices in dollars.

The town identified in the story by the letter "K" is almost certainly Koza, notorious for its many G.I. bars and brothels.

Dark Flowers

Kishaba Jun

. 1 .

BY THE TIME Nobuko opened her eyes, the sun was already high in the sky. Through holes in the closed shutters streamed rays of sunlight swirling with tiny particles like bluish smoke. She lay on her stomach between the dirty sheets covering the steel-frame bed and took a deep drag from a menthol cigarette. Something weighed heavily inside her numbed brain. Not only that, she felt like throwing up. These days even a headache was hard for her to bear.

Nobuko was exhausted.

The night before, she and Joe had drunk too much. Joe's black skin, big, broad shoulders, and flattened nose made him look like a prizefighter, but he had a gentle, easygoing nature.

"Joe, buy me a good pair of shoes, will ya? The cheap ones wear out too fast."

"Whew." Joe narrowed his eyes without answering.

Nobuko didn't really want a pair of shoes. What worried her was how little remained of the three thousand yen she'd gotten from Joe a week before to cover this month's food and rent. Now there was no way she could bring the two thousand yen her mother always pestered her for whenever she went home to the countryside.

"Nobuko, all you talk about is money. Money, money, money. I give you my *whole pay*. But, well, I guess we can get the shoes. Payday comes pretty soon now, so no sweat."

Joe put his arms around Nobuko's shoulders, pulling her into his lap, and pressed a glass of booze to her lips.

"No, don't." She fled from his black hands—those hands like polished satin. Moving away, she reached down to grasp a leg of the bed, then stared back at him. Joe's eyes were filled with the guileless disappointment of a child who had been teased.

It made Nobuko angry to think that probably all Joe needed from her was her body. He pretended not to care about money, but was such generosity just part of his easygoing nature? No, there was more to it. Underneath she could smell the pungent odor of that superiority complex exuded by these men.

She admitted to herself that there was something corrupt about what she was doing. But she felt that in the end, no matter what she talked about or did with them, her relationship with these men always degenerated into one between the strong and the weak. For them, she thought, a woman was just "my pet" and nothing more. Yet for some strange reason, she didn't feel this way so much with Joe.

"Michikō gets five thousand yen," Nobuko had wanted to tell him, but she couldn't bring herself to say it. Her close friend Michikō, who also came from Y Village in the southern part of Okinawa, was the mistress of a white man.

"Why are you crying, Nobuko? You know I love you. Let's go see a movie in K Town tomorrow. And I'll buy you those shoes."

Joe kissed her cheek, which jutted out sharply on her gaunt, bony face. He put his arms around her—she had now sobered up—and lay down with her on the bed. Then, just as always when he'd been drinking, Joe hunched up his shoulders and, in the husky voice of a man whispering to his lover, talked with his eyes closed and his hands waving about a girl who worked in a bar at a port in Mississippi. She was plump but beautiful, he said, and as soon as this war was over, he was going back to ask her to marry him. "Is your darling the same color as you?" Nobuko wanted to ask him, but cut off her words.

When she first met Joe, Nobuko had no idea where Mississippi was; if the people there were poor and unable to find work, like people here in Okinawa; or if, even without jobs, they could still eat.

But after hearing him talk all the time about his life there, she had figured out that he was a dockworker.

She listened drowsily now as he hummed a song. His humming echoed in the stifling air that hung in that dark room where, for Nobuko, the alarm clock seemed to stop ticking and the clock face seemed to drift out over the straw floor mats. In his song she heard the sadness of people who were resigned to hardship but determined to endure it—a sadness that refused to succumb to despair.

She wondered if Joe had learned this song from his father while picking cotton in the fields or from his coworkers on the docks in Mississippi.

Nobuko knew she couldn't go home to her family today. Before that, she would have to borrow some money from Michikō. Nobuko had been expecting her mother, Uto, to visit, but she hadn't come for the past two months. Whenever she visited, Uto always asked Nobuko for money. Then last week Nobuko had gotten a letter from her younger brother, Shinkichi, explaining that Uto couldn't travel because she'd been sick in bed for some time and asking Nobuko to come home for a visit instead. Nobuko knew this meant that she was supposed to bring money with her.

Nobuko ground out her cigarette on a dessert plate and buried her face in a pillow as her tears began to flow. She didn't know herself why she was crying. Then she crawled out of bed, lifted the teapot to her lips to gulp down some water, and peeked at herself in the mirror adorned with the photograph of a famous baseball player.

She was an ugly sight.

She tried pushing up the drooping strands of her reddish brown hair, but now she could see the black splotches dotting the chafed skin on her face, which looked gaunt and haggard with its protruding cheekbones. A lump like a man's Adam's apple bulging from her scrawny neck made her look all the more weary and emaciated.

Suddenly, terror ripped through her like a stone ax. "Could I have gotten . . ." Afraid to say the name of the disease, Nobuko hurriedly flipped the mirror over, facedown, and stared anxiously into space. As she pressed both hands to her chest, her fingers made a cracking sound. Hers were the bony hands of a farm girl, hands that still carried the smell of the soil. She wondered if the lungs beneath her breasts had collapsed, leaving an empty cavity. The noises that echoed from her chest when she tapped it with her fingers sounded pathetically hollow. Now she thought that quite possibly the fatigue in her leg joints, the excess of phlegm in her throat, the pain in her hips, and her lack of appetite could all be symptoms of that illness.

When Nobuko opened the shutters, the late-morning sunlight on this October day came glaring in.

Across the road, a giant gasoline tank stood on a hill surrounded by a wide green carpet of grass. Long rows of white barracks, separated by spacious lawns, stretched northward along the seacoast all the way to the end of the cape. The rays of bright sunlight reflecting in the barracks windows made her aware of how hot it was today.

Nobuko decided she would visit Michikō first, then go to K Town in the afternoon. Back when Michikō had a job as a housemaid, she had been raped by the man she worked for, but unable to decide where to go next, she ended up living with him for about a year and a half in N City. The man then left her with a red-haired daughter and returned to America. Michikō put the child in her parents' care for the time being and about three months ago began renting a room not far from Nobuko.

To get to Michikō's room, Nobuko had to walk along the asphalt military highway, turn at the corner gas station, go down a gravel road lined on both sides with tire repair shops, car washes, and other stores, then walk in the direction of the seacoast along narrow footpaths between rice paddies. Here and there among the paddies were rows of brand-new houses, built on gravel landfills, with gleaming red-tile roofs. It made for a weird landscape.

These houses, with their fancy roofs, stood in the marshes, paddies, and potato fields dotted with old tree stumps. They were owned by farmers who had moved here after being forced to give up their lands to "protect freedom from its enemies." It was the third time these farmers had been resettled.

They were, without a doubt, fine houses. But by this time none of the farmers, who'd been relocated here in this forced migration, were living inside. Instead, they lived in tin-roof shacks that had been built onto the kitchens or put up in the backyards. The interiors of these "fine houses" had been partitioned into eight-by-eight-foot private rooms where yellowed bras and dresses in many colors now hung outside the windows, fluttering in the wind. At night these "fine houses" became bars and cabarets.

Since the shutters on Michikō's window were closed, Nobuko thought she was probably still asleep.

"Mit-chan. Mit-chan."

Nobuko knocked two or three times, but no sound came from inside. Embarrassed to find that the door was locked, she smiled wryly. Just then someone turned off the music, an old popular song, that had been coming from the window opposite Michikō's, and a woman poked her head outside. It was Saako.

"You know where Mit-chan went?"

"Yeah. Come on in, Nobu-chan."

Saako smiled at Nobuko but seemed to be looking not at her, but up at the small *shiisaa* statue of a guardian lion perched on the roof of the house. This was because Saako was cross-eyed.

"If you come in, I'll tell you where Mit-chan went. And there's coffee ready, too. I get so lonely being here all by myself."

Leaning out of her window as she spoke, Saako seemed to be begging Nobuko to come in. Nobuko hated talking about anything personal with other people and really wanted nothing to do with Saako. But Michikō was out, so Nobuko couldn't ask her for the money, and she certainly didn't feel like going back to her room.

Nobuko sat down beside Saako on the bed. All the cups left on Saako's small mirror stand were filled with cigarette butts, and the corners of her room were littered with banana and mandarin-orange peels.

"About Michikō," Saako began. "Harris came to pick her up this morning. She told me they were going swimming at N Beach. She made such a fuss last night about borrowing a bathing suit. Mine was way too big on her, she said. Made her breasts look flat. Ha, ha, ha!" Saako laughed alone at this.

"But N Beach is only for foreigners. It'd be too bad for Michikō if they wouldn't let her in." Nobuko paused. "Still, she seems to be making a nice living these days."

"That's the *most* dangerous time," said Saako. "'Cause you never know how long it'll last."

Saako handed Nobuko a cup of coffee. Then, peering intently at Nobuko, she put her hand up in front of Nobuko's face as if to say that what she was about to tell her should go no further.

"Look, I bought a ring. This one's real expensive."

"What do you need a ring for? You getting married?"

"No, it's an investment. For my future."

They both gazed silently at the ruby ring. She had tried to make fun of Saako, but that word "investment" struck pain deep in Nobuko's heart. She wondered how long into the future her own dark and hopeless existence would drag on, and why she had to live this way. All she could think of was that it was because of her father's death, or the fault of the war. Later, on her way home, she regretted having talked to Saako.

"I'm going to America, y' know. I already got my family registration certificate and put in for a visa. Don't you think I can make a living over there one way or another?" Saako's voice with its thick southern Ryukyus accent and her smiling face with its crossed eyes had begun to grate on Nobuko.

. 2 .

K WAS THE main business district in the middle part of Okinawa Island. It had the shabby postwar look of a town born and grown up along the military highway that ran through it from north to south. Its streets were lined with a jumble of souvenir shops, movie theaters, foreign import-export companies, bars, game centers, vendors' stalls, and brothels—all fronted with signs written in English. Hidden behind its neat, modern buildings were countless one-story shacks. Clusters of men and women with various skin colors spilled outside onto the streets. Standing next to a bench in front of a restaurant, a boy with a

G.I. haircut chewed sticks of gum one after another, spitting out the leftover wads. He was clapping his hands as he peered into a barbershop where a woman, whose low-cut blouse didn't quite cover her breasts, could be seen reflected in the mirror as she sat in the barber chair.

K Town looked impressive on the surface, but it was missing the lively humming of machine belts from a lumberyard and the bustle of men in oil-spotted work clothes. Instead, a stale odor of corruption and listlessness hung heavy in the air.

Nobuko constantly watched her step as she walked awkwardly, staying close behind Joe. She wore an orange two-piece dress and a blue kerchief tied around her neck, making her look just like a turkey on its way to someone as a gift. Joe, worried about the way she was walking, reached out to take her hand, but she refused. Though still concerned about her, he now smiled wryly. Then, just as they turned off the pavement, Nobuko lost her balance and tumbled down, twisting her ankle. Joe roared with laughter, showing the whites of his eyes and his white teeth, then quickly bent over and took her hand gently. To Nobuko, he looked just like the old chef with the white cook's hat that she had seen in magazine ads, and, though angry, she was now smiling wryly herself.

At the movie theater the newsreel was just ending, and the audience was packed with G.I.s and their girlfriends.

"Doesn't my Tony look like Gregory Peck?"

"Maybe a little. But his eyes are different."

"Hey, isn't that Toyoko sitting next to the post over there?"

"It couldn't be. I heard she was in Central Hospital."

"Her lungs again?"

"She must've had a relapse."

The girls next to her were talking, but Nobuko kept noisily munching her cookies as she gazed listlessly at the coming attractions. Then the movie started, and the talking stopped.

Joe held Nobuko's hand.

On the screen, white people were riding in a convoy of covered wagons heading west. Leading the settlers was Gregory Peck. One day they were visited by a miner and a pretty bar hostess who the women in the covered wagons glared at disapprovingly. Later, the two men fought, and Peck ended up killing the miner and taking his woman. But there was worse trouble ahead for the settlers. First, they had to cross the wide, rugged prairie; second, a tribe of Indians living on the plains, who were determined to defend their homeland, vowed not to let the settlers set foot on it.

Now it became the primary mission of the men in the convoy to attack at dawn and get rid of the Indians. Peck, their courageous leader, rode alone into the Indian fortress, and in the true pioneer spirit, with arrows flying all around him, he shot hordes of Indians dead, beat others to death with the butt of his gun, and almost single-handedly annihilated the tribe. After this, the covered wagons proceeded to their destination of richly fertile lands where, against a backdrop of lush green fields, Peck and the bar hostess kissed so long they probably should have suffocated, and the women in the covered wagons offered their blessings to the happy couple. With that, the movie ended.

Why did the Indians have to be massacred, Nobuko asked herself. It had filled her with anger to see them desperately defending their homeland as old Indian women died in terror, young Indian men tumbled to their deaths from cliffs, and camera close-ups showed the faces of men trampled to death after falling from their horses. Why would Indians ever agree to perform in such a film, she wondered. The whole thing made her sick.

Walking away from the wide street where the lights had just come on, Joe and Nobuko turned into a narrow alley and entered a drab little bar where the sign in front said "Swan" in English. Inside, men the same color as Joe sat at the counter in the narrow barroom, joking with five or six bar hostesses.

"Hey, Joe. Where you been? That's a real pretty woman you got there."

"Sure is. That body looks like a gorgeous turkey, doesn't it? And she's got beautiful eyes, too. But she cries a whole lot. Always drags herself around moping, like a snake. She never laughs."

Joe bent over to kiss Nobuko in front of his buddies. Ignoring them, she sat sipping her beer in silence, so they soon went back to bantering with the hostesses, and the laughter never stopped.

On the way back, Joe and Nobuko parted in front of his military base. Then, walking alone, she again recalled the faces of the Indian men in the movie. They brought back a horrible memory. It had been a sweltering dawn in mid-July when she witnessed this brutal scene. Just before sunrise, across the military highway from her room, she'd seen the faces of men and women huddled together, trembling with rage. They had just been dragged outside the barbed-wire fence that now surrounded their land, and the young men among them were being arrested. She had seen it with her own eyes. And she could still hear the endless clanging of an alarm bell at dawn as everything these people owned was being taken from them.

"Gregory Peck, 'Mr. Handsome.' Hah! What a fraud," Nobuko grumbled to herself. As she passed in front of the gas station, she decided to visit her family the next day, no matter what. Then, recalling the silent treatment she always got from the villagers, a vague fear seized her. This had been the real reason she'd put off going home.

Anyway, now she'd be able to see her younger brother, Shinkichi, the person she was most fond of in this world. Though not yet twenty, Shinkichi had broad, powerful shoulders.

. 3 .

BOUNCED AND JOLTED for the hour-long bus ride, Nobuko finally reached the countryside she hadn't seen in six months. The bus bumped along gravel roads through the poor villages of southern Okinawa, which were planted with sugarcane and smelled of mud. She got off at the bus stop beside a ditch just outside her village.

As the sun set behind a hill, reddish brown rays from the glowing sky poured down onto the *susuki* grass that looked like it was burning in Tarumui Forest. From here it was twenty minutes to her village. Nobuko thought about taking the path along the ditch but set off through the forest instead. She didn't want to meet up with anyone, afraid that the villagers would start talking about her. The *susuki* grass grew high and thick on both sides of the path, which ran along a mountain ridge through Tarumui Forest and down toward the back of her village. Here and there on the mountainside were large Indian almond trees, newly dug grave mounds, and turtleback tombs with their doors open.

The war had once denuded this forest, shamelessly exposing the barren red soil. Gone for some time after that was the sharp smell of resin that drifts from the thick groves of red pines, which stay dark even during the day. Nor was there any sign of the red-bellied water lizards that hide lazily in the grassy shade. The roofless stone graves that had been used for storing guns when Nobuko was a child were covered now with *susuki* grass.

After passing the point where the dirt path turned into thick, slimy mud, Nobuko slipped several times in clumps of cow manure. In the lingering twilight, she peered down through a grove of acacia evergreens and saw the narrow, one-story elementary school that looked like a centipede crawling under its thatched roof.

A jet fighter roared overhead, then streaked out of sight.

Turning right as she headed down the slope, Nobuko finally came to the western edge of the village and felt relieved to see the familiar row of houses across the river.

At last, she reached the dirt floor entranceway of her family's home. The light coming from the kerosene lamp inside was veiled in thick, sooty smoke from the oven, and the silent house seemed deserted.

"Mom. Are you home?"

Nobuko waited, but there was no answer. White steam drifted from potatoes boiling in a pot. She put down her woven-bamboo handbag, along with her wrapping-cloth bundle, on the dirt floor of the entranceway, then grabbed a pair of rubber sandals and headed outside to the well. All at once she caught a glimpse of something black moving in the darkness behind the goat shed, but when she turned to look, it had stopped.

"Who's there? Yukio?" Now she spotted Yukio just as he started to run away.

"Yukio! What are you doing out there in the dark? Where's Shinkichi and Mom?"

Nobuko's bony face broke into a warm smile as she called out to him, but Yukio just stared back at her in silence. His rust-colored face wore a tense expression as he busily filled a bamboo basket, putting in and taking out artillery shell fragments, torn pieces of wire mesh, empty cans, and other items, in order to measure the day's harvest of scrap metal.

Later, as Nobuko was ladling soup from the pot and pouring the leftover potatoes into a bamboo basket, her mother and Tamiko arrived home carrying large bundles of dried *susuki* grass on their heads. They were soon followed by Shinkichi carrying a sack on his back filled with feed grass for the goats.

"How're you doing, Nobuko?" asked Mom. "Did you get the day off work?"

"Yeah," Nobuko answered. Uto used the word "work" because the truth about Nobuko was supposed to be a secret from Yukio and Tamiko. But, being sensitive children, they already knew about her. Yukio had even been skipping school lately because he hated being called "the whore's little brother."

"How're things going?"

"Well, you know, this house is getting eaten up by termites. And old man Maeda says we have to replace the beams 'cause they won't last through the next typhoon. Of course, he wants the money up front."

"Uh-huh. And how's the cane doing? There're not supposed to be any more typhoons this year, so it should be a bumper crop. Right, Shinkichi?"

"A 'bumper crop?' Hah! On this teeny-weeny plot? Then we have to pay all that money to the farm co-op for fertilizer. And, on top of that, there's the . . ."

"Aw, cut it out, Mom," said Shinkichi as he looked up at his older sister's bony cheeks. Nobuko couldn't remember when Uto had become such a complainer. Looking at her mother's drawn and sallow face, Nobuko thought for sure that Uto's illness must be either heart disease or hookworm. From her handbag Nobuko took out her purse and placed two bills on Uto's lap. Uto snatched them up, then stuffed them inside her kimono.

"Thanks, Nobuko."

Nobuko didn't tell Uto that this was money she had borrowed from Michikō.

Supper that night was potato soup flavored with canned sardines. At this rare gathering of the whole family, Shinkichi tried joking to cheer everyone up, but the laughter didn't last. Nobuko just kept sipping her soup and said nothing.

"Well, I guess you'll be staying the night."

Uto's barely mumbled words made Nobuko feel like a pebble that had been flung into a quiet pond, an intruder who had disturbed the tranquil, if somber, waters of this household. Uto had obviously meant that, in this house, Nobuko's presence was a problem.

Shinkichi looked sad now as he gazed again at his sister's gaunt face with its protruding cheekbones. He wanted to say something, but couldn't think of what.

When supper was over, Shinkichi took some books with torn covers and a stack of mimeographed pamphlets out from the cabinet housing the family's Buddhist altar, stuffed them under his arm, and stepped down into the dirt-floor entranceway where he slipped into a pair of sandals.

"Kichi, you better not go. That's no place for a kid. Maybe it's all right for Tat-chan at the store. But you'll just get chewed out again by old man Maeda."

"Hey, maybe I'm just a kid, but my teacher at school is young, too, and he's got some good ideas. Tat-chan's organized a reading circle at the store, and we're doing this book called *The New Farm Village*."

Shinkichi had turned shyly toward Nobuko but spoke with pride before disappearing into the darkness outside.

"They're always blabbing about 'organizing' and 'unions.' It's stupid if you ask me. Once a dirt farmer, always a dirt farmer. Old man Maeda told me they're just gonna get themselves in trouble."

Uto spoke with a look of uncomprehending despair in her eyes as she stared into the space Shinkichi had just left. Never one to mince words, her overbearing bluntness reflected the wily instinct for self-preservation of a woman who had been born and raised in poverty. That night she talked to Nobuko about what had happened recently in the village, but when she had exhausted this topic, she began to repeat over and over again in a weak and pleading voice how hard it was these days to find scrap metal.

By now Yukio and Tamiko were asleep.

Nobuko knew it was time for her to leave.

"You take care of yourself, now." Uto had come out as far as the front gate to see her daughter off, and, though Nobuko tried to refuse them, Uto stuffed some pieces of brown-sugar candy wrapped in newspaper into her hand.

The night was so quiet out here in the country.

At Tat-chan's store the shutters were closed, but Nobuko could hear voices inside. It was easy to recognize Tat-chan's voice, which carried over everyone else's. She imagined Shinkichi gazing in wonder and surprise as he listened to what the others were saying.

Turning the corner at Tat-chan's store, Nobuko came to a long hedge of hibiscus plants. She couldn't distinguish the blossoms from the leaves.

Nobuko remembered when, as a child, she and Tat-chan were playing house. Pretending to be "the bride," she had adorned her short hair with hibiscus flowers. Tat-chan's grandmother discovered them and gave the children a severe scolding, although Nobuko had no idea why. Crying bitterly, she ran home. Ever since then, Nobuko vaguely feared these red flowers. From their stamens oozed a sticky slime, and they had a dark aura about them. Were they, as Tat-chan's grandmother claimed, flowers for the dead, flowers of sadness?

According to what she had told them, these associations went back to ancient times during consecutive years of famine and plague. Farmers were not only assessed heavy yearly tributes on their crops, but were also drafted from districts far and near as forced labor to build the king's castle at Shuri. Day after day they marched in long columns, dragging logs and stones, and many died from starvation and sunstroke. There were horrible scenes of death. Under the relentless gaze of bailiffs, the farmers, nearly dead from exhaustion, collapsed in the shade of trees beside the road to give their bodies a brief rest. At such times they must have noticed these dark flowers blooming in the shrubbery.

Perhaps these shabby dark flowers reminded the farmers of their suffering. Oppressed and impoverished, they might have felt toward these poor, dark flowers a kind of communion and, at the same time, a repulsion that came from their own self-loathing.

Passing the hibiscus hedge, Nobuko turned onto a street leading to the path beside the ditch. In her mind's eye, the shabby town where she rented a room seemed to close in on her. But her vision of this worn-out town crawling under the sunlight, where she had to live, contrasted with a second vision of the impoverished little farm village where Shinkichi was determined to start a vigorous new life. The two images came into sharp focus as she remembered the many nights she had suffered in silence and anger.

She wanted to weep, to cry out loud.

But, no. She resolved, instead, to fight what was hateful to her with everything she had, and, like Joe, to celebrate what made her happy with a joyful smile.

TRANSLATED BY STEVE RABSON

Ōshiro Tatsuhiro (1925–)

Born in Nakagusuku on the main island of Okinawa, Ōshiro went to high school at an international academy in Shanghai. When World War II ended, he returned to Okinawa, where he worked in a government office and began writing fiction, drama, and essays that often had local subjects and settings. In 1967, he became the first Okinawan to win the Akutagawa Prize for his novella, Cocktail Party, *and he has since continued to win acclaim for his literature, which spans a wide range of genres. Ōshiro regularly publishes novels and short stories, including works of historical fiction. He also writes dramas and advises theater productions, many of which are performed in Okinawa dialect. And his critical studies of Okinawan cultural history have informed a wide readership both inside and outside the prefecture. Yet he also finds time to advise younger writers and to serve on numerous selection committees recommending publication and literary prizes. Today, he remains among Okinawa's most well known writers and is undoubtedly the most prolific.*

Ōshiro has drawn on his personal experience of the war and its aftermath, especially his years in China and early postwar Okinawa, for works offering an acute perspective on the psychological and moral implications of war and military occupation. "Turtleback Tombs" (Kame-no-kō baka) was first published in the regional magazine Shin Okinawa bungaku *(New Okinawan literature) in 1966. Ōshiro has often remarked that he considered this work to be more deserving of literary acclaim than was* Cocktail Party, *which examines the injustices of American occupation rule and the complex legacies of Japan's war responsibility. But he attributed the popularity of* Cocktail Party *among mainland Japanese readers to its obvious contemporary relevance and ready accessibility. In "Turtleback Tombs," on the other hand, Ōshiro experiments with the use of regional dialect and explores Okinawan religious practices, which are so unfamiliar to the average Japanese reader that he chose to incorporate explanatory passages into the text. English-language readers should know that during the Battle of Okinawa, it was common for families to take refuge in the caves and ancestral tombs scattered throughout the islands.*

TURTLEBACK TOMBS

Ōshiro Tatsuhiro

ON MOST DAYS, all Grandma Ushi and Grandpa Zentoku thought about was what went on inside the ninety square feet of their thatched-roof house on its quarter acre of land. Only on those days when they joined their neighbors to see soldiers off for the front or receive the remains of war dead did they think about "Okinawa Prefecture," "The Greater Japanese Empire," or "America." So they had no idea these things had anything to do with the noises they were hearing now.

First, a thundering seemed to shatter the air as their house shook. Outside in the goat shed, the horned male ran in panic three times around the post he was tied to, coiling the rope tightly around his neck. As Zentoku watched this, stunned, a man carrying a straw basket filled with grass appeared outside the front gate and shouted to him.

"Grandpa, they're gunboats. Gunboats firing. It's the war!"

Zentoku's hands, now motionless, had stopped weaving the straw mat he was holding.

"Gum boats?" What the hell did gum have to do with that crazy noise, he wondered.

"Not gum. *Gun. Gun*boats."

"What?"

"Battleships with cannons. Firing shells. The war's coming!"

After delivering this message, the man hurried away out of sight beyond the stone wall in front of the house. Now Zentoku dropped everything he was holding, stood up, and yelled toward the kitchen. "Hey, Grandma, gunboats. It's the war!"

Ushi had just set a wooden bucket down on the black-dirt kitchen floor and was stirring potato mush for the pigs. "What? Gunboats? War? Coming today?"

"Yeah, we've got to get out of here. Where're the kids?"

"At school, practicing for graduation tomorrow." Ushi rushed outside and looked up at the sky. But seeing nothing, she went back to the bucket in the kitchen. "I better make sure the pigs get enough to eat."

A moment later, as she stood in the pig shed behind the house pouring potato mush into the feed bucket, there were two more thundering explosions.

"Grandma, what the hell are you doing? Think of your grandchildren before you throw away your life like that!" Zentoku yelled at her from the window in the sitting room where he was lowering an oil can filled with rice into a straw carrying-basket.

"We're not going to die this minute, Grandpa. Besides, the pigs have to be fed before we leave. We don't know when we'll be back."

"Well, then, while you're at it, fetch all the goats' grass and toss it out for them. They've got to eat, too. Damn war makes trouble for everybody! Hey, how much of the kids' school stuff should we take?"

Ushi didn't hear him. She had walked around to the well in front of the house and was washing her hands, which were covered with potato mush. "Grandpa," she yelled back. "Go get Eitarō. You'll need his help. There's no way you can pack everything by yourself."

When he heard this, Zentoku slammed the blankets he was carrying down on the floor and dashed outside. "Hey! I told you never to talk to me about that rotten bastard!"

"Rotten or not, we've got no young people at home now. We need him, even if he does have only one arm."

"Then you're rotten, too! So what if there's a war? To go begging for help from that bastard shacked up with our shameless daughter. Could you live to face people after that?"

"Sure I could live. Shacked up or not, we need his help."

Again came the thunder, followed by a deep rumbling from behind the western hills that got louder and louder until it faded away to the east. Just as Zentoku peered up toward the noise, his graying eyebrows arching on his wrinkled forehead, an older man appeared at their front gate.

"Zentoku, I heard crows cawing. The hills are full of them flapping their wings. This is going to be a hell of a big battle. You folks have got to get out of here."

"Where's it coming from, Mr. Yamazato?" asked Ushi.

"America."

"I know that, but . . ."

"Look at the ocean. Full of battleships since last night. If those cannons start firing, we'll be wiped out."

"Where'll you go?" asked Ushi.

"Probably the northern countryside."

"That's far."

"The farther the better, where the guns can't reach us."

Ushi ignored his answer, which made Okinawa sound like a continent instead of an island. "Where should *we* go, Grandpa?"

"We'll decide that later," said Zentoku. "Right now we've got to feed the goats and pack our stuff."

After Mr. Yamazato left, Ushi shook the well water from her hands and feet. Then, just as she began wrapping her kimonos in a *furoshiki* cloth, the two grandchildren, sixth-grader Fumiko and fourth-grader Zenshun, came running up to the house.

"Grandpa, Grandma, it's war! War with America. We have to get away. The teacher says if we evacuate safely, we'll win."

"What'd she say about school?" asked Zentoku.

"It's war so there's no school."

"Then you won't graduate?"

"Graduate? In the middle of a war? Don't be silly, Grandpa."

"Yeah, and where's *she* going?"

"She didn't say where. Just that everyone should leave with their families and that we'd have school again after we won the war."

Again came the thundering.

"Fumi!" yelled Ushi. "Go tell Eitarō to come here." Ushi lifted the cooking pot off the dirt kitchen floor and set it down with a bang on the wooden floor of the house.

Fumiko's large eyes opened even wider as she stared at Ushi. "Are you sure it's all right to bring him here, Grandma?"

"Listen here!" shouted Zentoku. "Fumiko's old enough to understand." He gave Ushi another angry look. "So what if there's a war. Sin is still sin. How could we face our son if we did something so shameful in front of this precious grandchild he left in our care. You can talk that way about Eitarō because you're not a blood relative."

"What does it matter whose blood it is? Our lives are at stake. How can you complain about such things when we're trying to save lives?"

"Whoever said we should throw our lives away? Now let's get the hell out of here!"

"Oh, yeah? You think you can carry all this stuff by yourself? And just *where* are we supposed to go?"

"Hah! Asking at your age where to go and when to die. We'll move into the tomb, of course, and be with our ancestors."

"Into the tomb, Grandpa?" Zenshun let out a shriek.

"Sure, the tomb is our ancestors' home. They'll protect us."

"Won't it be scary?"

"Why should it? They'll chase away anything scary."

"Well, that'd make it even better," interrupted Ushi. "But how can you possibly open that heavy stone door by yourself? Better get Eitarō, Zenshun."

"Okay," answered Zenshun as he started to run off.

"Don't you *dare* go after him! What can he do anyway, with only one arm? I put that stone in by myself. I can take it out by myself."

"How old were you then? And now, past seventy. Even with one arm, he'd gladly give us the strength we need, especially to help his girlfriend's family. Nowadays we should consider ourselves lucky to have a young man around to rely on, even with a missing limb. Go get him, Zenshun."

"Huh?!" Zentoku seemed at a loss for words. Then, just as Zenshun started to run from the house, Zentoku's daughter, Také, rushed up to the front gate, screaming as she led her only daughter, five-year-old Tamiko, by the hand.

"Grandma! Where're you going? Please, take us, too!"

Now Zentoku was in a quandary. It bothered him that his daughter had called out first to Ushi, though she was not a blood relative. He knew this was because all he did lately was complain about Také. And when he saw the fear in Tamiko's eyes, his heart went out to his granddaughter brought here by this shameless daughter. Zentoku was still at a loss for words when the thundering roared again—sounding very nearby—so loud this time that the children shut their eyes tightly. At that same moment a man came flying through the gate almost as if blown in by the blast. With his one arm, he struggled gamely to carry blankets, pot lids, and other household goods. Zentoku looked at the empty sleeve where Eitarō's other arm would have been. It was flapping furiously in the wind and looked to Zentoku as if it were laughing at him.

"You . . . y-you . . ." Zentoku stammered.

"Hey!" Ushi yelled at her husband, who seemed to have forgotten all about packing. "If you're going to murder him, do it after we get this stuff to the tomb, okay?"

"What? Are you crazy? Talk about murder at the tomb and we won't bury you with the ancestors even if you die right this minute."

Ushi, stunned momentarily, could only stare at Zentoku. Among local farmers "murder" was hyperbole for punching someone, and she had said the word casually. But mentioning it in the same breath with "tomb" had been wrong, and now she hurried to explain. "No, I only meant . . ."

"Going to the tomb, Grandma?" Také interrupted Ushi as she tried to correct herself. "Then we'll go there, too." She nodded toward Eitarō, who put down their baggage with a clatter.

"You got a pole, Grandpa?" he asked. Without waiting for an answer, he walked into the storage shed, rummaged around inside, and came out holding a shoulder pole hung with two straw carrying-baskets. Then he gathered the things he and Také had brought and dropped them into a pile with Ushi's and Zentoku's belongings. After Také helped him pack everything into the straw baskets and tie it down securely, he hoisted the pole onto his shoulder. Zentoku, who had been watching them with a scowl on his face, now jumped down from the floor of the house and walked across the yard to the shed. From inside he took out a hoe and brought it back.

"Don't forget this."

"What do we need a hoe for, Grandpa?"

"Idiot! You're farmers, right? How're you supposed to eat if you move somewhere without a hoe?"

Silently, Eitarō untied the carrying-basket and opened it. Zentoku spoke again as he slid the hoe inside.

"We'll be bringing more baggage, so you go first. But don't open the tomb door. Wait in the grove next to it at the cemetery until we get there so you can't be spotted from the airplanes."

"That's enough stuff, Grandpa." Také spoke to her father for the first time. "The food and clothes are all packed. Our lives come first. We can't be too greedy with a war on."

"Who's being greedy? Even in a war, you try to live a normal life," said Zentoku as he walked defiantly in long strides toward the main house. Then, for no apparent reason, he stopped, turned around, and walked back. "Grandma, where's the crowbar?" he asked. "We need it to open the tomb door since he's only got one arm."

"Even with both arms you'd need a crowbar," Ushi said. "It's here, under the house." Stepping down from the wooden floor to the ground, she pulled out the crowbar, and Zentoku took it from her. Then Eitarō and Také, agreeing to leave for the tomb, walked out through the front gate with the children following, eldest first.

The whole family had been talking about "war" and "the battle," but none of it seemed real until they left home. Before that, war had only been something that kicked them in their sleep, that jolted them out of bed and spun them around. Now, as they walked together, time seemed to creep along until, suddenly, it was morning. Making their way from their front gate across the village grounds, they realized that war had come to the whole village. And when they reached the outskirts where the landscape opened before them, the whole world seemed to be at war. The village was surrounded by flat fields of sweet potato and sugarcane stretching 200 yards east to the sea. To the west, terraced fields and rows of tombs covered the slopes on a long line of hills—or could they be called mountains?—ranging to the north and south. Now the family set out on the 300-yard walk along a farm road that led to the tomb where their ancestors slept among the fields and occasional rice paddies extending into the distance, north and south. The refugees they met on the road were constantly looking around in every direction. Whenever the family passed people from their village or met people coming toward them on the road from other villages, they doggedly asked and answered the same questions over and over again, as if for the first time.

"Where're you going?"

"To the Yanbaru countryside up north," most replied, or "South to Shimajiri." A few with elderly relatives among them said "To our tomb."

When asked if the enemy had landed, most didn't know. But Zentoku heard one man say it would be the day after tomorrow. This man had been a village councilman until last year, and he carried a piglet in the basket hanging from his shoulder pole.

"The Americans are coming by sea the day after tomorrow," Zentoku shouted.

"Who told you that?" Ushi shouted back, and Zentoku yelled the man's name.

"But did he say where he heard it?" Ushi asked as she reached out to take her granddaughter's hand from Také, who had been leading Fumiko but now headed for the cane fields to pee.

Zentoku thought about this man who had finished two years of middle school, had been a village councilman, and, even at a time like this, had the presence of mind to plan for earning money from the piglet he was carrying. He must be possessed of wisdom beyond that of ordinary people and was surely right when he said the enemy would land the day after tomorrow. It shouldn't matter who'd told him, yet Zentoku couldn't shake off wavering doubts. Perhaps he had misunderstood the words "landing the day after tomorrow" that he'd heard only moments ago. When he turned to look back, the man was still carrying the piglet along in a rhythmic step, moving toward the village Zentoku had just left. But by now that village and the one beyond it must be nearly deserted. As the man headed toward them, he seemed to vanish slowly into the hazy, distant sky. Zentoku, growing more confused by the minute, could only shake his head.

Ushi, too, found herself in a state of confusion. She had taken Tamiko's hand and started walking ahead but changed her mind all at once, deciding to stop and wait for Také instead. Ushi worried there would be trouble if they got separated. Crouching down at the side of the road, she watched Také cross the ridge between two small potato fields and disappear inside a thicket of sugarcane. The moment she slipped out of sight, apprehension seized Ushi. It might have been the renewed thundering that made her think Také would never reappear. Until then Tamiko had been casually watching the sugarcane, waiting for her mother. But now Ushi wondered if some of her own anxiety might have affected the little girl, who seemed suddenly overcome with panic. Meanwhile, Eitarō, a man in his prime even with only one arm, was bearing the heavy load of their belongings and had gotten well ahead of the others. But now he, too, stopped and turned this way to wait for them.

Také must have been holding it in for a long time. The patch of soil she sprinkled inside the sugarcane furrow had turned a glistening black by the time she emerged, busily straightening out her work trousers tied at the ankles. Her face seemed to be tinged with an anxious shade of red as she stared up at the sky.

"Hey, hurry up!" Ushi yelled at Také. It was the first time she had felt like shouting.

Then Zentoku bellowed at Eitarō. "What the hell are *you* looking at, standing there like a zombie? Get moving!"

Listening to Zentoku, Ushi realized that from now on their lives would be like nothing they'd ever known before. It was strange enough with Eitarō barging unexpectedly into the family. But things were further complicated because, with Eitarō now in their midst, Také's relations with the others had changed, too. Perhaps because Ushi had come so far from home, things unreal and disconnected—like the refugees streaming in all directions as far as the eye could see— seemed to be driving the people in her family apart. Yet at the same time, Ushi felt that they were all clinging desperately to each other.

Zentoku had been wrong to yell at Eitarō, thought Ushi, but what she said trying to smooth things over could only have made them worse.

"He's right, you know. If we don't hurry, we'll end up in the after-world." As soon as she blurted this out, Ushi knew she'd misspoken again. But this time, because of what happened next, Zentoku didn't notice.

Walking close behind Eitarō, Zenshun had spotted a wooden headrest that had fallen by the side of the road. "Look, a pillow!"

"That old man up there must have dropped it," Fumiko added quickly. "The one carrying the futon."

"I'll bring it to him," Zenshun volunteered, and he was about to run off with it when Eitarō stopped him.

"Hey! Hold it right there, or those gunboats'll fire on you."

At that moment Také seemed to come to her senses. "Let's take it," she said. "You can use a pillow, Grandpa. In your big hurry, you probably forgot one."

"What! Use someone else's pillow? Throw it back, stupid. Don't you know there's a war on?"

But Také refused to give in, certain that Zentoku was being needlessly finicky. "You better take it, Grandpa. You're the one who can't sleep without a pillow, war or no war." She snatched the pillow from Zenshun and stuffed it into one of the two straw carrying-baskets hanging from the pole Eitarō was carrying.

Now Ushi spoke in a high-spirited voice, trying to cover her embarrassment of a moment before. "C'mon, everyone! This is serious. Let's hurry up and get moving!" She waved her hand furiously and pointed ahead.

Just then someone yelled from right behind them; a group of people, unnoticed, had caught up with them on the road.

"Grandpa Zentoku, you all going to the tombs, too?" It was Zenga, Zentoku's second cousin, who had been principal of the local elementary school twenty years before. Clustered around him were his daughter-in-law and grandchildren.

"Yeah. You too? It's just *awful*, isn't it."

Zentoku returned Zenga's greeting in an unnecessarily loud voice. After reaching down to roll up the cuffs on his serge trousers, Zenga picked up his walking stick again.

"When the American army lands, you have to keep going no

matter what. Dying in a war at our age would be a disgrace. Do all you can to get through it, Grandpa. Good thing you've got your grandchildren with you, and everyone's looking well."

Seeing Zenga's eyes fixed squarely on Eitarō, Zentoku seemed tongue-tied, so Ushi replied.

"Yes, and with this young man, we're stronger, too. Come on over and visit us."

"That was dumb!" Zentoku snapped at her in a hoarse whisper. "Visit us? In a war?"

Again Ushi realized she'd said the wrong thing, cheerful words spoken in the momentary illusion that this was just some communal migration on the way to a new village. Trying again to hide her embarrassment, she turned to the children. "Fumiko, Zenshun, don't get too far away from us."

Just as she spoke, from nearby the thundering roared again. Zentoku started to mumble as if he wanted to say something but cut it short, hurrying ahead with clattering footsteps. Only Fumiko, right in front of him, had heard the sound of Grandpa's voice emitting from his body like the meaningless grunt of pigs out for a walk.

THE tomb greeted the family as always, covered in a deep black coat of moisture. The three pine trees—in which of the family's generations had they been planted?—today reached a height of 30 feet, towering like guideposts at the cemetery entrance. Zentoku often spoke proudly of their majesty to all his relatives. Arriving on a hillside path, visitors to the family tomb entered the cemetery at the pine trees' roots and proceeded along a walkway 12 feet wide that resembled the front approach to a shrine. After walking 30 feet, they made a right-angle turn, then went another 18 feet to the tomb garden. The 450 square feet of lawn looked beautiful that day with its freshly cut grass. The large tomb within seemed to be leaning back against the hillside as it waited quietly for the family. It was called a turtleback tomb for the convex shape of its roof. On its mortar siding, which swelled voluptuously, curving lines branched out to the left and right, as if supporting that rounded roof, and coiled into whorls at both edges bordering the large stone slab that was the tomb's front wall. From there the lines flowed downward all the way to the ground, where they seemed to embrace the garden. People familiar with these tombs compare them to a woman's body, shaped exactly as if she were lying on her back with legs spread. They say that the "tomb doorway" centered at the bottom of the front wall—large enough for one adult to enter, crouched down—is designed like a vagina, representing the source of life to which a person is said to return after death. Besides turtleback tombs, there are also "gabled tombs" in Okinawa, named for their triangular roof corners. These look more like an ordinary house with a front entrance. Both kinds of tombs are scattered throughout the island in various settings—backdropped by rolling hills, enclosed in groves of trees, or nestled in fields. They signify, probably first and foremost, the ancestors eternally asserting their presence. And perhaps they embody the hopes of ordinary people, whose lives are hard in the present world, for prosperity in the afterlife. For some families these dwelling places for their ancestors' bones are far grander than the houses they live in. And on this peaceful island now besieged as if by evil spirits, these tombs served well as fortresses where people driven from their homes by the monstrous gunboat assault could find spiritual strength.

This family's tomb, resembling a woman's supine body, her legs spread open, now looked out on an ocean where enemy warships floated in the distance. Yet it greeted the ancestors' descendants serenely, as if it knew the incantation that brings eternal life. The deep spiritual exhilaration Zentoku felt in its presence even made the thundering seem to stop for a moment. Back when he was twenty-five, the tomb's stone siding had begun to lose its shape after many years of weathering. The family had reconstructed it at enormous expense by selling off some of their farmland. As part of the rebuilding ceremony, Zentoku had, for the first time, closed the massive one-piece stone door filling the tomb entrance. Since then it had been opened occasionally for funerals and for the periodic ritual of washing the bones of the deceased. Today Zentoku was moved deeply to think that fate was now making him open the door to seek protection for his own life. After thumping his shoulder twice with his fist, he grasped the crowbar and positioned it next to the stone.

The proper days for opening tomb doors are prescribed by the yin-yang principles of ancient Chinese philosophy. Ordinarily, Zentoku and Ushi followed these strictly, but neither even mentioned them today since there was, of course, a war on. In this emergency, with cannon fire thundering far and near, such grueling work required the utmost courage and concentration. Realizing that his aging body would no longer do what he wanted it to, Zentoku finally came to appreciate how Eitarō had, quite literally, lent them his arm. Yet even after the dark cavity lay open—today with new meaning—and he had hurried inside with the children, Zentoku again felt it was wrong for Eitarō, Také, and Tamiko to be inside the tomb.

"You all don't plan to stay here, do you?" he asked Také.

She had put her hand on Tamiko's shoulders, trying to calm the young child, who was glancing around fearfully. But as soon as she heard Zentoku's question, she looked over quickly at Eitarō and Zentoku, then yelled as if hurling her words through Tamiko's shoulders. "And just where are we supposed to go?"

"Any damn place!"

"Hah! You make us carry the baggage and open the tomb door, and now you want to throw us out."

"I never asked you to do it. You insisted, so I *let* you."

"All right then," said Také. "We'll leave. But if your granddaughter gets killed, it'll be your fault. So just make sure you apologize to our ancestors."

At a loss for words, Zentoku peered out across the 150 square feet of the tomb floor. Standing about three feet inside the doorway, he could see the stone shelves inside, built in levels like stairs from the floor to the ceiling, on which the mortuary urns of the family's successive generations were enshrined in their proper order of seniority. Most everyone Zentoku's age had memorized each of the ancestor's life stories. The family began seven generations ago with the marriage of the man who had established its independence. The history of succeeding generations included now familiar events in the lives of the family heads and, most important, where their wives had come from. Zentoku knew how many children each woman bore; that because one wife could not give birth, a child had been adopted into the family; that when this child grew up he had been fond of women and kept concubines, scattering his seed; and that when his illegitimate child died, the relatives had objected when he wanted to bury the child's bones in this tomb. Zentoku also knew that the head of the family in one generation had worked as a servant in the house of the village lord, accompanying him on a visit to the royal castle at Shuri, where the servant received a gift from one of the palace nobles for being clever and helpful. The gift was stored as a family heirloom, but this man, fond of nightlife, had sold it and spent all the money on drink. This angered the relatives and resulted in his banishment from the lord's house, after which he drifted to another village. Because of him, the family still went to that village to offer incense in his memory both on the *O-bon* holiday, honoring ancestors' spirits, and on New Year's Day. All these things Zentoku had fully memorized. The mortuary urns were called "little shrine pots." Though made of cheap pottery, they were elaborately engraved and ornamented with covers modeled pretentiously on roof tiles so they looked like miniature "antique" houses. Enveloped in a faint blue darkness and smelling like dead leaves, the urns stood lined up in rows like aging dignitaries, never moving as they radiated enigmatic expressions and an aura of authority that pressed in on Zentoku.

Zentoku had heard the thundering again just as he'd passed through the tomb doorway, but, looking up at the dignitaries, he was relieved to feel their protective powers. Now Také's words jolted him with the realization that these same dignitaries could convert their powers to condemnation. As he looked around at the ancestors one by one, observing them intently in their proper order of seniority, strange thoughts troubled him. What galled Zentoku most was his wanton daughter. Her husband had gone to war as an honored imperial soldier and given his life in battle. Even though he was dead, when the mother of his child took up with another man, Zentoku could no longer think of her as his daughter. Now it occurred to him that Také might have inherited the blood of that philandering ancestor adopted into the family long ago. And if so, then his blood could be flowing in

Zentoku's veins as well. This possibility disturbed Zentoku deeply. He had maintained strict chastity until he remarried after he was past sixty. Even then, he had taken a wife mainly to appease the ancestral spirits, since only the women of the house could conduct the family rituals. Still, he was unable to rid his mind of the thought that this ancestor's blood coursed within him, and he now found this adopted son from the past truly hateful. Yet he also knew this was not a time to be concerned about such things. It was just as Také had said. By refusing to let her and Tamiko stay here, he was putting them in great danger, for which the ancestors would surely condemn him. With the cannons thundering in his ears, he knew that if he was going to depend on the ancestors to save their lives, he couldn't hold a grudge.

Confused and unable to see clearly in the dim light, Zentoku gazed around at that silent group of his ancestors. Ushi, beside him, grasped a handful of rice from one of the carrying-baskets and poured it onto the overturned lid of the lunch box. She then placed this as an offering on the lowest shelf of the altar. Next she clasped her hands together in prayer, raised them to her withered lips, and spoke in a voice barely audible but with a rhythm that was steady and sure.

"Today America brings war on us with the violence of their gunboats. Help in any way you can, oh revered ancestors, to save your many descendants from harm."

AND so began the family's cohabitation with their ancestors. Ushi looked again at the clothes and food they had managed to carry here and reflected on how theirs had been a safe journey.

"I wonder if Zenga and his family had any trouble moving?" she asked worriedly.

"The shelling's just started," said Zentoku. "So what kind of trouble could there be?" Whereupon Zenshun piped up, "This is war. If the cannons hit 'em, it'll be sudden death!"

"Hey, that's no way for a kid to talk."

"Kids or grown-ups—with cannons it makes no difference."

Zentoku and Zenshun were yelling at the top of their lungs, determined not to be drowned out by the thundering cannon fire. Their voices echoed loudly inside the stone chamber.

"Hey, you two. Quit your hollering!" Ushi glared at them. "How can you say a bad word like 'death' in front of the ancestors?"

Zenshun, looking puzzled, gazed again at the rows of mortuary urns, and Zentoku glanced up to see Eitarō crouched in the far corner of the chamber. To Grandpa he looked like a freeloader who'd barged in on them and was now eating their food but doing no work.

If only Zentoku would resign himself to Eitarō being with Také, at least the adults could adjust to the family's cohabitation with their ancestors. But the two older children couldn't get used to this place, no matter what. Tamiko, the youngest, seemed to adapt right away because she felt secure just being with her mother, but Fumiko and Zenshun were obviously frightened to be in a tomb with human bones. As dusk fell on the first day, they edged closer to Také and Eitarō. Zenshun asked again and again about the mortuary urns.

"Are there really people's bones inside?"

"Well, we don't keep pig's bones in 'em." Eitarō tried to make Zenshun laugh but only got another glare from Zentoku.

"Zenshun, Fumiko. Come over here." Sensing that something had to be done for the two children, Ushi called them away from Také and Eitarō. Then Zentoku set down the wooden pillow he had carried over to make his point and lay down, squeezing himself into a narrow corner. This was also done to teach the children.

"This is how we'll sleep. Just like our ancestors. You don't have to worry. They aren't ghosts, you know."

"That's right," Ushi chimed in. "There's nothing scary about 'em. They're *helping* us." This was her belief. And though she had embraced it reluctantly at first, she was even more fervent than Zentoku now in trying to get the rest of the family to believe, too. Thanks to her faith, she appeared to be mostly at peace after entering the tomb, even when night fell and the thundering roared.

That night Ushi woke up after midnight. "Také," she called in a low, raspy voice that wouldn't echo in the stone chamber. Her words seemed to fade into the darkness.

"Oh, Grandma!" Také, startled, answered in a sudden shriek. At the same time, though Ushi couldn't see it, Také was pushing away Eitarō's hand, which was searching for her breast.

"How are the kids?"

"They're asleep." Také's voice had recovered its composure.

"What about Eitarō?"

"He's . . . uh . . . sleeping."

"Everyone's asleep, then."

"Yeah."

"Got to get a good night's sleep in a war. But how can you, with all these damn mosquitoes?"

At a loss for an answer, Také grabbed Eitarō's hand in midair as it reached toward her for a second time. Just as she did, there was a dull, wet thud outside. Ushi went over to peek out the tomb door as Také and Eitarō sat up automatically.

"What are those things?" Ushi asked no one in particular as she peered outside. "They look like a whole bunch of fire spirits," she said, comparing the streaks of light she saw to the wisps of luminescent phosphorous gas that sometimes rise from the mortuary urns as the bones inside decompose.

"They're flares. For night vision," Eitarō explained.

"Is that right? To see the battle even at night, eh?" As she spoke, Ushi straightened out her collar and skirt, which had ruffled up in her sleep. She seemed to be doing this as a precaution, lest certain exposed parts of her body be suddenly illuminated.

"Don't worry, Grandma. Fire spirits would run away in a war." Také sounded as if she were trying to force a laugh, and Eitarō cleared his throat to speak in a voice that sounded full of courage.

"Inside the tomb even fire spirits can't scare us. The dead are our friends now. Right, Grandma?"

Without bothering to answer, Ushi stepped out through the doorway.

"Grandma, where're you going?"

Také's voice seemed to chase after her, but Ushi had already slipped outside and was making her way over the flat pavement along the stone wall. When she came to the sleeve-like contours at the base of the tomb, she squatted down carefully. The wall, coming to right angles here, enclosed her body and made her feel safe.

Without knowing why, Také and Eitarō had followed beside Ushi. Now they watched in the starlight as she lowered herself, knees still drawn in, from a crouching to a sitting position, placed both hands in her lap, and quietly folded her fingers together.

"Také," Ushi called quietly as she stared into the darkness.

"Yes, Grandma."

"Keep your eye on the kids. If they die here, Grandpa won't put their remains in this tomb, and his ancestors would never forgive that."

"Does it really make any damn difference whose tomb it is in the middle of a war, Grandma?" Eitarō's tone in speaking to Ushi was much too familiar.

"It sure does. Are you crazy?" Ushi rarely spoke so harshly. "This tomb is Grandpa's. It's only right for you to go to *your* tomb."

Také and Eitarō exchanged glances in the darkness. Neither could make out the other's expression but thought it was probably gloomy.

"You've come here with us and don't seem to care about your own parents," Ushi explained. "There's nothing we can do about that now. But if you die here, your ancestors'll never forgive you. So you better live through this and go back to your family. And Také, you better apologize to *our* ancestors for the things you've done lately."

As they listened to Ushi's words, Také and Eitarō stared hard into the darkness out toward the distant sea.

THE thundering echoed day and night, with flashes clearly revealed after dark. By this time, countless warships, their cannons firing, clogged the ocean's surface. With a seemingly random violence, red gashes tore through the darkness as the thunder roared. An instant later, flare bombs exploded in the same patch of dark sky, lighting up grassy hillsides and potato fields below like faces pale and chagrined. The nocturnal landscape hid the real faces of living things, so only flashing patterns of light could be seen here and there, but the ghastly roaring echoed endlessly.

Now Ushi was thinking she might die here. Yet she wasn't

imagining her flesh torn apart by those thunderings into some hideous form so that she would end up like the pigs slaughtered in every household the day before the New Year's feast. Instead, her thoughts probably reflected her wish to die here rather than somewhere else. As Zentoku's second wife, she felt an especially strong desire to die at his ancestral tomb.

She had married him when she was past fifty, so she bore this family no children. Zentoku already had a boy and two girls by his first wife. The elder daughter had moved to the Philippines; Také was the younger daughter. When war approached, the son had sent his two children, Fumiko and Zenshun, to live at Zentoku's house. Ushi felt no connection with this son except through Zentoku and his grandchildren. And she wondered how much she could grieve if his son or elder daughter should die in some faraway place like the Philippines. Yet she knew she must be able to mourn like the others. It was another of the obligations and aspirations life had brought her during more than ten years in this family.

ZENTOKU had taken Ushi as his second wife so he could entrust to her the rites for his ancestors as well as those household chores that fell to a man living without a wife or daughter-in-law. Ushi understood this when she married him and had done her best performing the rites and doing the daily chores for Zentoku and his grandchildren. Being nearly sixty, she found her many obligations to Zentoku's relatives far less daunting than a young wife would have. And she was delighted with the respect often accorded her as the family matriarch.

In truth, she would have been in real trouble if she hadn't gotten on with them. When nearing age forty, she'd been turned out of the house by her first husband. She thought this was probably because the one child she'd borne him had died, but he also had another woman. She'd then returned to her parents' home, where she lived some ten years raising silkworms. But after passing fifty, she began to wonder where her bones would be placed when she died. One day at home she happened to ask about this and was told that if she died here, her remains would enter the family tomb but would be set in a special place. Though they might not end up in a separate row, a special explanation would be required of her descendants each time they opened the tomb. She would thus have to bear the disapproval of her ancestors even in the next world. How painful it was, having once left home for marriage, to return to her parents' house. Life was hard for a woman.

Then, as luck would have it, just at that time a proposal came for her to become Zentoku's second wife. She agreed not so much because she was eager to marry him, but at least partly because, after death, her bones could then be reposited in the normal way at his family tomb. Just as rumored, Zentoku turned out to be rather clumsy and stubborn, yet he seemed to have a boundlessly sunny disposition. Having been chosen by him, she decided that if she didn't do her utmost to serve his family, punishment would befall her. She would have no excuses when facing the ancestors of a family who had generously welcomed this "surplus person" to join them through marriage. And so she performed her duties with everything she had and was called "Grandma" by Zentoku's grandchildren as they came to adore her. Then, all of a sudden, just when she thought nothing would be lacking in her relations with the family's ancestors in the next world, her time for cohabitation with them had come early and entirely unexpectedly. Of course, it wasn't true cohabitation as long as she was still living flesh and blood. Still, she wanted to believe that somehow the ancestors had wanted it this way. And though she felt she might die here, this feeling was in no way at odds with her belief that these ancestors would save the lives of the family. For her, both came from her desire for "peace of mind."

But now, Ushi thought, there was the problem of Také and Eitarō. Whatever could be said about Eitarō, Také was being a most unfilial daughter. Zentoku had good reason to be angry with her. Yet Ushi could understand Také's feelings, too. As a man, her husband had been expected to go off to war and even to die, but Ushi could sympathize with the wife he'd left behind. Také was caring for a small child with no husband to rely on. He had been a second son, so she was spared the hardship of serving a mother-in-law. Yet this also meant that no property was passed on to her that could support them. Hers was a loneliness that Ushi, abandoned while still in her thirties, knew all too well. She could understand how Také had panicked when the war came and, ignoring shame and reputation, had rushed with Eitarō back to her parents. To take in this troublesome trio might be an imposition on the family ancestors, too, but with a war on, it couldn't be helped. Now it was more important that Také and Eitarō take every precaution not to die here. If they didn't somehow survive, there would be even worse troubles.

Unlike Zentoku, Ushi openly showed her feelings toward Také and Eitarō, always treating them kindly. Listening to Ushi, Také felt a rush of sadness and warmth and reached out toward Eitarō, who, she thought, was lying diagonally behind her. Instead, she grabbed his limply dangling empty sleeve and had to shift her grasp hurriedly. Eitarō helped her with his one hand until their two hands finally clasped together.

Just then the thundering roared again, this time from directly overhead, shattering the night sky with a bright red glare.

"Grandma!" Fearing for Ushi, Zentoku screamed from inside the tomb as if his heart would burst, and Ushi called back immediately.

"I'm right here, Grandpa!" Facing the tomb door, she had fallen down at an awkward angle, protecting her body with both arms. Také and Eitarō hugged each other tightly, keeping their eyes on Ushi, who held herself motionless as though glued to the tomb's stone foundation.

ON the morning of the third day there was an explosion so loud that the wobbling faces on the small shrines seemed to frown. At about this time everyone—young and old, male and female—began to feel a kind of unity. They all agreed when Zentoku said no one should go outside the tomb just to piss. But there was a momentary impasse when someone pointed out that this would be a problem for shit, since it couldn't be absorbed into the stone floor.

Eitarō tugged at Také's sleeve and whispered that the bottoms of the mortuary urn covers were hollow and could be emptied outside at night after use. But Také signaled him with a frown to keep his mouth shut. Then, in a low voice she told him that although this was a good idea, if either of them were to suggest it, Grandpa might find it blasphemous and get angry. Now, when everyone had just started to feel this new unity, it was better not to upset him for a while. Eitarō agreed. Yet perhaps because his clever idea had stirred the ancestral spirits lined up before them, the same suggestion came from the mouth of the eldest descended grandson, Zenshun.

"That's yucky!" Fumiko objected, her scowling face blackened with dirt. But from beside her, Ushi replied.

"He's right. There's nothing else we can do because this is war. Later, if we wash the urns clean, punishment won't come to us." Having rationalized her actions, she removed the cover from a mortuary urn within easy reach. Then, thinking she needed to show extra respect, she again set out some rice—only three grains this time—as an offering and pressed her palms together. As she clasped her hands in silent prayer, she worried that if prayers were needed again after tomorrow, there would be no more rice for offering.

Shut up inside the tomb, the family had no idea how the battle was going, but after seven days, they were so inured to the thundering that no one gave it much thought. For them, the war had become thunder, hunger, and shitting in the urn covers. Také and Eitarō regretted that sex was no fun on the hard ground and rather lost interest in it. But in a way things got easier for them because, under the circumstances, their love for each other could hardly be a secret anymore. With his combat experience, Eitarō worried that the enemy might have landed. He mentioned this to Také, but she couldn't feel any real danger. Like Ushi, she was most concerned about their dwindling supply of rice, sweet potatoes, and miso. Anticipating shortages from the first day, they had economized more and more, often leaving the children feeling hungry. In time, instead of crying, the children began sleeping longer, something that troubled Také far more than the approaching enemy. Having yet to see any soldiers, friend or foe, the possibilities of victory or defeat had little meaning for her. She couldn't believe the nation's fall was imminent as long as the rows of mortuary urns didn't crumble to pieces.

On about the fifth day they realized that for a half-hour every morning and evening, the ships' cannons would stop firing. After the war, it was learned that these had been the enemy's mealtimes. The breaks in shelling gave everyone a chance to forget their troubles and venture outside the tomb, where they felt slightly dizzy in the open air and the children played with pebbles.

It occurred to Eitarō that now he could walk out and shit leisurely in the fields. He found a suitable spot inside a thicket and, squatting down, gazed out calmly through the trees at the fleet of warships. For him they brought back childhood memories of the ships in long rows from Japan's combined fleet lined up in the bay. At night its search-lights had seemed like a reliable halo of protective power. But now he was looking at squadrons of the U.S. military, the bitter enemy well known for brutality. Yet it was too bad, he thought, that they had to be the enemy—those hundreds of warships lined up in rows of towering black silhouettes that hid the ocean horizon and seemed so full of con-fidence. The old adage, "Splendid, though an enemy" might be trite, but shut up by this war day and night inside a tomb side by side with other people's ancestors was starting to give Eitarō an inferiority com-plex. Now, as the dry spring wind played across his unwiped ass, he found physical pleasure in confronting this enemy. Thinking they could not see him, he had the illusion of being somehow on equal terms with them, and his spirits, too, were lifted.

Eitarō slipped back inside through the tomb door, still excited from his first sojourn outside, just as thundering broke out from resumed shelling. He and Také stared at each other in wide-eyed alarm. But the next morning he stayed outside longer, crouching down to face the enemy until the thundering started. Though he'd been ready to flee back to the tomb full speed at the first rumbling, he now embarked on a one-man insurgency. He stared out at the cluster of battleships, poised like a sprinter at the starting line, and let out a sudden cry, not knowing whether it was from shock or pleasure. In the next instant, countless cannons roared. It amazed Eitarō how the ships would lurch powerfully backward just after spewing their shell fire. He stayed put, as if held there by some mysterious force, concealing his lower body in the shadows of a nearby rock as he gazed far out into the ocean. The battleships were moving forward rapidly now, one after another, belch-ing fire and lurching backward with a roar that split the sky and made its colors seem about to dissolve and float away. Eitarō had seen combat in China, but from childhood he could only think of the sea, the sky, and this land now before his eyes as things of beauty. Witnessing this awesome destruction, he felt no panic, but was filled instead with a sense of wonder, as though he'd discovered some freakish form of life on earth. In the next moment a rush of power surged through his body with a strange crackling sound, and an unexpected desire welled up inside him. He ran back, waving his one arm wildly, and could feel all his muscles stiffen as he grabbed Také. Of course, she resisted, thinking he'd been frightened by the shelling.

Then Ushi hollered at him. "Maniac!" Her voice sounded weak. "How can you be so selfish, not even thinking of the children! Instead of doing that, you'd better start hunting for sweet potatoes tomorrow. The ones in the field below here should be ready to eat."

At first Eitarō thought he was being scolded for grabbing Také, but from Ushi's manner he realized she was telling him not to risk his life so recklessly. Still, apparently unable to cool his excitement, he did not respond to her. Meanwhile, Zentoku slept, looking very cramped with his body all curled up. Only his pillow lay straight.

Ushi and Také agreed to wait for the evening break in shelling to go out for sweet potatoes. Také told Eitarō he had to go, too, but he remained silent.

That afternoon things took an ominous turn. Along with the roar of cannons, they began to hear the popping of rifle fire nearby and the buzzing of airplanes. Inside the tomb they couldn't tell which direction these sounds were coming from, but every time the airplanes buzzed closer, after a few seconds, the thundering got closer, too. After listening for a while, Eitarō whispered, "Contact probes."

"Contact—what?" asked Také, but Eitarō didn't answer. Now there was more gunfire. Then came a noise they heard for the first time.

"Chase guns." Eitarō spoke again as a veteran of the fighting in China. He usually talked in Okinawa dialect, but he said the words "contact probe" and "chase guns" in standard Tokyo Japanese. For a moment he forgot about life inside the tomb and spoke of his combat experience with a certain wistful pride. Yet what he was saying mattered little to Ushi, Zentoku, and Také.

None of them thought about what these changing circumstances meant in the unfolding strategy of battle. But with the noticeable lull in conversation, fear seemed to be pressing in on everyone. That evening, for the first time, there was no break in the shelling.

"I guess we can't go hunting for potatoes, Grandpa," Ushi said as she peeked outside.

From his pillow Zentoku half-opened his eyes and answered with what sounded like a groan.

"Sounds like the battle's starting, Grandma," said Eitarō.

Again, he spoke as a combat veteran. At this point Zentoku finally took the trouble to sit up. "Hey, you can't even fight," he bellowed. "So what the hell are you blabbing about?"

"Grandpa, ease up on him," Ushi scolded. Eitarō, looking embarrassed, muttered softly so only Také would hear.

"Yeah, but for this family, even someone like me is handy to have around sometimes."

Také knew he was right and that she would have to convince Zentoku and Ushi of this. Fortunately, the next morning the cannons stopped shelling at the usual time. Rifle fire continued but seemed to grow distant, though they might only have imagined this. Také took this opportunity to speak up so everyone could hear her.

"Eitarō, let's go dig for potatoes," she said. "If we take the straw baskets, we can bring back enough food to last a while."

Without a word, Eitarō grabbed Také's hand, and together they slipped outside. "The baskets! Get the baskets!" Také tried to remind him, but Eitarō never even glanced back as he led her hurriedly through the tomb garden and into a thicket of trees.

"Look at those battleships!" he said. "Pretty, huh. They're really beautiful with their guns firing."

His tone was strangely passionate. Without knowing why, Také did as he said and peered out at the cluster of battleships lined up like a row of islands floating on an ocean so serene it seemed unreal. Until this moment she'd been overwhelmed with worry, cooped up inside that tomb with the old folks, the kids, and this man. But now the vast, open landscape before her seemed to bring a sudden feeling of release.

The smell of green leaves mixed with a burnt odor coming from no-where in particular awakened in her an almost forgotten desire. The momentary calm on the battlefield took her mind off the fear she had felt for her life and, at the same time, emboldened her to forget all con-straints. Eitarō's one hand began groping here and there on Take's bare skin. As his movements grew more fervent, she helped him to embrace her with his one arm by wrapping both her arms around his chest. Just then someone called from the other side of the thicket.

"Mommy!"

Tamiko's voice startled Take more than thundering cannons, and she struggled frantically to pull up her half-shed underwear.

"Those cannons'll hit you out here! Go back to Grandma, damn it. Hurry!" She had shouted with unintended anger as if the cannons really were about to fire on them. Then, suddenly frightened, she bolted out of the thicket and grasped Tamiko's hand without even a glance back at Eitarō. Though worried about losing this chance to gather potatoes, she hurried ahead and inadvertently let go of the child's hand. Then, just as she made her way through the tomb door, there was a dry, whooshing sound, as if a large package had been hurled down on the stone pavement behind her. Thinking this was a strange sound for a child falling, she turned around instinctively. At that same moment Eitarō, who had been following behind her, cried out in astonishment.

What looked at first glance like a package turned out to be a Japanese soldier. He'd tumbled down from the tomb roof just as Take was passing through the door, just missing her back but knocking Tamiko over as she ran behind her mother. Then, still tightly grasping his rifle, he'd fallen facedown on the gray stone pavement. When they saw both the fallen soldier and the child he'd knocked down lying motionless, Take and Eitarō stood in shock—one inside the tomb, the other outside. The thunder roaring at that moment brought the loud-est screams yet from Take and sent her cringing backward. Zentoku, realizing something was wrong, leapt to his feet and ran toward them from the rear of the tomb. Reaching the door just as Take was backing away from it, he slammed into her from behind and their bodies tangled, falling in a heap on top of Ushi. Now Ushi lay on her back, looking squashed, and yelled out between gasps. "Wh-what happened? Where's Tamiko?"

Hearing Ushi's words, Také leaped to her feet in fear for her daughter just as Eitarō came through the door carrying Tamiko.

"We can't stay shut up in here anymore with this war right on top of us. We've got to get out of here." Eitarō spoke as he lowered Tamiko to the ground, but no one was listening to him.

Také clutched her child with both hands, making sure Tamiko was warm and breathing. Then, after feeling her pulse, she asked, "Was that really a Japanese soldier?"

Eitarō nodded.

"Maybe this means Japan's losing the war."

"C'mon. Wars aren't lost because one soldier dies." Eitarō stared up at the ceiling as if straining to listen for something.

"No, I guess not," said Také, fervently shaking Tamiko, who lay motionless.

Yet a Japanese soldier falling from the tomb roof and dying right in front them seemed like a terrible omen, frightening everyone. Tamiko soon revived but cried for a long time afterward. Now they could hear the loud droning of airplanes, and Ushi hurried to cover Tamiko's mouth, but the child twisted away and cried even louder. Her voice seemed to stir a desperate anger in Zentoku.

"Her spirit's gone! It must be brought back!" he yelled, and Ushi tossed him a look that told him she already knew this without his having to say so.

It is believed that when children are frightened after, for example, stumbling in the street, falling from a tree, or being bitten by a dog, they lose their spirits at the site of the accident and their bodies become like empty shells. At these times a *yuta* shaman is engaged to offer prayers at the site to restore the child's spirit. Ushi had thought of doing this as soon as Tamiko came to but realized at the same time that their situation would make it extremely difficult.

If no shaman were available, someone in the family would suffice, but Ushi had never used anything but rice for the required votive offering, and besides, going out to the site where the child's spirit had fallen was out of the question.

"There's no rice and we can't go outside. How can we bring back this poor child's spirit?" Ushi wailed, stroking her granddaughter's dirt-smudged forehead.

"You can use miso or potatoes. And today we'll just have to send our prayers from here," yelled Zentoku.

Ushi knew he was right, especially since he was speaking in the presence of the ancestors. With two fingers, she scraped out what remained in the miso jar and spread it on a lunch-box lid. Then, turning to face outside in the direction of Tamiko's lost spirit, Ushi set down the miso offering and brought her palms together in prayer.

"Do we pray for the dead soldier? For his 'eternal good fortune in battle'?" Zenshun asked, raising himself slightly as he lay on his belly. His face, blackened with dirt, wore a serious expression

"You can't have 'good fortune in battle' after you die," said Fumiko. "Pray for 'his soul to rest in peace.'"

Fumiko repeated a phrase she'd remembered from a memorial service, and then Ushi spoke.

"This soldier was sure to be punished, after causing another family's child to lose her spirit and then defiling their tomb."

Ushi resumed her prayers.

When everyone had fallen silent, the constant noise of airplanes and gunfire—fading away for a moment, then coming closer again—made them feel as if they were in the middle of a war being waged around this one tomb. And the presence of the soldier who had died right before their eyes made things seem all the more ominous. Fumiko and Zenshun took turns poking their faces outside the tomb door to check on his corpse.

"He's still there," said Zenshun fearfully for the umpteenth time.

"Well, I guess punishment hasn't come yet," Také murmured for no particular reason.

"Whose punishment are you talking about, anyway?" Eitaro scolded her in a low voice, and Také wondered if it would be the soldier's own punishment or the family's punishment that he would suffer. She turned to look back at Eitarō, her eyes like a weary chicken's, but, thinking she would only get confused trying to answer his question, she said nothing.

"Eitarō!" Zentoku called out, and Eitarō wondered how much Grandpa had heard of their whispered conversation.

"Yeah!" Looking startled, Eitarō answered Zentoku crisply for the first time since they'd left home.

Ushi turned toward Eitarō, taking a break from her praying.

"We've got to give him a proper burial." Zentoku spoke to Eitarō, also for the first time, with a note of authority in his voice.

"Bury him? Where?" Eitarō answered more earnestly than he'd intended.

"Can't put him in here, so we'll have to dig a hole."

"But if we just lay him outside somewhere, the body will decompose on its own."

"No. That would bring punishment on us. After all, he's a soldier of our nation, fighting for us. He's got a hometown and parents somewhere. We'd be punished for sure, and all those ships would come shooting their cannons at us."

"You're right." Eitarō agreed so readily he even surprised himself. Yet all at once things seemed to be just as Zentoku had said. Grandpa's words echoed in Eitarō's mind as he recalled the brutal sight of the soldier's corpse, which he'd seen before anyone else. "But I can't do it alone," he said, making every effort now to look earnest.

"Of course not," said Ushi. "Grandpa will work with you. And if you need someone else, Také can help. The corpse is still fresh, so with a proper burial done right away, no one will be punished."

As they listened to this judgment pronounced with such apparent confidence, Eitarō and Také exchanged glances, remembering that just moments before, Ushi had predicted punishment for the soldier. Yet she seemed unaware of any contradiction. Stranger still, Eitarō now found himself staring intently at Ushi and nodding in agreement. She pressed her palms together, then turned again in the direction of the soldier, who looked as if his soul were caught in limbo between this world and the next. In Ushi's mind the soldier's punishment had already become one with their own. She didn't know where this punishment was coming from or who was meting it out, but she was sure that unless they acted now, those cannons and rifles were destined to come and make hideous corpses of them. Ushi prayed for her granddaughter's spirit in the firm belief that she was also praying for the soldier's spirit and that the two would merge with the spirits of the rest of the family and be calmed. In this way, her prayers extended to the soldier's burial. And, though they didn't understand what seemed logically inconsistent, Eitarō and Také felt somehow reassured by the faith Ushi and Zentoku shared.

That evening, with the break in shelling, Zentoku motioned emphatically for Eitarō to get the crowbar, and, with Zentoku carrying the hoe, the two of them hurried out of the tomb. Finding a place to bury the corpse wasn't easy. Though it looked like there was plenty of open space, the nearby trees had spread thick, hardened roots under most of the ground. Zentoku soon lost his temper.

"What the hell is taking you so long to find a spot?"

With Zentoku yelling at him, Eitarō began wandering around in confusion and came inadvertently to the place where he had stroked Také's bare skin earlier that day. Just as he was wishing he had avoided this spot, Zentoku spoke again.

"That's fine—right there. Now get out of my way!" Pushing Eitarō aside, Zentoku raised the hoe, but his aging body, deprived of food and sunlight for some ten days, staggered after just one swing.

"Let me do it, Grandpa."

"Oh yeah? With one arm?"

"Sure. I lay a woman with one arm. No problem digging a hole."

Zentoku glared at Eitarō, ready to scold him again, but Eitarō seemed unconcerned now as he snatched the hoe from Grandpa and raised it with his one arm. Though his stance looked precarious, he didn't miss his target. Zentoku stared, mouth open, at Eitarō's one-armed swing and at his other shoulder where the arm had been severed. His voice came out in a low monotone.

"If you hit any rocks, I can yank 'em out with the crowbar."

"No rocks, Grandpa. You just stand there." Strong as he was, Eitarō's voice came out in half-gasps as he swung the hoe down again and again, remembering all the while that this was the spot where his lovemaking with Také had been cut short. He was also remembering how the soldier's corpse had fallen into their midst, and now the two events seemed oddly linked by destiny. Yet as he continued to dig, cursing and spitting, he could feel the weight of that destiny lifting bit by bit. Then, just when he'd dug deep enough to bury the corpse's shoulders below ground level, the thundering rang out again.

Eitarō gazed at the ocean. In the deepening dusk, flashes of fire from the roaring cannons lit up the sky with a red brighter than morning. But now, far from exciting a desire for lovemaking, the scene reminded him of the soldier's corpse. And the terror he'd felt a few years before on the battlefield in China flashed back inside him, ripping to the very core of his body.

"Grandpa, the shelling's started!"

"So what? We've got to keep digging and bury him before the day's over. Gimme that hoe." Grabbing the hoe, Zentoku let out a yell as he thrust it into the ground. "Hurry up and bring the corpse. Get Také to help."

Scowling as his last words were drowned out by the thundering, Zentoku swung the hoe upward only to have his own momentum spin him around and hurl him down on his rear end. After helping him to his feet, Eitarō took a deep breath, then dashed back toward the tomb where Také was waiting. She'd been poking her head out of the doorway, peering cautiously, but when she saw Eitarō motioning to her with his one hand, she rushed out toward him.

Wearing full combat gear, the corpse was too heavy to lift, so Eitarō pried the rifle from its grasp and hurriedly took off the steel helmet. Shorn of his helmet, the soldier's eyes seemed to bulge glaring from his head, and Také let out a shriek. In too much of a hurry now to remove the leather belt and ammo pouch, the two of them grasped the corpse by its arms and legs. Dragging it across the ground, they had to change grips constantly, and Také kept her eyes shut most of the time as she struggled with the weight and her fear. By the time they reached the hole, the corpse's head was covered with cuts and scrapes.

"Just a little more, Grandpa," yelled Eitarō.

"Yeah, the hole's almost ready."

With her nerves raw from fear, Také could sense in the men's voices an unexpected warmth between them. She stared intently at Zentoku's face and suspected that the two had been crying as they spoke to each other. "I'll finish it, Grandpa," she said, snatching the hoe from his hands.

"Okay. It's almost done." Zentoku staggered as he stepped aside, and Také's face, tightly drawn as though she, too, had been crying, now broke into a smile.

"Eee-yah!" Také seemed to imitate Zentoku, letting out a yell as she swung the hoe down into the soil. "Keep an eye on Grandpa, Eitarō," she said.

"Sure thing," he answered, then walked over to where Zentoku was sitting on the ground and stood beside him protectively.

About the time they finished burying the corpse, shells fired from a battleship exploded over the thicket, spreading a red glow through the treetops and making them look like they'd caught fire.

"Grandpa!" Také's instinctive shriek was so piercing that it still echoed in everyone's ears even after they had made their way stumbling back to the tomb. Inside, Ushi greeted them and, with devoted hands, began gently patting and rubbing their bodies, which trembled from fear and exhaustion.

"Anything left to eat?" asked Zentoku, still trying to catch his breath. He turned his head to look back at Ushi as she massaged him.

"There's a little more miso, Grandpa," she said apologetically.

Zentoku tried hard to make out Eitarō's profile in the near-total darkness. "What'll happen to us now?" he asked in a barely audible voice.

"Listen, Grandpa." Eitarō also kept his voice down. "The battle's coming right at us. We can't stay here any longer, even inside the tomb."

"You mean the Americans are coming here?" asked Ushi.

"The gunfire's still a ways off, so I can't be sure. But if the Japanese soldiers run, the Americans will come after them. And before that happens, we've got to get the hell out of here."

"Would Japan just run away?" This was Zenshun's question.

"Well, I . . ?" At a loss for words, Eitarō realized he'd never seen a battle with America attacking and Japan fleeing. But all at once he found himself able to imagine the Japanese army in retreat, maybe because he was hearing gunfire and had seen nothing of this battle except one dead Japanese soldier. The sight of the corpse had affected him deeply, but it wasn't only that. Ever since he and Zentoku had risked their lives burying the soldier, Eitarō felt as though some fateful force were pressing in on him. He stared into the darkness. "Japan might retreat for now but will surely win in the end."

"Retreat where?" asked Zentoku.

"Can't tell now if the attack will come from the north or the south, though we may know by tomorrow morning. That'll be the time to get the hell out of here, Grandpa."

Nodding meekly, Zentoku agreed that what Eitarō said made sense, though of course none of the others could tell he had changed his mind about their leaving. Nor did anyone hear the words he spoke next in a thin, wavering voice that sounded more like Ushi when she prayed.

"I still want to stay here."

THAT night it rained.

"Eitarō," Zentoku called out suddenly through the darkness. "It's raining. Let's go dig some sweet potatoes."

At first Eitarō only groaned sleepily, but he'd understood Zentoku immediately. "In the rain?" he asked, and both men sat upright.

"That's why we've got to do it now, before the storm gets worse. We should leave at dawn, but we can't travel on empty stomachs. Besides, the shelling's let up. Now's our chance. What time is it, anyway?"

Since he was only slightly drowsy, Eitarō figured it must be close to dawn, but he didn't answer. He'd decided to do what Zentoku said, convinced that Grandpa was talking to him more now because the older man's feelings toward him had softened. He also sensed in his tone that Grandpa had decided that when the time came to leave, everyone would go together. Still, Eitarō wondered why Grandpa was so worried about digging sweet potatoes now. If they couldn't stay here, surely they could find food at the next place, so wouldn't it be better to look for it after they got there? Zentoku's strict sense of pro-priety—insisting they go to all this trouble just to bring potatoes along from their own field—seemed more than a little strange under the circumstances. Yet, again, it seemed better to go along with him for the time being. Besides, Eitarō also realized that by eating and traveling together with this family, he was obligated to do what they asked of him.

"You'd better get going now," whispered Také, and Eitarō complied, following Zentoku outside through the tomb door.

What Grandpa had said, about the cannon fire letting up, turned out to be an illusion. Earlier, the sound of the rain had diverted their attention from the noise and light flashes of a relentless bombardment that shattered the night nonstop. Now it was the shelling that diverted their attention, and they barely noticed the rain, which made for treacherous footing in the muddy soil bulging with slippery rocks and tree roots.

"Grandpa!" Eitarō called out in vague apprehension. In the light flash of a bursting shell he saw Zentoku flip the straw baskets over the carrying pole and hoist it onto his shoulders.

"You know that field just below here?" asked Zentoku. "Under the 'Navy Commander'?"

"Sure, I know all your family's land, Grandpa." With the same left hand that held the hoe, Eitarō brushed away the slimy, wet *susuki* leaves that were slapping at his face as he raised his voice proudly over the noise of the rain to answer Zentoku's question. On their way down the embankment, Eitarō came dangerously close to slipping into a huge hole made by a cannon shell. As soon as he regained his footing, he was worried again about Zentoku. "Grandpa!"

"Yeah?" Zentoku called back from far below on the slope. He'd already gotten well beyond the shell hole and had climbed down to the billboard painted with the figure of the "Navy Commander," which was the trademark for Jintan breath mints. Now there was another flash and Eitarō could see the commander in his old-fashioned commodore's hat, wearing a look of robust good health and a serene expression on his face.

"I'm putting the baskets down here. We can toss over the potatoes we dig up." Zentoku's quavering voice revealed that he was already exhausted.

"I'll dig, Grandpa. You cut the vines."

This time Zentoku accepted the easier job without a word, unlike before when they'd dug the hole for the soldier. But as he started digging, Eitarō's frustration mounted because the hoe handle he grasped in his one hand was soon slippery with rain and mud. On top of that, he had to scrape off the mud that clung to every potato he dug up before heaving it toward the baskets.

"Don't bother with the mud," Zentoku yelled. "Just toss 'em over. I'll scrape it off later." Having forgotten his sickle at home, Zentoku had to stop at each plant and crouch down, using all the strength in his legs to rip the potatoes out of the ground. Thrust backward by his own momentum, he fell down again and again on his butt. "Goddamn it!" he cursed to himself, scowling each time he got to his feet.

When dawn started to break, the potatoes Zentoku had managed to scrape off were just beginning to form a mountain-shaped pile. "That's enough for now," he called out in a voice weak from exhaustion, then gazed off absently into the distance around him where several people stood in the fields within his view. From far away, everything looked calm and he felt somehow relieved. But what he saw a moment later instantly swept away all his sleepiness and fatigue. "Hey, that's Zenga, our school principal!"

Looking where Zentoku pointed, toward the opposite corner of the family's potato field, Eitarō was shocked to see Zenga now standing there, digging in the ground.

"What'll we do, Eitarō? He's stealing from us!" On this dimly lit battlefield, Zentoku had now run into a problem that, in his mind, was far more serious than all the trouble of digging up sweet potatoes.

"Aw, let him take some, Grandpa. We've got plenty."

"But he didn't even come to ask permission. And he's the school principal!"

"The cannons might have blown him away if he'd tried to get here. Besides, he's a relative."

"Yeah, but he's still the principal. So what the hell do we do now?"

Thrown into confusion by this unexpected betrayal of trust, Zentoku had forgotten about the rain. Several times he started to get up, then changed his mind and sat down again. Now he was remembering someone else—the village councilman carrying a piglet—who they'd happened to meet on the road the day the family left home. Zentoku had felt a vague admiration watching him walk away because he was, after all, a man of learning. But these days such learning was no longer respected. Carrying a piglet marked him as nothing more than a jittery old tightwad, and the principal was further proof of what things had come to. "Being a principal or a village councilman just doesn't matter anymore," Zentoku muttered in a hoarse voice heavy with regret.

Hearing this, Eitarō wondered if the village councilman might have joined in the thievery and looked out to survey the scene again. At that moment Zenga finally noticed them. At first he swung around to face them, then quickly turned his back. Hunching down, he started edging away in short, quick steps while hastily wrapping an armful of sweet potatoes in what looked like a man's kimono. Then, tossing the bundle over his shoulder, he took off in a staggering run in the opposite direction toward a nearby thicket of sugarcane.

"Hey, he's gonna get away!" yelled Zentoku, and without thinking, he started after him.

"Grandpa! No!" Eitarō dashed after Zentoku to stop him, but his foot caught on a potato vine and he tumbled down hard. At that instant he heard a shell explode with a roar and Zentoku scream.

Shrapnel from a battleship cannon had ripped a clump of flesh the size of a fist from Zentoku's back. Eitarō tried desperately to help him to his feet and saw that the upper half of his own body was smeared with Zentoku's blood. He tried shaking Grandpa and yelling to him, but he didn't move. Through it all Zenga had not even turned around once and seemed to have blended in with his surroundings as he stood among some local farmers.

By this time the morning sun had risen, bringing daylight, and Eitarō saw a shell explode against a hilltop just ahead, spouting debris. Below, where a thin mist hovered, was Zenga's family tomb. Eitarō wondered how long it would take Zenga, after "stealing" all the potatoes he could carry, to get down there. How many times would he fall on the way? And, most important, could he make it safely? By now he was probably scrambling away on the other side of the sugarcane field, and as Eitarō imagined Zenga stumbling along, he barely suppressed an urge to yell at him. Though managing to lift Zentoku's body, already grown cold, off the ground, Eitarō was dripping with sweat and covered with mud, so, with only one arm, it took him a very long time to hoist the body onto his shoulder. Just when he thought he'd gotten it up there, it slid off and fell to the ground. Then he lifted it too far to one side and it slipped over his armless shoulder and fell again. Once he was on the verge of going back and bringing Také to help but decided it would be unforgivable to leave Zentoku alone even for a minute. Besides, he had an ominous premonition that, if he brought her here, the next shell would kill them both. At last he was able to hold Zentoku up on his shoulder by grasping him upside down, legs pointed upward. It took all his strength to crawl to the top of the embankment, where he took a few slow steps on the ground as he fought a crushing exhaustion that seemed to shatter into splinters, piercing his body from shoulders to feet. Suddenly a violent gust of wind sent him reeling, but as he started to tumble back down the embankment, his fall was checked just in time by the "Navy Commander" sign.

The moment he finally reached the tomb after his long struggle back, the wailing of Ushi and Také that greeted him made the whole ordeal seem worthwhile. He knew he had done the right thing and looked forward now to their appreciation and sympathy. So when the two women pushed him aside and abandoned themselves to weeping over poor Zentoku, Eitarō wanted to throw himself down and cry. But, resisting this urge, he soon felt a strange rush of pleasure welling up inside him.

It came most of all from the powerful solidarity he felt with Ushi, Také, and the children as they grieved together for Zentoku before the bones of their ancestors inside that cramped, narrow tomb. Knowing this precious unity was possible only because he had risked his life through rain, mud, and shelling gave him renewed energy and an unexpected sense of pride. *Starting today, I'll lead this family safely out of this battlefield,* he vowed silently. And thinking how reassured they all must feel to have this young man with them enhanced his pride and sense of responsibility. He remembered now telling Také that "even someone like me will come in handy for this family someday." But soon his pleasure turned to loneliness as he realized sadly that his sense of fulfillment had come as a result of Zentoku's death.

Eitarō also knew that the only thing he should be feeling now was sympathy for Zentoku and his family. The moment of Grandpa's death replayed slowly in his mind, along with the painful memory of Zentoku's chagrin over a school principal who would steal when, according to Grandpa, even in a war he should have made the short trip to ask his relatives' permission. Grandpa was so old-fashioned to worry about such things at a time like this, thought Eitarō, feeling mildly dizzy from hunger. Maybe Zenga had no fields near his tomb and had decided that if forced to steal, it would be better to take from a relative. If only Eitarō had explained this to Zentoku in time, Grandpa might not have died so suddenly. Such thoughts were Eitarō's way of offering his sympathy to the two grieving women and expressing his devotion to this family. Taking responsibility for the family now, he told himself, would ease the women's minds. And, as their sobbing abated, he started to explain what had happened.

"I'd never expected it," he said, beginning his account from the time when he and Zentoku had set out from the tomb. But he quickly ran into the dilemma of many witnesses to tragic events. Though he tried hard to offer an objective, even scientific, explanation, the experience had been so personal—so solitary—that he found himself constantly digressing into a haze of subjective impressions. He clearly remembered falling down and feeling exhausted, but everything else he'd been through seemed shrouded in rain and darkness. When he came to Zentoku's final moments, Ushi wanted to know more and interrupted him with questions, her tear-stained eyes opening wide.

"Where were you when it happened?"

Eitarō answered without difficulty at first, guessing from memory how many feet he'd been from Zentoku. But when she asked this same question for about the fourth time, he stared at her intently, as though suddenly fearful. It was obvious that she was pressing her frantic

ŌSHIRO TATSUHIRO · 149

inquiry to make sure Zentoku's death had been truly unavoidable. And behind her questions loomed a heavy sense of responsibility that was now, unmistakably, shifting to Eitarō. Though he did not fully grasp her intent, he tried to evade this disturbing inquiry and rationalize his actions by plunging into a minute description of events. When he reached the point where they had spotted Zenga, his explanation became even more detailed, until he finally ended his account.

"So there was no way the principal could have known Grandpa died. And then I carried him back here, getting all sweaty, as you can see."

Eitarō tried to end the story in a way that avoided the issue of his responsibility, though he might have been overreacting to Ushi's questions.

"Well then, nothing could have been done. It was heaven's destiny," Ushi finally said while she finished wiping her tears. And, as though adding a last refrain, Také sobbed once more in a high, wailing voice. When she had quieted, Ushi spoke again, softly but forcefully.

"Now let's bury him."

Eitarō and Také both nodded. Yet hadn't they only last night finished burying a soldier whose name and hometown they never knew? Eitarō's heart sank as he remembered that ordeal. But at the same time he knew Grandpa would have to be buried, especially after all he'd gone through to carry Zentoku back to the tomb so he could lie with his ancestors. Lacking a coffin, they could bury him now in the garden out front, then re-inter him later with a proper ceremony when the war was over.

"All right, I'll get the hoe," said Eitarō in a tone of resignation as he got to his feet. The hoe and baskets were still out in the field.

"Let me go," offered Také.

"No, never mind. I know where I put it. And I can bring back some potatoes, too." Still covered with sweat, Eitarō shook himself as though warding off the cold. Then Ushi spoke.

"You'll have to go around to the relatives, too."

"Huh?" Také and Eitarō gasped simultaneously.

"First to Zenga's place. Then to Zenchō's. He's probably staying at his family's tomb on the hill right behind us. Then to Zenshin's. Oh, and Zensei's wife is probably at her family's tomb. Just go see the people nearby. Can you think of anyone else, Také?"

"Grandma, this is hardly a time to be visiting relatives," Eitarō said, his voice wavering with shock and dismay, but Ushi was unmoved.

"With Zentoku dying like this, his ancestors would surely condemn me if I didn't give him a proper burial." She looked around intently at the rows of mortuary urns, then continued. "It's even more important because Zenga still doesn't know Grandpa died. We can't leave things the way they are or Grandpa will go to the next world bearing a grudge. And if he tells the ancestors there, it'll be awful for Zenga. No. As Zentoku's second wife, there would be no place in this family for me if I failed now in my duty to our relatives."

Her words came amid the relentless cacophony of exploding shells, droning airplanes, and pouring rain. Také and Eitarō looked at each other, their mouths tightly drawn. Both were remembering what Ushi had said to Eitarō with such fervency their first night in the tomb: "If you die here, you'll never be able to face your ancestors." Surely she had not forgotten her words then. So why was she sending him off now to risk his life on these errands?

"Oh, and Eitarō. There's one more thing." Ushi peered gently at Také and Eitarō, whose eyes were fixed on her. "Grandpa forgave both of you before he died. So burying him properly is your last filial duty."

Také burst out wailing in a voice so loud she seemed to explode. "Dad! Oh, Dad!"

Clinging to Zentoku's body, she barely wrenched out the words through her uncontrolled weeping. As for Eitarō, his face gradually settled into the expression of a wayward youth who had just vowed to reform. Their suspicion of a moment before over Ushi's apparent inconsistency had quickly evaporated, and they were now resolved to carry out the mission she had assigned them. Though unaware of it herself, Ushi's real purpose in asking them to perform "their filial duty" was to apologize to her own ancestors. The possibility that, in carrying it out faithfully, they might be killed by cannon fire never entered her mind. Meanwhile, the mortuary urns peered down at the three of them, as always, in silence.

Five more minutes passed and then Ushi, feeling now that she had made full atonement to her ancestors, clasped her hands together in prayer. By now Eitarō and Také had decided which relatives each should visit. Eitarō had assigned himself the more distant Zenga and was running along the top of the embankment. He turned back to look at Také, but she was hidden from sight in the shade of some trees. At that same moment a nearby tomb was blown to smithereens, and the wind from the blast sent him tumbling down the embankment. After getting to his feet, he realized that at long last the rain had stopped. Surely, he thought, this was help from heaven to carry out his filial duty. And he looked up to see that the clouds hanging over the nearby ridge of hills were rapidly floating away. But now, smoke spewed up from those hillsides each time they were pounded by shells. Momentarily forgetting the danger of being exposed in the middle of a field, Eitarō stood upright to gaze out at the ocean. A battleship was burning in flames that shot upward as airplanes swarmed around it in the sky overhead. Seconds later one plane swooped down at the battleship in a sudden nosedive, and, from the place where it disappeared, more flames spewed upward. Eitarō gasped. Then, with a courage surging inside him more powerful than any he'd ever felt before, he took off trampling through the field at top speed. After about fifty yards he came to the sugarcane field where Zenga had hidden that morning. He could see that taking a shortcut through it would be much faster than running along the top of the embankment. But the going was rough inside, where the ground was furrowed with ridges and the cane leaves bore tiny teeth that slashed his hands and face, smearing blood all over them. Still, he was relieved to know he was concealed from view. Coming to the edge of the field, he paused for breath. Then, looking up ahead, he was thrown into sudden despair. Before him lay a river about thirty feet wide that he had to cross to reach Zenga's tomb, but the bridge had collapsed into the water.

Remembering that this was the only bridge, he took a deep breath, then started climbing down the embankment, letting himself slide the last few feet to the bottom. Near its banks the river came up only to his waist, but it got deeper as he moved out toward the middle and would soon be over his head. Still, even with one arm, Eitarō was a confident swimmer, certain that the swift current couldn't stop him, though it might deflect him a little. Bracing himself, he felt his way along with his feet, reassured that he was safer in the river than he would be out in the open on land. But having misjudged the riverbed's depth, he suddenly felt his whole body sink underwater and his feet catch in the mud. He gulped down several mouthfuls of water before floating back up to the surface.

"Damn it!" he yelled, and after swimming a few more seconds, he finally reached the opposite shore. He had stopped to rest on the bank and catch his breath when all at once, from behind him, he heard an absurdly loud roar and saw countless clumps of earth hurtling through the air. He turned back to see that the spot of ground inside the cane grove he'd just left was entirely blown away. Now he could look all the way through to the fields beyond and noticed that the "Navy Commander" no longer stood in the place where he should have been. Perhaps he, too, had been blown away. The many clumps of earth that had just fallen into the river made the water even muddier in the quickening current.

But now Eitarō saw worse trouble ahead. Even if he somehow managed to climb the embankment looming before him—about 300 yards wide—and make it safely to Zenga's tomb, how could he ever bring the old principal back across the river?

He'd worried only about getting through shells, mud, and filthy water. And now, standing knee-deep in the river, he cursed his lack of foresight.

Nearby the thundering roared again, followed by more wind from the blast. Eitarō tightly clutched the weeds growing on the embankment and set his feet firmly in the riverbed. "All right! If I have to die, I don't give a shit where they bury me. But before that, I've got to get to Zenga."

Slipping and sliding through the mud, his legs smeared with blood, Eitarō finally climbed to the top of the embankment. Now he threw himself down to lie flat on the ground and turned to look back the way he'd come. Along a distant ridge of hills he saw something moving in the direction of the tomb where Ushi quietly clasped her hands in prayer. At first he couldn't tell what it was, but soon he heard heavy thuds in the surrounding area that sounded much more like trench mortars than battleship cannons. And when the smoke cleared, again there was movement. Soldiers! Eitarō could see now that a huge force was moving in and realized he might not be able to make it back to Ushi.

With his last ounce of strength, he dragged himself to his feet, his body feeling like it would disintegrate. All he could think was that unless Zentoku and his ancestors acknowledged the loyalty he had rendered them even at the risk of his life, the family would be punished.

Knowing nothing of Eitarō's ordeal, Ushi waited impatiently inside the tomb for her loyal relatives. Together with her grandchildren, she gazed at Zentoku's remains while outside, slowly but surely, the firing line approached.

TRANSLATED BY STEVE RABSON

SHIMA TSUYOSHI (1939–)

Shima Tsuyoshi is the pen name of Ōshiro Masayasu (no relation to Ōshiro Tatsuhiro). Born in Tamagusuku, Shima graduated from Waseda University in Tokyo. While working for the prefectural Office of Education, he has written dramatic works, film scenarios, and historical studies in addition to fiction. His historical survey, Okinawa in the History of the Shōwa Era *(Shōwa-shi no naka no Okinawa), was published by Iwanami in a best-selling series on contemporary social issues. He has also written several historical studies of the Battle of Okinawa and was an editor of the multivolume* History of Okinawa Prefecture *(Okinawa-ken shi), published by the prefectural government.*

His stage dramas and films often depict Okinawan civilians who fled U.S. enemy forces during the Battle of Okinawa and sought shelter in caves, where they were threatened, beaten, and sometimes killed by "friendly forces" of the Japanese Imperial Army

"Bones" (Hone) appeared in the Ryūkyū shinpō *in 1973 and was the first work to receive the newspaper's annual Short Story Prize. Readers should note that it was published only one year after Okinawa's reversion to Japan. Reversion opened the floodgates for massive economic investment from mainland Japan, and the resulting construction boom generated tremendous excitement and optimism among Okinawans—at least for a while. As this story suggests, however, eager Japanese developers and local construction crews sometimes unearthed more than just soil.*

Bones

Shima Tsuyoshi

The work crew had arrived at the construction site and was taking a break when a yellow safety helmet swung into view at the foot of the hill. The man in the helmet was moving at a fast clip as he made his way up the dirt road that cut through the pampas grass. Right behind him was an old woman. She relied on a walking stick, but she dogged him like a shadow.

The construction site was situated atop a stretch of foothills from which one could see the entire city of Naha in a single sweep. Long, long ago the area had been covered in trees, and many a tale had been told about the ghosts who resided in the dark, densely wooded hills. But that was until the war. The heavy naval bombardment from offshore had leveled the *akagi* forests down to the last tree. And then came the postwar expansion of the city that had altered the way the land looked down below once and for all. It was as though the whole area had been painted over in colors that gave it a bright, gaudy look. The denuded slope was like a halfpeeled papaya. The top had been lopped off, and from there to the road a quarter of the way down the hill, the red clay was exposed to the elements. According to the notice posted at the construction site, the hilltop was slated to become the site of a twenty-story luxury hotel.

The five men in the work crew were from Naha City Hall. Sitting under the shade of a giant banyan tree, they gazed at the city as it stretched before them. The plain was flat and dry and looked as though it had been lightly dusted in a silvery powder. The August sun had risen to a point in the sky where it was now almost directly overhead. As the light danced over the whitecaps that broke against the coral reef lying offshore, it seemed almost playful. It was as though the sun had come to make fun of the men and the bored, fed-up expressions they wore on their faces. Meanwhile, some forty to fifty feet from the tree sat a big bulldozer. It was resting quietly for the moment, but the prongs on the shovel were pointed this way. It was just about there, too—the spot where the bulldozer was parked—that the bones had turned up the day before.

The man in the yellow safety helmet nodded in the direction of the assistant section chief as he approached the work crew from city hall. He was the man in charge of the construction site, and the company name, "TOA ELECTRIC," was embroidered on his breast pocket in fancy gold letters. They glittered in the sunlight.

"Well, where are the bones?" asked the assistant section chief, a round-shouldered man. He had grabbed a shovel and looked as though he was ready to get to work right away.

"I hate to say it, but there's been a new hitch." As the construction boss turned and looked behind him, the metal rims of his glasses seemed to flash as they caught the light of the sun.

There was the old woman—her neck thrust forward, her withered chin jutting out prominently into the air. She was out of breath from keeping up with the man in the yellow safety hat as they had climbed the long incline.

"So where is it, this spot you're talking about?"

There was a razor-sharp edge to the man's voice as he turned to address the old woman. With that, she lifted her walking stick and pointed it at the men from city hall.

"That's it there. I'm sure of it. Because the tree marks the spot. Any place from the tree to where you've got your bulldozer parked over there is where you'll find 'em. Yes sir, underneath it's nothing but bones. I know 'cause I saw it all with my own two eyes. There's no mistake. I'm absolutely certain of it."

The construction boss could hardly believe what he was being told and turned to the assistant section chief with a look of total incredulity.

"I never thought I'd have a mess like this on my hands. It wasn't until this morning that these people let me know there was a *graveyard* up here."

The construction boss introduced the old woman to the assistant section chief. She was the former owner of the property, and her family name was Higa. Higa Kame. Her given name sounded the same as the word for turtle, and the boss could not help feeling there was something tortoise-like about the old woman's appearance.

The turtle woman cut him short. "No, Mister, this is no graveyard. We just dug a hole and threw the bodies in. That's all there was to it. We were in the middle of a war here on the island, and nothing more could be done."

"But that's exactly what I needed to hear from you. Why in hell didn't you say something about graves before now? Letting heavy-duty equipment sit idle even for one day costs a fortune. We're taking a big loss."

The anger in the man's voice was countered by an equally furious look from the old turtle woman. Her aging, yellowed eyes had peaked into small triangles, and her lips were tightly pursed. The assistant section chief tossed his shovel aside. He knew trouble and could see it coming now.

"What kind of numbers are we talking about here?" he asked uneasily.

"Thousands. The mayor had us gather up all the bodies from around here and put them in a pile. There were so many you couldn't begin to count 'em. . . ." The old woman waved her stick in the air as if to make her point. Doubtless she was having trouble expressing herself in standard Japanese and felt the need to emphasize what she had to say.

"That many, huh?" A look of despair crossed the assistant section chief's face.

"There were so many bodies they wouldn't fit in the hole. Later on we used gasoline to burn them and then buried the ashes. The mayor said he'd look after the upkeep of the site, but then we never heard another word from him. Pour souls. There was no one to care for them when they died, and now their bones have been completely abandoned."

"That's not how I heard it. No siree, that's not the story I was told." The frustration and anger in the construction boss' voice was almost palpable as he spat out the words in his own local Osaka dialect from mainland Japan.

No, that was not the story.

It was a line from the script recited to him by the people down at city hall. But the line was supposed to be delivered by them to him, not by him to someone else.

It was yesterday when he had phoned them from the construction site to say unmarked graves had been uncovered on the hill and that the company was asking city hall to step in and deal with the problem.

"Unmarked graves are the responsibility of the Health and Physical Education Section," he was told. "They're the ones to handle it."

But then again, if he was talking about the bones of war dead, "Well, *no, that was a another story* altogether."

"Where's a phone around here?" The assistant section chief seemed to have decided on some plan of action and needed to report it to the office.

The boss took the lead as the two men headed up the red clay slope of the hill. The others remained seated on the ground, watching the boss and the assistant section chief disappear into the distance.

The first to speak was the oldest member in the group. He was wearing a pair of rubber work boots. "Ma'am, when you say 'bones,' are you talking about the bones of mainland Japanese?"

The turtle woman inched her way under the big banyan tree. Her lips were in constant motion. It was as if she were chewing on something or muttering to herself. "Hell, what does it matter whose bones they are? They all died in the big battle. Japanese. Americans. Men. Women. Even little babies got killed while they were still sucking at their mothers' breasts. We dumped them all together into this one big pit."

"You mean there really are thousands of bodies buried under here?" This time it was the fellow with only one eye who spoke. He could hardly believe what the old woman had said.

"They talked about putting up a memorial stone. That's what the mayor told us, and that's why my father planted this tree to mark the spot."

Without thinking, the men let their eyes scan the tree that branched overhead. Now that she had mentioned it, there *was* something strange about a banyan tree growing here. But there it was, standing in the middle of a field of pampas grass. It had been free to grow as it pleased, and, tropical plant that it was, it had shot up to a height of ten yards. From its boughs hung a long red beard of tendrils that reached all the way to the ground.

"That means it's twenty-eight years old." The one-eyed jack blew a puff of smoke from his lips. He sounded impressed at the thought of how much the tree had grown.

"And, ma'am, that means when you got the boss here to buy the land you pretended not to know about the bones, right?" This time it was the youngster in the group who spoke up. What with a crop of whiskers on his chin, he looked like a hippie, and there was a smart-alecky grin on his face.

"No, idiot. The reason the company got the property was . . ." The old woman sprayed the area with the spittle that flew from the gap between her missing two front teeth. "It was all because of that dumb son of ours. He let the real estate agent pull the wool over his eyes. We tried to educate him. We tried to get him to understand what sort of property it was and that it ought not to be sold, but he never got the point."

It was not long before the assistant section chief and the construction boss were back. They both looked agitated.

"We've got no choice. We're the ones who will have to step in and deal with the problem, and that's that. The government is ducking it at both the national and prefectural levels, saying there's no budget. Or no manpower. That means we're elected for the job. So let's get to work." The assistant section chief turned to his men and addressed them in a voice that was more mature than expected for a person his age.

But no one moved. The men continued to sit, smoking their cigarettes and wearing the same dull expression that had been on their faces all morning. The construction company boss studied them with a forlorn, even helpless, look. "Just how many days is this going to take, anyway," he asked.

"Hmm, I wonder. After all, these are the only men we could muster from the city's Disinfection Unit. With such a small crew, there's no telling how long it might take," replied the assistant section chief.

The construction boss walked in a circle, trampling the thick clumps of summer grass underfoot. It appeared he had some sort of plan in mind. Suddenly he stopped in his tracks and looked up, turning the full force of his charming baby face on the crew. "First, I must ask you men not to let anyone from the newspapers get wind of what's happening here. Once the press gets to shouting about it, we'll have a real mess on our hands."

The assistant section chief had a questioning look in his eye as he closely studied the construction boss' face. He seemed to be stumped and not fully prepared to digest what the boss might say next.

"We don't want any news to get out that will damage the future image of the hotel."

The assistant section chief nodded in agreement. Clearly, something in the boss' argument had impressed and persuaded him.

But by then Hippie-Beard was already on his feet. "Here we go again. And whose ass are we wiping this time? I can't believe we are going to do this." His heavy, gong-like voice resonated in the air. Yet if he was being sarcastic, his remarks seemed aimed at no one in particular.

"It's a helluva lot better than having to dig up undetonated bombs," piped up One-Eyed Jack.

All the men from city hall knew what he was talking about. They also knew he had a history of dropping explosives overboard in the ocean to catch fish illegally, and this was how he had lost an eye.

"Anyway, we start work right after lunch," announced the assistant section chief.

But Kamakichi was in no hurry, and he was the last member of the crew to get to his feet. The shadow that the big banyan tree cast on the ground had shrunk to nothing by now. In the distance, the cicadas were droning away. The mere thought of what was about to unfold was enough to make Kamakichi depressed. And, try as he might, he could not help feeling this way.

I⊤ was a little past noon the following day when the first bones began to surface. The men had been digging all morning, and until then the only noticeable change had been in the color of the soil as it turned from red to gray. As they dug deeper, they began to find some white things that looked like pieces of broken clamshells scattered in the powdered soil. Perhaps they only imagined it, but the earth seemed to give off the odor of rotting flesh.

"It's like the old woman said. The upper layer is all ashes."

The assistant section chief directed his crew to spread a canvas tarp along the edge of the pit. Kamakichi and the man in the rubber work boots were put to work doing the sorting. When each spadeful of dirt and ash was shoveled out of the hole, their job was to pick out the pieces of bone and put them in a burlap bag. Because the small, cremated pieces of bone had been reduced almost to a powder, it was impossible to identify any of them as belonging to a particular part of the human anatomy. Kamakichi closed his eyes. It was with a sinking feeling of dread and disgust that he forced his hands to sift through the piles of ashes.

The work went at a livelier pace once whole pieces of bone began to emerge from the pit. The gloomier the job became, the more it seemed, paradoxically, to raise the men's spirits. From out of the ashes came two round objects about the size of Ping-Pong balls.

"What're these?" When Kamakichi showed them to the man in the boots, Rubber Boots laughed and thrust them in the direction of Kamakichi's crotch.

"Fossilized balls."

All at once the men roared with laughter.

"No, no. It's not right to laugh at the dead. They're all bodhisattvas now, you know." The assistant section chief looked very serious, befitting his position of responsibility, and there was a mildly admonishing tone in his voice. "That's the hinge ball where the femur attaches to the hipbone."

"I bet you were born after the war," said Rubber Boots to Kamakichi.

Kamakichi felt as if the older man was trying to make fun of him. As for the war, he had no memory of it. "I was two when the war ended."

"Why, it's practically the same thing. If you ask me it seems like, ever since the war, we've all kept on living here in these islands by picking our way through a huge pile of bones. That's what's kept us going."

"Back then, nobody batted an eye at the thought of sleeping with a corpse," chimed in One-Eyed Jack.

Rubber Boots went on with what he was saying. He spoke with the authority of an older person who was the senior member of the work crew. "I was in the local defense forces when I was taken prisoner. One day I discovered a patch of big, white daikon growing in a field not far from the POW camp. But when I went to dig them out of the ground, I found they were growing on top of a huge mound of bones."

"Did you eat 'em?" asked Hippie-Beard.

"Of course I did. What do you think?"

Once again the men roared with laughter.

"It's the dead protecting the living," said One-Eyed Jack. The tone of his voice was almost reverential.

"This here banyan tree is a lot like us. It's had good fertilizer." Rubber Boots stretched himself upward from the waist and craned his neck to peer up at the tree.

"It's the same for everybody here in Okinawa," added One-Eyed Jack, sounding almost as if he were making excuses for himself.

"That may be true, but what about the others? You know, the ones who've used their fellow Okinawans as bonemeal to feed off them and make themselves rich and fat." It was Hippie-Beard speaking up again. He had been born after the war but was determined not to let this conversation pass without putting in his two cents.

"So just who is it you're talking about?" One-Eyed Jack had turned serious.

But now Hippie-Beard got flustered, at a loss to explain.

As Kamakichi sorted out the pieces of bone, he could feel the gorge rise in his throat, and he had to swallow hard from time to time just to be able to keep working. He felt oddly out of place amid the lively banter of the other men in the work crew. What they were saying struck him as terribly disrespectful, even blasphemous, toward the dead. At the same time, he kept trying to tell himself that the bones were just objects, no different from what one might find in an archaeological dig of an old shell mound.

In the afternoon, as the men began to let their pace slacken, all at once the old woman silently reappeared, as if out of nowhere. They welcomed her back, trying to joke with her about the job they were doing. But she would have no part of it. She hunkered down next to Kamakichi and began to study the pile of bones. As always, her mouth was in constant but wordless motion.

"Hey, ma'am. Afterwards we want you to do a good job of saying prayers for the dead buried here to rest in peace. Otherwise, there'll be hell to pay if so many lost souls get out and start wandering all over the place." The assistant section chief seemed to be in an uncharacteristically jocular mood.

But the old woman said nothing, and presently she began to help Kamakichi sift through a pile of ash. She worked with the deftness of a farm girl trained to sort beans of different sizes. As her fingers sifted, her mouth in ceaseless motion began to form words that she muttered to herself. "You poor, poor things. Whose bones are you, here in this miserable place? Look what's become of you. Who were your parents? And who were your children? It's all so sad."

Her mutterings were like a pesky gadfly that flitted about Kamakichi's ears. As he watched the deft movements of the old woman's withered hands, suddenly he was reminded of his mother. And then he remembered the three stones she had told him about. She said she had collected them at the bottom of the precipice at Mabuni. That was the place where Japanese soldiers had jumped to their deaths rather than surrender to the enemy at the end of the Battle of Okinawa. But he knew that the story about the stones was no more true than the inscription "June 23rd," the last day of the battle, that was written on the back of his father's mortuary tablet as the date of his death in the war. He recalled the photograph placed on the family altar of his father dressed in the uniform for civilians in the Okinawa Defense Corps. His father had been taken from his job at the town office and conscripted into this citizens' army, which was supposed to be the island's last line of defense. It had all happened so very long ago that, to Kamakichi, it seemed like some ancient, mythical tale that had no connection with him now.

Just as the men were about to finish for the day, the construction boss showed up. The straps of his safety helmet were, as always, tied firmly in place, and there was a folding ruler in his breast pocket.

"Looks like it's going to take a lot longer than expected." There was an arch look on his face as he peered down at the men in the pit.

"Look at it, will you? There are thousands of bones down here." Such was the cheerless reply the assistant section chief shouted back from the bottom of the hole.

Hippie-Beard shoveled a spadeful of bone and ash over the edge of the pit. "Wiping the ass of people who make a mess starting a war is no picnic, you know."

"This area here will be the front of the hotel's stroll garden," announced the construction boss as he walked around the pit one more time. "The landscape design is going to be quite elaborate."

"The view will be wonderful," said the assistant section chief, picking up on what the boss said and complimenting him.

"That's why, starting tomorrow, if it's okay with you, we'll get to work with the heavy equipment in the area next to your crew. As things stand now, we're way behind schedule, and it's time to start construction on the hotel."

"That's fine with us," replied the assistant section chief without a moment's hesitation.

That night Kamakichi sat drinking *awamori* at an *o-den* restaurant in Sakae-machi. It was his first night out in quite a while. But he had no appetite. It was almost as though his stomach were no longer his own. The mutterings of the old turtle woman continued to resound in his ears no matter how hard he tried to tune them out. Little by little, and long before he realized it, he had drunk himself into an alcoholic haze. He thought of his father, and the memories came back fast and furious, without letting up.

The bulldozer went to work in the area adjacent to the pit on the crew's third day at the site. The loud, ferocious roar and the perpetual cloud of dust it generated assaulted the men mercilessly. Their mouths filled with grit, and they began to feel sick. It was as though something had swept them up in the air and was shaking their internal organs violently. To make matters worse, what had been the sole source of pleasure in their lugubrious task was now denied them because the bulldozer obliterated all possibility of conversation. Indeed, it stamped out anything they tried to say in much the same way it trampled the weeds growing on the hillside. The men now fell into a dark, sullen mood, and as the temperature climbed and their fatigue increased, they became wildly careless wielding their shovels. As they spit and tried to clear their parched throats, they felt a rising anger directed in equal parts at the steel-monster bulldozer and the idiocy of the assistant section chief.

The old woman was back again to help, having arrived in the morning. On the one hand, the din generated by what she called "the bull" made it impossible to hear her and thereby saved Kamakichi from having to listen to her gadfly-like mutterings. On the other hand, the lack of conversation or any other diversion left him all the more vulnerable to his private fantasies about the bones, causing him to withdraw into ever-deeper introspection.

It was a little past noon when the men began to uncover bones in the shape of whole skeletons. If not apparent earlier, it was now all too clear that excavating the gravesite would be far more time consuming than originally anticipated. The bones were solid, each one a heavy weight. In addition, buried along with them were all sorts of paraphernalia. Metal helmets. Army boots. Canteens. Bayonets. The mouth of the pit looked like a battlefield strewn with the litter of war.

All the bones had turned a rusty red. Collarbones. Shoulder bones. Thighbones. Rib bones. Tailbones. Skulls. One after another, bones like those Kamakichi remembered seeing in high school science class were chucked over the edge of the pit. Each time he went to pick one up, he could not prevent his mind from clothing it in fantasies about the living human flesh to which it had once been attached; and when he went to toss it in the burlap bag, he could not avoid hearing the dry, hollow sound it made. At times it seemed to him as if the bones were quietly laughing, their laughter not unlike the sound of a stone rolling over and over, or of a cricket chirping.

A skull cracked in two right before his eyes. As he looked at the jagged edges, he felt he was about to be sick. He had been suffering from a hangover since morning and was sure his stomach was about to go on a rampage. In the midday heat, his head felt terribly heavy.

A tattered pair of army boots was slung over the edge of the pit. As Kamakichi went to set them aside, he saw a perfect set of foot bones inside. Each and every white piece of bone was intact, arranged in five neat little rows. As he began to pull them out, he heard one bone that had stuck to the boot's inside sole snap and break off with a crisp, popping sound. He felt his fingers go numb. And suddenly, his chest began to heave. The nausea swept over him like a great wave that rose from his stomach and then surged forward.

The old woman was collecting skulls from which she painstakingly wiped the dirt. No matter what skull she picked up, it always seemed to have the look of a living human face. Although everything else had turned a rusty red, the teeth eerily retained their original shining white. It was if they were alive and wanted Kamakichi to know how hungry they were. He remembered the words his mother had said so many times. "War is hell. And, in that hell, no one escapes becoming a hungry ghost." She, too, had known what it was to fall into that hell and live among the hungry ghosts. Once, at the bottom of a dark cave at Makabe, she had taken a fistful of dirt and stuffed it into her little boy's mouth. Kamakichi was just a baby. He would not stop crying, and this was the only way she could silence him. She had seen a Japanese army officer silhouetted in the light at the mouth of the cave. His sword was drawn, and she knew that meant he would kill the child if he did not stop crying. And so it had become her habit to say to her son, "That's what war is like."

Doubtless these bones had been on the verge of starvation when the people died, and even now they wore a hungry look. Kamakichi's hands ceased to move, and kneeling there in front of a skull, he mentally traced on it what he could remember of his father's face.

Just then a canteen came rolling over the edge of the pit. Casually, Kamakichi picked it up, then realized he could hear water still splashing inside. He felt as if his face had been dashed with cold water, and a terrible chill ran down his spine.

At the 3:00 P.M. break the assistant section chief asked if the men had come across any gold fillings. The engine on the heavy-duty equipment owned by Toa Electric had been switched off, but still the men made no effort to reply. "It's amazing. All these bones and not one gold-capped tooth in the lot. I wonder why." The answer to this question he had posed like some mysterious riddle was patently obvious, but something kept the men from speaking up. It required too much energy.

That was when Kamakichi happened to notice a flat piece of bone sitting right in front of him. It was shaped like a spatula, and a fragment of rusted metal protruded from its surface. When he picked it up and looked at it closely, he could see that a sharply pointed blade had pierced all the way through to the other side. "It must have hurt like hell," he said, muttering almost to himself. Even he was shaken by the implication of his own words.

What was that? Suddenly he was overcome by a hallucination that his father was lying right next to him. Yes, there he was, lying on his side. Kamakichi had never thought much about his father until now. It had always seemed natural for his father not to be around. Except once—and that was when he had gone for an interview at the bank and they had rejected him for the job. He had resented being a son with a father who had never been more than a fleeting figure—a ghost—in his life.

Before anyone knew it, the construction boss was back, standing around and talking with the assistant section chief. It appeared they were discussing the next step in the project. Since there was no sign that "the bull" was about to start up again, the men in the city hall work crew stretched out and decided to relax for a while.

"Cut it down?" They could hear the high-pitched voice of the assistant section chief.

"The landscape people will be here tomorrow to do their survey, and we can't wait any longer. We're way behind schedule."

"But what a waste. You can't just cut down a tree as big as this one. And didn't you say this spot was going to be part of the hotel garden?"

"But that's exactly why it's in the way. Besides, it's only a local tree that grew here naturally. We'll be bringing in coconut and fern palms as part of the garden's motif."

The assistant section chief made no attempt to question the construction boss further.

"Since it has to be cut down, we might as well do it now," the construction boss said. "Then, starting tomorrow, we'll put up a tent over there for shade at break times."

"Damn it. This is an outrage! It's out-and-out violence, that's what it is. Now you've gone too far." Suddenly Hippie-Beard had leapt to his feet.

Startled by the young man's voice, everyone started to get up. But his expected protest did not last. And, looking as cool as could be, the construction boss ignored him.

"Our company has no intention of doing anything to inconvenience you."

Just then, the old turtle woman pushed her way through the men and stepped to the front of the group.

"Well, Mr. Bossman. You say you're going to chop down the banyan tree? And just who do you think it belongs to? That tree there was planted by my father. What's more, it has come to be possessed by the spirits of thousands of dead people. That's where their spirits live. Don't you have any common sense?"

There was something of the shamaness about the old woman. Her raised eyebrows floating high on her forehead and her old, yellowed eyes coated with moisture gave her the look of a woman possessed.

"I can't say I know much about the customs in these parts," said the construction boss. "Besides, the title to the land has already been transferred, and . . ."

"I'll never permit it. Never. Because this tree here is my father's. Don't you have any appreciation for all the hardship and suffering people had to go through in the past?"

"We can't allow you to interfere with our job. No matter what you say."

The men continued to stand where they were, silent and expressionless. The construction boss' face was full of anger as his eyes surveyed, one by one, the row of apathetic faces before him.

At last the assistant section chief spoke. "Isn't it possible to move the tree somewhere else?"

"There'd be no problem, if it were all that easy. But look, I only work for somebody else, just like you."

The turtle woman stepped between the two men. "Look here, you. If you so much as lay a finger on that tree, there will be a curse on you wherever you go in Okinawa, and, before you know it, bad luck will come crashing down on that head of yours."

Kamakichi leaned back against the banyan tree as he studied the withered nape of the old woman's neck. Given his druthers, it was a scene he would have preferred never to have witnessed. How much better it would have been if he had averted his eyes and looked the other way. He felt his head grow feverish, and from time to time a knot tightened in his chest that made him feel as if he were going to be sick at any moment.

The surface of the banyan tree was rough to the touch, and it hurt when he rubbed his back against the trunk. Still, there was something about the tree that made him feel cool and refreshed. It made him think of his father again.

For no apparent reason he reached up and tore a single leaf from the branch overhead. Almost automatically his fingers went to work, and after trimming off the edges, he rolled the leaf up. Then, pinching one end of the rolled leaf between his fingers, he blew through it as hard as he could. The piercing screech it made took everyone by surprise. Even the construction boss' yellow safety helmet appeared to flash and—bang!—explode in the bright sunlight as he turned toward the sound of the whistle.

TRANSLATED BY WILLIAM J. TYLER

Nakahara Shin (1949–)

Nakahara Shin is the pen name of Yamazato Katsunori. Born in Motobu, he is currently professor of American literature at the University of the Ryukyus. After receiving a B.A. from the University of the Ryukyus, he attended graduate school at the University of Hawaiʻi and the University of California–Davis, where he earned a Ph.D. in English. A member of an Okinawa writers group that meets regularly to critique each other's work, Nakahara has recently completed a book-length study of American nature writing and has written extensively about poet Gary Snyder. He has also coedited a volume on postwar Okinawan culture and writes as a literary critic for local newspapers and magazines.

"The Silver Motorcycle" (Gin no ōtobai) appeared in the Ryūkyū shinpō in November 1977 and won the newspaper's Short Story Prize that year. It alludes on page 186 to the famous ryūka poem quoted on page 16 of the introduction. The translation below is, to our knowledge, the first time that a Japanese fiction writer has published an English translation of his own work.

THE SILVER MOTORCYCLE

NAKAHARA SHIN

. 1 .

SHE DIED NEARLY ten years ago, toward the end of a summer when it had hardly rained at all. Like sparrows at sunset, people had flocked together and gossiped about how she had been a little strange.

That summer everything dried up. She had been proud of the big rubber tree at her gate, its leaves covered with fine white dust. The leaves turned yellow, then gradually brown as they fluttered in the wind until at last they fell straight down with a dry, rustling sound onto the pavement in front of the garage. And they kept falling, one after another, whenever the south wind blew hard, carrying with it a vague feeling of nostalgia.

The sofa in her living room was also covered with dust. She kept the curtains drawn, but the dust that blew off the street behind her house got in through small openings in the windows.

I worked for her that summer, taking care of her yard every other week. She had enough money from what Harry left her and got a check from America once a month. She couldn't spend it all by herself and was never stingy when it came to my wages. A little patience and I could get that motorcycle. "Just wait," I told myself, "and that shining 125-cc bike will be yours." I'd found the secondhand bike at a motorcycle shop near my house. The owner, a friend of my father, said he would keep it for me until I saved up enough money. The woman I worked for knew why I had taken the job in her yard, so she always gave me more than we had agreed to. My father was going to put up most of the money for the bike.

I always avoided the woman when I went to work. I tried to stay out in the yard as much as possible because I didn't like the way she looked straight into my eyes when she talked to me. It was my mother who made me take that job. "You should feel sorry for your aunt," she told me.

. 2 .

IN THOSE DAYS I was mad at myself for being so shy. I'd get embarrassed because I couldn't quite figure out what she was saying to me and would answer her sullenly.

"Is it raining? It must be raining."

"No."

"It must be raining. You'll catch a cold if you get wet."

"No, it's not raining."

"Not raining? You must be kidding."

"Take a look for yourself."

She spoke from beside the window where she sat with her eyes shut tight. I had tried to sound mean, telling her to "take a look for yourself," but my voice turned hoarse when the words came out. Even so, they'd had an effect, and I could see her back twitching. She knew I was watching her and wasn't about to give up the argument. Though she seemed to be searching for the words to throw back at me, she was obviously beaten, unable even to look out toward the yard. After sitting up very straight for a while without saying anything, at last she pulled the curtains shut and withdrew inside the house. Victorious, I glared at her from the other side of the curtains. "There's no way it's going to rain," I told myself. "But if it does, let it pour down on this thirty-nine-year-old woman and wash away this obsession of hers."

As I pushed the lawn mower, I wondered why I felt this strange antipathy toward her. She had started talking about rain a couple of years after Harry died.

Harry never left Okinawa and ended up dying here. After coming back from Korea, he'd moved into one of the houses built for Americans on the hilltop in Ginowan. Years afterward, he came back early from Vietnam, got out of the army, and turned into a hopeless alcoholic. He would scare little children at the local clinic where he went to the doctor. When he saw a child crying, he would dance up to the kid, wagging his hips, and blow whiskey breath in the kid's face. Or sometimes he would gently bite a kid's ear and yell, "Who's giving Mama a hard time?" Of course, the doctor told him to stop drinking, but he was always dead drunk by the time he got to the clinic, making the kids bawl and their mothers worry. And when he got tired of that, he would amuse himself talking to a black man who was just as drunk, also waiting to see the doctor.

One day a nurse called the woman to complain, and after that she went with Harry to the doctor. He'd sit quietly whenever she was with him.

But now the black man got bored. A fat man with a thick neck, he would come over to wag his butt and twist his torso in front of them. The woman reached out with her left hand and tried to push him away. But he only laughed in a low voice and twisted his hips even more feverishly, dancing nimbly with his butt pointed toward them. She couldn't stand it anymore, she said, and tried to hit that big butt of his. But the black man was too quick, and her hand hit only air. Now Harry broke into loud laughter, pounding the sofa with his right hand. And the black man laughed, too, his whole body convulsing. Soon she was left alone in the waiting room, exposed to everyone's probing eyes.

Whenever she talked about this, her eyes got a little wild and she cursed the black man.

Harry died suddenly.

She insisted he had died because of the black man. "Harry always thought he might die at any time," my mother said to her, and then added in a whisper, "That's why he told you to go to the hospital."

"No, he just didn't want that baby," she replied, tugging gently at her hair.

"I'll never understand why he had to die in Okinawa, coming here all the way from that fine country of his," said my mother as she munched on peanuts coated with brown sugar.

In those days, I couldn't tell whether the woman was sad or not. It seemed as if she were trying hard to look calm, and she came often to see my mother, but I never saw her crying. The only difference was that whenever the wind picked up or there was a slight murmuring outside, she would always ask if it was raining and didn't seem to care if her question interrupted other people.

The leaves rustling on the row of palm trees in the yard did sound a lot like the showers that come suddenly on a summer evening. But she was the only one who always mistook the wind for rain. In the late afternoon, whenever the withered banana leaves swung listlessly, her ears would be deceived by the wind. And when she realized it wasn't raining, she would stare at us intently.

Drinking coffee, she would chat for hours. Sometimes she went to see a *yuta* fortune-teller and then brought my mother the latest news. Harry had ignored the important news from the *yuta*, so now she talked about it excitedly to my mother, who was always an eager listener.

My mother, who burned incense twice a month in front of the gas stove and prayed to the fire goddess, would encourage the woman to tell her everything the *yuta* had said. And my mother often nodded with satisfaction at the *yuta*'s interpretation of things that had been worrying her. "Well, that's a relief," she would say, firmly committing the *yuta*'s words to memory. "It was just as I'd imagined."

But for the woman it was all just talk, and she never followed the *yuta*'s instructions. Whenever my mother tried to set the day for a pilgrimage, the woman would complain that walking made her tired, adding that even if they drove, it was still a long walk to the family's tomb, a hollow carved out of a cliff surrounded by rocks. Besides, she said, the silk trees growing along the path would scratch our arms and shoulders, and she got goose bumps just thinking about those mosquitoes that were nearly the size of your fingertip. "When Harry was alive, he never let me open the screen even for a second." She could think up any number of excuses for not going. And my mother used to say that it was just a waste of money if you didn't really believe what the *yuta* said.

In those days I was rather serious about my studies and stayed home every day. When I got tired of studying, I'd have a cup of coffee and listen to them talk. I came to think of her as "that stubborn, rain-crazed woman" and tried to avoid eye contact with her. Sometimes she teased me and would say something out of the blue. "You have a nice masculine voice. The girls must like that." Then, when she stared at me, I got all flustered and clammed up. My mother winked at me, stifling a laugh, and said, "He's just shy, you know," which made me mad. Sometimes, all at once, the woman would start talking feverishly. She would speak about things from deep inside the burning core of her memory and seemed to forget about everything around her, including us, as if she were talking to herself.

"I sure hope it'll rain soon. Remember when we went to the hospital? Ever since then I've felt the rain coming. It's strange, though, because that was so long ago. I know the rain will be heavy, and before the downpour, it will get very dark. We'll see the lightning flashes all around, and the thunder will shake everything. The rain will start far away, but I can feel it coming closer and closer to where I'm standing. I can smell the earth now as big raindrops begin to hit my face. It hurts so much that I have to open my eyes, but I can't see a thing through the heavy rain. I'll catch the thick drops in my palms, cupping them together until rain pours from my hands. Harry told me to go to the hospital, so I had to, but ever since then I've been feeling that a heavy rain like this would start any time. Well, he never came to visit me there. I guess he thought it would be all right because you were with me. It was humid that day. Now, if it rains . . ."

Unless my mother yelled at her to stop, she would go on and on like this, talking to herself. Whenever she started, my mother always tried to divert her attention. "Let's talk about what we did after the war," she would say. "About when we came out from hiding in the hills."

Then they would sip coffee and talk about my grandfather, sometimes cursing him, sometimes pitying him.

"By now there must be lots of fruit on the Indian almond tree behind our old house. Remember how we used to eat it? I want to go pick some now, but I feel like that old drunkard is still there."

"That's no way to talk about him. Everyone becomes a god after they die."

"That's easy for you to say, since you moved away to Koza after you got married. That old drunk was always waking me up in the middle of the night. Mother died too soon, while Seiichi and Keiko were still crawling around."

My grandmother died of encephalitis five years after the war. She died singing "coloring the flowers, coloring the flowers" in a soft, clear voice. According to my mother, the memory of that voice and her song haunted my grandfather, and he became a hopeless drunk.

After my grandmother died, the woman worked for about a year under the big radar dish at the American base on top of Mount Yae, near the town of Motobu. She washed and dried soldiers' uniforms, always noticing that Harry's was the biggest. Harry was kind and generous to her. It wasn't that she was tired of paying for my grandfather's liquor or taking care of her little brother and sister. So she didn't think it was wrong to say yes when Harry asked her to marry him.

But when she told my grandfather, he grabbed the pole he used to carry baggage and tried to club Harry with it. Then she ran out of the house, following Harry, and never went home again.

My grandfather died of appendicitis. He had tried to ignore the pain, dulling it with liquor, and got peritonitis. He died in his futon, sucking a thick sugarcane leaf. There was already a bad smell coming from his guts, and it filled the house. He wasn't really the kind of man to die miserably like that, my mother had said. She came back after his death to put away the futon while the men there laughed and drank.

These are the things I heard them talking about as that summer came to an end.

That summer had constantly betrayed the woman as the days came and went uneventfully. The typhoons that suck in all the energy and then explode off the water skirted the island many times. But the heavy rains she was waiting for never came. The ocean, dyed a dark red in the light of the setting sun, rolled on and on with a sense of promise. And the clouds skirting southward thrilled her. At night they would sweep across the sky, sucked in by the approaching typhoon. And behind them the moon shone, flickering like the giant inflamed eye of the universe as it gazed down at humanity and its puny rebellions.

But the typhoons only pretended to attack and retreated without striking. One of them could easily have landed, raping the island, yet even if it had, the woman would have just stared calmly into its face. But then it would only pass by, front paws extended, back stooped over. Or it would run out of breath and drift away, panting toward the distant southern seas?

. 3 .

SHE ALWAYS ACTED bossy inside her house, except that the telephone would startle her. But if it was a wrong number, she would chew out the caller. A man with a gravelly voice dialed the wrong number many times that summer, maybe because it had been so hot.

She liked to make fun of Gravel Voice. He seemed sincere when offering a lengthy apology. But her voice, when she answered "That's perfectly all right," sounded so phony it made me angry.

Sometimes, though, Gravel Voice seemed to learn from his mistakes. He could apparently tell by the tone of her voice whether he should apologize politely or just hang up quietly. When he didn't apologize, I would always have to listen to her bad-mouthing him. He even seemed to know that he should hang up on the days she spent manicuring her nails over and over. On those days I would be sure to stay outside in the far corner of the yard.

I just couldn't figure her out. She would stop drinking her freshly brewed coffee to complain that the clock's chimes were too loud. She accused the clock of playing innocent while it cut everything short, ticking toward some final goal. The clock fooled everyone, she said, because it looked so ordinary. Then, grumbling about how we were all being deceived even as we sipped our coffee, she would empty her cup into the sink.

"Listen, it's a race, okay? You'll be tricked if you just keep sipping coffee. The moment you close your eyes and say 'ah, that's good,' you've already fallen way behind. Doesn't it just wear you out, trying to keep up with everything?"

"But I heard things were easier for you, living by yourself."

"Who said that?"

"My mother."

"That stupid woman."

She always talked in riddles. But all I could think of was the shiny 125-cc silver motorbike, so for me, the things she said and did were just a nuisance. I was supposed to report them all to my mother, but there was no way I was going to try deciphering all that mumbo jumbo she threw at me.

Stripping off my undershirt, mowing the grass, gulping down water from the hose, then splashing the water on my face, neck, and shoulders all helped to relieve the oppressive feeling I got from talking to her.

Summer grass grows faster than you realize. Every other week, when I went there, I was surprised at how tall it had gotten. But she never cared about the grass. It would grow very early in the morning or very late at night, while she was sleeping. Just after she fell fast asleep or before she woke up, those blades fed off of the sunlight they snatched during the day. Or, giggling among themselves, they imbibed what they could find groping inside the dry soil. The summer grasses, too, seemed to be outwitting her.

I pushed the lawn mower hard when I cut the grass. The wilder the grass grew, the harder I pushed. The motorcycle was shining brilliantly in the sun, in a future not too far off. Stretching out my arm, I could almost touch it. Every time I pushed the lawn mower, I advanced a notch along the flow of time. The stiffness of each stem of grass only made those notches more tangible. When I cut the grass, I held my breath and felt I was controlling the flow of time.

Cutting the grass was all I had to do, I thought. But now I know I was wrong. That summer, I was determined to cut down every blade of grass in her yard until I got that 125-cc motorbike, no matter how uncomfortable I felt talking to her and how quickly the thriving grass outwitted her.

Toward the end of August, when its growth slowed, she started wearing gaudy clothes in bright primary colors and let her hair grow long. I would walk straight to her yard, pull out the lawn mower, and try to avoid talking to her.

Since it was too hot during the day, the best time to work was between five and seven in the evening. Mowing the grass on a hill in her yard, I could see the sun sinking over Kerama Island, squatting out in the ocean. A little past seven, the red-hot sun would start melting. As it dipped toward the horizon, its core turned fluid and it could no longer hold its neat midday perimeter. The cloud castle towering in the western sky seemed to catch fire, and the white cement walls on the island smoldered silently. A lonely pine tree writhed as it burned, and a coral reef emerging from under the sea seemed annoyed that it had dried up. That's when I noticed that the upper half of my body, too, had gotten burned. Feeling for a moment like the whole universe was on fire, I watched the bloated sun sink into the horizon.

Seeing everything aflame as I stood leaning against the lawn mower, I repeated many times in a small voice, "Oh, gods, if we're all going to die, please let the red-hot sun burn us up."

It was around this time that her hair got really long. Toward evening, she always took a shower. Then she would sit with her shiny dark hair wrapped around her slender neck, gazing at herself in the mirror. Her bedroom faced the yard, and when she pulled open the drapes, it made me uncomfortable to see her large almond eyes peering up at the mirror. I pretended not to notice her, but she insisted on talking to me. As she put on her makeup, she told me about her plans for excursions, which of course never materialized. Or, she talked about some poor heroine in an old movie whose lover pushed her off a bridge. She cursed the man's cruelty but seemed to enjoy telling his story. Then she frowned and said how she hated April evenings when the southern breezes start blowing. "After the kids run off, you can hear the *sanshin* in the dark. 'Oh, Kana, my love, how well I remember your face. . . .' Oh, yes, even I know that song. Grandpa was always singing it, playing his *sanshin*."

She went on muttering while she made herself up. "Oh, you that I love, if only you could love me." Leaning her head to one side, she slowly brushed her hair. "Please come to my village." I stopped the lawn mower, telling myself I should say something nice. Suddenly she turned toward me, noticing that the lawn mower—Harry's lawn mower, rusty from years of use—had stopped. She pointed at me with her index finger curved slightly downward like a witch and said, 'I'll get mad if you keep calling me Auntie. From now on call me Masayo, like Michiko does. I'm Masayo Kinjō, okay? Well, Masayo Thompson is fine, too. Listen, I haven't dried up like Mrs. Jones and Mrs. Scott. You know what I mean, don't you? Probably not."

Her laughter sounded rough and mean. Finding no words to throw back at her, I stood in silence as she turned again to face the mirror and began reciting a Ryukyuan poem in a high-pitched voice. "O, you that I love, if you love me, too, please come to seek my hand at the village of Ishadō blooming with flowers in Nakagusuku."

. 4 .

BY THE END of August everything had dried up. I watered her yard furiously, but the whole island lay parched, waiting for rain. The American military seemed aloof to the problem at first, but finally the high commissioner (or some other high officer) made an announcement that a rainfall operation would be attempted over Yomitan. They were going to scatter chemicals over the clouds to make rain.

She came to our house early on the day of the rainfall operation. Her Plymouth stopped with a squeaking sound, and when she opened our front door, her eyes were sparkling. A telescope hung from her shoulders. It had belonged to Harry and was especially powerful and of high quality. She wanted to go to Yomitan with my mother to see what she called "this great operation." She wore a long, loose-fitting purple dress that looked like an evening gown. Whenever she dressed like that, my mother talked to her as if she were her dumbest daughter.

"It's not going to rain, you know. The newspaper says they're only making a trial run. Just look at the sky. They aren't magicians, after all. I'm not going."

"The military can do it. I'd even bet on it. I'm driving, so come with me. Just to watch the airplane. See, I brought my telescope."

"Hey, there are things even the military can't do. You just don't want to go by yourself. But I really can't make it. They're supplying water today, and I need it to do my laundry."

"Michiko, you only do what I ask when you need something. Well, from now on I'm not doing *anything* for you."

"C'mon, you know I'll be in trouble if I don't fill my buckets with water. Seizō, maybe you should go with your auntie. I mean, if you're not studying today."

Hearing this, the woman and I both frowned. But my mother started winking at me as she always does, and in the end I had to go. So I went out and got into the woman's Plymouth.

We whistled as she drove north on Highway One. Obviously in high spirits, she leveled her intense gaze at me and asked if I could whistle. It was embarrassing to listen as she soared easily up to the high notes. My whistling stayed low and somber, never reaching those joyful heights.

"I bet it'll rain."

"I wonder."

"I'm sure of it. I trust my sixth sense. Harry told me once that the air force always makes it rain in California. I know it'll rain today."

"Well, if you say so, but . . ."

"But what?"

"Never mind."

"You should act like a man and not be so wishy-washy. Maybe that's why you failed your entrance exams."

"Well, what are you going to do? I mean, if it doesn't rain today?"

"Now you're mad."

"No, I'm not."

"If it doesn't rain, I'll give you the telescope. I'm taking you away from your studies today, so you can have it."

I didn't answer.

"Now what's the matter?"

"But I thought you really liked that telescope."

"Hey! You're a strange kid, thinking it's already yours. Now what are you going to give me if it *does* rain?"

"I'll cut the grass for nothing and wash your car, too."

"Now you're trying to be stoic. Just buy your motorbike, and if it rains today, you can give me a ride when you get it."

She was speeding way over the limit on Highway One, and I was worried the MPs would stop us. Driving along, she whistled short, high-pitched melodies as if reminiscing about something. In the bright, transparent daylight I could see the downy hair on her rounded lips.

That morning was terribly humid. The oleanders planted along the fence inside the military base were blooming in bright red clusters. I only glanced at the flowers from our passing car, but they seemed to be floating before my eyes all the way to Yomitan. Every time I thought of how the oleanders burned even redder under the summer sun, it felt like sweat was breaking out all over my body.

The sky above Yomitan was covered with clouds. Through the openings between them I could see chunks of blue sky that, with their ragged cloud perimeters, looked like slices of bitter melon that someone had shoved inside. But those clouds seemed much too high for rain.

She decided to park her Plymouth on a small hill to get a good view of the airplane. Veering recklessly off the road, she drove around in search of a vantage point until she finally came to a stop on a slope covered with rocks. Coming out of the car, she saw a boulder nearby as tall as she was, and, pulling her dress up to her thighs, she hurried into a shaded spot underneath that was just big enough for one person.

The operation was scheduled to start at eleven, and she waited without saying a word. She never seemed to think about anyone else. Wherever I saw her, she always made me uncomfortable.

A little after eleven, from out of nowhere we heard the roar of an airplane. She looked up at the sky through her sunglasses, but neither of us could spot it. The plane sounded as if it were determined to keep flying above those clouds. And, listening to that faint but persistent drone, I began to think that it might actually start raining, that maybe the American military really *could* make it rain.

The sun was right above us. There was sweat on her forehead. I could smell gasoline from her car, and the air was filled with the pungent odor of grass. Small insects flew all around, annoying us. The smell of tires. Flies. Rocks baked hot in the sun. Naked . . . . Harry and his friends had been naked above their waists. Small bottles of beer. Strong American men pouring beer over each other in the late-afternoon sun. Clarinets, saxophones, and trumpets wailing frantically in my ears. Roaring laughter. A hairy chest. The small carton of ice cream Harry had given me that I hid under the sofa, where it melted and turned into bubbles. Harry's yard. That close-cropped lawn with the bittersweet smell. Harry's hard body conquering and taming the grass with the obstinate violence of iron. The late-afternoon sun beginning to bloat. Someone's back starting to sweat. The smell of beer. The rasping of a trumpet. A languid saxophone. "Harry, Harry! The ice cream is melting. It's all melted!" "Oh, no," she says. "I told you put it in the fridge. I'm not going to bring you here anymore if you don't do what I say." "But if I put it in the fridge, it won't be mine any more." "What a dumb kid," she says. Harry and his friends roar with laughter. After tossing me around playfully from one to the other, they give me a big box of ice cream. But, oh no, that's melting, too and will be all gone unless I do something. Ice cream melting in the heat and changing into white bubbles. Noisy flying bugs. The scratch I got from a twig begins to hurt. The smell of gasoline. Water. She drinks from her cupped palms. The smell of burning tires. Sunglasses. Telescope. Clouds. And, oh yes, the roar of an airplane. The roar . . .

We waited for two hours but never saw the plane. And there wasn't even the slightest hint of rain. Apparently the operation had ended in a fiasco.

"So this is what you call an 'air force,' a 'great operation,'" she said angrily.

But she kept looking up at the sky, and I hesitated to say let's go home because she seemed to be challenging something up there. She wasn't just looking at the clouds, but at something beyond the clouds, higher and deeper.

Strangely, at that moment I could feel her strength. Then, maybe because the telescope was too big for her, I felt like laughing. It hid her pale, white face completely. I decided to tell her I wouldn't take the telescope after all and that she could ride the motorbike whenever she wanted.

The warm southern wind swept over the hill, rustling the hem of her long, loose dress. It was a beautiful sight, I thought.

The next morning the newspapers reported that the cause of the fiasco had been "low cloud density." Maybe so, but it just shows that making rain is no simple matter.

A few days later my parents went on an overnight trip. I'd caught a slight cold and had to stay home in bed. My father said he couldn't postpone the trip because he'd already scheduled his annual paid holiday. He was grumpy that day because my mother had been pestering him to go, and he had finally given in.

My parents had asked the woman to come and stay with me.

As soon as she came into my room that evening, she held her nose. I had sweated a lot sleeping in my room, which was baked by the sun during the day. That night I had a fever. She had kept telling me to take a shower, and after I did, I ran that fever and my eyes got bloodshot. I knew she was upset, but I didn't say anything and just stayed in bed.

A little after ten o'clock, she told me she would be staying overnight because it looked like rain.

It was the first heavy rain in ages. After clouding up in the evening, it began pouring after ten o'clock. When the rain started, she sat on the edge of my bed and softly sang a very old song.

I could hear thunder in the distance, and streaks of lightning slashed through the darkness outside my window. Then I heard the unmistakable sound of rain hitting the ground. She had waited a long time for this rain, but she greeted it silently. Though I told her not to, she began combing my hair with her fingers. A languid feeling came over me, and I kept my eyes closed.

After that I dozed off, though I don't know for how long. When I woke up, I saw her standing next to my bed. She was drenched with rain, her large eyes shining and her lips pressed tightly together. Raindrops were dripping from her hair. I looked up at her but said nothing, and then suddenly she threw herself onto the bed. She didn't seem to care whether I got wet or not as she wrapped her arms around me and pulled me toward her. My throat was dry, and I couldn't say a word.

Holding me softly, she put her nose to my neck and called a man's name I'd never heard.

Though wet, she felt warm to me and smelled good. She reminded me of my mother, who used to lie down next to me whenever I had a cold. It was the same warmth and smell. And she felt soft, too.

Outside my window it continued to pour.

Her voice moaned as his name tumbled from her lips. In her trembling body, I felt a sadness I could neither describe nor explain. Then my body began to tremble. I couldn't help it and didn't know why, but now I was shaking and crying, too.

Apparently startled, she pushed me back down on the bed and hurried out of the room. But I couldn't stop shaking.

It rained until the next morning.

Late that afternoon, my parents returned home in high spirits. But the woman stayed closed up silently in the room next to mine.

I couldn't explain why I'd cried so much that night, but I had strange dreams later, whenever I thought of her.

She is walking toward me, about to cross the Hija Bridge from Yomitan to Naha. A man is with her. She is wearing an old-fashioned white cardigan. She starts pleading that she doesn't want to go across the bridge. Her eyes seem like a rabbit's, meek and innocent, as she peers up at the man. Despair is written on his face, but he drags her toward the bridge. "I'm doing this for your sake," he says. He is heavyset and bowlegged with a sallow face, and he is a smooth talker. Yet he seems pathetic, too, a man whose whole life has been a failure.

Near the bridge, I see big, beautiful Ryukyuan pine trees spreading their branches. The moonlit night is tinged with blue. Yes, it is one of those April nights when the southern breezes begin to blow, making everyone restless. She is weak, going along with the man just because he yells at her. She is singing a song. I can hear your song, Auntie, if you sing it a little louder, just a bit louder. But, look, she is crossing the bridge. She fades from sight.

Next she is standing on the south end of Hija Bridge. She has draped a red cardigan over her shoulders and hides her face with a scarf. She wears black high heels. She is walking around rubbing her hands, waiting for someone. She is chewing gum. Here he comes. He is tall with a cold, indifferent look. She is trying hard to say something to him. But he only pretends to listen. She motions that she can't go to the other side of the bridge. The tall man laughs. The night is clear with no north wind. But the white road stretching north and south from Hija Bridge looks cold. Now the man is leaving. She is left standing alone in the moonlight.

Next I see my grandfather. He is drunk and trying to club someone with his carrying pole. He makes me want to laugh, and then I really am laughing. Now he collapses on the ground, wailing in that pitiful voice. Grandpa, where's your sense of dignity? I'm sick of your crying and wailing.

Still, she stands alone, stretching her arms outward into the slashing winds of purple time that swirl around her.

. 5 .

ON THE LAST Saturday in August I finally got the silver motorcycle. It had a black seat and a silver body that was light and sleek. Though a secondhand machine, its sturdy engine looked as though it would never stop running. And the tires were sharply notched with a deep tread that seemed sure to grip the road without slipping. This bike would run fast and proud on Highway One.

As I rubbed the machine all over with an oilcloth, the guys at the bike shop made a lewd joke about what I was doing. The owner laughed. "You be careful now," he told me. Later, when I was riding close to home, I shifted down and ran the bike for 300 yards in low gear. The heavy throbbing of the engine felt good and made me proud.

That day my father came back from his job at city hall before noon and said something that made my heart sink.

"Well, thanks to Auntie Masayo, you can ride that bike now even if you haven't passed your entrance exams yet. We ought to go show it to her."

"Hey, he worked long and hard in that blazing sun," my mother said.

"Aw, c'mon, he's already a young man. The heat shouldn't bother him."

"Oh, yeah? It'd wear *you* out in half an hour."

"Hey, everybody at city hall tells me how tough I am."

"Well, then, why don't you cut down the branches in the yard once in a while on Sundays instead of lying around the house all day."

"A section chief's job is demanding. Exhausting."

"Oh, sure. Sitting at your desk, puffing on cigarettes. Isn't that really all you do?"

"Smart-ass women. Think they know everything."

"That's right. We know *all* about it."

"Hey, why do you have to talk to me like that?"

"Well, *excuse* me. I'm *so* sorry. . . ."

It was true that the woman they called Aunt Masayo always made me feel strange. Yet she threw herself into everything she did and seemed more sincere than either of my parents.

That afternoon my father drove our mini-car along the highway just ahead of me riding my motorcycle. My mother, who sat beside him, kept turning around to look back at me. She was talking to my father and smiling, but he wouldn't answer and just stared straight ahead. She seemed proud of me. My father stayed in the far right lane, driving ten miles below the speed limit. It annoyed me. I told myself that after showing the woman my bike, I would drive out to the reclaimed shore land and open it up as fast as it would go. It took us half an hour to get to her place.

After making us wait a long time, we were stunned when she finally opened the door. My father grimaced, and my mother's shrieking laugh sounded almost hysterical. I felt like hugging the woman and vomiting at the same time.

She must have thought she looked "cute." She wore a white cotton shirt and red short pants covered with little pale printed flowers. She had laced her white leather boots extremely tight. She wore no lipstick but had put on thick eyeliner, and her shiny dark hair hung down her back.

My parents looked disgusted but went inside without saying anything. Meanwhile, I couldn't take my eyes off her. Under her thin cotton shirt, I could see the shapes of her breasts. If I cupped my right palm, it would just cover one of those poor little breasts. While my father spouted polite clichés, thanking her for the motorcycle, she seemed restless, walking back and forth over the tile floor in her squeaking boots. She had longer legs than I'd thought, and seeing how thin they were made me angry. Her small waist made me sad, though, and I wanted to howl like some wild animal.

Without asking anyone's permission, my mother went about making fresh coffee and was soon sipping it with my father. When the two of them started talking about old times, the woman got bored and said she wanted to take a ride on the motorcycle. Though the long downpour had ended, the island was still covered with thick clouds, and it rained off and on. But she was no longer preoccupied with rain, her interest having already shifted to the silver bike that was now mine. Before my last day working in her yard, I had explained how to ride a motorcycle. I told her how to start the engine, release the clutch, and apply the breaks. She insisted that I accept her telescope or she wouldn't take driving lessons from me. But I was stubborn, too, when it came to the telescope. So we made a compromise and asked my mother to hold on to it for us.

That day she got off to a shaky start. At first I had to hold on to the seat from behind so she could keep her balance. She sat there, laughing happily, but looked funny because she was leaning too far backward. I kept telling her to bend forward. After driving only four or five yards she fell off because she had accelerated too abruptly. But she didn't seem to care that her left knee was skinned and just got up and grasped the handlebars again.

We decided to take a break, and I explained again how to control her speed by balancing the clutch and the accelerator. She was so cheerful she seemed like a different person. She listened to me attentively, stroking her hair and leaning her head to one side. She looked very funny, I thought, like a high school girl. But she was so serious that I couldn't possibly laugh.

After the break she tried again. I decided I would let her drive today as much as she wanted. She went a hundred yards this time but fell again on her way back to where I was standing. She'd hit her right elbow hard on the ground and there was a lot of blood. I ran to her and reached out my hand to help her up, but she slapped it away and averted her eyes. She gazed squinting into the distance as if to watch a rival who had passed her up and was now driving a motorcycle far away at full speed.

She wore the look of a young girl determined to win.

There was no way I could stop what happened after that. Suddenly she got up, straddled the silver motorcycle, and took off at full speed. The whining roar of the engine stabbed me in the stomach. In the next moment she shifted quickly from second to third, then bolted ahead.

She was racing after someone, speeding toward some unreachable goal.

Her hair fluttered wildly in the wind.

At the next curve she failed to make the turn, plunged off the road, and crashed into a stone wall. The collision hurled her down onto the asphalt in a flash of silver light.

TRANSLATED BY THE AUTHOR

SHIMOKAWA HIROSHI (1948–)

Born in Yokohama, Shimokawa earned a B.A. in French literature at Waseda University, where he also did graduate research in French drama. He has worked in the past as a preparatory school teacher and today is thought to be living in Tokyo, although he has dropped out of sight during the past decade. Shimokawa is the only writer included in this anthology who is not himself Okinawan, and he appears to have published little fiction since "Love Letter from L.A." (Rosu kara no ai no tegami). Yet this story received high praise from Okinawan critics for its compelling portrayal of a woman's experience of the U.S. military presence in Okinawa after reversion. Published in the Ryūkyū shinpō *in November 1978, "Love Letter from L.A." was awarded the newspaper's annual Short Story Prize.*

LOVE LETTER FROM L.A.

SHIMOKAWA HIROSHI

. 1 .

FOR THE FIRST time in many years, Tomiko saw Sueko again. That night she was out with her boss, Yoshida, and they happened to stumble into the one bar in all of Naha that Sueko was running. Tomiko was less than overjoyed about bumping into someone she knew because Yoshida, in addition to being her boss, was also the married man with whom she was having an affair.

Only a few days before, Yoshida had learned that he was being transferred back to the company's main office in Tokyo. Come to Tokyo with me, he had told Tomiko. I'll divorce my wife and we can be together, he promised. To Tomiko's chagrin, Yoshida insisted on talking about his imminent departure and his grand plans for her in public, right there in a bar, no less.

When at one point both Tomiko and Yoshida sat silently, staring at their drinks, Sueko seized the opportunity to join the conversation.

"Excuse me, are you Matayoshi Tomiko?" she asked hesitantly. Tomiko was at a loss.

"You remember me, don't you? I'm Kinjō Sueko, from junior high school. We were in ninth grade together. We both went on the school trip that year, don't you remember? I'm so glad to see you. It's been ages! Ten years, at least," she spouted perkily and smoothly, as if she had been rehearsing these lines for a cameo appearance in a soap opera. All of her reminiscing gave Tomiko the creeps. Although she responded pleasantly to Sueko's animated banter, by the end of the evening, Tomiko had vowed to herself that she would never come to this bar again. She hated being seen with Yoshida. In the city, you would never bump into an old schoolmate like this, but this wasn't Tokyo, as Tomiko had been made painfully aware by the stinging rumors that had spread once before when she had been seen out with a man.

To Tomiko's surprise, Sueko called the very next day and invited her over to the bar. Yoshida apparently had left his business card with her. Furious though she was at Yoshida's lack of discretion, Tomiko could think of no excuse and decided to make a night of it anyway.

She felt uncomfortable at first, unable to guess her hostess' intentions, but then Sueko welcomed her with such enthusiasm (and a meal of sushi and tempura) that Tomiko let down her guard. She felt ashamed that she always assumed the worst about people.

Though Tomiko enjoyed reminiscing about their school days, she found herself struggling to revive memories of Sueko. Tomiko had always been an excellent student, bound for high school and college, while Sueko belonged to the vo-tech group, destined for the working world. Tomiko wondered if she'd ever had so much as one conversation with Sueko during their junior high school days.

One thing she did remember about Sueko was her fondness for animals. Indeed, the only relevant photo in Tomiko's album of memories was a shot of a smiling Sueko sitting in one corner of the school yard playing with a rabbit. Even now, at nearly thirty, she still had the same sweet dimples in her cheeks, big eyes, and broad face common among Okinawan women. But Sueko also had many wrinkles, which made her appear much older than Tomiko.

"I always looked up to you," confessed Sueko. "You were so attractive."

"Sorry I'm not anymore."

"That's not what I meant! It's just that I wasn't one of the popular kids in junior high, so I knew that you would never pay any attention to me. But look at me now. It's like a dream come true."

"I'd hardly call it a dream."

"And remember, on the school trip, how I got my first you-know-what. I felt like crying because it felt so icky and smelled so bad. . . .

Maybe I did start crying, I don't know. But then you saved me. Remember how you gave me that sanitary napkin? You just came up and slipped one to me, real discreet."

Tomiko didn't remember any such thing. If it actually had happened, Tomiko doubtless hadn't acted out of kindness. If anything, she probably was exasperated by Sueko's lack of resourcefulness and preparation. Or perhaps she couldn't stand the stench of blood anymore.

"So, tell me, are you married?" Sueko inquired.

"Not yet."

"Have you been abroad?"

"No, I haven't. Why do you ask?"

"Because I have. I've been to the States. And I got married, too. I was in Los Angeles—you know where that is, right? Isn't that a scream, that I've done all that, and you haven't? And I'm supposed to be the loser."

Tomiko could only smile. Sueko spoke with extraordinary enthusiasm, without a trace of malice.

"I'm not making it up."

"What?"

"That I got married in the States."

"Really."

"You think I'm lying, don't you?"

"No, I don't," Tomiko retorted.

"I have a picture to prove it," said Sueko, reaching into her purse. The picture showed a young Westerner with a buzz cut. He wore a U.S. Marine uniform and was smiling, but his smile was twisted and rather mean looking.

"Try and guess what he does for a living."

"I have no idea."

"He's a really good—what do you call someone who paints houses for a living in English?"

"A painter."

"See how smart you are? I know, I know! When you say painter in English, it can mean someone who paints pictures, too, right?"

"Right."

"But another fancy way to say painter in English is aa—"

"Artist."

"That's it. Anyway, he'd get mad if you called him a painter. He'd say, 'I'm an artist, not just some lousy painter.' But I didn't see anything wrong with calling him a painter. You should have seen the pictures of Mickey Mouse he used to paint on the walls. They were fantastic!" A bit tipsy, Sueko rambled from one topic to the next.

When Tomiko stood up to leave, Sueko grabbed onto her arm and would not let go. "You've got ice water running in your veins, don't you, Tomiko?"

"But it's really late and I have to go to work in the morning," explained Tomiko.

"That's not what I meant at all."

"We can talk again some other time, okay?"

"Oh, sure we can. I bet you'll never set foot in here again. I know what you think of me. You think that he left me, right? You think I'm ridiculous. I can tell."

"Why would I think that?"

"You can't fool me. It would be strange if you didn't wonder what I was doing here in Okinawa. Right? Of course you want to know why I'm not in the States."

"I've wondered about that some."

"Not just some. A whole lot, right?"

"Whatever you say."

"So you do think he left me. You think, that's what happens when a girl like me gets hitched to a Yankee. Admit it."

Having been pushed this far, Tomiko had no choice but to go along with her. "Okay, so that's what I think. So what?"

"Thank you. That's all I wanted to hear," said Sueko, and, grasping Tomiko's arm even more tightly, she pressed her plump, voluptuous body against her. Her mouth brushed up against Tomiko's ear and the smell of whiskey was overwhelming. Tomiko felt revolted but didn't try to push her away.

Not one to hold back, Sueko whispered into her ear, "We're friends, so let's not hide things from each other. Tell me what you're thinking. If you don't, our friendship doesn't mean much, does it?"

"I thought it would be rude to ask too many questions."

"It doesn't bother me. Go ahead and ask me. Ask me if he abandoned me," said Sueko.

"Okay, okay. So, tell me, what happened to your husband?"

"You're driving me crazy, Tomiko. I just want you to ask me if he left me. Go ahead."

So Tomiko asked, enunciating each syllable deliberately, "So, did he leave you?"

With that, Sueko let go of her arm and took a step back. Then she glanced up at the ceiling, much like a weight lifter does before picking up a huge barbell, and let out two big sighs. Next she narrowed her eyes and gazed intently at Tomiko. Her moves were so studied that Tomiko could tell this wasn't her debut performance. She must have done it before for her other friends as well, thought Tomiko, and she bowed her head in an effort to keep from laughing. Not one to be thwarted, and determined to have her audience's full attention, Sueko bent over and peered up at Tomiko's face.

"It's natural that people think such things about me, but, actually, he didn't leave me. And I didn't leave him. We still love each other very much—but we just have to live apart."

"Why can't you live together?"

"I'm embarrassed to tell you."

"Don't be. You can trust me."

"It's the English."

"What?"

"I can't speak English," said Sueko.

"You were speaking it a little while ago."

"I don't know how to put the words together into sentences, and I can't read or write either. It kinda makes life hard in the States."

Tomiko didn't know how to respond.

"I had a nervous breakdown when I was over there. Whenever anyone came up and talked to me in English, I'd fall apart. My legs would start shaking and I'd get all sweaty, and then I'd pass out. Nothing like that'd ever happened to me before. I was a total wreck. I'd rather have gotten attacked by a stranger on the street than have someone talk to me in English. You know those 'Don't Disturb' signs they have at hotels? Well, I got one of those and hung it around my neck. I must have been out of my mind. Anyway, finally, my husband took me to a mental hospital. In the States, people aren't ashamed about going to mental hospitals like they are here in Okinawa. To American women, it's no big deal, just like going shopping. You know, they have psychiatrists' offices right upstairs from where you buy your groceries. The rich ladies, they go up there for their appointment with the doctor, and they have a nice chat and go home feeling better. But not me. Like I said, I couldn't talk with the doctor if I wanted to, not in English, anyhow. The whole thing made me worse, and the doctor warned my husband. He told him that he had to send me back to Japan. Don't ask me exactly what the doctor said, 'cause he said it in English. So that's why we're not living together. Does that make sense to you?"

"Of course."

"I really want to go back to the States, so I've been studying English, but it's a lot harder than I thought it would be."

"Yeah, English's hard all right."

Sueko switched on her tape recorder so that Tomiko could hear her English lessons. She spent half her life practicing English with this tape, she had said, but Tomiko noticed that Sueko could barely repeat the simple English sentences on the tape. She started to wonder if, even back in high school, Sueko had known the difference between "to be" and other English verbs. Even though it depressed her, Tomiko sat late into the night, patiently keeping Sueko company as she practiced her English.

. 2 .

AFTER THAT NIGHT, Tomiko and Sueko became fast friends. Once a week, just around the time when Tomiko was getting ready to leave the office for the day, she would get a phone call from Sueko and they would arrange to meet on the weekend. Except for her trysts with Yoshida, Tomiko had little to occupy herself with in the evening. She had already graduated from the flower arranging and tea ceremony classes that single women took in preparation for marriage. At one time, she had even taught English classes at an evening cram school but didn't enjoy being around children, so she quit. The only child she did like was her nephew, but each time she went to visit him, she felt painfully conscious of the critical gaze of her grandparents. Even worse was her mother, who would inevitably whip herself into a tirade about her useless, still-single daughter. And, increasingly, instead of feeling unfettered and liberated when she got home to her own apartment, Tomiko would collapse under the weight of her own anxieties about the future and the past. She was thirty, after all.

Tomiko could not deny that she had been pampered as a child. During the American occupation her father was a high official in the civil administration, and thanks to him, she had the best of everything. All through school, and until she graduated from high school, Tomiko had ranked at the top of her class, right up there with the boys. She decided to reject the advice of those who urged her to try for a prestigious national university and chose instead to attend an elite women's college in Tokyo.

To Tomiko's chagrin, the time she spent on the mainland coincided with the years of great political and social turmoil in Okinawa. Tomiko came to see herself as a victim of the age. She felt humiliated when someone would single her out from a crowd for an opinion, as if her roots in Okinawa gave her special insight into the anti–Vietnam War demonstrations. When the time came for her to visit potential employers her senior year in college, everyone gawked at her, like she was some rare panda on display at the zoo.

Tomiko found such experiences trying in the extreme. She could hardly blame it all on Okinawa and the times, though. Her constitution was nothing like the willow branch that lets a strong wind blow by instead of snapping and breaking, and she was unable just to laugh off such incidents. It wasn't as if she desired obscurity, but rather it irked her that the attention she did receive was based on her origins, rather than her own achievements. Since she had no control over such matters, though, she came to the conclusion that she'd rather not be known at all than be labeled the woman from Okinawa. She tried to forget. But after an unhappy love affair, she began thinking of Okinawa as home again and made up her mind to go back. Once back, though, she immediately regretted her decision. Tomiko realized that she should have stayed in Tokyo and tried to lose her Okinawan identity. Such anonymity was Tokyo's only selling point. Tomiko did not find Okinawa an easy place to live.

At length, Tomiko started taking Sueko's place behind the bar pouring drinks and even began to hone her skills as a charming companion to the customers. It was great fun, and she fancied that she had discovered her own hidden talent. In the past, people had always considered her overly serious, but in front of tipsy customers, Tomiko would pull out one racy joke after another. Once she had learned blackjack from some customers, she turned out to be quite the gambler as well. No one could beat her, but she would magnanimously treat everyone to drinks with the loot she won.

No matter how much she denied it, some of her regular customers insisted that Tomiko must be the mama-san of the bar. This didn't bother Sueko in the least; in fact, she liked it. Business was good, and that meant Sueko could sit and talk endlessly about the man she had married in L.A. After the last customer left, she would pester Tomiko for an English lesson.

"Okay, okay. Repeat after me. Please show me the way to the station."

"Purizu shoo mii . . . what comes after that?" asked Sueko.

"The way."

"Za uweei. Go ahead."

"To the station."

"What does 'station' mean?"

Tomiko explained the meaning to her again.

"Tuu za station."

"Good. Try it again."

"Purizu . . . what's the next word? Purizu shoo . . . tell me how it goes again. Purizu . . ."

Frustrated, Tomiko slammed her scotch on the rocks down on the counter. Sueko peered fearfully at Tomiko's face, and the two were temporarily their childhood selves again. The clock had turned back.

Only one other time did Yoshida come to the bar. The moment she saw his face, Tomiko felt anger well up inside her, but she firmly suppressed it. She had refused to attend the junior high school reunions that her class faithfully held at New Year's and during the *O-bon* festival in late summer. The alumni group had no address for Sueko, so she never received the invitations, but Tomiko realized that she had no right to ask Sueko not to attend if she ever did get an invitation. Tomiko had no desire to become the focus of discussion during her classmates' drunken conversations, and she especially didn't want Yoshida's name to come up in such company.

That evening, she had another opportunity to introduce Yoshida to Sueko, but this time she made it clear that it was a working relationship. "This is my boss," she explained. For her part, Sueko showed no signs of curiosity about Yoshida, as if their previous encounter had utterly vanished from her memory.

To Sueko, even Yoshida was fair game, and she started out by telling him about her time in the States and then went on to describe her husband the painter, the psychiatrist's clattering false teeth, the troubles she had learning English, and her desire to return to America. Yoshida sat and listened agreeably to her banter. Tomiko felt relieved that the evening had gone so smoothly. When at last they were saying goodnight to him at the door, though, Tomiko reached over and gave him a sharp slap on the shoulder. Sueko made no further mention of his visit.

It was raining the night Yoshida left Naha. People from work had invited Tomiko to the last of a series of going-away parties for Yoshida, who had a ticket on the last flight bound for Tokyo that night. Just when everyone was heading out to the restaurant, Tomiko excused herself, explaining that she had something else she needed to do. As she was saying good-bye to Yoshida, she showed no emotion whatsoever. They had succeeded so completely in hiding their relationship from those around them that, even if she had cried a bit at their parting, probably no one would have suspected a thing. She assumed that after the party the people from the office would take Yoshida to the airport.

With an odd sensation of victory, Tomiko headed for Sueko's bar. Doubtless because of the bad weather, she found the place empty, except for Sueko, who sat alone at a table, listening to one of her English tapes. Tomiko helped herself to a scotch and water and then plopped down on a stool. She sat, her glass before her, twirling the ice cube around the inside of the glass with her fingers and taking only an occasional sip. She wasn't in the mood for drinking.

As the day of his departure drew closer, Yoshida stopped talking about divorcing his wife. Nor had he brought up the possibility of Tomiko coming to Tokyo with him. Not that Tomiko had intended to do so in the first place, nor had she taken his ardent promises seriously. She wished he had never even talked that way in the first place. If he felt compelled to be romantic, he at least could have been consistent about it until it was time for him to leave.

At the hotel the night before, Yoshida had barely said a word to Tomiko. What choice did she have but to remain silent as well? Any feeling that had existed between them was gone, and all that was left was an empty shell. Still, they mechanically went through with their final night together. Tomiko had wanted it to end passionately; she wished for an ending that touched her soul. But for that to happen, Yoshida would have had to love her much more. He would have had to feel some regret at their parting, or at least pretended that he was going to miss her. It seemed to her that the duty of the male of the species was to supply love and passion to the female. If Yoshida had remained silent and never made any rash promises to begin with, instead of changing his course midstream, then Tomiko might have been moved to action and pleaded with him not to leave. That is how the tug-of-war between men and women is supposed to work. But instead, thought Tomiko, he's left me in between, at neither extreme of joy or misery.

"Tomiko, is something the matter?" she heard Sueko say. "You don't look so good."

"I'm okay, really. I'm just a little cold from being out in the rain," replied Tomiko hesitantly.

"Your boyfriend's left, hasn't he?"

Tomiko did not respond.

"It was that fellow Yoshida, wasn't it?"

"Don't tell me you knew all along?"

"Maybe I should have said something. Of course I knew. You were so antsy the night he came. But you didn't say anything, so I pretended not to notice."

"And here I thought you hadn't caught on. You're a much better actress than I am."

"Why didn't you go with him? You love him, don't you?"

"There's nothing I can do."

"How come?"

"Because he walked out on me," said Tomiko brightly. She started laughing hysterically, which made her feel better, like a small ant that had bored a hole in a huge dam. Tomiko then let loose and told—virtually sang to—Sueko about her past with Yoshida. As she narrated it in terms comprehensible to Sueko, she came to see that their affair had been no different from any other, like a pebble on the wayside. Sueko cried for her, tears pouring from her large, dark eyes. In the midst of their talk, a customer walked into the bar. Confronted by the sight of two women, one laughing, one crying, and not another soul around, the man beat a hasty retreat. That made Tomiko laugh even harder. Sometimes her laugh sounded desperate, and that made Sueko cry even harder. Tomiko, still smiling, finally reached the end of the story.

"So like I told you, he left me. What else would you expect with an Okinawan bride, anyway? We abandoned women should stick together—don't you agree, Sueko?"

Abruptly, Sueko stopped her crying and shook her head several times in disagreement. Looking straight at Tomiko, Sueko's eyes glistened strangely, but this time not because of her tears. "That's not what happened to me and you know it," she said in a deep voice.

Tomiko instantly regretted her words.

"I wasn't abandoned."

"I'm sorry, Sueko. I said the wrong thing."

"He didn't leave me, I tell you. But that's what you've been thinking all along, isn't it? You never believed what I told you in the first place."

No matter how many times Tomiko apologized, Sueko refused to forgive her and stubbornly stood her ground, like a soldier protecting herself with the mightiest of shields. Tomiko started to lose her patience as Sueko repeated the same words again and again, like a spell, like a record skipping.

"He didn't abandon me. It's not the same situation. We got married, but when I got sick, we couldn't live together anymore. We love each other, you know, and when my English gets better, I'll be able to go back to Los Angeles."

That was enough. Tomiko decided that she had to destroy the shield that Sueko held before her and make her listen to the truth.

"Do you want to hear what I think, Sueko? I think that he did leave you. How long did you say it's been since you came back to Okinawa? A year? A year and a half? Have you heard from him at all during that time? Have you? I bet you haven't. Don't you think that's strange? If he loves you so much, why hasn't he called or written that whole time? You're sick. You need help."

Sueko bit into her fist, and a single tear streaked down her cheek.

"And besides, he doesn't even send you money. You told me that you opened this bar with money you got from him, but that was a pay-off, wasn't it? Don't pretend you're so innocent that you don't know the difference.

"Forget about the bastard. You're hardly the first woman in Okinawa to get left behind. Welcome to the club. At least you got a nice trip to the States out of it."

Sueko raised her hand and slapped it hard against Tomiko's soft cheek, and then she sat back, looking rather surprised at herself. Tomiko tried hard to remain calm.

"And that's not all. Do you want to hear what I really think of you? That you're making the whole thing up. Where's all the stuff you got when you were in L.A., anyway? I don't see any of it here. I think it's all a fantasy, all that about going there and marrying an American."

With that, Sueko bolted out of the bar into the pouring rain. Tomiko grabbed an umbrella and ran out to search for her. When she finally caught up with her and offered the umbrella's protection, Sueko snatched it and angrily threw it on to the ground.

"Why did you do that?" asked Tomiko.

"It hardly ever rains in California, but when it does, no one ever uses an umbrella. Those people there just walk along in the rain, that's what they do," Sueko told her.

Because Tomiko had also heard the saying "California shower," she could hardly brand this another lie. They crossed Route 58 and walked aimlessly along International Street, the center of Naha's shopping district. They were both soaked, and Tomiko felt dismayed that her favorite dress had been ruined. But when she looked over at Sueko's profile, dimly spotlighted by the headlights and streetlights, she found her pensive face rather lovely.

. 3 .

A FEW DAYS later, Sueko called to ask for Tomiko's forgiveness. Tomiko had no reason to apologize, Sueko said humbly, for she herself was the one who didn't know when to leave well enough alone. Tomiko privately regretted having been so coldly blunt and wondered if she had a drop of blood left in her veins. When Sueko told her that she had a favor to ask, Tomiko agreed to meet her at the bar. She assumed that Sueko probably needed to borrow some money, and she wanted to help out in any way she could.

The bar was quite cramped, and even a friend would not have credited Sueko with good taste. The chairs were old and beat up, and pink lightbulbs hung over the rickety tables. That night, the bar looked a little different. Tomiko noticed that a ten-gallon hat had been added to the decor on one wall, along with a toy rifle, and she guessed that Sueko had tacked them up herself and had done so in a hurry. Glaring white patches of plaster showed through gaps in the grubby wallpaper. Looking around, Tomiko spotted a new framed photograph as well. It showed Sueko and her husband smiling, arm in arm, standing next to a wooden sign that read "Death Valley." The picture was grainy, perhaps because it had been enlarged.

A photo like that would have been fine as part of Sueko's bedroom decor, but Tomiko was surprised to see it hanging in the bar. Everyone in this business knew that customers were interested only in a woman's present, not in her past. Tomiko felt her face flush as she recalled the cruelty of her accusations on that rainy night. She felt terrible.

"I wrote a letter," said Sueko, "and I want you to translate it into English for me."

Tomiko agreed to take on the task but then asked Sueko, "Why didn't you hire a translator? Why ask me?"

"I've been thinking about it. Maybe you were right. Maybe I was abandoned. I don't want other people reading my letter. It's too pathetic. Anyway, I don't know English, and so I can't call him on the phone. When I was leaving Los Angeles, I couldn't tell what he was feeling about me. All I know is that he kept saying 'I love you, I love you,' up until the minute I got on the plane. Is that what a man who's about to dump you would say? He was so sweet. He must have told me fifty times that he wanted me to come back to L.A. But you are right, you know—it's strange that he hasn't been in touch. You think it's okay for me to contact him, don't you?"

"Of course," agreed Tomiko, and she hastened to add, "The quicker you find out what's going on, the better." *I wish she would wake up from this dream,* thought Tomiko, but she said nothing.

Sueko's letter was full of mistaken and missing characters, but her handwriting was surprisingly good.

Dear Donald,

How are you? I am much better. When I arrived back here, I felt relieved to be able to speak Japanese again. At first, it was a little rough. Dr. Fletcher told me that I should go see a Japanese doctor about my fainting, but I didn't because I knew it wouldn't happen again. I've been studying English every day. I opened a little restaurant in Maejima (that's in Naha) with the money you gave me and my savings that I had in the bank here. The rent is very low because the manager of the Rose Room (where you and I first met) put in a good word for me. Every time I see the manager, we talk about you. He told me that he loves the portrait that you painted of him. I should have had you paint one of me, too. I wish I hadn't been so shy about it. But I did put up our honeymoon picture in my restaurant. That was fun, wasn't it? The manager is also very proud of the sign that you painted for his place. I think it's a million times better than any other sign you see around here. I did feel sad when I saw it the other day, though, because it had faded a little. With the Vietnam War over and all the soldiers gone, the town is desolate. The manager seems to be having a hard time of it. I respect him so much.

I have been spending a lot of time with a friend of mine from junior high school recently, and that makes me feel better. Have you made up with your brother? Please don't fight with him anymore. After all, he is taking care of your mother.

Also, after I got back to Japan, I remembered all the things I'd forgotten to do before I left California. I never paid Mrs. Canoldo for doing my hair that time. Could you please give her some money for me? I owe her three dollars. She has so many kids and depends on her hairdressing to get by. Please also give my best to the Gazolinis. Mrs. Gazolini was so nice to me. She also made delicious spaghetti. I've tried to make spaghetti like that here, but it never turns out like hers. They don't sell those funny-shaped mushrooms here in Okinawa. (What were they called?) Please thank Nick and everyone for lending us the car. Thank Mr. Cohen's aunt for looking after the house. Please thank Mrs. Spelvin for the refrigerator she gave us.

Please tell Dr. Fletcher not to let his dentures fall out of his mouth when he's with patients. And also tell him how much I appreciated his help. Don't forget to say hi for me to your mother, your brother and sister-in-law, Raul, and little Cary. I want you to take good care of yourself. I'm not worried about you drinking too much, because you never did. Remember, drugs will make you lazy. Please attend an anti-smoking group meeting once in a while so you won't smoke too much at work. Good-bye for now.

Yours truly, Sueko

Tomiko took the letter and went home, only to find a special-delivery letter from Yoshida in her own mailbox. It contained nothing that surprised her—lines such as "I'll always remember you fondly" and "I hope you will find a nice man to marry some day." His glib, flowery words made her feel more empty than angry. The noncommittal expressions of goodwill hurt her most. *He doesn't care what I feel at all,* she thought as she ripped up the letter and threw it into the wastebasket.

As for Sueko's letter, it occurred to Tomiko that it did not contain one affectionate phrase. After she read it the first time, she mentioned to Sueko that for a love letter it lacked passion. Sueko had smiled sadly and explained that she was worried that Donald might have forgotten her and she didn't want to overwhelm him. A line from a poem by some French woman painter flickered through Tomiko's head: "In this world, the most melancholy woman is one who has been forgotten." Sueko didn't need to end up that way.

Tomiko translated the letter as faithfully as possible, and then added a postscript below Sueko's name at the bottom. *If Sueko won't say it herself, I've got to write it for her:* "P.S. Why haven't you written to me or called me up in such a long time? You've forgotten me, haven't you? I need and belong to you. I can't live without you. I'll kill myself if you should leave me!"

Tomiko planned to explain the meaning of these words to Sueko if she asked, but Sueko happily took the English letter from Tomiko and raised it up with both hands, as if it were a precious gift. She didn't ask anything about the postscript. Tomiko had written the letter nicely so that Sueko could send it as it was, but Sueko insisted on copying it over in her own handwriting. Her childish, round letters improved as she copied, and the final product was not half bad. It took her a full week to finish it. She even imitated the suggestion of spontaneity in the writing that Tomiko had used for the P.S. I-need-you-and-belong-to-you part. Tomiko had purposely avoided using the word love because she thought Sueko might recognize it and realize that something had been added, but Sueko was so innocent that it likely never occurred to her that Tomiko might go to such lengths.

They were friends, after all, so Tomiko was doing her a favor. Or, depending on how one looks at it, she was meddling in something that was none of her business. Indeed, her motives were less than pure. She had added the P.S. partly because she wanted to expose Sueko's true feelings for all to see. It was cruel of her, she realized, and she felt guilty at what seemed to her a terrible betrayal of their friendship. But it really didn't matter in the end, Tomiko told herself, because nothing would come of the letter anyway, whether it had that P.S. or not. So she would be forgiven.

The two women went to the post office together to mail the letter. Sueko was strangely excited, as if she had accomplished some great feat.

"He'll write back some day, don't you think? Don't you?" she asked, hoping for a positive response from Tomiko.

All Tomiko could do was smile ambiguously. Sueko would not stop pestering her for a definite answer, so she finally replied curtly, "Something will come in about a month, I suppose." Then, with greater clarity, Tomiko spit out, "But if you haven't gotten anything by then, then just give up on it, will you? Admit that he left you."

Sueko stopped and looked reproachfully at Tomiko. Then, pulling herself together, she again sought Tomiko's agreement. "I think it'll be fine, don't you?"

She said nothing.

"Okay, let's bet on it," said Sueko defiantly. "Let's bet on whether he'll write back or not."

"Fine," replied Tomiko calmly. "What shall we bet?"

"My bar—I'll bet the bar." She was serious and stood holding her breath.

"You must be kidding. You bet the bar, and what am I supposed to bet?"

"Nothing. You don't have to bet anything."

"What kind of bet is that?"

"It's fine with me. Anyway, what's the point of having the bar if I don't have my Donald?"

At the post office counter, Sueko handed the letter to the postal clerk and then bowed her head and clapped her hands together, as if in prayer at a shrine. Surprised, the clerk averted his gaze, as if he thought Sueko were possessed. Tomiko also looked away. She couldn't look Sueko straight in the eye because she felt certain that mailing the letter made her the winner of the bet, prayer or no prayer.

. 4 .

AFTER MAILING THE letter, Sueko said no more about the States. She also pledged to the local shrine that she would abstain from drinking, cigarettes, tea, and rice. To make up for the lack of oral gratification, she would sit in the corner of the bar, nibbling on peanuts or some other snack. She went to the bank and got a big calendar so that she could cross off each day since mailing the letter, counting the days until a month passed. Each time Tomiko visited, Sueko would point to the calendar and grin.

"How many days left?" she would say, as if marking off the days until the 1970 World's Fair opened in Osaka. Her obsessiveness gave Tomiko the creeps, making her tense when they were together, so she stopped by the bar less often. After a time, Tomiko got sick. Tomiko was slender yet hearty, and normally she could recover from a missed night's sleep. But something like this happened to her about every two years. Her body constantly felt heavy, and she lost her appetite. It felt as though all the water in her body was going to evaporate, and she grew frantic worrying that her face would shrivel up into a mass of wrinkles, like an old woman's. She kept waking up at night and was unable to get back to sleep. Like a pregnant woman, she craved sour foods. What had happened with Yoshida made it worse—in fact, Yoshida was the cause of her malady. She dragged herself to work every day, but finally one day she could not summon up the energy and stayed home. Instead of staying in bed as she should have, though, Tomiko paced around the room all day.

And the letter from Yoshida that she had torn up and thrown away—it was still in the wastebasket. Tomiko fished it out and taped it back together. She read it closely, devoured it again and again, in an attempt to sniff out his feelings for her between the lines of ink. She experienced all of the unavoidable delusions that plague abandoned women.

She came to the simple conclusion that she was in love with Yoshida, but the very mundaneness of her state drove her to distraction. She dozed off and dreamed about encountering Yoshida's wife (whom she had never actually met) and having a fight over him. In her dream, this, too, was a dream. Then she heard a loud knocking on the door, and she stumbled out of bed. It was light outside. She couldn't tell whether it was the next day, or the same day she had fallen asleep. She pulled on a robe over her pajamas and went to answer the door, her hair wild from sleep.

"Are you okay? I went to your office and they said you'd caught a cold. I haven't seen you for so long that I was starting to wonder if you were still alive. I was worried about you."

There stood Sueko, a basket of fruit in one hand. Tomiko dragged her fingers through her hair and squinted out into the bright daylight.

"Is that the only reason you came?"

"I got a letter," said Sueko, her face glowing. Then, remembering her original mission, she hurriedly expressed her wishes for Tomiko's speedy recovery, at least three times. She deliberately made no attempt to show the letter to Tomiko, but instead forced Tomiko to become her patient. She put a pot on the stove so that she could make some curative rice gruel and peeled an apple for Tomiko. Once Sueko had finished bustling around, Tomiko again brought up the topic of the letter, but Sueko was totally unresponsive. Finally, when Tomiko, impatient, raised her voice and demanded a response, Sueko answered faintly, "Actually, I'm scared."

"Of what?"

"I've decided not to open it."

"You mean you're never going to read it?"

"He wrote back to me, Tomiko. That means he hasn't forgotten me. That's all I need."

"That's ridiculous."

"You think so?"

"Of course I do. It's not as if you had written to President Carter and gotten something back from him, you know. A reply in and of itself is no reason for celebration. Stop being so childish. Pull yourself together. Of course it's important to find out what's inside. Open it up and I'll read it for you."

Tomiko was amazed that he had actually written back. So perhaps they had lived together in Los Angeles. Tomiko guessed that the couple had never legally married, though, because the procedures were complicated for a Japanese marrying a foreigner. It had been an ordeal for Sueko just to write a letter to him, much less file all the papers needed for a legal marriage. She was such a child. If they were married, there would have been a clean break much sooner than this. Tomiko had always found her stories to be suspicious, and this made no sense either. In any case, she felt certain that Sueko would not be happy about the contents of this letter.

She started to read the missive from Sueko's husband, Mr. Donald Stroud, which opened with the words, "I'm sorry it's taken me so long to write to you." At first, Tomiko had intended to translate the letter line by line, but she looked over and saw Sueko sitting with her eyes screwed shut and her hands pressed tight over her ears. If she were ten years younger, she might look cute in that position, thought Tomiko, and then she decided to read the letter start to finish silently to herself.

The English was simple, with no difficult words to look up in the dictionary, and the handwriting easy to read. Tomiko could immediately tell that Donald was a kind and gentle man, and as she read further, she realized that her predictions had been off the mark. This is what the letter said: soon after Sueko left, Donald had fallen from a stepladder and injured his back. He was then in the hospital for a long while. He had not written to Sueko because he didn't want her to worry, and with his injury, he was not able to send any money, either. He finally recovered and is now well and has a job. He made up with his brother. He relayed all of Sueko's messages and her thanks to everyone. Everyone there wanted Sueko to come back to L.A. soon. The letter ended with these words:

I work hard every day. So I'll be able to visit Okinawa to meet you by next summer. I need you, too. Don't kill yourself! My pet Sueko!

After she finished reading the letter, Tomiko let out a loud laugh. *These Yankees are really something, aren't they?* It was just like a sentimental love poem. Tomiko laughed until tears streamed down her cheeks. Sueko sat staring blankly at her. Finally, she asked, "What does it say? What does he say?"

Tomiko sat silently, staring back at her, and watched cowardice well up in Sueko's eyes as she sat waiting for a response. Tomiko felt disgust for her.

"What does he say? Tell me. Tomiko, you've got to read it to me."

"He's getting married next summer."

"Married? Who's he marrying?"

"Another American, I suppose."

Where this lie came from, Tomiko did not know. Her mood had turned black. Sueko's face hardened and the dimples disappeared from her cheeks. Pools of tears started to well from the lower rims of her large eyes, threatening to become a flood. That set off Tomiko, and she said the first thing that came to her mind.

"He doesn't want to bother with the details of the divorce himself, so he's hired a lawyer. He wants to know if you've heard from the lawyer yet. He says that he'll always remember you fondly, and he hopes that you will find a nice Okinawan man to marry someday."

Sueko had still not started to cry. The tears were brimming in her eyes, and her feelings were very close to the surface. *It won't be long until the bomb explodes,* thought Tomiko, and then she muttered, "Am I such a heartless woman? I should tell her the truth."

"What? What did you say?" said Sueko desperately. *This woman still has hope.*

"Nothing. I was talking to myself."

Finally, Sueko started to weep. Tomiko sat watching her for a while.

"Well, that's the end of that. Sorrow becomes Okinawan women. You stop your crying now," said Tomiko, flinging out the words harshly. Such was her attempt to comfort Sueko.

TRANSLATED BY ANN SHERIF

YOSHIDA SUEKO (1947–)

Born in Motobu, Yoshida Sueko has spent much of her life in northern Okinawa, where she continues to live today. She has published fiction in several magazines, including Shin Okinawa bungaku, *which awarded her its literary prize in 1984 for "Love Suicide at Kamaara" (Kamaara shinjū). Yoshida is currently writing more stories about prostitutes in postwar Okinawa.*

This story is set in the Kamaara district of Koza, which has grown into Okinawa's second-largest city. Koza is the main shopping and entertainment destination for the many American military personnel and families who live on the nearby U.S. bases. In fact, Gate Street, mentioned in this story, connects Kadena Air Base (the largest U.S. air base in Asia) to the town's main intersection, Goya. The story also refers several times to B.C. Street (Business Center Street), which runs parallel to Gate Street. These two streets appear in countless works of postwar Okinawan literature, since they served as the shopping and entertainment center for G.I.s from the 1950s through the Vietnam War. English-language signs announced the restaurants, souvenir stores, pawn shops, bars, and strip clubs that lined these two streets. Many of Koza's establishments continued to conduct transactions in U.S. dollars, even after Okinawa's reversion to Japan designated the yen as the official currency. In an effort to shed its image as a base town (in both senses of the word), the Koza City Council changed the municipal name to Okinawa City in 1974. Later, Gate Street was renamed Airport Road, and B.C. Street became Central Park Avenue. Despite the efforts to reshape the town's image, the American bases remain, and as this story reminds us, they have fostered some surprising legacies.

LOVE SUICIDE AT KAMAARA

YOSHIDA SUEKO

. 1 .

KIYO WAS AWAKENED by the sound of the lighter hitting the floor. She opened her eyes and saw a faint wisp of smoke drifting toward the sunlit ceiling. Glancing over at the other side of the bed, she saw Sammy looking at her with a cigarette between his teeth. He must have been watching her sleep for some time. Kiyo rolled over and faced the wall. She knew he'd been getting an eyeful of her hair, which was starting to turn white at the roots, and at the lusterless nape of her bony neck. She felt painfully exposed and pulled the blanket up above her ears.

Sammy wanted to leave. Kiyo knew that. She could see it in the frown on his forehead and in his eyes that avoided looking at her. They were the eyes of a restless spirit. Above all, his face told Kiyo that he had begun to hate sex with her.

Sammy wanted to go back to his unit. He'd grown tired of his life as a deserter, tormented by the unexpected boredom and daily humdrum. This was obvious from the listlessness in his speech, the irritation in his walk, and the occasional disgusted glances he threw at Kiyo. The M.P.s were not going to come looking for him. The police were not going to send out a fleet of patrol cars to track him down. He realized now that being a deserter was far more tedious than he'd imagined, and the daily monotony had become a hell for him.

When Sammy left, he would probably head straight for that drab little shed that was the front gate of Camp Courtney, the base where he'd been stationed. There, he would be arrested by the M.P.s and thrown into the stir cage. Yet even with what awaited him, there was no doubt he was going to leave. She didn't know if it would be today or tomorrow or ten days from now, but one day soon he was going to get up and head straight for that little shed with the brick roof, and there was nothing she could do to stop him.

Kiyo heard Sammy get up to open the window. Bright light poured across the back of her neck, and she pulled the blanket up over her head.

He's avoiding me.

Now she was angry. Sammy had again moved evasively so that he wouldn't have to be near her. He seemed to dread even the possibility of touching her.

The ashtray clanked softly, and then there was silence. Until only recently, Sammy would stub out his cigarette and slip into bed next to Kiyo. The squeaking in the ashtray had been Sammy's signal, but somewhere along the line, that, too, had stopped happening.

From under the blanket Kiyo watched Sammy as he stood at the windowsill gazing outside. His thin, pale neck disappeared behind his disheveled hair parted down the middle. She looked at his large ears, which seemed to jut out abruptly from the sides of his head, and she felt the loneliness of morning.

"Sammy."

"Yeah." He turned back to look at her.

"Close the window and pull the curtains. It's too bright."

Sammy got up, closed the window, and drew the curtains.

"Come here, Sammy."

Sammy stood at the side of the bed. Kiyo reached out with one arm and put her hand on his pants.

"What time did you get back last night?" she asked.

"I think it was around twelve, or maybe one."

"You went to sleep without taking off your pants?"

"Uh-huh. I couldn't be bothered."

Kiyo knew that Sammy had not come back until dawn, around 5:00. "Where were you?"

"At Jim's. Jim Oblender's. I told you before, about the guy from my hometown in the air force here at Kadena."

"It's okay to hang out at your friend's house, but if you wander around outside too much the M.P.s will catch you," she said.

As she spoke, she thought how strange the American military was. It had been almost half a year since he ran away from his unit, but they didn't seem to be looking for him. And Sammy didn't act like a deserter, casually walking around outside day and night, pretty much wherever he liked. If she hadn't seen it in the newspapers, she probably wouldn't have believed he was a deserter.

"Undo your belt."

Sammy did as she said, rattling his buckle as he unfastened his belt, and lowered his pants a bit so that Kiyo could slip her hand in easily. Kiyo took hold of Sammy from the opening in his olive-drab G.I. underwear.

"Come closer," she said.

As Sammy drew closer, Kiyo slipped his underwear down and pulled him out. She sat up and buried her face between the perspiring boy's legs. She licked him, then held him in her mouth. Once inside, Sammy got hard. Kiyo put her right hand around his back. With her left hand she slowly rubbed the skin around his navel and then lowered her hand to cup him where he was soft and rounded as she gently pushed upward. Sammy groaned faintly and fell on his back. Kiyo lay on her stomach, and as she buried her face at the base of his legs, Sammy lunged suddenly with such strength that Kiyo felt he would thrust through the back of her throat.

The erect Sammy, his youthful vitality aroused inside Kiyo's mouth, trembled. He thrust himself upward with awesome power as if to penetrate Kiyo. He was life itself, and when Kiyo held him in her mouth, her aged cells were restored, as if she were being rejuvenated. Injected with pure youth, she felt imbued, through her lips and her cheeks, with that young vigor. The powerful force that raged inside her mouth made her want to suck in this essence of life with all its youth and joy and make it her own. Kiyo's eyes glistened in the darkness as she engulfed Sammy.

Sammy's hands, grasping Kiyo's cheeks, tightened their grip. Kiyo was lifted up as he turned over and pushed her under him. As his liquid life came rushing impatiently into her body, Sammy convulsed violently, and then it was over.

With both of her legs still pinned between Sammy's, Kiyo groped for the head of the bed. She lit a cigarette. Sammy's body jumped at the sound of the lighter, and his legs parted. Sammy turned over. Kiyo gazed fixedly at his profile, which was shaded from the bright light. Sammy's beard, to which he had not put a razor even once in the last half year, flowed from his chin onto his chest. Kiyo thought it heightened the sharpness of his chiseled features. He looked exactly like the picture of a crucified Christ she had once seen. After Kiyo lit the cigarette, she pushed it between Sammy's lips.

. 2 .

WHILE SHOWERING, KIYO wondered absentmindedly what she would do all day. Her money had run out. Not one yen left. Until yesterday, she'd had at least two thousand yen but spent it last night at a nearby supermarket to buy three bottles of beer for Sammy, potato chips to snack on, and bread for breakfast. Now the two thousand yen was all gone, and this morning she was broke.

Kiyo stood in front of the mirror, wiping herself dry with a small towel. Her face was discolored and bloated, perhaps from lack of sleep. It was a loathsome face. Her neck had become even scrawnier recently. Not only was it thinner, but it had lost its color. The yellow, wrinkled skin clinging to her neck hung down, sagging lifelessly. A trace of her youthful past remained in her thin arms, but veins floated on the backs of her hands, and her yellowed palms were pitiful. Her chest, too, was bony, having lost its glow, and her flabby belly was covered with fine wrinkles. She was acutely aware that she was no longer young, which made her feel all the more ugly. Looking in the mirror, she carefully applied her makeup. At least she had to look as young as possible, for Sammy's sake. She couldn't let this Adonis of hers, who seemed to have slipped out of a Greek myth, know the hideousness of her old age.

She opened her dresser and changed into a two-piece outfit. Sammy was still in bed, now fast asleep.

It was drizzling when she stepped outside. She thought about going back to the apartment for an umbrella but felt suddenly anxious and changed her mind. Sammy might be awakened by the sound of the door opening, and if he woke up, he might leave and never come back. So Kiyo gave up on the umbrella and set out across the pavement of the neighboring vacant lot. She walked slowly at first, and as she walked, she thought of Sammy.

THEY had met in the shadows of Pinocchio Burger where she always stood. As usual, she was there propositioning customers. Soldiers would float up like bubbles from beside the bottle palm trees on B.C. Street and stand in front of the small counter. After being handed their hot dog or hamburger wrapped in a napkin, they would stand there and begin chomping on it. Kiyo would watch them from the shadows. When they finished eating, they would wipe their mouths with the napkin, throw it in the trash, and begin heading back into the sea of lights.

"Hey."

It was at that moment that she'd call out. A soldier would come over, usually look at Kiyo's face and body, then start walking away in disgust. At that point, she would yell out, "Ten dollars" as cheerfully as she could. Ten dollars was less than half the market price, so a soldier short of cash would stop in his tracks. Kiyo would then rush over and grab hold of his right arm. This required considerable skill. If she were too quick, she would be brushed off, and if she were too slow, he would escape. It was all in the timing, and at first, before she had it down, she lost many customers.

It was close to midnight when Sammy appeared, around the time Kiyo was beginning to think about going home. As she emerged from the shadows and glanced up, she saw a slender soldier standing at the counter. Kiyo paused, thinking that he would be the last one tonight. When the soldier had finished eating his hot dog, he began walking over to Kiyo. He looked young enough to be in high school.

"Ten dollars," Kiyo said to him.

"Five dollars," the young soldier quickly replied.

Does he really think he can have a woman for as little as a thousand yen?

Kiyo's anger was mollified somewhat by his innocent, childlike face. She had a weakness for pretty, young boys. But even so, she would not usually have been so taken by a boy's looks to have agreed to five dollars. It wasn't until they got back to her apartment that she realized this boy was truly an unspoiled Adonis.

That night Kiyo had been standing in the shadows of the hot dog stand for nearly two hours and was exhausted. All she'd wanted was to sit down somewhere. She would even have agreed to go for free just to be tucked into a warm bed with a man. Strangely, it was just when she'd begun to lose hope that Sammy appeared. He was by himself. It was rare for a soldier to be walking alone at that hour.

Passing the hotel on B.C. Street, Kiyo brought Sammy to the Kamaara Apartments. When they entered her apartment, she stuck out her hand and said, "Five dollars."

Sammy reached into his pants pocket, took out a frayed five-dollar bill, and placed it in Kiyo's palm.

"You sure you don't have any more?" she asked.

"Really. This is all I've got left."

"Then how are you going to afford a taxi back?"

"I'm not going back to my quarters."

"What do you mean . . . not going back?"

"I've deserted."

"Well, well."

Kiyo gazed at the boy. A fringe of chestnut-colored hair covered his forehead, below which his thin face was smiling awkwardly.

"Which base are you from?" she asked.

"Camp Courtney."

"A marine."

"Uh-huh."

"What are you planning to do now?" "

"Earn some money and go up to the main island."

"To Honshū, the main island of Japan?"

"Yeah, from Honshū I'm thinking of going over to North Korea or the Soviet Union."

"You must be kidding!" Kiyo raised her voice but did not return the money.

After taking a shower, Kiyo approached the bed. The young soldier, his shoulders bared, looked out from beneath the sheets as if to appraise her. Their eyes met. He hurriedly averted his gaze. At that moment Kiyo felt a heart-wrenching sorrow. In spite of herself, she was overcome with the irresistible urge to embrace him and hold him close to her. It might also have had something to do with the lighting in the room, but the boy's face filled Kiyo with a strange sense of pity that awakened her maternal instincts. His gray eyes, though radiating a mysterious quietude, showed fear.

Kiyo got in next to Sammy. He clung to her tightly. Kiyo felt the boy tremble as he clutched at her breasts. When she reached out her arm and put her hand between his legs, he pulled his hips away in surprise. Sammy had never been with a woman. Kiyo suddenly turned toward him and pushed the timid Sammy inside her. Sammy's face contorted, and before she knew it, he had finished and become dead weight on top of her.

That night Kiyo let Sammy, who had nowhere to go, stay in her apartment. The next morning he left with no particular destination in mind. The following day, there was a small item in the newspaper about him. Kiyo read it on the second floor of the beauty parlor.

"Marine at Camp Courtney Stabs Sergeant and Flees"

Only a few lines in a small article, but Kiyo knew right away it was Sammy.

"A Camp Courtney Marine, Private First Class (age 18), got into an argument in the training area at Camp Hansen with his platoon leader, Sergeant John W. Anderson, over a minor matter, stabbed the sergeant in the abdomen with his bayonet, and fled. It is expected that Sergeant Anderson, who is seriously injured, will need one month to recover. The Marines have obtained the assistance of local police, and are investigating the boy's whereabouts."

Kiyo wasn't afraid of having slept with a person who would stab someone. She thought Sammy must have been seriously provoked to do such a thing. In the past twenty years, Kiyo had witnessed many brutal acts among the soldiers. She had even seen a man shot to death right in front of her, so a mere stabbing didn't frighten her in the least.

When Kiyo had finished getting her hair dyed and walked back to her apartment, Sammy was sitting on the front steps. He laughed weakly when he saw her, his face heavy with fatigue.

"Hi," she said.

"Hi."

Kiyo sat down next to him. His collar smelled of sweat.

"Where did you go?" she asked.

"Isahama."

"Isahama?"

"A guy from my hometown, Jim MacGuire, lives there, so I went over to his place. But I got thrown out."

"You were in the newspaper," she said.

"In the newspaper?" Sammy's lips trembled slightly.

"You stabbed your sergeant?"

"Just nicked him. He's not going to die or anything."

"They say it'll take him a month to recover."

"It was his fault, he—"

"It's okay, you don't have to tell me why. But if you stay out here, you'll get caught."

"Yeah, well . . ." Sammy's face was turning red. "Can you put me up for a while, two or three days?" Just until the money from his mother in the States arrives at MacGuire's place, he added.

Kiyo gazed at the boy's face, and Sammy blushed. Kiyo remembered his expression from that first time when she had turned toward him and pushed him inside her, and now she was getting hot. The sensation of the boy's trembling filled her entire body. The feel of his round, firm buttocks returned to the palms of her hands. That night Kiyo had held the boy down while he lay dead asleep and devoured him until there was nothing left. His response had been weak. As she had rolled around in bed realizing how wonderful intercourse between a man and a woman could be, she held Sammy's head in her arms and cried. She'd never been so thankful to be in the business of selling her body. It was her line of work that had made this experience possible. Otherwise, she'd never have had the chance to be held by a man like Sammy, not even in three lifetimes.

Kiyo stood up, opened the apartment door, and called out to him from behind as he sat on the steps. "It's okay, Sammy. It can't be forever, but you can stay here."

The next day Kiyo got up around 11:00. As she was brushing her teeth, the doorbell rang furiously. She looked out through the peephole and saw a police officer.

Here they come.

It was the same officer from the Goya police box she'd often seen on B.C. Street. She wondered how he knew to come here. After shaking Sammy awake, she helped him escape through the window, then opened the door.

"Excuse me," said the officer as he removed his hat and looked around the room.

"What can I do for you?" Kiyo was still holding her toothbrush as she looked up at the young officer.

"Are you Yafuso Kiyo?" he asked.

"Yes. . . . What can I do for you?"

"Actually, we're searching for a marine deserter. Do you happen to know where he is?" The officer got right to the point.

"So why did you come all the way over to my place?"

"To tell you the truth, an employee at Pinocchio Burger said he saw someone fitting his description. As you know, that's a popular gathering place for soldiers. The employee said he saw you heading for Kamaara with him. Do you know where he is?"

"When was this?" Kiyo asked, playing innocent.

"Three nights ago . . ."

"What does he look like?"

"He's still a boy, Caucasian. Marine private first class . . ." The officer described Sammy's features, adding that it was a particularly brutal crime for someone his age. He explained that this information came from the investigation request issued by the marines.

"Well, I did meet a soldier in front of Pinocchio, but the description doesn't fit," Kiyo said, still playing innocent. "His hair wasn't blond, but golden, and I think he must have been at least twenty-four or twenty-five. You'd better talk to that Pinocchio employee again."

"I see. Well, that's all I needed to ask you." The officer laughed as he was putting his notebook in his pocket. "In any case, he'll probably show up around B.C. Street, so it's just a matter of time until we arrest him. He's got no place else to go." The officer spoke as if he'd said these same words many times before. He apologized for having bothered Kiyo as he fixed his hat and then saluted, repeating that they were sure to catch him.

Kiyo watched from the window over the sink until the officer had turned the corner at the vacant lot. She felt a thin layer of sweat on her back. That night Sammy came back after sunset.

HALF a year had passed since that day. The officer didn't appear again, and the M.P.s never came around even once. They didn't even seem to be looking for Sammy. It surprised Kiyo that the American military could be so lax.

There was no sign that Sammy was getting any money from home. In all this time, he had not paid Kiyo a cent. Instead of receiving money, Kiyo had actually started giving Sammy spending money. Once, after the second or third month, she had demanded he pay her back, but now the circumstances were completely different. She had come to understand that this was the price an unwanted fifty-eight-year-old prostitute had to pay so she could embrace an Adonis young enough to be her grandson and handsome enough to be a movie star. And, if she thought about it, this was a bargain. Where else could a woman like her sleep with such an angelic boy for a mere ten or twenty thousand yen a month?

. 3 .

WHEN KIYO LOOKED at her watch, it was after 3:00.

Where should I go?

She could think of nowhere in particular.

I'll go out to the main intersection. Then I'll decide.

Kiyo walked faster. On her face fell a drizzling rain that was sure to ruin her makeup. She took a handkerchief out of her handbag and pressed it to her forehead.

After reaching the intersection, she turned onto a side street and stopped at a pawnshop, where she left her ring as collateral for a five-thousand-yen loan. It was a cheap ring, but she was able to borrow the money because she knew the owner, Mr. Shiroma, whose wife, like Kiyo, was from Tsuken Island. She counted the crisp thousand-yen bills, stuffed them into her purse, and went into a cafeteria for a bowl of Okinawan-style noodle soup with pork.

When she left the restaurant and looked at her watch again, it was after 3:30. The image of Sammy kicking back on the sofa watching television floated into Kiyo's mind. But all at once she was overcome with the anxiety that he might already have left the apartment for good. Kiyo stopped short in the middle of the street and considered returning home. Then, on second thought, she decided that he couldn't have left. After all, where could someone go who was homeless and penniless? Kiyo began walking again, trying to shake off her doubts.

She stood at the bus stop and thought of going to Nakagusuku Park. From atop the stone wall of the old castle there, she'd be able to see Tsuken Island. She wanted to look at the white crests of waves dashing against the far reef. On days when she felt down, she longed to see the outline of the island where she was born and would come to gaze at the ocean surrounding it whenever something was troubling her. Perhaps because she had fallen on hard times, Kiyo was often depressed these days. She constantly dwelled on the past, something she hated doing. Or maybe it was because she was getting old that she thought more and more about the past, especially about her husband and children, long estranged.

Since she'd left her island, Kiyo had seen her husband two or three times, but he was always so roaring drunk that she couldn't even have a conversation with him. Her two children had long ago passed their thirtieth birthdays. She heard they'd gone off to Kanagawa and Hyōgo on the Japanese mainland to get married, but they never came to see her or sent her a single letter. They must find her detestable, she thought. The realization that she must also have several grandchildren by now was almost too much to bear.

In the air-conditioned bus sat five or six passengers, all looking bored. When Kiyo sat down in an empty seat, her whole body felt heavy. She got off the bus at Ishinda, then hailed a taxi. By the time it reached the park and pulled up at the ticket booth, painted bright red just like Ryūgū Castle, the drizzling rain had stopped. There was no one in the booth, so she put two hundred-yen coins on the counter and went inside. Pale-skinned middle-aged men and women, typical tourists, came down the steep, narrow gravel slope holding on to each other to keep from falling. Kiyo stopped under a cherry blossom tree lushly covered with dark green leaves to let two of them pass, then headed up toward the castle rampart.

At the top of her climb, the gravel path opened onto a red clay courtyard framed by a grass lawn. The borders of the courtyard rose up in two or three tiers, and behind it the castle wall spread out its flowing hem in graceful waves of stone. Kiyo walked around the lawn and sat down on a bench. Two high school students, who seemed to be sweethearts, yelled to each other as they played badminton. Both were barefoot, and two pairs of shoes were lined up neatly on the red clay. For some reason, Kiyo got goose bumps and averted her eyes. She stood up hurriedly and fled.

From where she stood on the rampart, Tsuken Island was hidden from view in a mist. Beneath the low clouds, a large helicopter circled overhead, flashing a red light. A huge tanker was slowly heading out to sea below. A damp, dark wind had begun to blow, carrying big rain-drops.

WHEN Kiyo returned to B.C. Street, the sun was starting to disappear behind the clouds. The light from the street lamps, which had been turned on too early, played across the tops of the bottle palms in rows along the curb. Soldiers strolled peacefully in the soft breezes at twi-light. Some looked at photographs from the floorshows on signboards propped up against the entrances to bars and cabarets. Some lined up at the hot dog counter. Others leaned against the telegraph poles, cast-ing lonely gazes at passersby. One middle-aged soldier stood next to Pinocchio Burger with his back to the street. Kiyo approached him.

"Evening," she said.

"Good evening," he replied, in a more youthful voice than she had expected.

"Wanna make love?"

The soldier remained silent and shook his head.

"Suit yourself," Kiyo said, laughing awkwardly as she passed by. She regretted having spoken to him.

After she had been walking a while, she spotted two very drunken soldiers coming toward her. Kiyo stopped, said "Hi," then made her approach. "Hey, soldier, wanna come with me?"

"Where to?" one of the drunks stopped to ask.

"It's up to you."

An image of Sammy watching television floated into her mind. She had noticed lately that Sammy would sometimes watch television with tears in his eyes.

"Go with you and do what?"

"Make love, of course."

"With you?" He laughed loudly, dragging the other drunken sol-dier away. Kiyo turned her back on them. It was no use wasting her time on those drunks. She hurried away, heading back toward Pinocchio Burger.

Kiyo went up to the counter and ordered a hot dog. A man in a triangular hat silently wrapped the hot dog in a napkin and thrust it toward her. Kiyo withdrew into the shadow of the building and bit into it. Her money was fast running out. With what she had left, she couldn't even buy Sammy a pack of American cigarettes.

Lately there were fewer soldiers on the street. Maybe her "unemployment" continued because she was old and had lost her appeal. Still, how could anyone make a living in this business with so few soldiers around? A feeling of helplessness blew up from under her feet like the cold wind.

I could go to the black soldiers' district in Miyazato.

She heard that black G.I.s still came around sometimes where she used to work at the top of Miyazato Hill. Maybe guys who'd been turned away at the bars around Camp Hansen were there now, looking for a good time. Kiyo wiped her mouth with a napkin and hailed a taxi.

SHE got off at the entrance to the Ginten shopping street. The arcade was lined on both sides with shoe stores, coffee shops, stores selling household goods, and other shops. Kiyo dragged her feet slowly along the needlessly wide street. At the end of the arcade, she entered the area of bars where she used to work. She stepped onto the asphalt sidewalk and felt a slight pain in the pit of her stomach.

Kiyo turned the corner at the fabric store. From here, if she went down the side street, she would be at the place where she used to work. The smell of damp air assaulted her nose as she turned the corner. Kiyo stopped and looked around. Dirty cinder blocks. A rotting wooden fence. Houses with sagging clay-tiled roofs.

She climbed the gentle asphalt slope and recognized the little stone plaque marking the end of the street. Looking up, she saw the faded T-frame eave of the familiar Pittsburgh Bar that seemed to be looking down at her. Kiyo dusted off the stone steps in front of the rusted screen door and sat down. She took a cigarette out of her bag, lit up, and puffed on it a while, her eyes fixed on the far end of the alley where the veil of twilight slowly descended. Identical dirty cement buildings stood silently in a row. On the corner to her left was the bar Manhattan, on the corner to her right was the Niagara. Next to that was the Seven Star, and halfway down the hill was the New York. . . .

She recalled the face of her friend Sumiko, who worked the Manhattan. She wondered what had happened to Sumiko, who always used to talk about how she was going to save up the money to get her front teeth replaced. Then there was dim-witted Hiromi from Iheya who always used to talk about how she'd been sold off to pay her parents' debts, almost as if she was boasting. She got pregnant many times by black soldiers and always had an abortion. Once, she came to Kiyo to borrow money, saying that she was going into the hospital. She said Anderson would give her twenty dollars on payday, and she promised to return the money as soon as she got it from him. So Kiyo had lent it to her, but she never came around again.

Kiyo was reminiscing about acquaintances from the past as she peeled her nail polish when, out of the corner of her eye, she saw something small and black moving nearby. Next to some garbage bags at the end of the alley a cat was sitting with its front paws together staring at Kiyo. The cat was big, and Kiyo stared back for a while. It seemed interested in the plastic bag near her and was glancing back and forth between the bag and Kiyo's face. Kiyo glared at the cat, which got up, arched its back, and walked away.

After the cat had gone, Kiyo suddenly felt tired and wanted to lie down. She leaned up against the stone plaque and closed her eyes. From the top of the hill, she heard the sound of an empty can rolling. As she opened her eyes, an image of the cat flashed into her mind. She turned to look toward the garbage bags and saw an empty soda can roll slowly by, picking up speed as it tumbled down the asphalt street before falling into the gutter in front of the Niagara. When she looked back at the garbage bags, she saw that the cat had returned. Poking its nose into a hole it had ripped in one of the bags, it glared at her from time to time out of the corner of its eye.

"Ma'am"

Kiyo heard a voice and turned around. The blurred outline of a black face floated in the semi-darkness. The white eyes hurriedly looked away.

He must be disappointed.

"Excuse me?" Kiyo said.

"No, no, forget it." The soldier took two or three steps back as if to indicate that he had mistaken her for someone else and then turned around. Kiyo spit loudly at him as he walked away.

A pack of dogs ran right by Kiyo. The lead dog stopped, looked back at her, and stood motionless, watching her intently. Kiyo remained seated and pretended to pick up a rock. The dog turned and ran away, with the others following close behind, until they had all disappeared around a corner.

. 4 .

WHEN SHE REACHED the paint store on the corner, Kiyo saw a light coming from her apartment. She walked faster, entered the lot at the end of the winding asphalt street, and dashed up the stairs. Bright fluorescent light seeped out from the small window. She turned the knob and called out Sammy's name as she bounded into the room. There was no answer.

"Hey," she called out again, but there was no sign of Sammy. Kiyo stood paralyzed in the middle of the floor. She wondered if he had gone back to his unit. Maybe he'd given up his dream of crossing over to Honshū or Kyushu that he talked about so often.

Where could he have gone?

After a quick stop in the bathroom, Kiyo grabbed her handbag and dashed outside. She retraced her steps back to B.C. Street. Behind the Caravan bar was a house where Tom Moore, a friend of Sammy's, was renting a room. Sammy could have gone there.

Kiyo walked faster when she got to B.C. Street. Moore's room was just off the street. She went around to the side entrance of the Caravan and called out from under his window.

"Corporal Moore."

The window opened immediately. "Well, if it isn't Kiyo," he said.

"Sammy isn't there, is he?"

"Sammy?"

"Private Samuel Copeland."

"Oh, the deserter?"

"He comes around here a lot, doesn't he?"

"Yeah, but he hasn't been here today."

"Oh . . . thanks a lot."

"Is everything okay?"

"Uh-huh. He's probably at the pachinko parlor."

Kiyo rushed out of the alley. Where could Sammy have gone? She looked in at the nearby pachinko parlor but didn't see him. She went out onto Goya Boulevard to look in at each of the two or three large pachinko parlors there but saw no sign of Sammy. Where could he have gone?

I wonder if he went back to his unit.

Kiyo's legs trembled. She had heard that if a deserter returns to his unit he is immediately placed in a holding cell at Kawasaki and sent from there back to the U.S. Could Sammy have resigned himself to being sent back and returned to his company? No way. *Maybe he's already back at the apartment,* she thought. *Or maybe he's just taking a short walk around the neighborhood.* Before she knew it, Kiyo was heading back toward the Kamaara Apartments. Her pace gradually quickened. At the end of the winding road, she arrived at the front of the apartment building. There was a light in the window.

I thought I turned it off when I left.

Kiyo's heart danced. She rushed up the stairs and pulled on the doorknob. The door opened easily. The room overflowed with bright fluorescent light. Sammy was not back.

I guess I must have left it on when I ran out.

Kiyo threw her handbag down on the table and fell onto the bed. She lay facing upward without moving for a while. Then she got up slowly and lit a cigarette.

Where is he? Did he really go back to his unit? That boy who hated the military so.

If Sammy had returned to his unit, she would never see him again. Kiyo rose staggering to her feet as if she were losing her mind.

He didn't go back. He wouldn't . . . I know. He probably went to the yacht harbor. . . . But why would he want to go there in the middle of the night?

Suddenly the door flew open as if blown by a gust of wind and Sammy entered. Kiyo's slender shoulders dropped. She felt as if she were going to cry.

"Where were you?" Her voice was shrill and trembling.

"I went over to Gate Street."

"If you walk around too much the M.P.s will catch you."

"Never mind that," he said with resignation. "It's all over."

Sammy clasped his hands behind his head and fell onto the bed. He lay there without a word. Kiyo also said nothing. The silence continued for some time.

"Is there any beer?" he asked.

"No, should I go and buy some?"

"No, it's okay."

Again there was silence.

"You know, I . . ." Sammy raised his eyes to look at Kiyo. Kiyo quickly averted her gaze. She anticipated his words with her entire body. Her legs trembled.

"I made a phone call. . . ."

Kiyo said nothing.

"I told them I'd be at the front gate tomorrow morning at ten."

Kiyo felt as if she'd been hit over the head with a two-by-four. She saw stars before her eyes. "I see," she said.

She tried to laugh, but the skin on her cheeks only twitched. She tried to smile, but she couldn't tell if she was succeeding. As she lay next to Sammy and closed her eyes, she felt as if her body were sinking into the floor. Sammy's sweaty palm reached out for her thigh. When she opened her eyes, she saw his sullen expression. Kiyo brushed his hand away and got up. Her head ached to the core. She walked away from the bed, then turned around.

"Sammy, let's run away together. Let's go to my island. No one will come looking for you there. I know lots of empty houses," she said.

"To Tsuken Island, the one you're always talking about?"

"Yeah. It's got lots of abandoned houses. They're old, but they have gardens and fields. I'll cut the grass. And you can fix the broken storm doors and floorboards."

Sammy closed his eyes and shook his head firmly from side to side. "If they catch you, they'll send you home. You want to go anyway?"

"I don't care. It's all over," Sammy muttered, as if to convince himself, and turned his back to Kiyo.

KIYO stood under the shower. For some reason, she'd suddenly wanted to bathe. She washed her body carefully and then stood in front of the mirror. Wrapping her hair in a towel, she stared at her reflection. Her eyes sparkled inside the pallor of her face. She peered at herself and laughed, though it looked like she was crying. The bags under her eyes seemed to have doubled in size.

Kiyo wrapped herself in a towel. As she got out of the shower, she could hear Sammy snoring. Somehow it sounded louder than usual to her. She brushed her hair carefully, then tied it back with a ribbon as she listened to Sammy snore. The kettle whistled. She threw her towel down on the makeup table and poured herself coffee. After quickly finishing two cups, she put down the empty cup and opened her dresser. She took out a gaudy pink dress but decided against it. For some reason, Kiyo suddenly felt like wearing Japanese clothes. She took out her Kumejima kimono, which she stored at the bottom of the dresser, and stared at it vacantly for a while. The snoring stopped and Sammy turned over.

Standing in front of the mirror, Kiyo finished tying her obi and then meticulously applied her makeup. Next, she got up and closed the window. As she was locking it, she heard the thunderous roar of a jet testing its engine in the distance. Checking the lock on the door, she went into the kitchen, where she opened the propane gas jets, turning on all three. Then she walked back to the bed, leaving the kitchen door open, and lay down. Perhaps her state of mind caused her to feel she was quickly losing consciousness. She thought she'd try counting to a thousand. As she began, she suddenly felt thirsty and got up to take a drink of water. When she staggered back into bed, Sammy turned over again and began to sit up. Now Kiyo picked up the lighter that was next to the bed. Lying flat on her stomach, she placed a soft pillow on top of her head. Then, gathering her resolve, she turned the flint wheel with a click.

TRANSLATED BY YUKIE OHTA

YAMANOHA NOBUKO (1941-)

Yamanoha was born in Nago, in northern Okinawa, where she lives today. She is among a growing number of Okinawan writers, many of them women, who began publishing in local forums during the 1980s and whose stories focus not on the war or occupation, but rather on contemporary Okinawan life in relation to the natural landscape and traditional religious beliefs. As of September 1999, Yamanoha had written fifty-five stories, most of which were published in the small-circulation magazines of private literary circles. "Will o' the Wisp" (Onibi), however, appeared in the Ryūkyū shinpō in 1985 and won the newspaper's Short Story Prize for that year. This story draws on a local superstition that the ghosts of drowning victims pull others into the ocean to assuage their chagrin.

WILL O' THE WISP

YAMANOHA NOBUKO

MOMMY, MOMMY.

The voice was faint at first and didn't register. Through thick layers it reached her, jolting her to consciousness. She wanted to wriggle, but she couldn't move, as if steel reinforcements ran through the center of her body. She felt trapped in cement, gooey cement that had just been poured around her body without leaving her an inch of space. She opened her eyes suddenly, which smarted immediately from the cold. It was water, the weight of water that was constricting her. Saltiness assailed her nostrils and overflowed into her already open mouth. *The sea!* she shouted, and the pressure of the water thrust her upward, knocking her against some rocks. She felt the back of her head and her spine being gently crushed. Bubbles glistened in a row along a single strand of her disheveled, swaying black hair. There was no sunlight; only the glow of the water gave the dimness its form. A ceiling of stone; below, only the dark depths. Something like mist settled around her; shuddering, she felt as if goblin-like creatures were gushing from her in rapid succession. She floated face down, her arms extended above her. Fishes of all sizes and kinds schooled around her, nibbling on her body. She felt no pain—only a strange lingering itchiness. Looking around, she saw innumerable small bugs squirming everywhere in the water, drifting and dissolving in it as if they made up its very substance. The bugs, forming a ring and coiling around her like smoke, pricked her skin. The itchiness abated. It was as though the water bugs had settled in her central nervous system. She felt as cold as if she had been shut up, half-cooked, in a freezer. This was the middle of an ocean begging to be described as muddy, it was so filled with tiny living things. There, in a tunnel connecting the *yato*, the big hollows in the immense reef: that's where Yūko was. Perhaps she had drowned; her body seemed swollen, and her clothes were torn.

Where are you? Yūko asked, searching for the voice.

I'm here! In here.

The voice came from her belly. "Ah!" she gasped, startled. She noticed her body, plump like a *medaka* fish, a vivid reminder that she was seven months along.

Am I . . . not going to be born?

A boy's voice called from inside her. The voiced seeped through a membrane in her belly, a membrane not quite yellow though not transparent either, a membrane oddly sticky like the film on milk.

Oh? You're a boy. Can you see Mommy? Yūko was shocked to hear the word "Mommy" coming from her own mouth.

I can't see you, but I think I understand.

I see.

She felt a strange tickle. A child was definitely growing in her womb—a boy, the child of Nakajima Kazuhiko.

Mommy, am I not going to be born? the voice in her belly asked a second time.

Could she give birth to this child?

Yūko looked on as a fish chewed off pieces of her flesh. Her skin, as white as if bleached, split open here and there like a ripe pomegranate, and blood oozed out from one vein after another only to vanish. Her body felt slippery like a fish. She had a twinge of apprehension as the black wall of water beat against her. Staring at the large fish directly in front of her eyes, Yūko thought, *Maybe this little boy is merely borrowing the sack in my belly. If my belly were ripped open, he would be sucked out into the water and could be raised by fish, like a baby raised by gorillas in the jungle.* By this time, she could clearly see the little boy floating in the sac. *Does he want to be born that much?* Yūko asked herself, now feeling a touch of envy.

You'll be born, I'm sure.

Just as you can make a cookie of any shape with the right cookie cutter, at the right time and place, you can tell any lie.

Your father's a charming man. And he's a policeman. You understand, right? A fine person.

I have a father?

Of course you do. I'm sure he'll be happy, too.

But even as she spoke, Yūko knew it was unlikely that Kazuhiko would be happy. If Yūko had drowned, why hadn't he saved her? Or, if Kazuhiko had drowned with her, why was he nowhere to be seen? An indescribable anxiety overcame her.

I . . . I know all about it. As the child spoke, he seemed on the verge of laughing.

Know what? Yūko asked dejectedly.

That Daddy said to get rid of me.

Yūko hesitated. The child had obviously overheard her conversations with Kazuhiko.

So what did you think, honey? Were you sad? she asked caustically.

I don't know. I guess it doesn't matter either way.

His answer relieved her. Yet this time she'd really wanted to have the baby, no matter what. She didn't care any more that Kazuhiko had a wife and children. It wasn't that Yūko wanted a child so much. But his wife was pregnant, too. It just wasn't fair that she could have a child and Yūko couldn't. So even when her belly had begun to show, she had brushed aside his comments, saying she'd gained weight. Kazuhiko's eyes revealed his mounting suspicions, and finally the day came when he blew up. When Yūko told him she was much too far along for an abortion, he had screamed, "Get it taken care of, even if it means a stay in the hospital!" Retorting that this was not the sort of thing that he could resolve by shouting, she had felt calm and cool.

"Even if I have the child, I won't bother you. I can handle raising one kid." Yūko spoke confidently as she placed her hand on her belly.

"Don't be a fool. You know taking care of the child isn't the problem. You just try raising a kid on your own. It'll grow up like a broken bauble. It might be okay shut away in your private treasure box, but it won't make it in the outside world. Think of the poor child!"

"I see. So you're saying children are just adornments for couples?"

"That's not what I meant. . . ." Kazuhiko rubbed out a cigarette he had just begun smoking and lit another.

"I'm not even asking you to admit you're the father. Don't jump to conclusions. That's what you were thinking, right? I mean, I'm not asking you to walk around with a sign announcing that you're his dad. That would be even harder for the kid."

Then, making the most of Kazuhiko's silence, Yūko pressed on.

"By now, you ought to know better about women's bodies. I've been scraped out twice already and you're telling me to get rid of it again? This is a child with human form, arms and legs all in place. You think only wives are worthy of becoming mothers? No way—you won't treat me like some dirty old rag."

Kazuhiko had said nothing.

"It's not that I don't know how you feel. You're just like other men: you don't have what it takes to juggle two women. I was just a convenient midnight snack, isn't that right? I knew it all along."

Silence.

Seeing that Kazuhiko, who had stood up, was now slouched over in distress, Yūko wanted to drive him even further into a corner. She felt triumphant, as though she'd caught a demon by the tail. Kazuhiko had never once hinted at marriage. While she hadn't really been deceived, she felt betrayed. It was as if she'd been made to wear a yellow dress she'd been told was white.

Even if Kazuhiko hadn't asked her to have an abortion, Yūko was planning to get one right away. And if she hadn't bumped into Kazuhiko's wife at the hospital, she probably would have gone ahead without thinking much about it . They were both three months along. Kazuhiko's wife had said "Thank you," politely bowing again and again to the plump doctor. As Yūko's mask, so like a ceramic doll, began to crumble, she sensed that something she held dear had shattered. Now she wouldn't care if some incident were to turn everything on its head.

"Have a child, and next thing you know you won't be able to get married. I won't give you any trouble. Just get rid of it."

Kazuhiko was only repeating the usual platitudes, but his words "next thing you know" stung her. His ego, swollen like a convex mirror, gave her a feeling of loneliness she was determined to overcome. No, I won't do it, she said curtly. Then Kazuhiko calmly tried to persuade her, explaining that he didn't like children himself and hadn't had them because he wanted them, but only because a married couple wouldn't look like a married couple without them.

"Well, I've done it twice already. So I guess I can get rid of a third." The words were on the tip of her tongue, ready to come out, but she swallowed them and only nodded slightly. Kazuhiko, seeming entirely reassured, got up from the sofa and came over to her.

"You're always driving yourself crazy by trying to add something to your life, you dummy." He poked Yūko's forehead as he spoke. Kazuhiko's crude words grated on her like whiskers scratching her skin.

Why was Yūko attracted to this man? The reasons were murky, like sludge in water's depths. . . . She had passed her first year with him dreaming foolish dreams; the second, in contrast, feeling like the firm leaf of a *fukugi* tree; the third and fourth, flushing away blood clots. Then the fifth year a scab formed from the pus of dreams and love and blood. Could that be it? When she totaled the pluses and minuses, it all seemed so simple, but each time she stopped to think, she only ended up starting from zero again. Everything had happened inside a ball filled with air, a ball that never let anything in from the outside. She felt only explosive ennui and kept staring at those round walls.

One reason they had met was that Yūko's house was behind the police box. But the most important factor in their relationship was that they were simply a man and a woman: they had joined like a twisted doughnut and exuded a shameful animal odor, ugly and intense. Who the partner was made no difference.

After Yūko's mother died, leaving her alone, Kazuhiko came sneaking into her bed night after night, rushing away when the phone in the police box rang. Nearly all of their rendezvous were limited to his days on duty; that's how timid a man he was.

If I am born, will I get to see both Daddy's face and Mommy's face? the voice in her belly asked. Yūko remained silent, lost for an answer.

I won't get to? the voice in her belly asked once more, sounding worried.

Honey, do you want to see us? Yūko asked.

Uh-huh. The boy sounded thoughtful at first but then spoke emphatically, saying, *Yes, I want to see you.*

Why? she asked. He must surely know he won't be welcomed.

Because not seeing you makes me anxious.

Yūko was alarmed. Had this child been in her belly feeling anxious all this time, with that tiny little body? For the first time Yūko felt sorry about how she had treated him.

Don't worry. You're a good boy. Of course you'll see us, just as soon as you're born.

Yūko stifled an urge to cry. She sensed that the child in her belly breathed a sigh of relief and was smiling. That innocent smile weighed heavily on her. Why had a new life lodged itself in her body? Vague pangs of regret began budding within her.

There are still three months to go. Don't rush it. Once again she lied.

Okay, I won't. Do I have any brothers and sisters?

Yes, you do. A boy in second grade and a girl about to be three. And there's a child your age, too. You won't be lonely, I'm sure.

Yūko stopped there. She couldn't bear to imagine this scenario, one in which she played no part. She wasn't thinking of him as someone connected to her. She simply couldn't rid herself of the feeling that he was merely borrowing her womb. She lacked feelings of love for the child in the way that someone color-blind lacked a sense of color. She saw maternal instinct as something like packaged instant food (just add water); children were like sweet gelatin dissolved in one's hand, about which one could casually ask, should I eat this or should I throw it away? Kazuhiko had been on the mark when he had said that she just wanted to "add something" to her life. She had begun to feel burdened by the chore of speaking to the child sweetly.

When's Daddy coming? the voice in her belly asked.

Yūko felt like saying, *Be serious.* She wanted to organize her thoughts a bit. Being holed up in the water with this baby boy, just the two of them, was unbearably depressing.

Your Daddy got transferred to the next town. But he'll come once a week. He promised. Your Daddy likes fish. And there are so many fish swimming here, he'll come to catch them for sure.

Since his transfer, Kazuhiko hadn't come to Yūko's place even one time. They had spoken just once, and he'd asked her to meet him. That encounter was their last.

It wasn't clear in her mind whether there had been a call from Kazuhiko or whether she had called him; only the red-yellow-white-black-pink telephone passed before her eyes. Her memory was a fog, but she was fairly certain that Kazuhiko had never called her before that. Yūko had called him continually. During her lunch break from work, from the coffee shop behind her office, from public telephones on the street, and at night from her own place. Perhaps on that day as always Kazuhiko had just been calling her back. On those days he would say he was sorry and promise to call back in half an hour. Yūko, staring at the second hand on her watch, waited for the call. When exactly thirty minutes had passed, the phone rang. The sound of Kazuhiko's breath filled her ears. He said, "I'm leaving now so meet me—" at such and such a bus stop at such and such a time and tried to hang up. But Yūko hurriedly asked, "Are you on vacation?" Kazuhiko said that he was working but that he could take some time off, as long as he got back by tomorrow afternoon. Yūko was happy. She relished the feeling, which was like plunging her hands into the middle of a pile of precious metals and jewels, scooping them up, and letting them spill out between her fingers. They had lots of things to discuss. She had gotten carried away, talking and talking, when she heard a click as the coin fell.

At 9:00 P.M. Yūko walked to the bus stop behind her house. The road was paved and wide, but there were few buildings; it was surrounded by sugarcane fields. As she passed by an unusually large shop selling Buddhist altars, the smell of a strange incense wafted through the air. After its shutters clanged shut, the street grew dark. Next to it stood a newly built hardware store and a stationery shop, but their shutters had already been lowered. The deserted road was slightly eerie.

The round beam of her flashlight fluttered about. . . . After a bus, without a single rider and filled only with desolate light, passed, she was left in darkness.

Just as she arrived at the bus stop a dark car pulled up beside her. Kazuhiko, as if hesitating to pause there for even a moment, started accelerating as Yūko got in.

Yūko had planned what she was going to say, but the instant she saw Kazuhiko's sunken eyes, the words got stuck in her throat. Finally she was able to say, "I've been wanting to see you." "Me too," said Kazuhiko, but he brushed away her hand from where she had rested it on his thigh, and returned it to her own lap. She had the sensation that Kazuhiko's hairy legs, which she had felt through his pants, were slipping easily between her thighs.

Yūko looked straight ahead, silent. There was no music either; the car was filled only with the sound of the engine as it took the shoreline road. From time to time the lights of oncoming cars flashed across their faces. Kazuhiko looked at the ocean and muttered to himself, "I wonder if there's time before low tide." The sound of the waves, soft and shallow, droned on. To the left, ocean; to the right, mountains. At the base of the mountains where there was a cluster of houses, it was dark and hushed. Forlorn outdoor lights shone here and there. They passed a group of houses, and then another, but after twenty or thirty minutes, they had come to a place surrounded only by mountains and sea.

Kazuhiko drove the car into the woods and stopped. They were at the northernmost tip of the island; below them, the sea lay dark and stagnant. Kazuhiko, silent, drew Yūko to him. Yūko listened to the conversation of the waves and the wind and the leaves, and to the pounding in Kazuhiko's chest. Some soundless signal was being sent to her from inside her womb. She wanted to sigh with contentment. Kazuhiko promised that he would come around to see her once a week. He even touched her belly, if just for a second. At that moment, Yūko felt glad she hadn't given up the child. They sat in the car for about thirty minutes and then walked down a gentle stone slope toward the ocean.

They had come once last winter. She remembered being frightened at the total darkness. When she had dipped her foot in the water, all the hair on her body had stood on end, and she had shivered. The water surface was covered with innumerable ripples, sparkling brilliantly. It looked like molten metal, fluid as syrup, swimming about. Then it wrapped itself coldly around her ankles. She had raised her foot suddenly, splashing water around, and shouted with joy. She had felt afraid, afraid that some absurdly large slimy slab of a creature would grab her foot and pull her out to sea.

"WAH!" she had shouted, and Kazuhiko, laughing, yelled back, "What's the matter?" She felt as though she had been left all alone in the open sea. She clung to Kazuhiko's arms. As they moved farther and farther out, the waves, which had sounded so far away, began to resound like a storm right beside her. She had looked around. She couldn't see the mountains and didn't know which way the land was. All was endless space, blanketed in darkness. They were moving through a blackness like lacquer. All they had to depend on was the light they had brought. The sound of the waves had overwhelmed her; her ears began to ring. The chilly wind beat against her mercilessly. Her hair stood on end, wildly disheveled.

"The tide is coming in," Yūko kept screaming.

Kazuhiko had been calm. He just laughed and said, "Don't worry, don't worry."

He had stopped suddenly, catching an octopus by the head, or so she had thought. Nimbly, he spun his arms around and threw the octopus into the trap on his back. As if gasping for breath, the octopus spread its arms in the bottom of the trap and stuck them out through the openings. Its body changed color and made waves in the water. Kazuhiko had caught a lot of octopuses that night. Yūko had laughed bitterly to herself, wondering whom he had eaten them with.

But tonight when he had asked her to come to the ocean, Yūko still had nonetheless unwittingly given an enthusiastic reply.

"Today I'll take you to the *yato*," Kazuhiko said.

"What's a *yato*?" Yūko asked.

"It's a deep hole," he answered, "with loads of fish swimming in it. I'll dive; all you have to do is stand there and watch. It's incredibly beautiful."

The water was cold. Long-armed starfish were everywhere. The surging waves were so rough and loud that it seemed a huge wave could break over them at any time. Kazuhiko walked along, pulling Yūko by the hand. All they could see was the area lit by their flashlight. Beyond it was complete darkness. There weren't even any stars. But Yūko didn't feel afraid as she had the time before. Although only faintly, she could make out the mountains there, the beach there, Kazuhiko's car over there. She was wearing flip-flops, and she almost fell several times, only to be caught by Kazuhiko. She walked carefully, trying to avoid the slippery rocks. She felt happy and soon found herself yawning. "What's the matter?" Kazuhiko asked. "I'm a little sleepy," she said, feeling odd, as if she had been placed in the middle of a mirage. "All right, I'll give you a piggyback ride," Kazuhiko said, and quickly hoisted her up on his back. The pressure Yūko felt on her belly was painful. But soon she was giggling. She had a sweet drunken feeling, and Kazuhiko's broad shoulders felt sturdy, dependable. From her place on his shoulders she could see far off into the ocean. The sea, which should have been black, glimmered bright white as if ice were floating on it. From above the surface, a single leaf blew toward them, glowing with a flare of piercing green light, and finally blowing into her eyes. She clearly saw the notches like a saw blade around the edge of the leaf. The saw made a gnashing noise as it circled in her brain. Her skull cracked. There was no pain, but the sounds of flesh being ground to a pulp, of water gently splashing, and of the slicing wind—countless such sounds rang deep in her ears, and she became acutely conscious of a numbness enveloping her arms and legs. Yūko repeatedly opened and closed her eyelids, trying hard to say something. Her tongue was tangled and her consciousness had drifted far away. Occasionally she was aware that she was babbling incoherently. In a millionth of a second countless dreams passed before her eyes. Above all, she was sleepy. But if she went to sleep now, she sensed, it would all be over. In the corner of her mind, a voice shouted, *You can't sleep now, don't sleep now!* Under no circumstance should she sleep. But her body would not listen. She heard her own snoring and started awake. *It must have been that coffee, the coffee we drank in the car; it had poison in it! You're not tired, you're a man, and maybe you can take it because you're stronger. Listen, this is really weird! Are you listening? It's poison, POISON!* Yūko was trying to pound Kazuhiko on the back, but her body was heavy, or was it light? It might be heavy like lead, or on the other hand, light like a balloon. Perhaps her body had melted away, for she had lost almost all sense that she existed—not in the form of a surface, a line, a speck, or even a heat wave. She couldn't move, not even a wriggle. She had fallen asleep without seeing a single fish, it seemed. During her long sleep, she had been awakened for a moment by the terrible cold. As she kicked her legs wildly in a struggle against her unfathomable fear, she felt the salt water penetrating her throat like a rope. When she suddenly opened her eyes wide, Kazuhiko was pushing her head down. The light entered her pupils, and she thought she glimpsed a terrifying expression on his face.

Had that been a dream? Or was this a dream now? A moray eel, looking much like a log—it was nearly two meters long—came and nibbled on her ear. The moray had blue-black specks on its glossy white body, specks on its lips, and specks all the way inside its mouth. It spread its jaws wide, opening its tongueless and entirely flesh-covered mouth, and bit into the flesh on Yūko's arm; then it nibbled and swallowed, nibbled and swallowed. As it showed its rows of jagged white teeth, its lips wriggled like obese earthworms. Fuzz resembling the sprouts of rice plants clung to the chunks of meat slipping from its mouth and fluttering downward. *If they were thousands of times bigger, they might make a rice paddy,* Yūko thought hysterically. Fish suddenly gathered to devour the scraps of meat. Yūko's flesh had become merely feed for the fish.

Yūko's eyes were one with the water. Slowly but surely, her vision was growing clearer.

Light shone faintly from the dense layers deep inside a table of coral. There was also coral completely covered with protrusions as well as vegetable corals in green and pink; from between them peered other coral resembling a human brain. Sea grasses like blood vessels and ferns like braided hair undulated in the water. Soft cockscomb coral looked like smashed, bloody flesh; the starfish, like part of a woman's thigh; sponges and sea worms, like multicolored trinkets; a clumsy sea slug, like a worm that gnaws at putrid flesh. She surveyed the scene and mused to herself, *Just as the ocean has graveyards for coral, mightn't it have a graveyard for women as well?*

There were fish attired in brilliantly colored scales, sporting blue teeth, wearing green and yellow lipstick, making her think they had anticipated human fashions. And yet, seeing a school of fish with black striped patterns like prisoners' uniforms, she laughed sadly. There were some fish, looking so much like hand-blown glass, that calmly fluttered their dorsal fins as they cut through the water; other schools looked like glass fragments rising to the surface, their transparent bodies lighting up as they darted upward. Some sat motionless in dark places as if they had forgotten to swim, while others never tired of playing games of tag. There were not only bright red ones that looked as if their bodies were covered in blood and fat ones like lumps of flesh, but others wiry like string as well. Fish so black you couldn't believe their flesh was white, fish that looked as if they'd been painted fluorescent blue; purple fish, yellow, green, gold, silver, hundreds more colors, shapes, and strangely patterned dazzling creatures dancing about wildly. Seeming to envelop them were lozenge-like drops that floated to the surface.

No matter where you chose to look, the sea would be beautiful, but Yūko was bothered by the spotted fish in front of her. If it were going to delve into her body, it should go ahead and do so, but instead it kept its mouth open, opening and closing a bit of flesh that could have been either tongue or gums. It was making a low sucking sound. In addition to its large teeth it had a row of smaller pink ones. Its eyeballs moved continually, and when other fish approached, it wheeled around and chased them away. Somehow it seemed to think that she was food for it alone.

The light was fading. The sea around her grew dim, and finally pitch-black. The fish returned to their respective pods and slept, eyes open. Some slept wrapped in blankets of mucus. The big fish right in front of her was no doubt sleeping as well, but silver circles around its eyes shone, making it appear to be crying.

She saw flickers of light everywhere in the water. Waves broke and then vanished like the flow of the Milky Way. Though it was hard to make out, she could see green coral suddenly releasing a larva, which then began to drift. *It's a full moon!* Yūko thought. She had heard from someone that it was on the night of a full moon that the green coral released a larva, which would then set off on its own journey. For days, weeks, the larva would travel at the will of the waves, at the will of the tide—and if at the end of its travels it were lucky enough to attach itself to a rock bed, it would be able to go on living. Her little boy should have been able to go on living without parents, too. . . .

If tonight were a full moon, it meant it had been nearly a month since she had come here. She was fairly certain she had been wearing a watch, but she had taken it off and left it in the car with her rings. Even in the dark water she could distinguish night and day. It would have been simple to calculate the days, but at this point she thought, *What's the use?*

The water made a gurgling sound as it was sucked in with the ebb of the tide, and when it bubbled up that was the tide coming in. The tides, perhaps the breaths of the sea, continued their eternal motion. Yūko felt weary—from the water that wouldn't stop for even a moment, from the boy who wouldn't let her forget his presence for even a moment.

If her body would only float to the surface, someone might find her. She tried to escape the tunnel by riding on the tide, but her clothes might have been caught on something, for even when the waves beat against her, she merely floated around inside the coral arch. If she could only find her way to the *yato* she could float to the surface. In the ocean there were many *yato*, and they each had names, Kazuhiko had said. If lightning had struck there, Lightning *Yato*, if a foreigner had died there, America *Yato;* if she and the little boy were found, would it be called Mother and Child *Yato?* Then she began to think that her little boy probably wouldn't be able to breathe air in the other world. If he went to the other world as a seven-month-old fetus, he would remain a seven-month-old fetus, unclothed, with stiff arms and legs, eyes not yet open, with a childish charm as yet undeveloped. The umbilical cord still dangling, he would feel only that twinge of uneasiness. Her mind filled with these thoughts, she trembled.

Yūko had been five years old. She had been playing with her mother's hair. Then her mother, combing out the dandruff, had said, for some unknown reason, "If you get too much dandruff, you'll turn into a fish." For a long time, Yūko hadn't been able to forget those words. She couldn't stand pale-gray scaly dandruff flickering in front of her eyes. She had dreams in which naked people writhed all over the ocean floor, and innumerable flakes of dandruff shining in rainbow colors floated about in the water. Every day she worried that her mother was going to become a fish, and about what she would do if her mother became a fish. Could it really be true that her mother was going to become a fish? Someone else told her that fish scales were made of dandruff, and she began obsessing over whether this might actually be true. When she saw a fish on the cutting board, it seemed to have human form. She had felt a horrifying anxiety. Fish, big and small, of this kind and that, even though they had no voices, appeared to be talking about something, to be laughing among themselves. They looked content, probably because they could blow such foamy bubbles, but on the other hand they could have been complaining about something. Now her own flesh had become part of their flesh. Ultimately there had turned out to be some truth in her mother's words.

Did people worry from the time they were fetuses? Did they drag adult worries with them from the time they were sperm? Even now, dead, she was somehow fraught with worry. She wasn't worried by things with shapes, things she could see, things she could hear, things she knew. It was the things she couldn't see, the hazy, shapeless things, that unsettled her. She wasn't bothered by the boundless spray that enveloped her, every drop penetrating the tissues of her body, causing it to decompose. It was rather things hidden deeper within, goblins pushing her down just short of the point of no return. Whether they took the form of foam or ashes, the goblins continued to gnaw at her.

Yūko told herself that the little boy's uneasiness was not her fault. Even if she had given birth to him, could she really have raised him? She hadn't decided to give birth because she wanted him, or wanted to raise him, or because she saw some inherent value in life. No, it was just that she had wanted to test something. Even if the test had gone well and she had managed to bear a healthy baby, he might have been too much for her to handle and she might well have killed him. She knew that to her a child would be no more than a tool. *That's all your life would have been, honey,* she wanted to say to him. She was intensely lonely.

Mommy, said the voice in her belly once again.

Yūko pretended not to hear.

Mommy, Mommy, he continued to call.

Yūko was close to tears. *What's the matter, honey?* she answered.

It's dark, the voice in her belly said, and fell silent.

Yūko had the sensation that she could hear the boy's soft, tranquil breathing as he slept. Then, after a while, he called to Yūko again. He started calling perhaps every two or three hours. Yūko also had begun falling in and out of sleep.

As she was nodding off, suddenly she thought she felt someone open the door to the water and come bursting in. Someone was descending the water's shining white steps, bathed in moonlight. *Those footsteps, they must be Kazuhiko,* she thought. Yūko quickly spun her body around and lifted herself up like a snake raising its long neck or a tiger striking at its prey. She curled her ten fingers around imagined stakes and hurled them at Kazuhiko with both hands. Then she gestured as if pulling him toward her. Perhaps she had succeeded, for Kazuhiko moved nearer as if trapped in the net of her fingers. The first thing she noticed was the yellow slippers with the initials "K.N." Then she saw the gray pants and black belt, the gray jacket, the sadly smiling face, and the short hair; it was indisputably Kazuhiko. Yūko got up, her pure white veiled dress streaming, and showed Kazuhiko in. She spread her arms to greet him and stole a kiss. At that instant, he began to lose consciousness. In a flash, she ripped off his clothes and lifted his weightless body in her arms. After bathing him in a shell tub, she put him to sleep in a soft bed of sea anemones. The anemones gently stroked Kazuhiko's body with their innumerable manicured fingers. Yūko lay down at his side. The flames of candles fluttered everywhere in the water castle, and music was playing somewhere. A water iris became a gently swaying fan, and dazzlingly attired fish covered them with shining blue sheets of water. As Kazuhiko tossed in his sleep, he played with Yūko's hair.

"You're my sea-wife," he whispered.

"That's right," Yūko answered, and laughed alluringly.

The laugh woke her. But from somewhere she could hear Kazuhiko's snoring. A slight warmth lingered in the hand that had been stroking her hair. When she thought of Kazuhiko at her side, her garden as she had left it—filled with lilies and faded pink roses—flashed before her eyes. The white carnations she had cut and put in the shrine to her mother had probably all faded to a suntan beige. The clear droplets left on the flowers and leaves after the rain remained as they were, untainted.

She dreamt countless times that such droplets, without even a tinge of salty odor, were overflowing in her hands.

I want to wash my face with fresh water and rinse my mouth, she thought. She wanted to get rid of the slime on her body. She wanted to smell the fragrance of dirt. She wasn't certain that dirt had a smell, so she should have tried to really feel the dirt—to walk in the dirt barefoot as long as she could stand, to rub enough dirt on her body so that she would be bathing in it. As the beautiful ocean gradually opened up before her eyes, the desire to touch earth with her hands branded itself in her mind. She had longed for the sea, but she could feel her desire fade like the ebbing tide. Even the carved, beautiful shapes of coral now held less charm than a dead tree. It would be easier to love a poisonous mushroom than the abundant swaying seaweed, and though she was mingling now with the fish she had only been able to sigh over when she had asked their price at the market, they had no appeal. How sublime those insects had begun to seem! If she could become a mole and burrow her way under the soil at the ocean's bottom, she could reach the dry surface of the earth. If she could return now, she wouldn't kill a single insect, or pluck a single leaf. . . .

However, in the end, a dream was a dream; she didn't really care whether she was found and dissected on an autopsy table, or never found, just passed on over to the other world. It didn't matter. She just couldn't stand being exposed to the tides for weeks on end. The surface of her skin had transformed into the face of a ghost; it was not a good feeling to watch oneself be torn apart. She wanted to slip away like the sand in an hourglass.

"If I ever commit suicide, I'll do it in the ocean," Yūko had once said to Kazuhiko. "Why?" he had asked.

"I couldn't fail in the ocean. I can't swim," Yūko had said, laughing. Of course, she had meant it as a joke. She had also said that she didn't want a grave.

"Someone once said that the ocean is a grave without headstones. I think after I'm cremated I'll have my ashes scattered in the ocean."

Had Kazuhiko merely gone ahead and done what she had said she wanted? Not exactly, she thought. He had killed the child, not her, or so she wanted to believe.

Yūko passed the hours and days so bored she felt barely conscious. No one came. Sometimes a good deal of blood flowed from her body. When the water around her became bright red, Yūko had hallucinations she was being burned in an incinerator. *I'm being mourned by someone*, she had even comforted herself, but as ever, she remained submerged in water.

If I'm not discovered, then I'll have to entice someone and kill him, she vowed. Otherwise she and the little boy wouldn't be able to rest in peace. The laws of destiny were strange, but there was nothing she could do about them.

The water was tinged with dawn as the darkness receded. She could even hear the crowing of the cock, which should never have reached her ears. Day in and day out, watching the writhing of luminous bugs and shells, she waited for someone to come.

But many days passed and no one came. Yūko's and her son's bodies had vanished without a trace. Bit by bit, their flesh had turned into fish feed, or had decomposed and drifted away with the tide. Even the huge moray that had come nearly every day to eat Yūko's flesh had disappeared. Now she thought of the moray as a fond old friend. She had seen it off with a smile and watched it slither away, voluptuously twisting its dazzlingly shiny body. The fishes had eaten the little boy's flesh with relish as well. His gouged-out eyeballs floated in the water, pulled by a string-like substance. Yūko unconsciously lowered her gaze. The boy was looking at her. She was gripped by an inescapable agony.

Yūko's bones and her little boy's bones were now at the bottom of the ocean. The ocean floor was not silt like a river's bottom. There were mountains of coral blanketed in green seaweed, a carpet of white sand, thick seaweed filled with the tide, clams crawling with alluring tongues, innumerable fish of vibrant colors.

Yūko and her little boy escaped from the coral tunnel, leaving their grubby bones behind. They came out in a *yato* twisted like a map of the Japanese islands. It was low tide. Even so the *yato* was filled with brine. Blue flames floated everywhere on the sea's surface. Yūko and the boy were among them. They had become will o' the wisps skimming the surface of the ocean.

And then, Yūko saw Nakajima Kazuhiko, whom she longed for. Kazuhiko had come to dive for fish. Not far away large waves were thrashing wildly. He would dive for two or three hours until the waves closed in on him. It was a moonless, starless night, but each flame gave off rings of blue light. Kazuhiko was 200 meters ahead. He had a lamp on his forehead and wore a diving suit. He jumped into the water, making a loud splash. Coming toward her, he pointed an underwater gun straight in her direction. She feared she might be killed a second time. *That day, Kazuhiko had held my body down, hadn't he? Could it have been on purpose?* She still couldn't believe it, yet tears like the web of a spider covered her face in a veil.

Mommy, why are you crying? asked a tiny will o' the wisp.

Yūko's eyes were fixed on Kazuhiko. *See that person coming toward us? That's your daddy.* Yūko began to cry again.

If that's Daddy, why are you crying?

'Cause Daddy came just like he promised, and I'm happy.

Why don't you just call to him?

Even if I call him, he won't hear. Daddy can't see us. But we can pull him in. All you need to do, honey, is hold down his head.

Yūko was aghast. It wasn't Kazuhiko. She looked again, but it just wasn't Kazuhiko. It was a man she had never seen before. She started to say, *I'm sorry, honey, it's not your Daddy,* but she cut herself off. At this point, it didn't really matter. It didn't even matter much who the father was. Men spewed out countless sperm. All the creatures wriggling in the earth, all the creatures inhabiting the sewers—they were all men's children. But men no doubt saw them as wild grasses that had budded of their own free will.

The man in front of her might be a man she had never met, but she got the feeling that it wasn't a complete lie to say that he was the boy's father. Besides, Yūko wasn't at all sure it was Kazuhiko's child she had wanted.

It's really good that you're getting to see your Daddy, Yūko whispered fervently to the little will o' the wisp.

The small spirit flame cackled back happily.

For a long time the man writhed violently. Finally, when his strength and his body had sunk to the bottom, the two flames were able to escape from the water.

Afterward, the dazed ocean—cutting crevices in the pattern of waves, wrapping itself in whirlpools of light, in currents of light, in shimmering droplets—spread itself out, pregnant with living things, the sounds of waves, and even carcasses. On its surface floated countless will o' the wisps. The bluish white shadow of spirit flames, in the hundreds of thousands, cut their way deep into the bottom of the sea, fluttering, wavering, with enough force to swallow up the ocean. Perhaps they're acting as the eyes of the ocean, which shatter sunlight, moonlight, all kinds of light, the two spirit flames whispered to each other, emitting a bewitching glow and ascending to the heavens.

TRANSLATED BY MELISSA WENDER

MEDORUMA SHUN (1960–)

Born in Nakijin, Medoruma majored in Japanese literature at the University of the Ryukyus and currently teaches Japanese at a vocational high school on Miyako Island. Although he has been winning literary awards in Okinawa since his university days, Medoruma was largely unknown among mainland Japanese readers until "Droplets" (Suiteki) was awarded the Akutagawa Prize in the summer of 1997. Kōno Taeko, a distinguished writer of fiction, was among many critics who offered the story high praise, remarking that in her eleven years on the Akutagawa Prize Selection Committee, this was the most engaging work she had encountered. Even less enthusiastic critics acknowledge that few Japanese writers of Medoruma's generation have tried to tackle the complex and sensitive issue of "war memory." Medoruma is a reclusive man who has viewed his newfound fame with a salutary skepticism. When granting interviews, he has refused the use of television cameras; he also insists that critics and the media refrain from disclosing his personal name, a wish that we have respected in this anthology.

A central image in "Droplets" is the gourd melon (tōgan in standard Japanese, subui in the text's northern Okinawan dialect). Roughly the shape and size of a watermelon, the gourd melon is usually boiled and eaten as a vegetable in Okinawa. In one of his rare comments on this story, Medoruma reminds readers that shortly after the Battle of Okinawa, abnormally large vegetables began to appear, presumably nourished by the countless corpses absorbed into the soil. He then adds, in his laconic manner, that a similar phenomenon was observed in China only a few years earlier.

DROPLETS

MEDORUMA SHUN

IT WAS DURING a dry spell in mid-June, the rainy season, when Tokushō's leg suddenly swelled up. He lay napping on a steel-frame army cot in the back room, away from the scorching sun of the cloudless sky. The heat had subsided now that it was past 5:00, and he was sleeping comfortably when he was awakened by a feverish sensation in his right leg. He looked down and saw that the lower half of his leg had swelled up bigger than his thigh. Frightened, he tried to sit up, but his body wouldn't move, nor could he speak. Cold sweat trickled down his neck. At first Tokushō thought he'd had a stroke, yet he felt alert and clearheaded. As he stared at the ceiling wondering what to do, his leg swelled up even bigger, stretching his skin so tight that it became smooth and shiny. Then his leg started to itch as if an army of ants were crawling across it, and although he was desperate to scratch, he couldn't move a muscle. For nearly half an hour he just lay there, cursing until his wife, Ushi, came in to wake him. The sun's rays were gentler now, and Ushi wanted him to go back to the fields with her.

Tokushō's leg had already swelled to the size of an average gourd melon and turned pale green. His toes reminded him of a family of poisonous *habu*, the mother snake lying beside her offspring, spread out like a fan. The sparse hair on his leg made it look lewd.

"Grandpa, time to git yourself up. C'mon now." When Ushi shook his shoulder, Tokushō's head slid off the pillow and tears dripped from his eyes, wide open and glazed, while saliva drooled from his mouth. "Hurry up! Outta that bed, ya hear?"

Tokushō often feigned sleep to avoid work, so Ushi—thinking he was up to his usual tricks—grabbed him by the nose and pulled it so hard she might have been trying to tear it right off his face. Still, he showed no reaction. Sensing something wrong, Ushi looked him over and discovered what appeared to be a gourd melon left by a neighbor. Then she realized that it was Tokushō's right leg.

"Well, I'll be . . . what on earth happened to this leg?" Timidly, she reached out to touch it. The leg felt slightly feverish but firm. Then Ushi got angry when she remembered that she'd have no one to help weed the fields or cut the grass to feed their goats. "Damn! How come the lazy bum gotta go out and get some weird ailment durin' the busy season!" Ushi decided that the illness was a result of Tokushō's care-free lifestyle—the late nights spent singing and playing the *sanshin*, gambling and carousing with women—and she slapped his swollen shin with all her might. Tokushō's eyes rolled back into his head and he lost consciousness. The slap resounded pleasantly as the tip of Tokushō's big toe split open, spewing forth water. Ushi hurriedly moved his leg off the bed and put a pitcher on the floor to catch the liquid dripping from his heel. The liquid, which seemed to be nothing more than water, had stopped gushing, but it continued to drip steadily.

Mighty strange, thought Ushi, staring at the droplets of water that oozed forth and dripped down his foot from the split in his toe. Curious, she moistened her fingertip with the liquid and took a taste. It had the mild sweetness of the juice from an unripe *hechima* gourd. Ushi thought this odd since other bodily liquids such as blood, sweat, and urine were pungent, so she slipped on her rubber sandals and went off to call the doctor.

The following morning rumors about Tokushō's leg spread through the village. Curiosity seekers feigning concern formed a line outside the house, and by noon it was nearly fifty meters long. There hadn't been such a long line in the village since the American troops started passing out food rations after the war, and even those with little inter-est in the ruckus felt compelled to queue up. At first Ushi served tea and sweets to the visitors, thanking them for their concern, but she finally lost her temper when an ice cream peddler showed up at the scene.

"What do you think this is? Some kind of freak show?" she

shouted. Then she went to the shed, grabbed a machete, and began waving it around as she admonished the crowd. "Bunch of lazy good-for-nothin's!" The villagers knew how much Ushi relied on Tokushō; anyone who dared talk back risked serious injury, so they quickly dispersed.

After Ushi disappeared into the house, the crowd began to regroup in shady spots throughout the village—beneath the *gajimaru* tree in front of the farmers' co-op, under the eaves of the community center, on the benches shaded by the long branches of the *kuwadisaa* tree near the Japanese croquet field. Those who had actually seen Tokushō's leg dominated the conversations, describing its shape and smell, its luster and consistency, the disfiguration of the toenails. Some villagers re-counted earlier examples of swollen extremities and speculated about whether this was a good or bad omen; others began placing bets on when the swelling would subside.

By the time they started to debate the impact of Tokushō's leg on the village economy, evening had rolled around and the liquor was flowing freely. Before long they were singing and playing the *sanshin*. Then the dancing and karate performances began, prompting a candidate in the upcoming village council election to go out and slaughter a goat, which he offered as the evening's feast. Meanwhile, the man rumored to be his likely opponent sent his son off to buy liquor for the occasion. Unsold mangos and pineapples were peeled, their sweet fragrance mixing with the smell of canned mackerel and dried squid. Women surrounded the pot of goat stew, their faces glowing from the heat; children set off firecrackers; the young adults drifted down to the beach, where their bodies were soon merging together and moving in unison with the waves; dogs ran wild through the village with pig bones clutched between their jaws.

"Damn fools! Just don't appreciate a person's worries." Ushi stood at the window and shook her fist at the revelers in the distance. She then returned to Tokushō's bedside to change the ice on his leg. *How come this gotta happen to us?* she thought, lamenting her fate. After all, she had never failed to participate in the village religious rites and always looked after her family's ancestral altar.

Tokushō had only a slight fever, and his pulse was normal. He was snoring lightly and seemed to be sound asleep. His right leg was now the size of a large gourd melon. Ushi was tempted to take a razor blade and puncture the leg, but even she, known to be fearless, panicked at the thought that Tokushō might never regain consciousness. A droplet of water continued to ooze from his big toe at the rate of once every few seconds. Ushi placed a new bucket under his bed and emptied the water from the old one into the garden behind the house.

Ōshiro, the doctor at the local clinic, was a good-natured man in his mid-thirties. His gentle manner made him popular with the elderly villagers. After checking Tokushō's blood pressure, taking blood samples, and conducting an external exam, Ōshiro made no effort to hide his perplexity. The doctor was unable to diagnose the illness and recommended that Tokushō be admitted to a university hospital in the city where he could undergo a thorough examination, but Ushi instantly rejected the idea. "No sir! Not a chance!" she shouted, remembering how old villagers from the croquet field always said that "no one leaves them university hospitals alive." Unable to persuade Ushi to follow his advice, Ōshiro took out a small bottle and collected a sample of the water dripping from Tokushō's heel. As he put the bottle in his bag, the doctor once again urged Ushi to take Tokushō for a complete examination the following day and promised to check on him regularly.

Ushi and Tokushō had no children. They had lived together for forty years farming a small plot of land, and neither ever considered life without the other. Striving to convince herself that Tokushō was not in mortal danger, Ushi decided to care for him at home, and she went out to the shed for the machete to scare off the noisy villagers.

Starting the next morning, Ōshiro paid them house calls twice daily. Between his visits a nurse would come to replace the I.V. and to help change Tokushō's clothes. This gave Ushi a few minutes to go out and check on the fields. Four days after Tokushō's leg first swelled up, Ōshiro stopped by and announced that the test results were in. The doctor explained that he had asked a friend at the university hospital to analyze the liquid from Tokushō's leg. Ushi had served the doctor her homemade daikon pickled in brown sugar, and he sat on the veranda munching away while pointing to a sheet of paper lined with tiny numbers. "Basically, it's just water, although it appears to contain a slightly higher level of lime," he reported.

Ushi asked why the water was dripping from Tokushō's leg. "Yes, that's the mystery," the doctor replied with a friendly smile. Ushi was tempted to ask how he could call himself a doctor if he couldn't even tell her what was wrong, but she restrained herself. "The cause don't matter, but can't you hurry and stop that dripping?" she pleaded instead. Ōshiro simply repeated that this is why Tokushō must be admitted to the university hospital. "That won't do shit," Ushi muttered under her breath, remembering a rumor that university hospitals use their old patients as guinea pigs. Someone had mentioned this when the Village Senior Citizens Association took a bus tour of the island's war memorials. "Huh?" asked the doctor, but Ushi merely laughed and thanked him, deciding once and for all that the only option was to cure Tokushō by herself.

At first Ushi thought that Tokushō had caught parasites. When she was a child, there were several men in the village who walked with a limp, dragging behind them a bad leg that resembled the stump of a pine tree. Hanging out from their loincloth would be a testicle the size of a boar's. Especially famous was the Wheelbarrow Man, a traveling repairman who made rounds of the local villages. His enormous testicle was as hard as a rock and slightly flattened like a pumpkin. The village children delighted in watching him work, for he found countless ways to deploy this special tool. It served him as a worktable when he repaired pots and pans; he used it to fix umbrellas and even to sharpen knives. When he finished work, the man would load his testicle into the wheelbarrow with his other tools and move on to the next village. Ushi's eyes filled with tears of nostalgia as she remembered the sight of the Wheelbarrow Man leaving the village, his ragged kimono torn in back and his tiny figure retreating into the distance. Then it suddenly occurred to her that Tokushō's swelling might have reached his testicles, but she was relieved to find her fears unwarranted.

Tokushō's legs had never been especially hairy. Now that the hair on his swollen shin had fallen out, the leg was covered only with baby fluff. The greenish color had deepened, and if it weren't for the snake-head toes, Tokushō's leg would have been indistinguishable from a gourd melon. The water continued to drip with clock-like regularity.

One day some of Ōshiro's physician friends stopped by to examine the water, but Ushi didn't even let them through the door. Still, Ōshiro continued to visit regularly and gave no sign of having been offended. Ushi never mentioned the incident but did give the doctor a generous serving of her pickled daikon. Tokushō's pulse and temperature remained normal, and he continued to sleep well, snoring lightly during his afternoon naps, so Ushi began to spend more time in the fields. At night she placed a large bucket under Tokushō's foot and returned to her own room to sleep, as she had in the past.

Then the soldiers began to appear at Tokushō's bedside.

TOKUSHŌ had been alert and clearheaded ever since the day he was confined to bed. Even when he seemed to be sleeping, he could hear what was going on around him and could understand Ushi's conversations with Ōshiro. Yet he was unable to speak and couldn't even use gestures or eye movements to communicate with Ushi. At first Tokushō was depressed by the thought that, in addition to being paralyzed, he might be growing senile. As an inveterate optimist, however, he convinced himself that he would soon be cured, and instead of worrying he killed time composing imaginary letters of apology to the women who he supposed by now must be feeling neglected.

Ushi left the room, and Tokushō was just nodding off when he was awakened by an itchy and vaguely painful sensation in the big toe of his right foot. His eyelids opened and he was able to crane his neck forward. The room was filled with the glare of the fluorescent light, which had been left on.

"Hey," Tokushō managed to cry in a hoarse voice. "Ushi! Ushi!" he called, but his voice didn't reach the next room. Even so, Tokushō was ecstatic that he could move at all, and he turned his head, eyes panning the room, until he noticed several men lined up at the foot of his bed. The men wore tattered army uniforms that looked as if they had been drenched in muddy water. Each of them stared at Tokushō's foot, seemingly lost in thought. Tokushō again craned his neck forward and discovered another man, hair parted in the middle and head wrapped in a discolored bandage. The man was crouched down on the floor, his hands grasping the swollen ankle so that the water from Tokushō's heel dripped into his mouth. The man swallowed loudly, and the throats of the soldiers standing behind him contracted as they watched with envy.

There were five men in all. Of the four who were standing, two wore helmets and two had bandages wrapped around their shaven heads. The bandages had turned a brownish color. The man standing in front had a splint on his right arm, and the second man balanced on crutches, his right leg cut off at the knee. The third soldier seemed to be a mere boy of fourteen or fifteen. The right half of his face was swollen and bruised, and three large gashes ran diagonally across his bare chest. Dried drops of purplish blood adhered to the wound like tiny mulberries. The fourth soldier was a handsome man with the facial features of a mainland Japanese. At first glance he seemed to have no wounds whatsoever, but a closer look revealed that more than half of his neck had been severed from behind.

The man who was crouching down put his mouth on Tokushō's heel and began licking. Horror, combined with the unbearable tickling sensation, made Tokushō cringe. Feeling as if he was about to lose his mind, he silently began reciting the lyrics to the village harvest song. After a while the soldier who had been drinking stood up. Without a moment's hesitation, the next man in line crouched down and started drinking. The soldier who had just finished paused and looked longingly down at Tokushō's foot, but he soon stood at attention, saluted Tokushō, and bowed. Slowly, he then turned away and vanished through the wall on Tokushō's right. At nearly the same time, from the opposite wall another soldier appeared and took his place at the end of the line. The new soldier seemed to be over forty. He looked around the room as if beholding some rare spectacle. When his eyes met Tokushō's, the man's bearded face broke into a smile, and he bowed slightly. Tokushō had a vague recollection of the man but couldn't remember where he had first seen him.

The boy with the bandage around his head groaned as he brushed his hand over the wound on his chest. Huge maggots fell to the floor one after another. The animated, ivory-colored maggots instantly began crawling toward the bed. A hoarse cry escaped from Tokushō's throat. After creeping forward about twelve inches, the maggots turned into dark blotches and vanished.

It was not long before the second soldier finished drinking, saluted, bowed deeply, and disappeared into the wall to the right. Just as before, a new soldier appeared out of the opposite wall and took his place in line. This continued until dawn.

The soldiers were all well mannered, and Tokushō soon got over the fear that they might harm him. Each man was so seriously wounded that he could barely remain standing. Tokushō was moved to pity by their miserable condition and polite bows as they disappeared, one after another, into the wall. Among them were men so pathetic that Tokushō was forced to avert his eyes. One soldier, about twenty years old, had his flesh torn away from his throat down to his collarbone, and with each breath, countless bubbles of blood floated out from his lungs. Yet even soldiers in such a condition would drink desperately.

Tokushō looked at the clock on the wall. Each soldier took an average of two minutes. The water, which dripped slowly, could not seem to quench the men's thirst. Often they were rushed along by the next man in line, and when their turn was up, they would look longingly at Tokushō's foot. If the dripping slowed, some men would lick the sole of his foot; some even took his big toe into their mouths and tried to suck the water out. At first Tokushō found the tickling sensation unbearable, but he eventually got used to it and would drop off into a light slumber.

It was not until 5:00 A.M. that the soldiers stopped appearing out of one wall and disappearing into another. As streaks of blue brushed the dawn sky, the last man finished drinking and, leaning unsteadily on his cane, disappeared through the wall. Tokushō slowly shook his woozy head and looked at his leg. The swelling had noticeably subsided, as had the dripping. He was ecstatic and would have shouted for joy, but he was too sleepy to utter a word. He then mustered all his strength and tried to sit up, but a searing pain shot through his foot from his toes to his groin. Water poured out from the tip of his big toe, and Tokushō, his mouth still open, lost consciousness.

THE swelling that seemed to have subsided returned by noon the following day.

Ushi had tried every possible cure. She visited the female elders of the village and at their suggestion fed Tokushō the extract from a brew of worms and paddy fish. When she heard that a butterfly on the brink of death had been rejuvenated after imbibing the water from *fuba* grass, she gathered some of the seaweed from the rocky shore and made Tokushō swallow the extract. After hearing that the meat of a sea turtle would surely cure Tokushō's ailment, Ushi procured the rare meat. She applied cold packs made of aloe and tried acupuncture and moxibustion. She even tried bleeding the leg. She was afraid that blood or water would shoot out once she pierced the smooth skin of Tokushō's bloated leg, but when she gently applied the razor, only tiny beads of blood oozed forth. Ushi collected the blood in a cup and studied it. She was relieved to find that the color and consistency seemed perfectly normal, and there were no apparent impurities. Still, there was no sign that Tokushō's condition was improving.

At the urging of the old women of the village, Ushi called on a highly reputed *yuta*, but this only made her more miserable. Besides charging an outrageous fee, the shaman scolded Ushi for neglecting her ancestral spirits, and she ended up ashamed of herself for relying on a shaman in the first place.

"Poor Tokushō. I just can't seem to cure you," muttered Ushi, gently rubbing his leg. Hearing her words, Tokushō was overcome with emotion.

NOW the soldiers began to appear nightly. Around midnight, Ushi would change the bucket and return to her room. Then they would emerge, one after another, from the wall to Tokushō's left. During this time Tokushō was able to move his head and eyes freely. The soldiers rarely looked at him except when they saluted before and after drinking. Their wounds were so severe they could barely remain standing, and their eyes were always fixed on Tokushō's big toe.

Tokushō noted that the soldiers were members of the Japanese forces. All had suffered serious injuries, and roughly 80 percent seemed to be from mainland Japan. Their ages varied widely. Among the Okinawans drafted into the island's Defense Force were men so old their hair had turned gray. The soldiers rarely spoke to one another. They simply stood in line, silently waiting their turn. Those unable to stand were supported by the others. After a while Tokushō could no longer bear to look at them and closed his eyes, praying for sleep.

It happened on the third night after the soldiers first appeared. Toward dawn Tokushō awoke from a light nap and gazed groggily as a soldier disappeared into the wall to his right. When the next soldier emerged, his eyes downcast, Tokushō suddenly groaned, "Ishimine!"

Tokushō and Ishimine were the only students from their cluster of villages who had gone on to the teachers higher school in Shuri after graduation. They had both been recruited into the Blood and Iron Imperial Service Corps and had stayed together throughout the battle. Now Ishimine stood before Tokushō, exactly as he had when they parted. Wrapped around his stomach in place of a bandage was one cloth legging, soaked in dark blood. The legging had been Tokushō's, and he had used it to bind Ishimine's wound. It was Tokushō who had made the splint from a pine branch that supported Ishimine's crushed ankle. As Tokushō stared at Ishimine's downcast eyes and delicate profile, he was at a loss for words.

Although Tokushō and Ishimine were from the same group of villages, they hadn't met until entering the teacher's higher school. Yet after less than half a year in the corps, they were sharing their innermost thoughts, relying on jokes to disguise their growing intimacy. Ishimine rarely spoke and always had his nose in books, so it was Tokushō who did most of the talking. But Ishimine's replies were succinct and insightful, and while Tokushō tried to appear nonchalant, he would listen intently to his friend's remarks.

When the Battle of Okinawa began, Tokushō and Ishimine were placed in the same company of the Blood and Iron Imperial Service Corps, where they were assigned to messenger duty and munitions transport. The Americans landed in the central part of the island and worked their way south. Tokushō's company ended up facing them on the front line, and after the second firefight had been all but annihilated. Tokushō and Ishimine fled south with a small group of *yamatonchu* (mainland Japanese) soldiers, making their way from cave to cave. Then on the night that Ishimine was hit in the stomach with shrapnel from a naval bombardment, they got separated at the southern tip of the island.

Now the soldier who had been drinking stood up, saluted Tokushō, and disappeared. Ishimine, supporting himself on the shoulders of the man in front of him, dragged his right leg and took two steps forward. No new soldier appeared from the wall. It was nearly dawn. Gradually it became clear to Tokushō that Ishimine had recognized him but was pretending not to.

These were the soldiers who had been left behind that night in the cave.

Now the pain returned to Tokushō's right leg. When Ishimine's turn came, Tokushō lifted his head in an effort to speak, but Ishimine kept staring at the floor. Unable to utter a word, Tokushō let his head fall back on the pillow and shut his eyes. Two cold palms grasped his swollen ankle. The thin lips parted and engulfed his big toe. When the tip of the tongue brushed across the wound on his toe, a tingling shot up from his foot through his thigh to the root that had hardened in his groin. A small moan escaped from Tokushō's mouth, and his aging body emitted the scent of young grass.

"HEY, how're you doin'? Long time!" said Seiyū, suddenly entering the room.

Ushi, who had been wiping Tokushō with a towel, glared at him. "What in hell's name you doin' here?" she demanded.

Seiyū, his face flushed from liquor, responded to Ushi's barb by forcing a smile and presenting a white plastic bag from the supermarket. "Just payin' a visit to the invalid. Just a little visit. This here's a gift." Ushi was sure that the papayas and *gōyaas* Seiyū pulled out of the bag had been stolen.

"We ain't takin' nothin' from you. Put that away and make yourself scarce!"

The papayas he had placed on the table were overripe and had begun to rot. A moldy odor wafted through the room, and a drone beetle crawled out from one of them, splitting its orange skin. Seiyū caught the insect between his fingers and threw it out the window. It then turned a luminous green and flew off into the blue sky.

"Where'd ya swipe it from?"

"C'mon, Ushi. You know I bought it."

"That's a damn lie," said Ushi, looking disgusted. Seiyū leaned against the window frame, smiling obsequiously. Ushi hadn't seen him for nearly six months, and as he scratched his head she noticed how thin his hair had become. Surprised at how much Seiyū had aged, she began to feel a bit sorry for him and decided not to throw him out after all.

Seiyū and Tokushō were cousins. Although they were the same age, Seiyū had never married. Sometimes he would go off to mainland Japan to work, and other times he'd find work as a day laborer in Naha. When the traditional New Year's celebration approached in February, he would always return to the house that his parents had left to him in the village. There he would earn daily wages cutting sugarcane. Tokushō and Ushi had worried about Seiyū this year, since he hadn't returned for the New Year's celebrations, but when Ushi actually set eyes on him her first reaction was disgust. Seiyū's scrawny body and impoverished features had earned him the nickname "Rat," although his big, strong teeth looked more like those of a horse. He wore pants with a sharp crease (obviously U.S. military surplus), and his gaudy T-shirt looked like those hawked to tourists at the beach. Seiyū stared at Tokushō, mesmerized at the strange sight.

"Ya old fool—nearly seventy, and look at you," Ushi said to Seiyū. She had always blamed him for her husband's obsession with drinking and gambling.

Seiyū approached Tokushō and was about to remove the towel covering his leg when Ushi grabbed a nearby fly swatter and slapped his outstretched arm with all her might.

"Hey! What's that for?"

"Keep them rotten hands off!"

"Ushi, I'm just worried about him. . . ."

"Your worryin' ain't gonna change nothin'. Hands off!" Ushi waved
the fly swatter menacingly, and Seiyū fled to the opposite side of the
bed. From there he had a good view of the water dripping from
Tokushō's toe, which was white and swollen. Droplets formed at a
small slit in the toe, then rolled down the sole to his heel, where they
fell into the bucket.

"Is it water?"

Ushi didn't answer. Ripples spread across the colorless, transparent
liquid, which seemed purer than water.

"Hey, what're ya up to now?" Seiyū had leaned over to get a closer
look when the fly swatter descended on his head.

"Git the hell away from there. You're gittin' on my nerves!" Ushi
grumbled as she kicked him in the behind. Then with both hands, she
took the bucket from under Tokushō's foot and carried it to the window, where she paused for a moment before lifting it. Seiyū stepped
forward to help, but Ushi rebuked him. "Outta my way!" Seiyū could
do nothing but lean against the window frame and watch as the bucket
was emptied into the garden behind the house.

The weeds in the garden had grown thick, and even hard-working
Ushi couldn't keep them under control. Branches jutted out every
which way from the hedge of the Chinese hibiscus, its red flowers shining against the blue sky. Entwined with the hedge was a vine from
some type of gourd, perhaps a *hechima* or a pumpkin, and on the vine
bloomed two radiant yellow flowers. Seiyū stood absorbed at the sight
of the enormous yellow flowers until noticing that only those sections
of the garden that sparkled with the water droplets from Ushi's bucket
had grown irregularly. Weeds were sparse in those areas untouched by
the water, and dry sections of the hedge retained their shape as if they
had recently been trimmed. Seiyū was still puzzling over the scene
when a voice assailed him from behind. "Hey, if you ain't got nothing
to do, why don't ya just hurry on home?" Ushi sat in front of the fan
beside the bed, glaring at Seiyū.

"Ushi, ya shouldn't let the weeds grow like this."

Ushi glared even more menacingly, and Seiyū noticed that she was blushing. He knew how ashamed Ushi felt to have weeds growing in her garden, so he entered into negotiations delicately. "Ushi, how's about hirin' me to help out with the garden and fieldwork? I'll also lend a hand in takin' care of old Tokushō here. Ya don't need to pay me much, though I'd be mighty grateful if you could fix my meals."

The glare still on her face, Ushi pondered Seiyū's offer. In fact, she had wanted someone to help out, since she couldn't spend enough time in the fields, nor could she keep up with the weeding. Even when it came to caring for Tokushō, she hadn't been able to do everything she'd wanted, such as turning him over regularly to prevent bedsores. The next-door neighbors had offered to help, but Ushi, not one to rely on outsiders, had turned them down. While she hated the idea of re-lying on Seiyū, she agreed to hire him at one thousand yen and three meals per day, adding the threat, "I'll break every bone in your body if you slack off or try swipin' anything from this house."

Ushi gave Seiyū his instructions for the day. He was to change the bucket whenever it filled up, turn Tokushō over in bed every half hour, and cut the grass. If there was a problem, he was to call her immediately. Then she got into her tiny, low-horsepower car and raced off to the fields, twice nearly hitting groups of children on their way home from school.

Seiyū sat near Tokushō's pillow, scrutinizing his leg, and tried to strike up a conversation. He quickly grew bored, however, since Tokushō couldn't respond. So, after turning up the volume on the radio that was tuned to the station playing Okinawan folk songs, he leaned against the wall and drifted off to sleep. After an hour or so, Seiyū awoke with a chill in his lower body. When he looked down, he thought for a moment that he had wet his pants while sleeping. Then he jumped up and hurried to change the bucket. The water from Tokushō's big toe was dripping more rapidly and had filled the bucket, which was overflowing onto the floor.

"Oh my god! What's goin' on here?" he shouted, throwing the water out the window and then rushing back to wipe the floor. "Never saw nothin' like this before."

Seiyū gasped and stared at the water dripping from the split in Tokushō's big toe. Not long before, the back of Seiyū's hands had begun to itch unbearably, and now they were covered with black marks. The marks looked like tiny insects, and he had tried to brush them off but couldn't get rid of them. Then he shuddered, realizing that the marks were actually growing on his hands. Like Tokushō, Seiyū had always had sparse body hair. At one time they both had tried shaving their arms and chests, hoping to make the hair grow thicker, but nothing came back in its place except the same baby fluff. Now stiff roots of dark, lustrous hair covered Seiyū's fingers and the backs of his hands.

As Seiyū stared at his hands, a glint of light caught his eye. He went to the window and looked at the garden. The water he had just thrown out sparkled in the sunlight, and the grass stood erect, emitting a peculiar scent. The flowers growing on the hedge shone brilliantly in reds and yellows. Seiyū rushed back to the bucket, dipped in his hands, and patted some water onto his balding forehead. It took less than five minutes to take effect. His forehead began to itch as if tiny insects were crawling under the skin, and when he rubbed it, he felt the stiff roots of what seemed to be soft, thin hairs. Barely containing his excitement, he cupped his hands and scooped up some of the liquid from the bucket, yet it had no smell and seemed no different from plain water. Seiyū cupped his hands again and caught some of the water dripping from Tokushō's heel. Timidly, he stuck out his tongue. A mild sweetness spread through his mouth; it was less bitter than he had expected. Now he tried more, swishing it around with his tongue. Suddenly he felt a burning lump forming around his anus, and then his entire body felt flushed. A pleasurable throb surged through his pelvis. The front of his pants bulged. Seiyū had been impotent for the past few years. Whenever he found himself a woman, his pathetic member assumed the shape and size of a dead sparrow's head; now it had grown to a good-sized pigeon's head, its long neck throbbing back and forth.

"Hallelujah!" shouted Seiyū, piercing the air with three quick karate punches. Then he bounded out of the room in search of a container for the water.

Tokushō awoke to the sound of laughter and to the sensation of his big toe being sucked. The soldiers were on their third round. When he realized that these were the same men he had left behind in the cave, Tokushō thought they might kill him. Yet it soon became apparent that he had nothing to fear, and he decided that relieving the soldiers' thirst was the only way to atone for his sins. Eventually, Tokushō even began to take pleasure in having his toe sucked, but at this point he still found it utterly repulsive.

Starting with their third round, the soldiers began behaving differently. Whether they had regained some energy or simply grown accustomed to being in the room, they were often engrossed in conversation while awaiting their turn and at times laughed so loudly that Tokushō thought the neighbors might overhear. Tokushō was both eager and anxious as he stared at the door, expecting Ushi to wake up, but there was no sign of her. The soldiers seemed completely oblivious to Tokushō. They continued to salute him before and after drinking, and they would look down in deference when approaching his leg, but otherwise they paid him no notice whatsoever. Besides Ishimine, Tokushō had spoken to several of these soldiers in the cave, and he was not pleased that they now ignored him.

"What did I do to deserve this?" Tokushō lamented dozens of times each day, yet he never sought the answer. He was afraid that once he started to think about it, all the things he had kept buried deep within him over the past fifty years would burst out like floodwaters. Tokushō remembered the elementary school students who, accompanied by their teacher, paid him a sick call one afternoon. Over the past ten years, whenever June 23 approached and Okinawans prepared to commemorate those killed in the war, Tokushō was called on to speak at the local elementary, middle, and high schools about his war experiences. Under normal circumstances at this time of year, Tokushō would be busy making the rounds of the local schools. The students who visited him this year were from the very first school where Tokushō had spoken ten years ago, and no matter how busy he was, he always made time to visit their school.

It was a teacher from the village who originally proposed that Tokushō talk to students about his war experiences. Until then,

Tokushō had tried to forget about the war and had always turned down similar requests. But the young teacher, a man named Kinjō, was persistent. He had just graduated from the university and never seemed to have doubted the righteousness of his intentions. Kinjō was accompanied by two female students who had participated in the oral history project, and when the two girls bowed repeatedly, begging Tokushō to share his war experiences with their class, he found himself unable to refuse.

The first time Tokushō stood in their sixth-grade classroom, he read from a paper he had prepared, not once looking up. Unaccustomed to speaking in standard Japanese, he raced through the paper, finishing what was scheduled to be a half-hour talk in just over fifteen minutes. After concluding, Tokushō timidly looked up at the students. A brief moment passed, then the classroom burst into applause. Tears still streaming down their faces, the students were clapping with all their might. Tokushō was bewildered; he couldn't understand what had so affected the children. Then he started receiving requests to speak at the village's other elementary and junior high schools, and he was even asked to speak at the high school in the next town.

At about the same time, the village's board of education had begun compiling oral histories of the war, and this brought Tokushō to the attention of newspaper reporters and university research teams, who soon began showing up at his door. Tokushō was even interviewed several times by television stations and was asked to speak to school groups visiting Okinawa from the Japanese mainland. At first he spoke with blind intensity, but eventually he began to grasp what his audience wanted to hear and learned not to appear too glib. At those times when he did forget himself, he would suddenly look up at the intent faces of the children and feel ashamed or even frightened.

Angered by this, Ushi would warn, "You start fibbin' and makin' up sorry tales to profit off the war and you'll get your fair punishment in the end." Tokushō hardly needed her warnings, for as soon as he finished a lecture he always vowed to make it his last. Yet after hearing the applause, being handed a bouquet of flowers, and getting showered with the children's kind words, Tokushō felt truly contented. *This must be how it feels to have children or grandchildren,* he thought, and tears even filled his eyes. He took special pleasure in opening the envelope containing his honorarium after he got home. Tokushō squandered most of the money on liquor and gambling, but he also managed to buy a new *sanshin* and an expensive fishing rod with his earnings.

The children visiting Tokushō kept peeking at his leg, which was draped with a large bath towel. "Please get well soon," they said, one after another, leaving him flowers and origami cranes, the folded paper birds symbolizing restored health. For a moment Tokushō was ready to apologize for all of his lies, and he almost confessed about what he actually did on the battlefield. Almost, but not quite.

Ushi's words came to mind: "You'll git your comeuppance for tryin' to profit off people's sufferin' in the war."

A soldier stared at Tokushō. The man's frightened eyes seemed vaguely familiar. He appeared to be about twenty years old. Unlike the others, who now had gentle expressions on their faces, this particular soldier still looked tense. The young man bowed deeply, put his hand on his chest, and grimaced, then slowly knelt down and began to drink.

After their company had been destroyed, Tokushō and the remaining troops kept moving and reassembled in a cave on the southern part of the island. The cave served as a field hospital, and the wounded were cared for by high school girls who had been conscripted as nurses. After they arrived at the field hospital, the girls, together with their teachers, checked to confirm who among their acquaintances in the cave had survived. In the days that followed, they were kept busy with messenger duty, carrying water and food supplies, and transporting corpses.

Tokushō had encountered this particular soldier while carrying a trough of urine and feces out of the cave. As he passed the wounded in their beds lined up against the wall, Tokushō did his best to knock away their arms that stretched toward him, but one hand managed to grab the edge of the trough, causing the contents to spill onto the face of a wounded soldier. Tokushō cringed, expecting a harangue from the man. The soldier was near the entrance to the cave, and a dim light revealed his face, drenched in urine and excrement. He stuck out his tongue and licked the foul water that surrounded his lips. The bandage wrapped around his chest moved ceaselessly. His head rotated slowly, and Tokushō saw the man staring at him from the very depths of his eyes. *Surely this man won't last until tomorrow,* thought Tokushō. "I'll bring you water right away," he said, stepping forward, but Tokushō never carried out his promise.

Now this man's teeth rubbed against Tokushō's toe as he sucked, and it hurt. The dripping seemed to have slowed. *Perhaps now I have fulfilled my promise,* thought Tokushō. But his sense of relief was outweighed by the fear that the ghosts of these soldiers would haunt him forever.

A soldier with a dented skull pressed his knee against the shoulder of the man in front of him. Reluctantly, the man stood up and, with fear in his eyes, looked at Tokushō. Then he bowed and disappeared through the wall, clutching his chest. The next soldier kneeled down and frantically began sucking on Tokushō's toe. A fly zoomed off the wound on the man's dented skull, buzzing around his head for a while before landing on the bed sheet and disappearing. This soldier had also grabbed Tokushō in the cave that day, begging for water. The tall soldier standing behind him, and the Okinawan soldier hidden behind him, and the one-eyed soldier who just now appeared out of the wall—all had been in the cave, extending their arms as they pleaded for water. Tokushō felt as if he was being dragged back into the cave's shadows once again.

Sensing someone outside, Seiyū hurriedly gathered together the money he had spread out on the floor and hid it under his floor cushion. Then, taking the flashlight, he peered through the window into the garden, closed the shutters, checked the latch, and again counted the money.

The water proved even more effective than Seiyū had imagined. Within a mere five minutes, fine hairs began growing on the freckled head of a man who had been bald for the past fifty years. A young high school teacher with thinning hair, who had initially scoffed at Seiyū's claims, tried the water and, within three minutes, handed over nearly all of the money in his pockets. When applied to a person's face, the rough epidermis would crack and peel off, replaced by a smooth and lustrous layer of new skin. When imbibed, a certain part of the anatomy that had dangled limply for years would now raise its head and reach for the abdomen. Skeptical customers had only to witness the eighty-seven-year-old man who stood rubbing his crotch, eyes twinkling like a contented elephant's, before they, too, rushed off to purchase the water. Seiyū had originally thought that ten thousand yen for a small bottle might seem unreasonable, but he sold out in less than an hour.

During the first couple of days, Seiyū stood at an intersection in the next town and sold the water out of small *sake* serving bottles he had scrounged up. Starting on the third day, however, he ordered special brown bottles and attached red labels with "Miracle Water" written in gold ink, so that the product resembled a Chinese herbal medicine. He also moved to a new location, setting up shop at the corner of the town's commercial district. Although he intended to be open for business between 7:00 and 8:00 in the evening, he always sold out in less than a half hour. Rumors spread quickly, and people began lining up at noontime. Even though Seiyū set a limit of one bottle per customer, there were never enough to go around. Frustrated customers would shout at him and refuse to leave, but he finally managed to assuage them by passing out "reserved" tickets for his next sale. Then he tried doubling the price and reducing by half the volume per bottle, yet the number of customers kept growing. A few customers claimed to have had the contents analyzed and found that it was nothing more than water. Though they accused him of fraud, the product's effectiveness was undeniable. One group of old men even began to worship Seiyū as if he were a god.

Seiyū put the money he'd made in his bag and chuckled as he looked at his savings account passbook. Then he began to think of what he should do next. There was no doubt that the *yakuza* would soon get wind of the potential profits and demand a cut. The mass media had already been around twice to do stories on the water, and it seemed prudent to think about skipping town for the mainland before the local tax office and health insurance bureau caught on. The dripping from Tokushō's toe had slowed recently and barely filled three buckets per day. If Seiyū raised the price further, he could pull in ten thousand dollars in sales, but Rat smelled trouble around the corner. While the *yakuza* and tax bureau scared him, he was even more afraid of what Ushi would do if she found out, so he was careful about how much water he took each day. Only a few more days, he decided. Having dispensed with that problem, Seiyū lay down, using his carrying bag as a pillow. He drifted off to sleep imagining all the massage parlors he would visit as he traveled from southern Kyushu all the way to Tokyo.

Two weeks had passed since Tokushō's leg had swelled up. It was July, and the cries of giant cicadas showered down on the sweltering summer days. The villagers had grown accustomed to Tokushō's condition and now inquired about him as if asking about any bedridden elderly person. They seemed to have consigned his illness to that category of tales about villagers who suffered strange fates: for example, there was the story of the man who was blinded by a red *habu* snake hiding at a sacred site in the forest; and the old woman, Makato, who is said to have grown horns on her head after turning 110 years old. Tokushō's illness was unusual but not implausible, and the villagers nearly forgot about him.

Ushi had returned to her usual morning routine—waking up before 6:00, sipping tea while sucking on a chunk of brown sugar, and then setting out for the fields to work before it got too hot. Seiyū would show up while Ushi was still drinking her morning tea and stay through the late afternoon. When he wasn't taking care of Tokushō, Seiyū did the shopping, cut grass for the goats, and cleaned the house. He worked so hard that Ushi began to think he had lost his mind. It is true that the garden had become overgrown, and she warned him about it once, but he answered that no matter how often he cut the grass it would grow back by the following morning. Although she thought he was lying, Ushi let the matter drop, since he was working so hard at his other chores.

Ushi would return home at 6:00 p.m. and relieve Seiyū. After washing Tokushō, changing his clothes, and taking a bath, she ate dinner. Then she would sit by his bed and listen to the radio while telling him what happened in the village that day. Ōshiro from the clinic stopped by regularly, alternating with the nurse. In addition to the I.V., they had placed Tokushō on a liquid diet, which was fed to him through a tube in his nose. Although he was somewhat thin, his skin actually appeared healthier than before, and since Tokushō couldn't smoke or drink, his blood pressure had also improved. His leg was still swollen, but the dripping seemed to have slowed, especially during the night, although no one was quite sure what to make of this.

Every time he visited, Ōshiro recommended that Tokushō be admitted to the hospital. While she continued to insist that "you can't trust them big university hospitals," Ushi privately began to waver. Tokushō's condition wasn't worsening, but there was no sign of improvement either. When she considered the possibility of his current condition lasting for the rest of his life, Ushi began to feel desperate and admitted to herself that she didn't know what to do. Even during the war Ushi had never shown any weakness.

That night, just as Ushi left the room to go to bed, the soldiers appeared. As if he had been waiting since the last time, the first soldier rushed to place the toe in his mouth. The man's mouth was so cold that it made Tokushō shudder, and he was so acutely aware of the movement of the soldier's lips and tongue that he couldn't sleep. Irritated at the banter of the other men, Tokushō tried yelling at them several times but could only squeeze out a hoarse whisper, and the soldiers paid him no heed. *If this goes on much longer I'll go crazy,* he thought. He was unable to cover his ears or bury himself under the blankets, and several times he was awakened just as he'd been on the verge of sleep. When Tokushō thought he heard a distant bell ringing at 5:00 A.M., he noticed Ishimine standing before him. Only the two of them were in the room. Until now, Ishimine had always averted his eyes, staring down at the floor, but now he looked directly at Tokushō. Tokushō craned his neck forward and tried to speak, but no words came. Ishimine looked down again, grabbed onto the metal bed frame to support his unsteady body, and slowly crouched down. Gently, he took Tokushō's toe into his mouth and licked it, though there was little water coming out.

Tokushō recalled the night that he and Ishimine separated. They had left the cave to get water when a rocket fired from a battleship exploded nearby. The three schoolgirls helping them were killed instantly. Ishimine's stomach was split open by shrapnel, and Tokushō was the only one left who could move. Ishimine was moaning and gripping his stomach. Between his fingers oozed something that looked like the guts of a slaughtered pig or goat. Tokushō untied his cloth leggings, wrapped them around Ishimine's stomach, and dragged him back to the cave. As soon as he set foot inside the cave, Tokushō was assailed by the soldiers' demands for water and food, so he left Ishimine lying near the entrance and hurried out to draw water.

That night the cave got noisier. The soldiers had been ordered to redeploy, and everyone able to walk was to take whatever he could carry and head south.

Cries for help of soldiers afraid to be left behind and the angry reprimands of their officers mingled together in the pale shadows. Sounds of men packing supplies mixed with the patter of the rain that had begun to fall, echoing in Tokushō's ears as he sat beside Ishimine. Tokushō was trying to think: he knew there was something important he should do, but no matter how hard he tried, he could not figure out what it was.

The cave, formed by Ryukyu limestone, was located midway up a small, forested mountain. The pouring rain fell on the tree leaves, where it turned into a fine mist and then seeped into Tokushō's and Ishimine's skin as they hid behind a stone wall near the cave's entrance.

Two sentries took their rifles and quickly moved down the hill through the forest. The redeployment had begun. One after another, dark lumps would appear from the shadows and slowly assume a human form before descending the slope. Tokushō held Ishimine in his arms and pressed against the wall, hardly daring to breathe as he watched the soldiers go. Few of the men could walk normally, so they supported themselves on each other's shoulders or with canes. As they slid down the slope, they became entangled and cursed each other, then exchanged muted cries of "Shut up!" The girls from the Student Nurse Corps passed by carrying one of their wounded comrades on a stretcher, then a shadow approached from the group. It was Miyagi Setsu. After learning that Tokushō and Ishimine were from her own group of villages, she had always stopped by to say hello. "How is Ishimine-san?" she asked. Ishimine leaned against the stone wall, letting out shallow breaths. He looked as if he would fall to pieces if not supported. Tokushō shook his head at Setsu, who asked nothing more. Coarse fingers gripped Tokushō's wrist, squeezing hard. A canteen and paper bag were forced into his palm. Tokushō tried to refuse, pushing her hand away, but Setsu brought her face close and said, "We're heading for the field hospital in Itoman, so be sure to follow us!" She spoke forcefully, grabbing his shoulder. Then she reached out, gently touched Ishimine's face, and said good-bye. Tokushō watched her pigtailed figure slide down the hill and disappear into the forest shadows.

Tokushō wasn't sure how long he had been sitting there. The shapes of the men passing before him had flattened and twisted. Soldiers leaning on canes were now replaced by those crawling on all fours or dragging themselves along on their stomachs, shadowy figures squirming forward on arms and legs like half-submerged amphibians. Mixing with the sounds of men wriggling through mud were the curses, cries, and pleadings of those left behind. Tokushō listened vacantly to the moaning of those soldiers who had slid off the cliff and couldn't climb back up.

"Tokushō," someone called faintly.

"Ishimine . . ." Tokushō spoke directly into his ear, but there was no reply. He brought his head closer and could hear shallow breathing. Tokushō turned around and lay Ishimine on the ground. The makeshift bandage he had wrapped around Ishimine's stomach had become twisted and was making a slight sound. Tokushō took out a piece of dried bread from the paper bag Setsu had given him and placed it in Ishimine's hand. Tokushō then poured some water from the canteen into his own palm and let it drip between the rows of white teeth that shone through Ishimine's parted lips. The moment Tokushō saw the water overflow and drip down Ishimine's cheek, he could no longer restrain himself. He put the canteen to his own mouth and gorged himself. When he caught his breath, the canteen was empty. The droplets of water spread through his entire body, creating a searing pain as if they were tiny shards of glass. Tokushō fell to his knees and stared at Ishimine, who lay on the ground where he was slowly absorbed by the shadows and muddy water. He looked too heavy to carry. No voices could be heard in the shelter. Tokushō set down the empty canteen beside Ishimine. "Forgive me," he said.

Tokushō slid down the slope, tree branches whipping him in the face, then took off running through the forest. Moonlight shone on a white limestone path, and fallen soldiers lay humped over like dark shellfish. Across the path he could see the tail of a black snake, its scales peeling off one by one. Tokushō ran after it and tripped over the outstretched arm of a soldier who looked dead. But then the man began crawling toward Tokushō, who pushed his arm away and stood up as a sharp pain shot through his ankle. Tokushō was now terrified that he would be left behind. Dragging his leg, he took off running again. An explosion suddenly ripped through the air behind him. Flashes of light pierced the middle of the forest. Afraid of being left behind, Tokushō continued to run, cursing those Japanese soldiers along the way who had killed themselves with hand grenades.

Four days later, Tokushō was taken prisoner by the Americans at Mabuni on the southern tip of the island. He had lain unconscious on the beach, waves lapping beside him, when he was rescued. During his time in the internment camp and even after returning to the village, Tokushō worried that someone might suddenly appear and accuse him of abandoning Ishimine in the cave.

Roughly one week after returning to the village, Ishimine's mother came to visit. She brought potatoes and canned goods saved from the rations issued by the Americans and rejoiced at Tokushō's survival as if he were her own kin. Tokushō found himself unable to look her in the eye. He lied, saying that he had lost sight of Ishimine as they fled and didn't know what had become of him afterward. In the hectic years that followed the war, Tokushō tried to erase his memories of Ishimine.

No one knew the whereabouts of Tokushō's father, Shūtoku, after he first went off to serve in the Defense Forces. Tokushō's grandfather and two younger sisters all died following their release from an American internment camp, so his only close relatives left were his mother, grandmother, and infant brother. His mother, Tomi, had always been sickly. She could not produce enough milk to feed his brother, whose face was covered with sores and was constantly surrounded by flies.

His brother died before reaching his first birthday. Tokushō relied on his grandmother to care for Tomi, who could barely get out of bed. Claiming to be older than his eighteen years, Tokushō found work during the days carrying freight on a U.S. military dock; in the early mornings and evenings he worked in the fields. Two years later Tomi died, leaving Tokushō alone with his grandmother.

Several times Tokushō tried leaving the village. He tried working as a day laborer in the thriving base towns concentrated in the center of the island, then as a house painter in Naha, but he never lasted long in these jobs. At twenty-five he returned to the village and built a rowboat out of an empty U.S. military fuel tank, and when he wasn't working in the fields, he'd take the boat out for spearfishing to make some extra money. At twenty-seven he met and moved in with Ushi, who peddled fish from door to door in the village. His grandmother couldn't have been happier. Ushi was two years older than Tokushō, and although she was a strong-willed woman, she had a big heart. During the next three years until Tokushō's grandmother died, Ushi took even better care of her than she did her own parents. After his grandmother's death, Tokushō and Ushi lived alone. Tokushō began drinking more heavily and started gambling as well. Ushi attributed this to her infertility, and she secretly began visiting a clinic for treatments.

Yet there was another reason for Tokushō's heavy drinking. At the ceremony commemorating the forty-ninth day after his grandmother's death, he overhead a conversation among the old women of the village and inadvertently learned what happened to Miyagi Setsu.

By the time Tokushō reached the cave that served as an infirmary, it had already been bombed. The Americans had used the "horse rider strategy," in which they straddled the top of the cave and pitched explosives inside. Tokushō could not discover Setsu's whereabouts and was forced to flee to Mabuni Beach at the southernmost tip of the island. The previous day, Setsu and her group had traveled nearly the same course and reached the cliffs at Mabuni. Atop the rocks, less than 200 meters from where Tokushō would later lie unconscious from a bomb blast, waves lapping at his body, Setsu and her five classmates took out a hand grenade and killed themselves.

After his relatives and the others returned home, Tokushō walked down to the shore alone. Setsu's face appeared before him. It was she who had given him the canteen and dried bread, she who had placed her hand on his shoulder. Sadness and then rage welled up inside him, and he was suddenly overcome by a desire to kill those who drove Setsu to her death. At the same time, he was forced to acknowledge a sense of relief that no one was left who knew the truth about Ishimine. Tokushō wanted to sob, yet no tears would come. It was then that he began drinking heavily. Since that time he thought he had succeeded in forcing the memories of Ishimine and Setsu from his mind.

Ishimine wrapped his palms soothingly around Tokushō's ankles and was drinking intently. A cool breeze blew through the room. From outside the window and across the sea, Tokushō sensed a glimmer of dawn light. Normally the soldiers would have disappeared by this time. Tokushō's robe had fallen open, revealing a stomach flabby from drink. He found the sight repulsive—the pale skin of his stomach, the sparse hairs surrounding his navel, and his right leg swollen up like a gourd. Tokushō realized that he was growing old fast, and he feared having to spend the rest of his life in bed, face-to-face with those memories he had repressed for over fifty years.

"Ishimine, forgive me!"

The color had begun to return to Ishimine's pale face, and his lips regained their luster. Tokushō, despite his fear and self-hatred, grew aroused. Ishimine's tongue glided across the opening on his toe, and then Tokushō let out a small cry with his sexual release.

The lips pulled away. Lightly wiping his mouth with his index finger, Ishimine stood up. He was still seventeen. A smile took shape— around those eyes that stared out beneath the long lashes, on the spare cheeks, on the vermilion lips.

Tokushō burst into anger. "Don't you know how much I've suffered these past fifty years?" Ishimine merely continued to smile, nodding slightly at Tokushō, who flailed his arms in an effort to sit up.

"Thank you. At last the thirst is gone." Speaking in well-accented, standard Japanese, Ishimine held back a smile, saluted, and bowed deeply. He never turned to look back at Tokushō as he slowly vanished into the wall. A newt scampered across the wall's stained surface and caught an insect.

At dawn, Tokushō's wail echoed throughout the village.

Seiyū arrived at the house earlier than usual and was surprised to find Ushi sitting near Tokushō's pillow and crying. Seiyū had never expected to see tears from Ushi, and at first he thought that Tokushō might have died during the night. He timidly took a peek and found Tokushō's eyes wide open and turning toward him. "All cured," announced Tokushō, his unshaven face breaking into a grin. Then he said no more and closed his eyes. Seiyū looked down at Tokushō's leg to discover that the swelling had completely subsided and the dripping had stopped. Roughly a centimeter of water covered the bottom of the bucket. In the water floated a few dead insects. Seiyū tried to tiptoe out of the room, but Ushi noticed and called him back in. Breaking into a cold sweat, Seiyū turned around. Ushi stepped toward him, not even trying to wipe the tears that stained her face. Seiyū was ready to bolt, but Ushi grabbed his hand and held on tight.

"I just wanna' thank ya. It's on account of your help that he's all better." Then she took an envelope out from her bosom and bowed as she pressed it into Seiyū's hand.

"He's my cousin, ain't he? Hey, anybody'd do the same thing," said Seiyū, forcing a smile. Then he promised to return later. As soon as he left the room, he took off running for his house. Now that the water had stopped dripping, there was no reason to stick around the village. He picked up the tote bag containing his money and a change of clothes and went to the public phone in front of the village co-op to call a taxi. The cab was comfortably air conditioned, and as Seiyū caught his breath he remembered the envelope in his pocket. He peeked inside and found three ten thousand-yen notes. For Ushi, this was quite an extravagant display. Although he felt a twinge of guilt, Seiyū reminded himself that he had actually helped take care of Tokushō. He told the taxi driver to hurry. He had reserved an airline ticket but still had one week before his flight and planned to spend the time at a hotel in Naha. He rubbed the carrying bag on the seat beside him. In addition to the five hundred thousand yen in his carrying bag, Seiyū had over ten million yen in a bank account. Yet his bag contained more than just cash and clothes. He had also stored some of the "water" in four stainless-steel thermoses. Now he opened one of the thermoses and took a sip, together with a swig of whiskey. Before he knew it, an itching began in his crotch. Seiyū thought about his travel plans and laughed as the taxi headed for the next town, where he planned to close up his shop.

When Seiyū saw a rowdy crowd of several hundred gathered in front of his shop, he closed the taxi door. At first he thought they were waiting to buy the water, but as he was deciding whether or not to get out of the taxi, he saw something ominous about the crowd. Everyone was covered with hats, masks, or sunglasses, and some people even carried steel bats and martial arts weapons. Just as Seiyū was urging the driver to leave, someone noticed him. In an instant the taxi was surrounded, and Seiyū and his bag were dragged out into the street. Someone held his head. He tried to crouch down, but several hands pulled him to his feet.

A man yelled into his ear, "Git up, you rotten bastard!"

"Yeah, what's really in this water, anyhow?" A bottle was thrust in front of his eyes, and at the bottom a small amount of water sloshed back and forth.

"Yes, that's the miracle water. . . ." replied Seiyū, but before he could finish, a woman's hand slapped him across the face.

"Miracle water, my ass!" The woman tried to grab Seiyū, but the others restrained her. The tip of a high-heeled shoe then struck Seiyū in the shin. Groaning, he bent over to rub his shin, but a man standing directly in front of him pulled him up by the collar.

"You son of a bitch! Take a look at what that rotten water did to me!" The man removed his hat and mask, then took off his sunglasses. His head contained only a sparse covering of a repulsive baby fluff that resembled moss, and his face was covered with splotches and wrinkles.

"What are you going to do about this?" Half-crying, the man shouted at Seiyū. It was the high school teacher, Seiyū's second customer to purchase the water. One after another, those in the crowd removed their hats, masks, and sunglasses. Both the men and women had lost their hair, and with their splotches and moss-covered faces they all looked like eighty-year-olds. Seiyū quickly brought his hand up to his own head, and the hair fell out between his fingers.

"Oh, my god!" Seiyū's cry was cut short by a fist, and he was pressed up against the door of the taxi. His face, reflected in the window glass, seemed to crumble before his eyes. His tote bag was torn open and money floated through the air. Cars stopped, causing a pileup, and people on their way to work rushed to the scene. As horns blared and curses flew back and forth, Seiyū, down on all fours, tried to crawl away, but someone grabbed him by the collar and shoved him down on the sidewalk. Martial arts weapons, high heels, and fists as bony as bird's feet continued to assail Seiyū, who was crouched down like a frightened mouse. A woman who had lost nearly all of her hair and whose wrinkles were so deep that her flesh dangled in multiple folds, took three of the canteens and climbed atop the taxi, where she began sprinkling unsuspecting bystanders with the water and laughing at the top of her lungs. While the mob went wild, overturning taxis and police cars that had rushed to the scene, one of the canteens rolled away. It passed through the legs of the crowd and fell into the river, where it floated out to sea, sparkling in the early morning sunlight.

Ten days had passed. Tokushō gazed out the window at the summer grass in the garden. The soldiers had ceased to appear since the dripping stopped, yet Tokushō was afraid to sleep alone, so for the first few days he had Ushi sleep beside his bed. And, though she protested, Ushi did not mind doing this one bit. Tokushō kept the light on at all times and listened as Ushi told him everything that had happened in the village while he was bedridden. Tokushō had trouble deciding whether to tell her about Ishimine and the other soldiers who came to drink each night, but ultimately he couldn't bring himself to talk about them. In fact, he realized that he would probably never be able to tell her. Once his strength returned, however, he did want to visit the cave together with Ushi. He would merely explain that he had hidden there during the war. They would offer flowers and look for any human bones that still remained. Having made this decision, however, Tokushō was afraid that he'd start putting things off and allow his memories to fade—that he would again try to forget about Ishimine. He even began drinking again despite his repeated vows never to touch another drop. When he went to pay a sick call on Seiyū, who had been confined to bed since his beating, Tokushō ran into some of his old drinking pals who had stopped by, and he ended up joining them. Seiyū had to drink the *awamori* through a straw, since both his arms were broken, but the party continued even after he passed out. Then someone brought out the cards. The next morning Ushi found Tokushō asleep outside the gate in front of their house. She gave him a sharp kick and headed for the fields without saying a word.

"Starting tomorrow I'll go out to the fields and work," Tokushō told himself. He decided to cut the overgrown grass in order to regain his strength, so he went to the shed, got out the sickle, and stepped down to the back garden. The grass had grown as high as his waist. He was amazed at its vitality but also worried that a *habu* snake might be hiding there. Taking a stick, he started beating around the roots. Then he hit something firm and the stick rebounded. Sifting through the grass, beneath a hedge of Chinese hibiscus, lay an enormous gourd melon too big for even Tokushō to carry.

Fine hairs glistened on the deep green skin. Tokushō gasped in surprise, then gave it a kick, but it wouldn't budge. A long vine, thick as a thumb, grew from the gourd to the hibiscus. At the end of the vine, a yellow flower swayed against the blue sky. The flower was so bright it made Tokushō's eyes brim with tears.

TRANSLATED BY MICHAEL MOLASKY

Matayoshi Eiki (1949–)

Matayoshi Eiki is the most prolific and successful Okinawan writer of his generation. Born in Urasoe, he graduated from the University of the Ryukyus and has spent nearly his entire life in Okinawa. Matayoshi regularly publishes fiction in prominent national magazines and has several volumes of stories to his name. He has received literary acclaim from both regional and national forums, having won the Ryūkyū Shinpō *Short Story Prize, the Kyūshū Arts Festival Literary Prize, and the Akutagawa Prize. Despite these accolades, Matayoshi has not "played it safe" by sticking to successful themes or comfortable points of view in his stories. On the contrary, he is constantly experimenting: he has narrated the experiences of a paranoid G.I. in Okinawa during the Vietnam War, a Korean man accused of rape, and Okinawan bar hostesses.*

In "Fortunes by the Sea," Matayoshi brings a deft, humorous touch to this depiction of Kazuhisa, a young Okinawan man who finds himself in the unaccustomed role of the bored and frustrated househusband. Kazuhisa's marriage brings about a reversal of traditional gender roles because he has given up his name and other patriarchal prerogatives by marrying into his bride's family. Although less common today than in the prewar era, this practice continues in mainland Japan as well as in Okinawa when a family without male offspring wants to maintain its family line—and succeeds in attracting a willing groom. Kazuhisa's predicament is exacerbated by geographical isolation: he lives on a small island off the shore of northern Okinawa (which itself is largely rural), and this offers few opportunities for suitable work.

As with many of his recent stories, "Fortunes by the Sea" refers to local customs and religious beliefs. Since Matayoshi writes for a broad readership, he often provides explanations of such material through paraphrase, glosses enclosed in parentheses, or other means. Readers of the translation below should assume that most explanatory passages are contained in the original Japanese text and have not been added by the translator.

286

FORTUNES BY THE SEA

———⋙⋘———

MATAYOSHI EIKI

. 1 .

THAT THE MARRIAGE came about quickly was due to a lack of concern over "blood," given how many degrees of kinship separated them.
The other reason was that the ridiculing by the young unmarried men
here on T— Island had gotten to be far too irritating.

On T— Island, there were no playhouses or movie theaters where
the two of them felt comfortable just sitting together silently for any
length of time. There were a few coffee shops. But these, while pro-
claiming themselves coffee shops on signs out front, were also bars that
served *awamori*. Five young men, having an afternoon drink at one
such place, noticed Kazuhisa and the girl there drinking coffee and
started teasing them. All five of the young men were three or four years
younger than Kazuhisa, who was twenty-two. None of the five had
made it as far as high school.

Kazuhisa and the girl often went for drives. A few days before,
when the two of them were driving along the twelve-or-so-mile road
circling the island, a large black car pulled up beside them. The five
young men thrust their heads out the windows and started giggling
girlishly, mocking them. Their car was traveling in the oncoming traffic lane. At a big curve in the road, it nearly collided head-on with a
small pickup truck driven by an old man on his way home from work
in the sugarcane fields. Pulled sharply to one side to avoid colliding,
the car ran off onto an expanse of exposed coral rock, the sharp teeth
of which blew out the front and rear tires. Concerned they might be

hurt, Kazuhisa stopped the car, but Misako said, "They had it coming to them." And then she said, "Frustration sure is a problem. By themselves, each of them is a weakling, but the five of them come together and they get like that."

She was dark-skinned and, rare on the island, had narrow eyes and eyelids with no fold. Five feet two, her arms were slender and her breasts rose soft and full. Her straight hair fell down her back, and she had a headband across her forehead.

"Too bad. It was a nice car."

"They're all farmer's kids; they've got money," she said. "The poor people have all left the island. It's only the rich that stayed. Come on, let's go."

It really wasn't much of a drive: half an hour took them all the way around the island and back where they had started. Kazuhisa felt most comfortable when he was driving, but since he couldn't just circle round and round the island, they usually parked the car under a tree or in the shadow of the rocks on the shore and ate the lunch Misako had prepared or played cards or something. They never did really talk.

There was no need to. Kazuhisa was only two years older than Misako, so they had often seen each other when they were in their early school days. At the springtime feast at the ancestral tomb, at New Year's, the summer *O-bon* festival, and other traditional gatherings of the *munchuu* (the full kin group), Misako sometimes came up to him to strike up a conversation. When adoption became a possibility, Kazuhisa found himself recalling Misako back then: in bobbed hair, long eyelashes over narrow eyes, and her single-fold eyelids; and later in her schoolgirl's sailor blouse and skirt, her long hair tied in back.

There were no schools on the island past junior high school, so to go on with schooling, you had to travel to the main island of Okinawa. Kazuhisa and Misako both went to the academic prefectural high school located at the neck of Motobu, the northern peninsula on the main island that their own island stood offshore from. A ferry made the trip back and forth several times a day, so they could have commuted from home, but Kazuhisa, naturally shy around strangers, took a room in a small boardinghouse run by an old woman. Misako, who was relaxed and open around people, lived in the school dorm. After graduation, Kazuhisa entered Okinawa International University, a private university in Ginowan, in the central part of Okinawa Island. Misako returned to their home island and got a job in the village office. She confided to Kazuhisa at the time that the head of the village council, a distant relative, had used his influence to get her the job. There were not many jobs on the island for women, most of whom went off to the Okinawan capital at Naha, got work as shop clerks and such, and almost never moved back.

The reason Misako had come back, Kazuhisa imagined, was to "take in" a husband. Her parents had had difficulty producing children. It was in the twelfth year of their marriage that they had finally managed to have Misako, and only after consulting a *yuta* and following her advice. The aged *yuta*—as Okinawan shamans are called—died soon thereafter.

"If only that *yuta* were still alive," Misako's mother often complained to her husband. "It's all because you didn't go back while she was still alive and find out what to do."

"She already told us," the normally unresponsive husband defended himself. "After the first child came, she said, it would be like the dam had burst and they'd be coming one after another."

Misako's parents were obsessed with their desire to have a son to inherit the family mortuary tablets and property—the family house and the lands they leased to the U.S. military. Even after Misako had entered junior high school, her parents, still at it, had gone with another *yuta*—this time from the main island of Okinawa —on pilgrimages around T— Island and to spots all over the main island as well. They prayed for a son at the various *utaki*, sacred places where supplication is made, marked by no more than an incense burner located below a crag jutting out over the sea, at the bases of cliffs, or under trees the Okinawans consider sacred, such as the *gajumaru* and the fan palm. After Misako, however, there were no more children, not even daughters. Her parents sought desperately to recall conditions at the time of Misako's birth and tried each and every thing they could think of, but none of it worked.

The families of Kazuhisa and Misako went down to the beach, put charcoal in the barbecue they set up there, and had a get-together over beer and the beef and chicken they cooked. This beach party, Kazuhisa surmised, was to arrange the marriage, or at least begin talking about it.

Kazuhisa had a mother and four older brothers; his father had contracted tetanus and died when Kazuhisa was a still a baby. Three of his brothers lived on the main island of Okinawa. The only brother left on this island was the eldest, who lived with Kazuhisa and their mother. There had been no girls; their father and mother had had five boys, each time hoping the next would be a girl.

With five boys on her hands after the death of Kazuhisa's father, his mother was thrown into despair. A proposal to adopt Kazuhisa came from his father's childless younger brother and wife when they visited to offer incense for the departed. A woman raising five boys by herself was just too much, they argued, and asked his mother to let them know after the forty-ninth day memorial service had passed. Kazuhisa's mother wavered for weeks, but in the end she declined politely, saying that children should be raised by their own mother and that no matter how poor they got to be, she would raise them herself. She began working the vegetable fields left by Kazuhisa's father and sold household goods door-to-door when she had time.

When he was in junior high school, Kazuhisa was told by his next older brother that it was his fate to become an "adopted husband." He had to look the words up in a dictionary to find out what they meant. It was a mystery to him at the time why he, of all the brothers, had been singled out. Gradually, he came to accept the possibility that it was his fate to be adopted, but even so, the very idea continued to nag at him. One thing or another kept bringing it to the fore. It might be for the same reason, he speculated, that he felt such boyish awkwardness around girls. Of course, thinking he was shy only made him that much more so. Later, on three separate occasions when he was a college student, female classmates came on to him, perhaps attracted by his strong physique or by his gentle personality. Each time he bungled things, had no idea what to say, and ended up shrinking away in retreat. From then on he was convinced that he was to have no luck with the girls.

Misako's mother, whose health had been declining for some time, was discovered the year before to have cancer of the pancreas. Misako and her father kept the news secret from her, but the mother, sensing the end was near, wanted to see her own grandchildren, or if that were impossible, at least have the satisfaction of seeing Misako in her wedding dress. She wasted no words complaining of her illness; instead she pleaded with them, arguing that she couldn't bear to have a complete stranger walk off with their property and that Misako's distant relative, Kazuhisa, was a quiet and a fine young man and they should propose adopting him as Misako's husband. Informed by the doctors there was nothing more they could do for the woman, Misako and her father tearfully agreed between themselves to have the wedding as soon as possible, bring peace of mind to Misako's mother, and send her off thus on the journey to *gusō*—the next world.

Kazuhisa was twenty-two years old when the proposal for adoption came. His mother and four brothers took the view that he was entering into marriage rather than going off into adoption. For Kazuhisa, who graduated from college that same month, it was as if something long expected had finally come. He had the vague feeling that marrying Misako was the best way to wipe away his perplexing feelings of inferiority around women. He concluded that this was how things were meant to be for him. It also occurred to him that being an adopted husband would not be without some interest of its own.

From his mother and brothers Kazuhisa was urged over and over to accept and "go into adoption." He thought it right that he should, and then, one day, he sought the opinion of the *kami*. He was partly serious about this and partly just going through the motions; mostly he just wanted to put the responsibility on someone besides himself.

There was an old, large nonflowering male *deigo* tree on the edge of the village. People said that the *kami* that came to rest there prophesied the future of anyone happening to fall asleep in the tree's shadow. Kazuhisa ordinarily cared little for such notions, but when he actually stretched himself out under the tree, he felt his heartbeat quicken. The breeze gently stroking his body was cool and refreshing, yet he was in such anticipation of the dream that he had trouble falling asleep. After a half hour passed, he got up, bought a few cans of beer at the village general store nearby, and returned to his spot under the tree.

Forcing himself to drink in the middle of the day had the intended effect. His body took on a warm glow, and drowsiness soon overcame him. It was a wildly disconnected dream he had. In one fragment he was writhing in agony on the ground after Misako, convinced there was a carrot missing from the crop, kicked him in the crotch. In another, he was left behind, in tears, at the top of a cliff as his mother and brothers receded far across the dark sea. It was days before these dreams finally lost their firm hold on him. The message, apparently, was that he could not expect a happy married life. This was disheartening, but he had no choice now but to give his consent.

A few days before the exchange of wedding gifts, Misako's mother took a turn for the worse and was taken to the big general hospital on Motobu. Misako, who was now working at the village office, used vacation time to take off work every day at 4:00, make dinner for her father and a packed meal for herself, and then take the 5:00 ferry to the mainland. She put up a folding lounge chair beside her mother's bed and tended to her through the night. In the morning, she took the first ferry back to the island and used another hour of vacation time to begin work at 9:30. She kept this up for more than three months. Anyone serving her mother with such devotion, Kazuhisa reasoned, will surely do well enough by me. His confidence in the decision strengthened.

A lull in the illness allowed Misako's mother to return home. Soon, however, the pain worsened. "Let me go back to the hospital," she pleaded with her husband and daughter. "I can't go on like this. Please, let me die." She thought hospitals were where you went to die. Her husband, a fisherman and man of few words, consoled her as best he could; clinging to one last hope, he returned her to the hospital. The doctors decided on final, radical measures and were on the point of proceeding when Misako's mother, so thin and frail now she seemed the ghost of herself, slipped out of the hospital alone, boarded the ferry, and returned home. "Hospitals take you away from everyone" was the reason she gave.

And so in the end it was at home, in the room housing the family altar, that she died. For days she appealed to the ancestors enshrined at the altar. On the eve of the day she died, almost wholly without consciousness now, she took hold of Misako's hand. Stroking her cheek with it, she opened her sightless, film-covered eyes and muttered over and over, *"Wan chakushi, wan chakushi"* (My son, my son). Consciousness slipped slowly away; by dawn she was dead. Misako told Kazuhisa that at first she felt resentment that her own existence had been ignored at the final moment. But then it struck her just how badly her mother had wanted a boy, and she felt sorry for her. Later, Misako told him, she began to suspect that her father had blamed her mother for their failure to have a son.

The wedding was held one month after the initial forty-nine-day period of mourning, at around dawn, to coincide with high tide. Misako's father dismissed the timing as superstition, but Kazuhisa's mother and brothers, harboring some apprehension perhaps, insisted on it. Only close relatives were invited to the reception.

The marriage of Kazuhisa, fresh out of college, and Misako, who had just celebrated her coming-of-age ceremony, resembled a piece of unripe fruit fallen to the ground. Misako, full of life and energy and giving not a hint of it in her expression, was in fact terrified of sex. Running off to meetings every night, as she began to do, might be explained as her escape from this fear.

. 2 .

IT MIGHT HAVE been the quality of Kazuhisa's cooking that had the newly married Misako eating so much. She was helping herself to seconds, even. Kazuhisa was happy to see her take such pleasure in the things he prepared, but the spectacle of a woman feeding herself with no thought of how it might appear to others impressed on him how oddly pathetic his situation was. It irritated him and made him lose his own appetite. He cooked two meals for them every day, but both Misako and her father took this as a matter of course, it seemed, never offering so much as one word of thanks or appreciation.

It also didn't really matter what Kazuhisa cooked. Misako said nothing, neither praising nor finding fault with the meal. She would simply finish, put on her heavy makeup, and in buoyant spirits leave the house. Kazuhisa had imagined that once they married, they would be able to go out together all they liked. As it turned out, however, night after night Misako attended meetings of one group or another—clubs for people with this or that shared interest, groups of people working in some movement or other. She even became the leader for some of these groups. She was out of the house nights and on her days off. Sometimes when she came back home she'd still be dressed for the group's activity, in a hula skirt, for example, or in an outfit for dancing to American country music.

When they went out on dates before they got married, Misako often wore neatly ironed skirts, but now when she went to work in the village office she went in jeans. She wore them tight around the waist, making her belly stick out. Kazuhisa thought a skirt would be better but soon convinced himself that it was all right.

The reasons given for his adoption were that there was no male child to inherit the family property and that there was no one to look after the family mortuary tablets once his father-in-law died. But far from receiving any of the family assets, Kazuhisa got no more than an allowance and had to keep a record of all his purchases to boot. Such matters as family property and mortuary tablets were far in the future; for now, he had only to keep an eye on how his silent father-in-law was doing and see to his needs.

Kazuhisa never once opposed his father-in-law, nor did he ever complain to his mother or to his brothers about the situation they had put him in. As a consequence, he acquired a reputation around the island as being a fine young man. Inwardly, however, he was not at all content.

On nights when there was little to cook, he would take a lesser portion than his wife and father-in-law, even though it was he who had prepared the meal. When this happened, he got hungry during the night and went downstairs to nibble on a meat or fish-paste sausage that he pulled from the kitchen shelves or from the refrigerator.

In time, Kazuhisa came to consider the cooking a remedy for his boredom and so ceased to be bothered by it, but shopping at the small grocery store a short distance from the house made him feel self-conscious. The heavyset woman in her seventies who ran the store, with few customers and much time on her hands, talked so much whenever Kazuhisa appeared that it seemed to him she'd never hand over the things he had asked for. In fact, she did remember exactly what he had requested and, after chattering on for a good long time, fetched the things from the shelves behind her. In exasperation, Kazuhisa sometimes drove the pickup truck east for the fifteen minutes it took to get to the supermarket near the harbor. Although he was a longtime customer and well known in the store, the young girls working there never went beyond a simple "Thank you very much." He could get the things he wanted off the shelves for himself at that store. But he found the curt manner of the clerks not really to his liking, and since there was no one left for him to talk to once Misako and his father-in-law left for the day, Kazuhisa headed over to the general store.

It was his habit each day around 2:00 in the afternoon to nap in the shade of the male *deigo* tree on the edge of the village where he had received his dream oracle. When he opened his eyes an hour or so later, he'd find himself feeling sluggish and listless. At such times, hearing the old shop lady's talk reinvigorated him. There were vending machines in front of the shop. Kazuhisa would gulp down a Coke and then go inside.

One day when he was there shopping, the woman started telling him about herself. Her husband had been a fisherman. When he was out in the open sea working the nets one day, he was attacked, she said, by a man-eating shark. The children, three boys and two girls, each received their share of the inheritance and left for the main island of Okinawa or for the home islands of Japan, and not one of them, she told him, had ever returned. After hearing her tale, Kazuhisa came to feel a bit of affection for the old woman.

The old woman didn't restrict herself to her own tale; she relayed gossip about the people in the village, too. This included tales about Kazuhisa's wife and father-in-law. For some reason Kazuhisa found it distasteful to learn these secrets; and before she got too deeply into them, he would force a change of subject. It was more natural, he thought, to learn these secrets little by little as he went on living with them. It didn't matter that he didn't learn everything; he could just as well live the rest of his life without knowing. Discovering what you had to know prior to a marriage was one thing, he felt; but afterward to be told all their secrets and shortcomings did no one any good.

In point of fact, his father-in-law was someone Kazuhisa hardly knew. There was something unapproachable about him. Kazuhisa's own mother and brothers had been quite active in pushing for the adoption, but, Kazuhisa couldn't stop thinking, his father-in-law had seemed much less enthusiastic. Only recently had Kazuhisa finally been able to address him as "Father." "Father" would come home from fishing, eat the dinner Kazuhisa had prepared, and then drink *awamori* and play the *sanshin*. It was especially hard to talk with him at this time. After he lost his wife, he began playing the *sanshin* and singing every night. It wasn't that Kazuhisa lacked musical skills; it was just hard to join in with him.

Kazuhisa always wondered if his father-in-law's true intention was to make a fisherman of his college-educated son-in-law. *There are few college graduates on the island, so I should be able to get good work, and if I do*, Kazuhisa thought, *Father will surely think better of me.* The household could easily live off the enormous amount of money they received each year from land leased to the U.S. military, but his father-in-law continued to fish, and Misako worked at the village office. Since Kazuhisa did nothing but the housework, he was convinced that his wife's relatives thought he had married for the money. There were two or three women in the neighborhood who spent all their time each day learning how to make pottery at the community center. Kazuhisa was incapable of doing that sort of thing.

He had taken his degree in sociology. His classmates were now teachers in junior and senior high schools. He didn't feel cut out to be a teacher, and so he hadn't gotten his credentials. He did take the prefectural civil service exam but failed it. He noticed how popular an interest in the local history—in bringing to light local customs and traditions—had become. The public offices on the island had not yet published a local history. He knew the village office did not take on new hires unless one of the older employees died or someone retired, but one night, after Misako returned from an activity of the Smart Consumers Club, he broached the subject. "Does the village office have any plans to put together a village history?" He was at his wit's end trying to come up with something but tried not to show it. They discussed in some detail the importance of village histories and where other localities were in their publication efforts. She readily agreed with his idea, told him to come to the office around 10:00 the next morning, and then, apparently tired from her activities at the Smart Consumers Club, went to sleep.

On the second floor of the village office the next morning, there was only one employee of Kazuhisa's age, a young woman. The five or six middle-aged female employees, taking their fifteen-minute morning break at 10:00, sat together eating cookies they had brought from home and the different varieties of rice crackers visitors from outside the island had given them. They talked on without letup over the noise they made munching their snacks. Kazuhisa sat on the black seat in the hallway and waited to be called by the head of the general affairs section. At 10:40, Misako emerged from the vice mayor's office and sat down beside Kazuhisa. She had talked not just with the head of the general affairs section, she said, but also with the vice mayor and the mayor. "It's premature to consider publication of a village history at this time, and, furthermore, employing a husband and wife in the same public office violates equality of opportunity" was all the answer she got. Misako seemed unaffected.

"You don't necessarily have to work, you know. I'm working, and Father gives us money every year from the military rentals."

"You say I don't have to work, but cooking and washing the dishes and doing the wash . . ." Kazuhisa stopped, concerned someone might overhear him.

"That's why I said you don't 'necessarily' have to. I'm not telling you to sleep all day morning till night. In my case, I'm at this office during the day, and then at night I'm on the staff of all sorts of organizations. Two of me wouldn't be enough to keep up with it all."

"And if bad rumors? . . ."

"What's bad? Cooking? The wash? Nobody thinks anything of it. It's you who are making a big fuss. No one thinks anything of it, so there's no way rumors'll get started. As long as there's nothing funny, nothing strange, no one's going to spread any rumors and no one's going to listen."

Kazuhisa said nothing.

"If there were any rumors, I would have heard them long ago. I see and talk with lots of people every day. You shouldn't be thinking such things."

Neither his wife nor his father-in-law pressured Kazuhisa to "give heart and soul to work," as the expression has it. So he continued making their two meals a day. In the afternoons, after eating some breakfast leftovers for lunch, he sat in the shade of the male *deigo* tree where he received his dream oracle; late at night he went fishing. It occurred to him from time to time that his real work was probably just to make his wife pregnant with a child she could leave the family property to.

People say that after marriage it's the woman who becomes absorbed with sex, but Misako, for whatever reason, seemed very little interested. By 10:00 most nights she had gone to sleep on her own, exhausted from her meetings and activities. Kazuhisa's interest focused on late-night fishing. The hour or two before and after midnight were the best time for catching *taman*, the most highly prized fish. The nightly schedules of Kazuhisa and Misako took them away from each other, but neither thought much of the matter, and both went on with their new life together, such as it was.

But in the abundance of time he had, Kazuhisa eventually fell to thinking, as he sat idly one day under the male *deigo* tree, of the dream oracle. Why was it that his wife went to sleep so early? Before they married, Kazuhisa had not been all that attracted to her, but once they had, his sexual interest in her increased by the day. For her part, Misako seemed unable to erase the impression she had of him as just an older brother she had known from childhood.

. 3 .

MISAKO'S FATHER FELT very beholden to his wife and thus meant to please her, but even while she was still alive he never missed his nightly drink of *awamori*. Misako recognized something free and easy about him after her mother's death that was at odds with his loneliness.

All of a sudden one day, his drinking increased alarmingly, numbness of the limbs and confusion in his speech soon followed, and so Misako made him go with her to the hospital on the main island where her mother had stayed. Early-term alcoholism was the diagnosis, but Misako let him continue his evening drink anyway. Since he went out fishing every day and never failed to have his two meals each day, she claimed, whether or not he drank at night should be left to him. Kazuhisa thought his eating wasn't the issue; he had been worried for some time about the dangers of letting an old alcoholic go out fishing. And indeed, as he left the house with his fishing gear and the lunch Kazuhisa had made him under his arm, there was a wobble in his father-in-law's walk, and his head swayed from side to side atop a very uncertain support. In this condition, it was only a matter of time before he fell into the sea.

After dinner one night, Kazuhisa and Misako went upstairs. It was one of the infrequent nights when Misako did not go to one of her meetings.

"Don't you think it is dangerous to let Father go out fishing in his condition?" Kazuhisa chose what seemed the right moment to ask.

"He'd only get worse if he weren't allowed to work," Misako said. "He's a fisherman, so he's not going to fall in. It's his body, not his head, that knows what to do. You needn't worry. It's because I want him to live long that I let him go out fishing."

"Why not suggest he cut back on his drinking?"

"That would only make him drink more. And he'd start hiding it from us. Are you prepared to stand watch over him all day long? I don't think you could do that. Just imagine—Father feeling guilty and having to sneak around like a criminal to have a drink. I don't want to ever see him like that."

"I know, but he's drinking more now."

"It'll go down again. If he thinks he won't be able to fish anymore, he'll cut back by himself. Father can't live without fishing. He may not know that himself, though. It's the blood, I suppose—it's the body that knows."

Kazuhisa had no answer.

"Look," she continued. "What do you think would happen if he quit fishing? He wouldn't have to worry about falling into the sea then and so he'd drink all the more."

"He doesn't take any with him when he goes fishing, does he? That is tea he has in his flask."

"But when he's at home, he's drinking the whole time."

"So it seems."

"Days he can't go out fishing, keep an eye on him, will you?"

"But your father never talks. Nothing but food and drink all day—the two of us will end up being domesticated pigs. That's an idea for you—two men becoming domesticated pigs."

"A man should work, right up till the day he dies."

Kazuhisa said nothing.

"Don't you take up drinking at night."

For the first time in a long while, Misako went into the kitchen and began washing the dishes. Kazuhisa sat at the low dining table and drank one cup of tea after another.

Several days later, Kazuhisa sat under the male *deigo* tree of the dream oracle and fell to daydreaming. The idea came to him that if he joined his father-in-law in his nightly drinking and chatted with him as they drank together, then the amount his father-in-law consumed might be reduced.

"I think I'll start drinking with Father every night," Kazuhisa ventured to propose to Misako on another night she hadn't gone to one of her meetings. She had just finished her bath and her hair was wet.

"Father likes to drink by himself. He's talking to Mother; he's singing songs for her. You'd be getting in the way. He doesn't want to talk with me, either. We shouldn't spoil his routine. During the day he goes fishing, and at night he drinks and talks with Mother. Do you understand what I'm saying? We really shouldn't disrupt this routine as long as Father lives."

Kazuhisa doubted that he really did talk with his dead wife. If he did, it would show somehow—his eyes would be moist, or there'd be some trace of nostalgia in his voice—but all Kazuhisa could see was a man having a drink and playing the *sanshin*. The only way to find out if he really was talking to someone in the realm beyond was to ask him;

what anyone else had to say about it, Kazuhisa felt, got you nowhere. He didn't say this to Misako.

The conversation now took an unexpected turn.

"If you become a good fisherman, Father would feel confidence that he had an heir. And, if that were the case, his drinking wouldn't get any worse even if he didn't go out fishing."

"Me become a fisherman?"

"He'd see himself in you doing the fishing. The more fishing you do, the more life you'll give the fisherman in Father.

What, Kazuhisa asked himself, *could she be talking about? I'm a college graduate, and I went to college precisely to avoid such backbreaking work. It wasn't to succeed someone as a fisherman that I came here as an adopted husband.*

"Look," Misako continued, "I'm not telling you that you have to become a fisherman, but if you can do it, I hope that you will. My grandfather was a fisherman too, and I have great respect for it. It's work that's good for you as a human being. If I were a man, it's what I would do."

Misako seemed to penetrate into Kazuhisa's innermost thoughts with these words.

Introverted by nature, Kazuhisa had no particular desire to be talking with his father-in-law. He sensed, though, that if he went out fishing, it would elevate him in Misako's eyes. He had gone fishing with his father-in-law four times since the marriage. He had learned how to work the engine and even how to steer the boat, but each time he had gotten seasick. Talk then was the furthest thing from his mind—it was all he could to do just to endure the agony he was in.

Fishing itself Kazuhisa liked; it was the seasickness that was the problem. He was given lots of advice: eat dried plums, for example, or look up at the clouds rather than down at the water. He tried all of these things, but none of it worked. Eating dried plums was in any case thought to jinx a fisherman and keep the fish away, and whenever you fish you're always looking at the water rather than the sky. He was not superstitious, but again and again he stole off to pray to the *kami* of safe sea passage enshrined on a small rock near the fishing harbor. Needless to say, this, too, did no good.

Kazuhisa told himself that the only way he would ever get used to the sea was through persistence. He just had to keep going out on the *sabani,* the small boats Okinawan men used for fishing. And then, once he could hold his own on the water, he'd have the respect of his wife and of his father-in-law.

A precocious fellow one year ahead of him in grade school had once told Kazuhisa that if you kept thanking the fish as you fished them, then you'd never get seasick. Maybe you could do that with a dog or a goat or some other animal that takes to humans, Kazuhisa thought, but how could you even be serious in doing this with something like a fish, which didn't even have arms and legs.

On Kazuhisa's third time fishing, his father-in-law entrusted him with steering the *sabani,* his idea apparently being that if Kazuhisa was concentrating on something, he shouldn't get seasick. But Kazuhisa did get sick, nearly ran the boat aground on the reef, and got himself yelled at by his father-in-law.

. 4 .

MISAKO WAS AT a welcoming party for temporary employees at work, held at the island's one large restaurant. Kazuhisa, at home, felt how burdensome it was making dinner. As he prepared the fish his father-in-law had brought home, he felt the urge to telephone Misako and tell her to come home. Was it good for them to go on like this? Then he realized there was another way. "If we have a child, both Father and Misako will change. I don't know just how they'll change, but surely change there will be. I'll be freed from doing the housework. And, if there's a child to raise and Misako has to quit her work at the village office, then I'll have to get a regular job. But there are no regular jobs on the island besides fishing. . . ."

Kazuhisa reminded himself how much he liked to fish. If he could somehow overcome the problem of his seasickness, he could do it as a regular job. But even if he did, how could he ever support an unemployed wife and the child they'd have by the sort of fishing his father-in-law did? He seemed only to be fishing for the sport of it, with that ice chest of his and the bamboo poles and reels loaded on his *sabani*. Occasionally the catch was big enough to take over to the cooperative, but more often he had only enough to sell privately to the boarding-house. His father-in-law had the land he leased to the U.S. military. The site of a U.S. military communications station at the northern end of the island was held in his name. During the course of the year, he received quite a large amount of money in rent. If Misako quit her job at the village office, then her father, Kazuhisa allowed himself some hope, might give this money to them. As he placed a fish in the pan, oil splattered and raised a great noise. The sound was pleasing to him.

When he ate the fried fish later with his father-in-law, Kazuhisa told him he would go fishing with him the next day. His father-in-law mumbled, barely audibly, that he thought he'd just get seasick, but he offered no opposition.

Kazuhisa got up at 5:00 the next morning and made lunches for the three of them. His wife helped for the first time in a long while. "I hope you won't be getting seasick," she told him. She didn't say, "Because I'm counting on a big catch from you." It was taboo to say this to a fisherman.

The two of them left the house. The hands of his alcoholic father-in-law were shaking so much that the small things in his gearbox rattled around noisily. He sometimes lost his balance, bumping into Kazuhisa or brushing into the low branches on the trees.

At 7:00, his father-in-law unsteadily boarded his *sabani*, which they had launched from the sandy beach. The beach, located a short distance from the fishing harbor, was lined with screw pines. "Shall I steer?" Kazuhisa asked. His father-in-law started the engine without answering. Within a few moments, his body displayed a strength that made him hardly recognizable. His back straightened, his head ceased to sway, and his eyes remained fixed on the surface of the sea in front of him. The *sabani* sliced through the water, pressing forward with great speed. The sun was up in the sky now. Beneath the clear blue water, myriad varieties of coral were visible.

The instant they passed the reef and were out in the open sea, Kazuhisa got sick. His face lost color and he broke out in a cold sweat. He felt sick in his stomach and in his chest. "You'll feel better if you throw up," his father-in-law told him, but he showed no signs of turning back to the beach. The spray from the prow of the *sabani* as it cut through the water struck Kazuhisa in the face. The strong wind quickly dried off the moisture, leaving his face sticky from the salt.

"Whoever heard of a man getting seasick," his father-in-law ridiculed him. "Is this a woman that's married into the family?"

"Before agreeing to this, I never promised I'd do any fishing," Kazuhisa tried to defend himself. He was having such a hard time breathing and moving his mouth, and the boat engine and strong wind were making such noise, that his words failed to reach his father-in-law's ears.

Why, Kazuhisa wondered, had he ever let himself become an adopted husband? If he hadn't, he wouldn't be suffering as he was now. The idea even came to him that he'd be better off letting himself fall the foot or so down the side of the boat and into the dark blue sea.

At long last, the *sabani* came to a stop. The spray ceased striking Kazuhisa in the face and neck. While the *sabani* was proceeding on its course, it was generally dipping fore and aft, but now it began pitching and rolling wildly in all directions. Kazuhisa's body, now devoid of all strength, pitched and rolled in rhythm with it. The engine was silent, but in its place Kazuhisa could hear, from deep within his ears, the sound of his own heart beating. The noise of the engine and the water spray on his face, Kazuhisa realized, had effectively diverted his attention from his nausea. Now he heard the sound of the water softly lapping the side of the boat and then the sound of vomit heaved up from his stomach.

His father-in-law prepared his equipment. He was going to fish with pole and line, using a simple pole and reel of the kind people had taken to during the recent fishing craze. He used the common sort of sinker and hook available anywhere. Kazuhisa had assumed from this that his father-in-law had not been fishing all that long, but in fact, he had known nothing but fishing since the time he was ten years old.

His father-in-law took a handful of krill and shoved it into his bait pouch. The putrid stench overpowered Kazuhisa; vomit heaved up and out his mouth in one rush. The discharge fell onto the surface of the blue sea, quickly dispersed, then disappeared.

After thrusting his rod into the water, his father-in-law began scattering the bait on the surface and then turned to Kazuhisa. "You put a rod in, too. You'll get better if you catch something."

Kazuhisa shook his head with all the strength he had. He wanted to say that seasickness was not something so easily cured, but as he opened his mouth, the nausea again overwhelmed him. His father-in-law rubbed Kazuhisa's bent-over back. The hand bore the awful stench of the bait. Kazuhisa became even more sick. Rubbing his back improved nothing, but his father-in-law kept rubbing all the harder. Kazuhisa raised his head and looked at his father-in-law.

"I'm all right now."

"Put your rod in the water. Then you'll be all right."

His father-in-law stopped rubbing and handed Kazuhisa a carbon rod that had an attached reel. Kazuhisa did as he was told and grasped the rod firmly. "Stick the krill into the bait pouch," his father-in-law said. The plastic bucket he handed Kazuhisa was packed, disgustingly so as far as Kazuhisa was concerned, with the dark red krill. He tried to catch his breath. But almost immediately he lost control and in a single massive gulp filled his lungs with the stench. Nausea overpowered him again. Kazuhisa decided not to use the krill but instead to bait the hook with shrimp. In an instant, the line attached to the sinker disappeared deep into the water.

Kazuhisa sat bent over like an invalid and grasped weakly the fishing rod that lay between his knees. He had lost the will to do battle with the fish. He prayed that he wouldn't catch anything and that the time would pass by quickly. But neither the sun with its blinding brightness nor the pile upon pile of white clouds in the sky moved at all.

Kazuhisa also prayed that his father-in-law caught nothing. He figured that if he wasn't catching anything, he'd give up and they'd go back in. In answer to these prayers, there was no movement on their rods for more than half an hour. His father-in-law turned on the engine and the boat started to move. Kazuhisa gave a sigh of relief. The sea spray splashed in on them, and the *sabani* dipped low between waves, then rose again, as it moved steadily forward. *I've made it; I just have to hold out a little longer,* Kazuhisa told himself.

A large rock near the shore came into view. Kazuhisa recognized it as the rock near the cape, directly opposite the beach they had set out from that morning. What little strength Kazuhisa had managed to hold on to now deserted him completely. His father-in-law wasn't taking the boat in; he was just moving it to a spot farther out. Turning the *sabani* this way and that, his father-in-law scanned the surface of the water, searching for the spot he was after. There were no rocks or coral on the bottom, no current in the water, and to Kazuhisa's eyes, it was everywhere the same solemn sea showing no variation in color anywhere.

His father-in-law, however, seemed finally to have found what he was looking for, maneuvered the boat delicately, and then dropped anchor. The water wasn't deep. He again shoved the foul-smelling krill into the bait pouch and dropped it in the water. This time Kazuhisa prayed that he'd catch lots of fish. If he had a big catch, his father-in-law would be satisfied, he'd be able to boast of his catch to Kazuhisa, and they'd go back sooner. Sure enough, before many minutes had passed, the fish came, lured by the smell of the krill. Three, even four, of them at a time caught onto the same hook. Kazuhisa couldn't take his eyes off the fish as one after another their faces rose to the surface of the blue sea. He felt sick but thrust his own pole in. The fish caught on his line, too. Almost all were of the same kind and of about the same size. Some jumped into the air, their scales flashing bright in the light. Kazuhisa was exhilarated. When he removed the fish or impaled the bait on his small hook, however, he still felt nauseous.

At 12:00, his father-in-law put up his reel and ate his lunch. Kazuhisa didn't put any food in his mouth. When his father-in-law finished eating, he started up the engine again.

Finally, a little after 2:00, they arrived back at the beach they had left that morning. Kazuhisa got out of the boat, felt dizzy, and so squatted down in the surf. The water covered him up to the waist. He lifted his head. His father-in-law was pushing the *sabani* from the tail end. Kazuhisa stood up, clenched his teeth, took up a position beside his father-in-law, and pushed with all his might. His father-in-law said nothing. Kazuhisa had no idea if he had any strength or if what he was doing was having any effect, but he continued pushing. "That's enough," his father-in-law finally said. Kazuhisa felt deflated, thinking he had been of no help. But the boat was now up on dry sand. His father-in-law fastened the cable from the boat to a post on the beach.

His father-in-law took up the gearbox and the lunch boxes; Kazuhisa picked up the fishing rods and the ice chest containing their catch and followed a few steps behind. From a path through the screw pines they came out onto a farm road. The road, a simple one with no turnoffs, had a light covering of sand on it. The two of them walked along silently. The awkwardness of this silence bothered Kazuhisa, but every time he tried to talk he felt a little nauseous.

They entered the village. They soon came to an intersection with stone walls around the residences at each of the four corners. His father-in-law, saying he would sell the fish at the guest house, took the ice chest from Kazuhisa, ran a wire through the gills and out the mouths of several of the fish, handed these to Kazuhisa, and entered an alleyway leading to the main street. Kazuhisa took a shortcut through the tree-lined windbreak and headed for home.

It occurred to Kazuhisa that today, at least, his wife might be doing the cooking. Maybe she had come home for lunch, he thought, and while she was at it might have prepared dinner for them already. It was only 3:00 and he couldn't expect her home yet; nevertheless, he called out that he was back as he pulled open the sliding door at the front of the house. He announced himself again as he entered the kitchen. There were no signs that she had eaten there. He put the fish into the refrigerator. A piece of paper on the table in the living room caught his eye.

"There's a meeting at work, so I'll be home tonight around 10:00. I'll have dinner out," it read. He looked in on their bedroom. He could see that she had come home during her lunch hour and changed her clothes. Kazuhisa took a shower.

He stretched out on the bed. The ceiling was moving; his body was swaying. He wasn't hungry, but he figured that he had to make dinner for his father-in-law. The thought of fish guts only intensified his nausea. His father-in-law, perhaps drinking with the man who ran the guest house, was late getting home. Kazuhisa thought it would be fine if he stayed gone two or three days. But as he drifted off to sleep, Kazuhisa heard signs that his father-in-law had come back.

. 5 .

MISAKO WAS EATING and sleeping so well that she gained more than ten pounds before the marriage had gone on three months. The fleshiness in her cheeks and jaw made her face round and the slits of her eyes that much narrower. She was also now wearing her hair short and had gotten a perm. She had suddenly acquired quite an imposing presence. If she was just going to fatten herself up like this, Kazuhisa sometimes felt, then it was ridiculous for him to be doing the cooking. "A wife who can't cook loses her husband: if the food's no good at home, a man seeks it elsewhere and finds a new woman along with it." He had heard these words somewhere and they often returned to him. Still, he'd go off to the kitchen and make the meals. Washing the dishes was the one thing he felt embarrassed to do while she was in the house, so he looked for times when she was out, reminding himself as he washed them that it was, after all, work he had to do.

He felt he could somehow put up with his life even if he didn't feel that he fit in; what he couldn't endure was if this were to continue into the next life. Given his shy, unsociable personality, he couldn't bear the thought that after death he would be for all eternity among complete strangers in Misako's family tomb. This was something that he had to bring up with her.

"Misako," he said to her one night when they were upstairs together after dinner. "I hope we'll have a tomb just for the two of us. Either that or I'd like to go back to my family's tomb."

"What do you mean? Of course, of course." She looked up at Kazuhisa as she put on her makeup. She was getting ready to go out. "We'll be together forever. In the same tomb—my family's tomb. There are great numbers of people there. But don't worry; I'll introduce you to everyone. They're not all complete strangers to you. Some of them know you already, and lots of them know your father and grandfather."

Kazuhisa wanted to talk with her about it some more. As he hesitated, she finished changing her clothes and left for her meeting at the community center.

Kazuhisa's anger built up little by little. It occurred to him to go back to his own family. They might not be wealthy like his adopted family, but they weren't so poor one more person would make any difference. Kazuhisa wondered why, since they were no more than a couple of miles away, neither his mother nor any of his brothers had visited him since the wedding. Maybe they were ashamed. Or maybe they were afraid that he would go back home. An adopted husband coming back home would make them laughingstocks.

Night fishing, he figured, might be the only way to take his mind off these things.

His father-in-law's fishing during the day and Misako's activities earlier in the evening had sunk both of them into deep, comfortable sleep. Kazuhisa left the house at 11:00. In the early days, Kazuhisa had gone out only when he and Misako were at odds, when things were strained between them; but now, taking off every night had become a habit with him. It was the energy and power that passed to his hand at the moment the fish got hooked that drew him. The fishing harbor was only ten minutes south of the house.

Kazuhisa attached a green fluorite light to the end of his fishing pole and positioned it through a gap in one of the concrete tetrapods forming the breakwater. He then sat down atop the seawall and concentrated all his attention on the dull green light. Good-sized, choice *taman* were easiest to catch in the hour or so before and after midnight. Talk had it that the nocturnal and nervous *taman* were scared off by the faintest light, even that of a cigarette. To have any hope of catching them, you had to refrain from smoking the whole time you were out there.

The dull fluorite light remained immobile. Over and over Kazuhisa hissed his displeasure at the cowards. Eventually, he realized, he was hissing at himself, not the fish.

There was a lighthouse nearby, the beacon light from which illuminated the sea, the seawall, and Kazuhisa at regular intervals. Kazuhisa stood up, pulled his fishing pole out, and laid it down at his side.

Two women came up to him.

"Catching any?" one asked as she squatted down beside him. "If you don't stand your rod up, they'll just eat your bait, you know."

It was true that the *taman* picked off the bait and quickly swam away from shore. The beacon light brought the woman into view. She had on a pair of shorts like men's swimming trunks and was wearing a T-shirt. Her soft-looking breasts showed themselves clearly. At a loss for an answer, Kazuhisa turned his head slightly, in the direction of the woman behind her.

"My sister," the crouching woman said. "Junko, sit down."

Junko was wearing a long violet-colored sleeveless dress. It looked to Kazuhisa like a negligee. She tucked in her skirt and sat down. Her feet were in red sandals. The medium height and slim figures of both women were very similar. Their fingers were slender and white, suggesting to Kazuhisa that they were strangers to any physical labor or housework.

"How about a beer?" The woman held out a can. Kazuhisa took it.

"Beach party?" he asked as he opened it.

"Yeah, it's our club association." A hundred yards from the seawall there was a fire going and a *karaoke* machine was playing noisily. A dozen or so people were there moving about. Being close to these young women and their sweetly fragrant perfume made Kazuhisa thirsty. He drained the can of beer. It gave him a slight buzz.

"Your name is Junko, I just heard, and you, the older sister, are . . ."

"Me? Who do you think? Rie, of course."

"I'm Kazuhisa. My family . . ."

"Never mind the family name."

Kazuhisa sighed softly, realizing he had been on the verge, thoughtlessly, of identifying himself by the name of his adoptive family. He reeled in his fishing line.

"Did you catch something?" Junko asked enthusiastically.

"Look at the end of the rod," Rie told her. "Is it bent? If it's not bent, then there's no way he could have caught anything."

There was no evidence of any nibbling on the slice of pike Kazuhisa had used as bait, but he changed it for a fresh piece anyhow, stood up, and, telling the women to look out, turned to face the dark sea and swung the rod in a wide arc. He put too much into it and missed the spot where he had previously caught *taman* by a good twenty or twenty-five yards.

"Junko, bring over a couple of six-packs of beer—nice cold ones."

"OK." Junko rose and, on somewhat unsteady legs, set off for the beach.

"What's your type?" Rie asked abruptly. Kazuhisa didn't know what she meant.

"Your blood type."

"B . . . why?"

"Just wanted to know if we match." She looked up into Kazuhisa's face. "We match. You and I."

Kazuhisa could very well have put down the rod with its fluorite light, but he remained holding it tightly.

"I have a small bar over in Motobu—the two of us, me and my younger sister. We divide the money equally between us, no matter who does more work or draws in more customers. One of us always keeps the place open, no matter what—like when I had to be at the hospital taking care of my child for lots of days, and when my sister left home for a long time because of an old boyfriend she couldn't leave. And then when we each took turns having babies, and when I took care of my father-in-law when he was sick. Doesn't matter how much either of us works. We get the same pay.

"The town of Motobu is on a peninsula our island lies offshore from. The town has a fishing harbor, a ferry dock, and a flourishing bar district.

"I'm twenty-six years old now. When I was eighteen, I got married. I got pregnant, too. Then last year my husband disappeared. I had some inkling what was up, but still, you know, it was a surprise. I've looked all over Okinawa but couldn't find him. His family—they live in Naha—say they don't know where he is, but I think they're hiding something. It's been six years, so there's only one to go. After seven years you can get a divorce automatically. If you like, you can be a candidate for my second marriage."

The way she said this showed she didn't care if Kazuhisa was already married or not. Kazuhisa set his fishing rod down.

"I have a pretty good idea what happened," she continued. "He started having sex with one of my friends and now they're living together, in Osaka or Kawasaki or somewhere. I think they even had a kid."

Kazuhisa said nothing.

"But I'm not going looking for them. In these past six years I've learned what happens between men and women. If you want to find out yourself, come over to the bar sometime. . . . Ah, here's my sister."

Junko had brought a *sanshin* back with the beer. Kazuhisa and the two women touched cans in toast and then each swallowed down a mouthful. Junko began playing the *sanshin* and singing an Okinawan folk song. The moon wasn't out, but the song told of love on a moon-lit night. Kazuhisa wondered vaguely what might be coming next. As she sang, Junko circled around the other two. With this much noise, Kazuhisa was thinking, even the smaller fish wouldn't be coming near, to say nothing of the *taman*.

But just then the five-foot pole flew from Kazuhisa's side and skipped across the surface of the concrete. Kazuhisa leapt up and chased after it. The women ran after it, too. Kazuhisa feared it would fall into the sea, but although the pole was lurching this way and that, it didn't fall in. The line was caught on a breakwater pod. Kazuhisa turned on a flashlight, handed it to Rie, and then nimbly disengaged the line and reeled it back in. His hands felt the tremendous force of the living thing at the other end. Sipping her beer, Rie gazed out onto the dark surface of the sea, intrigued. Junko softly played the *sanshin*. The force of the living thing struggling desperately to free itself from the line wholly absorbed Kazuhisa. It was a *taman*, he realized. He reeled it in by sheer force. Little by little, the *taman* drew closer to the breakwater. There was not the least sign that its strength had diminished; it pulled wildly from one side to the other. Kazuhisa sprang back and forth along the breakwater in step with the fish. His foot nearly got caught on the mooring post. Junko, continuing to pluck the *sanshin* with her fingers, peered at the water's surface. Rie, down on her hands and knees, also had her eyes fixed on the water, which she illuminated with the flashlight.

It occurred to Kazuhisa that the fish, frightened by the light, might struggle all the harder, but just as he was about to say something, Junko called out, "There it is, there it is."

"It's a *taman*, I'm sure of it," Rie cried out as loudly.

"My sister can foretell things," Junko said. "She gets it right all the time."

As if to give Kazuhisa strength, Junko began to pluck on the *sanshin* more lustily. He was annoyed somewhat by the music, but Kazuhisa moved to its rhythms and then heaved the *taman* out and up onto the breakwater. It was magnificent. The two young women were jubilant. Junko strummed away on the *sanshin;* Rie danced, working her hands and arms and chanting to the rhythm. Kazuhisa was also excited but didn't let it show.

Rie knew all about *taman*. "It's the best-tasting fish there is," she said, as if telling Kazuhisa something he didn't already know. "They serve it in the really fancy restaurants."

For a short while, the three of them stared in silent wonder at the fish lying on the concrete before them. Kazuhisa felt a bit triumphant before the women. Junko was wearing a band in her hair. Fluorescent paint she probably put on it made it glow with the same subdued light as the fluorite. Her broad forehead was white, her large eyes with their double lids were wide open. The women shared a strong resemblance in the eyes; it was the lips that differed. The younger sister's were just a bit thick; the older sister's were thinner and long. People said that a woman with long, thin lips was apt to be a talker; such in fact seemed to be the case with Rie.

Kazuhisa imagined how overjoyed his wife would be when he showed her the fish and suddenly wanted to get home. On the other hand, he recalled people saying that *taman* were always with at least a few other of their kind, and he wanted to present each of these strangely attractive women with a fish of her own. He baited the hook with a slice of mackerel and, using all his strength, cast the line out to the spot where it had been before.

Still squatting, Rie took the fish by its tail and hoisted it high in the air. "It's a good one, don't you think? It's got good shape. Junko, look."

Junko crouched down beside her and drew her face close to the fish. "It's really big. What kind is it?"

"*Taman.* Didn't you hear us saying so already? You wouldn't know because you never cook. The younger sister should do the cooking, you know; preparing food for her older sister is the Way for her."

"You call everything the Way when it suits your own purposes."

Worried where the two women might be headed with this, Kazuhisa momentarily gave up concentrating on his fishing.

"Everything has its Way. Even the fish. This man cast his bait to that fish's Way, and so he was able to catch it. Isn't that right, Kazuhisa?"

Kazuhisa nodded. His eyes remained fixed on the water.

Rie began walking out toward the end of the breakwater. Her gaze roamed the surface of the water as if she were literally looking for the fish's Way.

"Well, I was right, wasn't I? It was *taman.* Like I said, my sister does have the ability to see into the future." Junko seemed intent on persuading Kazuhisa. "She gets going with it after the customer starts feeling his liquor. She gets a little tipsy herself. It's then, she says, that both of them can set everything else aside and talk about what's really on their minds. Her head becomes very clear then, she says, and she can hear many different voices. Of course these are her own voices inside her. If you say they are *kami* voices or something, then people think it's just some kind of superstition. It's her own voice, and her own power, is what my sister says. Sometimes customers ask if she's a *yuta;* she tells them that just like they have the ability to be a section chief or something like that at work, she has the ability to see into the future. Isn't that good? I think she's right, right in that way of thinking about it."

Kazuhisa was now absorbed in the thought of the huge *taman* he was going to catch, but even in his excitement, her voice managed to get through to him.

"Why don't you give it a try—let her take a look for you? At your future wife and things like that."

I'm already married, Kazuhisa was on the verge of saying.

"You should come to our place sometime. Sister would like that, too."

"Is she usually right?" Kazuhisa turned his face up toward her.

"With other people, yes. With herself, she's always way off the mark. That's the reason she has no luck with men. I haven't had any luck with men either. But she could tell exactly what was coming, in my case anyway."

"Does she look into the future for the customers at your bar?"

"For those that want to know, yes. There are customers drawn to her sexuality and others drawn to her power to tell the future. But she never does it outside the bar. Business is business. If they buy drinks, then she does it for them."

"Which kind are there more of?"

"Customers? Half-and-half. Those not attracted to her physically believe in her power to see, and those that don't believe in her power find her physically attractive. Customers at the Garden of the Sea Hibiscus, our bar, are either one type or the other. How about you, which group do you think you're in?"

"Oh, I haven't yet . . ."

"I know. In a dark place like this you can't even see her face very well. And you've just met. You should come sometime to the Garden of the Sea Hibiscus. I hope you do."

It wasn't his fate in general that he wanted to know about; it was his fate as an adopted husband. He half-believed he had been fated to become an adopted husband, but he wanted to know for sure. Rie came back.

"My sister," Junko was saying, "has both sex appeal and the power to see into the future. I guess that's what they call a woman with both brains and beauty."

"Come to our place, please. I'll treat you like a man—about the future, sexually, whatever you like. Oh, by the way, what are you going to do with this fish? Sell it?"

As she asked, Rie lifted the fish by its tail and shook it slightly. Kazuhisa, who intended to take the fish home to his wife, shook his head. Rie misunderstood.

"Let's all eat it together, then. I'll cut it for sashimi."

Though muted, her thin voice had in it a curious energy and a kind of endearing trust. At first Kazuhisa tried to think up some excuse, but then he nodded his agreement. He could always catch his wife a fish the next night.

"Junko, go back to the beach and fetch the big knife."

"I know, the big knife." Junko rose in quick compliance.

"Not just the knife. Some paper plates and the *wasabi* and soy sauce, too. Everything that we'll need for sashimi."

"Okay. Chopsticks too, right?"

"Hurry. It's *ima-iyu* (fresh fish) we're having, so freshness is everything."

Junko wore her hair short like a boy, letting it fall in front across her forehead. As he watched her retreat, Kazuhisa thought short pants like Rie's would probably look better on her than the long one-piece dress she was wearing.

"That younger sister of mine, she dumped her boyfriend. She was engaged to the guy. But then for the longest time after she dumped him, she couldn't get over her feelings for him. To take her mind off it, she started going to a driver's training school and ended up marrying one of the instructors there. Married life lost its glow, and she came to realize how good the first guy was. All she ever talked about was how much she wished she hadn't left him. Then, apparently, she asked her husband for a divorce. He was completely against it and, nearly in tears, forced her into bed with him. Of course, I wasn't there to see any of this. But he seemed the kind of guy who thought that once he got married, his wife became his property. Maybe the old boyfriend wasn't much, but at least he was good to her. He was big-hearted, that's what made him that way. She keeps saying that all the time. "

"That's really bad."

"There's nothing bad about it at all. That's why I told you. The two of us in the bar, you see, we talk with each other hours on end waiting for customers to come. It's nothing, really. You should come sometime. I'll tell you everything if you do. Will you? I'll treat you to something good to eat, too."

Rie pulled a crumpled business card from her hip pocket and tucked it in the pocket of Kazuhisa's T-shirt. In the ocean breeze, her abundant, richly permed curly hair grazed against his forehead.

Junko returned. Rie took the plastic bag she had brought and spread it across a flat wooden board of the sort fishermen use to sit on or to cut up their bait. She then placed the *taman* on top of the plastic bag and, taking the large knife in hand, skillfully scaled the fish, cut open its belly, and scraped out the guts. The sashimi was ready in no time. Rie lifted up two pieces, dipped them in the soy sauce and *wasabi* Junko had mixed on a paper plate, and put them in her mouth.

"Tasty. Really quite good. Take some."

Kazuhisa and Junko ate.

"It's warm," Junko said.

"Of course," Rie told her. "It was alive just a few minutes ago."

Kazuhisa thought he preferred chilled sashimi to this fresh one. He put only two or three pieces in his mouth.

"It's really good; eat some more," Rie urged Kazuhisa. With some hesitation, Kazuhisa moved his chopsticks toward the sashimi.

"You're really eating a lot," Junko said of her sister. "You just had chicken and beef at the barbecue."

"Meat and fish aren't the same. And you almost never have the chance to eat fish that's just been caught. You eat some, too."

"I've had enough."

"Kazuhisa, have some more."

"I've had enough, too," he replied. "The way you gutted and filleted the fish—you're quite good at that. Did you grow up in a fishing village or something?

"No, I'm from the city—from Naha. The customers brought fish to the bar where I worked in Itoman, so I picked up how to do it. The mama there made me fix them. The young men in the fishing village must have thought it a crime or something to bring us other kinds of presents—jewelry or flowers or something. But I feel comfortable with straightforward men like that. It's the same with you—I can feel comfortable around you. You're from this island, aren't you? Island people are nice and straightforward. . . . Junko, eat some more."

"I've had enough."

"Kazuhisa, have some more. All island people must like sashimi."

"Thanks, but I've had enough, too."

"In that case, Junko, let's take what's left to the people on the beach."

Rie licked her index finger and then transferred the sashimi to a paper plate. "They'll be happy," she said. "Don't forget to tell them we just caught it."

"Okay," Junko said in English. She received the plate in a curiously reverential manner.

"Well, Kazuhisa, please be sure to stop by our bar. We'll have to be leaving now. We go back on the first ferry in the morning."

Rie extended her two arms, took Kazuhisa's cheeks in her hands, and lightly kissed him on the lips. Her hands smelled of the fish, but her lips were soft. Kazuhisa stood there in a daze. The two women made their way down the breakwater and onto the beach.

. 6 .

THE FOLLOWING DAY, Kazuhisa sat in the shade of the male *deigo* tree of the dream oracle and in a low voice asked if he should go see the two women. Then he closed his eyes. "Don't go," he seemed to hear a voice telling him. "The women are just ordinary human beings."

"You good-for-nothing tree," Kazuhisa muttered under his breath. It was this tree, he couldn't help but recall, that kept him from getting a job and that had him doing housework like some woman. And it was this tree that had him tell Misako they didn't have to have children and ever after had caused his desire to weaken. Kazuhisa got up and started walking down the country road.

His head told him that he wanted to know what his future as an adopted husband was to be. The indescribably soft sensation of Rie's lips came back to him and made his whole body quiver. Did she really have the power to see his future? Kazuhisa half-believed, half-doubted that she did. Perhaps he should take Misako with him to the Garden of the Sea Hibiscus. No, he shook his head slowly from side to side. Things do happen between men and women. If he was going, he should go alone. Surely Rie was no *yuta*. If she were, she would have the voice of the *kami*. She was just an ordinary woman. Bar hostesses, with their unhappy backgrounds, put faith in irrational things and have a fondness for fortune-telling and such things. They like to have their fortunes told, and they like to tell them for others. Rie's power, at best, was on par with divining someone's fortune using tarot cards. It wasn't something that could properly be called a power at all.

Kazuhisa imagined the earnest look in her painted eyes as she told the fortune of customers at the bar. Perhaps she really was a *yuta*, he thought. He recalled the old practice they talked about on the island of *yuta* offering up goats to the *kami* of the Dragon Palace below the sea. An altar was built on a *sabani*, and goat soup and *awamori* were placed on it. After the *yuta* prayed for good fishing, the people in attendance feasted on the soup. Then the idea came to him: he would present a goat to Rie. Maybe she wasn't a *yuta*, but she did have it in her nature to be one. A woman like her would find herself cut off from everyone if she worked in a company or a government office. Work as a hostess, where both she and her customers let the drink work on them, suited her much better.

Kazuhisa made up his mind to go to the Garden of the Sea Hibiscus. Since she wasn't a *kami*, she'd be shocked if he tried to make her a goat offering. Selling a goat to make his drinking money made more sense.

The number of goats people raise is not great, but the demand for them is. There isn't a restaurant serving goat that isn't eager to obtain more. The fat in goat meat apparently sticks to the walls of blood vessels; people with high blood pressure have been known from time to time to die from it. This fact did nothing to diminish the number of those devoted to the dish. You can get money for a goat anywhere, anytime. On several past occasions Kazuhisa had wanted to take his wife's bank passbook and seal from her drawer but never could accept the idea of throwing her money around, spending it on drinking and fooling around with some woman he hardly knew. Neither could he long entertain the idea of borrowing money from his mother or brothers at home.

Borrowing or stealing money from another person inevitably leads to trouble. He decided instead to steal the goat. He wanted to see Rie as soon as he could. The pure and simple Kazuhisa had almost never gone drinking when he was in college. To do so now, newly married, running off on his wife and father-in-law to some bar across the sea, and stealing a goat to boot, would be a momentous undertaking. His chest pounded and pounded. Such a venture, on the other hand, appealed to his pride. He felt driven now one way, now the other.

Before I could ever be a fisherman, he tried to convince himself illogically, *it's necessary first to become a man in my own right.* The ordinarily unfocused and irresolute Kazuhisa had now found something that completely absorbed him.

That night, after his father-in-law and Misako were sound asleep, Kazuhisa slipped out into the garden. He took his fishing pole and the ice chest from the shed. He set off at a quick pace toward the spot where he had been fishing the night before. His shadow followed him across ground that was covered with a thin film of sand. He sensed he was being watched by someone peering at him through the trees that lined both sides of the road. He felt guilty that the image of a young woman was drawing him away in the middle of the night. By now he could hear the sea's roar, drowning out the sounds of the insects.

He didn't see a soul on the breakwater or on the beach; the activity of the night before was gone completely. He felt silly being there alone putting in his line.

Drawn by the ocean's roar, he passed through a grove of small trees and out onto the stretch of beach where Rie and Junko had had their party the night before. He took off his sandals to get better footing and then set off. The sand was a pale white. The moonlight flickered silently across the water's surface, creating the illusion of large schools of small fish.

Kazuhisa took off his T-shirt and jeans. He hesitated a moment and then also removed his underpants. He entered the water and swam away from shore. The water was colder than he expected and gave him small goose bumps. His whole body tensed up. He could hear and feel the thrashing of the sea out beyond the reef. The moonlight followed his silent, swimming form and illuminated it. He stopped, pumped his legs to stay in place, scooped the water in both hands, and lifted it toward the moon. The water glistened with tiny points of light.

He dove underwater and swam with his eyes wide open. The moonlight did not get through, so it was completely dark. He rose to the surface and stretched out on his back. He gazed steadily at the moon. It was perfectly round, deficient nowhere. He did not want to leave the water. From where he was, it was the land, not the sea, that seemed unsettling. The slender leaves of the black screw pines hung limp, like human fingers. Large rocks and crags took on the shapes of cows and enormous turtles.

His body swayed softly to the movement of the sea. He drifted into a dream state. A naked female figure appeared, white and soft in the moonlight. Her black hair came loose and floated lightly on the water. It was Rie. She was floating on the water. On his back, his arms and legs fully spread, Kazuhisa released his semen. Immediately, he sank into the water. He resurfaced after a time and swam toward the beach.

When Kazuhisa sat under the male *deigo* tree of the dream oracle after lunch the next day, the scene of the night before came back to him. He knew how stupid his actions had been—vague feelings of incompatibility with his wife and father-in-law had made him seek out the woman from the beach, someone who could not possibly have been there, and then he had stripped naked and floated faceup on the sea. He tried to block out his feelings of stupidity by imagining the nakedness of a young, beautiful woman. Then Rie and Junko merged with the woman adrift in the water. The two nude women, lying faceup in the water, gazed at the moon.

Kazuhisa felt an aching throb in his body. He climbed into the *deigo* tree and, behind the cover of its dense leaves and branches, gave release for himself. The instant the strength left his body, Kazuhisa thought of his new wife and knew that he had done wrong.

He climbed down from the tree and leaned against the trunk. A cool breeze lightly brushed his body. An old man leading a white goat passed before his eyes. Kazuhisa felt himself being drawn into sleep.

. 7 .

THERE WERE OCCASIONS under the male *deigo* tree of his dream oracle when Kazuhisa's mind ran wild. Once he thought about Rie the time he went night fishing—thrusting her white fingers into the belly of the fish and pulling out its guts. This recalled to him a scene he had witnessed in elementary school: older island boys skillfully removing the entrails from the charred body of a goat and then dipping them in sea water to wash them off. He thought then of Rie's dexterity in gutting and filleting the *taman*. If his wife could cut up a fish like that, he'd have nothing to complain about. Rie must be serving sashimi to her customers at the bar every night. If Misako were Rie, then even if he were her adopted husband, he wouldn't have to do the cooking.

One of his distant relatives was an old man who lived alone and raised goats. This old man had one he called Cow. At a dinner party once, the conversation came around to the curious name he had given this goat. "I suppose there was a cow nearby when the goat was born," one of Kazuhisa's brothers speculated. "No, it's because his wife, who was no longer living, had that name," his mother informed them. In the old days, women often got names like Cow, Jug, Oven, Pot, and other animals and kitchen things familiar from daily life.

The old man raised goats for eating, but he was not a member of the T– Island branch of the Goat Meat Producers Association, made up of all the active producers. He did it to wile away the time in his old age and was thus unlikely to notice that one of his goats had disappeared. Kazuhisa renewed his resolve to sell the goat and see the two women. He'd heard there was a boom in goat soup going on in the amusement districts. The number of people with a long-standing love for the dish had not lessened a bit; and now young women and others had also taken to goat meat in great numbers, despite its very strong and distinctive smell.

There was a restaurant specializing in goat on the Motobu Peninsula that Kazuhisa had once eaten at when he was a college student. It was a small restaurant, under private management, and since it was in the amusement district, it had lots of customers coming in from the bars. If he took a goat there, he figured, surely they'd buy it from him right away. There were, of course, restaurants specializing in pork or in beef, but they were not in a position to buy living pigs or cows from individuals. A pig or a cow was much more likely to be receptive to people they'd never seen before, certainly much more than a goat would. . . . Then again, you could slaughter the goat to make it easier to transport, but then the selling price would go down. It would be a lot harder to handle, but the goat would have to be transported live. There was no avoiding the fact that, to one degree or another, he was going to have to contend with the goat.

Kazuhisa returned home immediately, got into the pickup truck, and headed for the house of the old man he was related to. On the way, his resolve began to crack. He tried to come up with a better plan. There must be some old man on the verge of senility raising goats, living way off by himself somewhere, he concluded. It wouldn't matter how far the place was from the beach where his father-in-law kept the boat. As long as he fed it, he figured, the goat wouldn't become too much of a problem in the back of the truck. He drove around the village, taking a look.

Most of the goat sheds were located by the road, no doubt to make it easy to unload feed and get the goats into vehicles. Kazuhisa drove slowly, trying to arouse as little suspicion as possible.

Close to the beach was a shed surrounded by trees. One goat there was pregnant, eliminating it from consideration. The old man there, who had piled up limestone from the sea floor to make the walls of the goat shed, lived all alone. The other goats also were about the right size. But the old guy was always talking to them, telling them to be sure to eat their fill and to get a good night's sleep, and other such simple things. It seemed weird to Kazuhisa, so he decided against the other goats, too.

There was another shed made from an abandoned truck left on the footpath between two tobacco fields. Thatch on the top helped ward off the heat. The windows had cloth shades on them and were screened. It was less a defense against theft, Kazuhisa assumed, than a way to keep stray dogs away. No people were in sight anywhere. Kazuhisa came closer. There were two goats. The smaller one had its face pressed to the window screen. Kazuhisa held his breath and tried to open the door on the driver's side. It may have been a dilapidated old wreck, but the door was firmly locked. He muttered something to the goats about how hot it must be in there in the middle of the day and went back to his own truck.

From a hill some distance away, he could see the goat shed of his relative, an old man. He stopped the truck to take a closer look. Probably because of the oppressive heat, there wasn't a soul near the shed, in the spacious yard around the house, or in the vegetable and sugarcane fields nearby. The storm shutters were all rolled back, leaving the house wide open. From outside, Kazuhisa could see nothing in the dim interior. He assumed the old man was in there napping. Now and again a goat poked its head out of the shed.

When all is said and done, Kazuhisa realized, his goat had to come from this house. But he still wavered. "I hope this old relative of mine is just a little bit senile," he prayed as he drove. "And that he's lost track of how many goats he's got."

He drove up the hill. There were family tombs on both sides of the road, but no guardrails. Kazuhisa very nearly ran off the edge, cutting the wheel back just at the last moment. He took a deep breath.

He avoided being alone that evening. Misako was at a meeting at the community center. As he ate his sashimi, he talked to his father-in-law about one thing or another, making little sense. The older man's expression showed he thought something was strange.

"Don't you get lonely with Misako away from home every night?" he asked at one point.

"You're the one who should be lonely."

"Did something happen today?"

"No, nothing unusual. No different today from any other day."

His father-in-law began playing the *sanshin* as he drank his *awamori*. Kazuhisa went upstairs. He wouldn't be causing so much of an uproar, he assured himself, that his father-in-law would be roused out of bed in the dead of night by the owner of the goat, the village headman, and everybody else once they discovered the theft. It wasn't murder, after all. Kazuhisa found himself as restless upstairs as he had been downstairs. It seemed to him that any moment he'd be hearing the village headman and the goat's owner announcing themselves in Okinawan— "*Chaabira-sai*"—at the door.

At 8:00, after his father-in-law had fallen asleep and Misako had not returned yet from her meeting of the women's club, Kazuhisa carried some rope and the grass and vegetable leafage he had cut that afternoon to the truck. He then set out for the old man's goat shed, going at a good speed. When he arrived after about ten minutes, the lights in the house were off and the old man was sleeping. Kazuhisa approached the goat shed, which faced a road in the fields. The goats were sleeping, too. The moment he turned the flashlight on, all three of them got up. There was a gentleness in their shining blue eyes. Their legs were slender, but their bodies were as hard as carved wood. He guessed that when he tried to seize one of them, the goat would spring up powerfully. He opened the door and offered them some of the feed he had brought. One of the goats, slightly smaller than the others, drew close. Kazuhisa very quickly dropped the looped rope around its neck. When he fished, Kazuhisa made no use at all of the power in his large frame, but now he drew on enormous strength—strength he didn't know he had in him. The goat resisted, bleating as it drew back. Kazuhisa pulled on the rope and on the goat's horns. Fear that the horns might poke him in the stomach called up even more of his strength. He managed finally to get it outside. Succumbing to his great strength, or maybe just lured by the feed, the goat emerged. When he got it along side the truck, Kazuhisa gave it more feed, tied its legs two and two, and then hoisted it up and into the truck. The goats left behind were raising a fuss, but this got no response from the house.

Ten or fifteen minutes later, Kazuhisa stopped the truck, pulled the knapsack filled with the feed onto his back, took the goat into his arms, and set out along a path through the screw pines. He very nearly tripped over the roots, which spread parallel to the ground like so many octopus legs. Startled, the goat thrust out its bound hind legs, which struck Kazuhisa in the pit of the stomach. The pain shot through his body and for several seconds took his breath away. He came close to dropping the goat but leaned forward slightly to control the pain, slipped through the screw pines, and finally came out on the beach. His father-in-law's *sabani* was there, afloat in the high tide. For a second, Kazuhisa thought he'd repay the goat for the kick by flinging it hard into the boat, but then he realized it would just be more trouble if the goat started struggling again, so he set it down gently inside.

He started the engine. The sound echoed off the rocks at the cape and leapt into Kazuhisa's ears. He worried someone would hear it, assume the boat was being stolen, and come in pursuit of him. He searched for a channel that would keep him in the darkness, but the moon was out that night. He wished it would conceal itself behind one of the gigantic columns of faint white clouds. Neither the clouds nor the moon was moving much. He got free of the shore. Sound was traveling across the water's surface rather than being swallowed up by the water. Kazuhisa felt relieved, though, figuring that from the shore it would sound like the roaring of the sea.

This was Kazuhisa's first experience in the *sabani* at night. The moon was now behind a column of clouds. The mainland, T– Island, and Oiwa lay as if stretched out asleep on the dark water. There was a solemnity in the soft, easy movements of the water; the waves breaking on the reef made no more sound than the rustle of a white kimono sash. Once he got through an opening in this white sash, he figured, he'd be okay. And later he realized that all he had to do was try, and somehow he could make his way through. He felt confident now. The goat, its legs bound together, struggled to escape, at times nearly falling into the sea; Kazuhisa would grab the horns or another part of the animal, pull it to himself, and hold it still.

About midway between the mainland and T– Island there was a current that flowed with the swiftness of a river. This water struck powerfully against the side of the boat, and the engine-laden *sabani* came dangerously close to capsizing. The goat lifted its head, bleating incessantly, and struggled to escape. Kazuhisa pressed some of the grass to its mouth, but the goat had not the least interest. A rope holding its legs loosened. Kazuhisa tightened it again firmly. The hard, stiff, pole-like legs were powerful, and they trampled all over the back of Kazuhisa's hand. Meanwhile, the *sabani* was making a wide turn in the water. Kazuhisa thrust the goat aside and grabbed the rudder. The *sabani* pulled out of the turn, but a few moments later Kazuhisa realized that he was now headed back to T– Island.

His presence of mind deserted him. Kazuhisa had no clear idea what course he was now on. A scraping sound came from the bottom of the boat. He was passing through shallow water above the reef. He hadn't noticed the reef's color, which differed from what it was in daylight. He knew that if he didn't remove himself from the expanse of coral quickly, he would surely run aground. Or worse, he would open a hole in the bottom of the *sabani* and sink. He had to do something quickly. He was about to cut off the engine. No, he immediately realized; if he did that, there was a chance the screw would get caught in the coral. If that happened, when he turned the engine back on the boat wouldn't move. The goat, frightened by the scraping sound, was making even more of a fuss, bleating hysterically. Kazuhisa strained his eyes to see. The moon emerged from behind the column of clouds. The light struck the surface of the water, and the distinction between the coral and the deep water became clear. Kazuhisa turned the bow of the boat toward the closest stretch of deep water.

When Kazuhisa at last got free of the coral, he collapsed over the rudder, drained of all strength. The grating sound from the coral against the boat had stopped, but the goat continued its bleating. For a moment Kazuhisa worried that he had opened a hole in the boat's bottom, but an examination of the boat revealed no signs of water coming through. A small amount of water had collected in the bottom, however; the moonlight glistened on it and on the water cut by the prow as the boat moved along. Kazuhisa placed some of the grass near the goat's mouth, but the goat's eyes seemed filled with contempt for him, and it kept its mouth shut tight. Kazuhisa set the grass down beside the goat and gazed out across the sea. The goat extended its hard pole-like legs and began rapping them on the boat's bottom. "You'll poke a hole through it, and then what'll we do?" Kazuhisa yelled. Seeming to understand, the goat became a little more peaceful.

To get to the mainland peninsula from T— Island, you normally traveled with the large rock they called Whale Rock on your right, but Kazuhisa was passing it on the left. Seen from the right, this large rock resembled the shape of a whale, the lone pine growing on top sug-gesting the spout of seawater. To Kazuhisa's eyes now it looked like a large rock and nothing more, so he let himself fall victim to the illusion that he was now heading away from the peninsula. Perhaps in fear, the goat had folded its body in on itself and huddled close to Kazuhisa.

But, Kazuhisa reasoned, if the boat had been turning every which way, it was odd that he hadn't become seasick. Whenever he went out with his father-in-law, the older man's marvelous control of the boat hadn't saved Kazuhisa from getting sick. Maybe it was because it was night now and he couldn't see things very well. It might also be because he was at the rudder, or then again, maybe because he was taking care of the goat. He could only guess.

Inevitably, just thinking about not getting sick made Kazuhisa feel nauseous. Before long he was unable to bear it. Since he and the goat were the only ones in the *sabani*, if he got seriously sick, then there was danger, he realized, of being swept far out in the open sea. He thrust a finger down his throat. The contents of his stomach rushed noisily out his mouth and into the water. The goat stared at him in apparent surprise. Kazuhisa thought of turning back, but he had already traveled for twenty minutes—all he had to do was endure another ten. If he turned back, he figured, it would take him even longer.

His seasickness made Kazuhisa think of all the other experiences he'd had with it when he was out on the boat with his father-in-law. As he struggled to ignore his discomfort, he thought of his father-in-law at home. He imagined his alcoholic body staggering along as he looked everywhere for him and the boat. Misako would be there, too, helping him stay steady. Her face was pale, her eyes cold and hard. From time to time, her father started talking excitedly about something or other. Kazuhisa closed his eyes, straining to hear what he was saying, but the voice did not reach him. If he returned and went up on the beach, he knew, he would hear it. *If he's speaking ill of me*, Kazuhisa figured, *I won't be able to say much in my defense, as sick as I am. And there's no chance Misako will be speaking ill of me.*

Kazuhisa started to turn the boat back to T— Island. *What in the world have I done*, he asked himself. The saltwater spray struck his face. This brought him back to his senses a bit. *Have I ever been able to actually do something, even once, in my entire life? What good*, he rebuked himself, *could it possibly do to turn back now? Why did I steal the goat in the first place? I'm making a big mistake.* Kazuhisa summoned his strength and turned the prow of the *sabani* back toward the peninsula.

The closer Kazuhisa came to the peninsula, the more he worried that a massive field of coral would rise up at him. The moon was now behind a column of clouds, and there was only very faint light. Kazuhisa concentrated as hard as he could, reduced the speed of the boat, and very carefully moved ahead. Lights shone here and there on the peninsula. With these as his guide, he moved forward. When he got closer to land he changed course, this time to avoid the light. He couldn't risk being seen by anyone. He decided to land on the beach, instead of in the fishing harbor.

The *sabani* ran up cleanly onto the beach. Kazuhisa still felt seasick but jumped immediately from the boat. He felt dizzy and had to sit down in the sand. After a moment or two, he rose unsteadily and secured the line from the boat to a large rock nearby. He then tied the rope from the goat's neck to the boat's anchor and removed the rope binding its legs. He took great care with the hind legs but got kicked in the hand nonetheless. He pulled the knapsack onto his back, grabbed a handful of grass feed, and, pulling the goat by the rope around its neck, made his way up the tide embankment, which was topped with beefwood trees. He then made his way past the fishing harbor facilities, which were deserted at night, and soon arrived at the bar district.

. 8 .

It was not yet 10:00, but the goat restaurant was closed. Kazuhisa pulled the goat around to the lot out back, where croton as tall as a full-grown man were flourishing. From the back, Kazuhisa could see that the lights in the restaurant had been turned off, too. He then searched for other restaurants serving goat but had no success. He walked along the street where the clubs were. Hostesses from the clubs eyed him with curiosity; a drunk petted the goat's head. Kazuhisa searched for Rie's club, the Garden of the Sea Hibiscus.

"Where is Welfare Office Street?" he asked a hostess standing in front of a bar. She was a middle-aged woman wearing a red sleeveless dress. She shook her head slightly from side to side.

"Well, then, where can I find the welfare office?"

"Not here any more," she answered. "What's with the goat? Something to do with welfare?"

"Where was it before it closed?"

"On the street behind here. You can get through from here. Not with a horse or a cow, though."

There was a gap between two buildings near where the woman was standing. Kazuhisa thanked her, pulled the goat along after him, and went in through the gap. "Be sure to come and have a drink at our club," he heard her saying behind him.

After walking along Welfare Office Street about five minutes or so, he saw the words "Garden of the Sea Hibiscus" on a neon sign. He pulled on the knob of the heavy wooden door; it had some kind of pattern carved into it like the front door of a magnificent house. Afraid it might be too conspicuous if left outside, he brought the goat inside with him. All was quiet there. An old popular song was playing on the cable radio station. There was not a single customer in any of the black chairs or in the shadows of the ornamental plants. Lights were on behind the counter, but there were no hostesses anywhere.

He heard, faintly, the sound of a toilet flushing, and then Rie emerged at his back as he continued peering behind the counter. She offered a cheerful greeting and then drew back in astonishment.

"What's with this?" she asked.

Kazuhisa was about to ask if she'd buy it from him.

"What's it for? The goat, I mean. It is a goat, isn't it?"

"I don't have any money for drinks, so I was wondering if you would take the goat in exchange." Kazuhisa had some difficulty getting this out.

"It's you—it is you. The one from T— Island. Am I right?" Rie was excited.

"This is the first time I've been in this club, but I met you when I was night fishing. . . ."

"I know. I haven't forgotten. You caught that fish and I made sashimi. Junko got the *wasabi* and soy sauce for us. Sure, I remember. But what's with the goat?"

"I brought it from the island. In the *sabani.*"

"It can't stay in here. There's a little empty lot out back. Tie it up there, will you?"

Kazuhisa, leading the goat, followed Rie out the back door, where cases of empty beer bottles and other things were stacked. They tied the rope from the goat's neck to a clothesline pole and then returned to the bar.

Rie put both her hands on Kazuhisa's arms and almost pulled him down onto one of the stools. She then went around behind the counter.

"You came to see me, didn't you?" she said as she put out an ashtray and a moistened hand towel. "We made a promise, right, the two of us. They say the men of T— Island keep their word, and so it really is true. What'll you drink?"

"The fine *awamori.* Ten years or older, if you have it." Kazuhisa, concerned how much the drinks would cost, was on the point of playing it safe and ordering beer, but then it occurred to him that even the best *sake* could not cost more than the goat. Rie took a bottle of *awamori* from the shelf.

"Make it on the rocks; it'd be a waste to dilute it with water," he told her. He got excited thinking he was going to be able to drink as much as the goat was worth. It wasn't that he liked drinking so much; he just had the feeling that if he drank, it would please Rie.

"Can I have one, too?" she asked as she made his drink. Kazuhisa nodded assent in an exaggerated way. Rie poured her own drink, which she lightly tapped against Kazuhisa's in toast.

"Today is my treat, so drink all you like," he told her.

They hadn't yet spoken about buying and selling the goat, but the sense of achievement Kazuhisa had from hauling the goat here elevated his spirits. He drank the *awamori* down in one swallow. Rie quickly made him another.

"Did you find it?" Rie asked as she filled her own glass. "Did you find the goat wandering around loose near the harbor?"

"The harbor?"

"They bring them in for the meat. Every once in a while they escape, apparently."

"I brought it over from T— Island. In the *sabani.*"

"Do you raise them?"

"I stole it. From an old man who's a relative of mine."

"You stole it? And brought it here? You've got a lot more nerve than I'd have thought. We don't get many customers these days; I guess it's the summer heat. But if I had some goat soup for them, then they'd be coming in for sure. This makes you something like the *kami* of Nirai-kanai."

Happiness, they say in Okinawa, is brought to people by the *kami* of Nirai-kanai, located out across the sea.

"I love it, I really love goat soup," she said.

The talk seemed to flow easily between them, and the pace of their drinking quickened.

"There's nothing wrong with you selling off a goat or two. The old guy just raises them to wile away his time anyhow. There was an old fellow in this town, too; he bred lots of goats, and he'd come around to buy women. He was overdoing it—ended up killing him. The old ones shouldn't be raising more than a goat or two; they shouldn't be wanting so much."

"By now I guess they're already searching for the goat."

"Don't be ridiculous. He's an old man! He's sound asleep—it's ten already. He won't discover anything until maybe five tomorrow morning. And if you're lucky, he's so senile he'll never notice."

"Maybe he'll have a heart attack when he realizes."

"He won't care. Goats are always reproducing. And in the end they just become meat for the table. It's not like they're pets, you know."

Kazuhisa said nothing.

"Keep bringing goats to me. And keep coming here to drink with me."

Kazuhisa could never have imagined someone urging him to steal goats.

"I'll buy them from you—I'll give you fifty, maybe a hundred thousand yen. And after you sell them to me, help out the business and do your drinking here. Of course, you'll have to take out the five thousand you'll need for the ferry to get home."

"I came in the *sabani*."

"That's right, the *sabani*. There's no way in the world you could have used the ferry to haul a stolen goat. But don't worry. Sleep here tonight. If you need money to get back, I can give it to you."

Kazuhisa nodded.

"Aren't you hungry? I'm starved. Let's get some sushi delivered. There's a good shop near here."

Rie telephoned the order.

Half an hour later, a young delivery boy with close-cut hair and wearing an apron placed on the counter his restaurant's finest *nigiri*, bowls of custard soup, fish covered in sauce, and a few other dishes.

He handed the bill to Rie, pronounced a lusty thank you, and made his departure.

"Have some," Rie said as she split a pair of chopsticks and handed them to Kazuhisa.

He thanked her, but he also had the feeling that payment for the meal was coming from the money for the goat. Rie took a mouthful of the sea urchin *nigiri*. She laughed softly, enjoying the taste.

"I can butcher goats, too, you know. The first anniversary since we opened this club is coming up. I can telephone the regular customers—invite maybe fifteen of them. That's not to say they'll all come. But all of them like goat quite a lot. They'll be happy. I guess I shouldn't be saying this, but I eat *nigiri* and other things with them all the time."

Kazuhisa worried that Rie, once drunk, might show rather too much consideration for him by announcing to her fifteen guests that the soup they were enjoying was from a goat he had stolen. On the other hand, it did give him a feeling of superiority knowing that stealing a goat and hauling it all the way over here was not something just anyone could do.

"Eat with us before you go."

"I don't think I'll be going back. At home, you see . . ."

"Well then, join me when I cut it up. It's your goat, so you ought to be there at the end. Tomorrow morning at ten, on the beach—the beach that you get to through the small stand of trees. We wouldn't want the police seeing us, you know."

"I'm no good at that sort of thing."

"You don't kill them because you're good at it; nobody prides themselves on killing for no good reason. Are you going to make me do it all by myself? That's fine. I will. All you have to do is help and do exactly what I say."

"How about your sister?"

"My sister? She won't be able to get free, what with her kid and her husband."

"It wasn't to kill it that I stole the goat."

"Then what did you do it for?"

"To see you." Kazuhisa felt embarrassed saying this, but he saw no way to hold back.

"To get the drink money. I thank you for that. But to get the drink money, we have to kill the goat."

"I meant to sell it to a restaurant."

"Stop deluding yourself. It's not like the goat is going to be any safer after you sell it to the restaurant."

"I just don't want to see the goat being slaughtered. Really, I don't."

"And that's what I'm telling you—I'll kill the goat and you can shut your eyes if that's what you want. Stop making me feel bad about it."

Kazuhisa saw there was no escape and that it was useless to say anything more.

"That's that, okay? We can leave that aside now. Tonight, let's just enjoy drinking together." She poured *awamori* into his glass. "I'll make us something else to eat. Wait here for just a moment."

Rie went into the back, behind the counter. Unable to forget that soft sensation when she kissed him on the lips, Kazuhisa had gone through his ordeal—nervously stealing the goat, hauling it all the way over here in the *sabani*—all in the hope that after he sold it, for one night at least, he could know the pleasure of being with her. And then after he had had his pleasure, so his plan went, he'd return the *sabani* to its place on the beach before his father-in-law went out fishing the next day. As things were actually turning out, here he was now, faced with the horrifying prospect of killing the goat with Rie. If he wanted to escape, now was the time to do it.

He stood up from the stool. His head was spinning. He leaned against the wall. The strength in his legs gave out and, his back pressed to the wall, he sank down into a crouch.

"What's wrong?" Rie had emerged from the back. She pulled Kazuhisa up by the hand and sat him on the seat. "I've fried some *maamina-chanpuru* (bean spouts), so eat up," she said, and then told him to hold on a minute.

She went in behind the counter again.

Minutes later, Kazuhisa and Rie were pressed close together on the seat, eating *maamina-chanpuru* and drinking *awamori*. Kazuhisa's fears about killing the goat gave way little by little. Things would happen as they were meant to, he told himself. For now, he decided, he should just enjoy drinking and talking with Rie. But the idea did keep coming back to him that it would surely be no easy matter to kiss a woman capable of killing a goat. The prospect of what might happen if he had sex with her sent shivers through his body.

As they ate the *maamina-chanpuru,* they were drinking even more than before. Soon Kazuhisa was excited by the idea of secretly taking the goat's life.

"The bottle's empty; I'll open another one. You've come all the way from T— Island, after all. It's not like you're one of the men around here who comes every day."

"Let's have a different kind this time—Zampa would be good."

"Zampa is good. Cape Zampa in Yomitan—do you know the place? Every day the rough waves on the deep water there crash against the jagged cliffs. The cliffs, though, aren't the least bit shaken—just like you."

Kazuhisa poured some Zampa into Rie's glass.

"You hold your *awamori* pretty well."

"I'm a woman; I take it all in."

"Is it only you here? Are there other hostesses? Who was the one who ate the sashimi with us the other night?"

"Oh, you mean my sister. She's busy all the time taking care of her kid. She got away to the beach party on T— the other night only by forcing her husband to look after the kid. They had a big fight about it when she got home."

"Does she ever work in the club?"

"Sure. She's off today, though. Even when she's here, she spends more time complaining about her husband than she does entertaining the customers."

"Bad for business."

"She's only twenty-one. She had her kid when she was eighteen and had no idea what it wanted when it started crying. She'd just hold the baby and rock it, and then it would open its mouth real wide and fasten its lips on her arm somewhere. No matter how hard she shook it, the baby wouldn't let go. When she'd try to force it to let go, it cried like crazy again so she had to let it suck on her as long as it wanted. The baby would finally tire and fall asleep, but my sister ended up with these red abscess-like things on her arm."

"That's really bad."

"No, not bad. What's bad is our own mother. She wanted to marry a guy so bad that she introduced us as her nieces. We were kept over at our grandmother's and whenever we went to our mother's place and the guy was there, we'd call her our aunt. We hated it at first; it was humiliating. But before long, even when the guy wasn't there we were calling her 'Aunt.' She never did get married with the guy but even now we call her 'Aunt.'"

"There's just the two sisters?"

"My sister and I? Yes, just the two. I'm five years older. My sister's what they call a *wari-gaami* (leaky pot)—give her a bottle of *sake* and she drinks the whole thing down. That's not to say she doesn't get drunk. When she gets home plastered, her husband gives her hell, so I have to go with her, you see, and coax him into taking it easy. I tell him anything I can think of, true or not. It's really bad, for me, too."

"Sounds really bad."

"Well, I've forgiven my mother. It was a difficult delivery when she had me, but she went through with it. The midwife kept telling her that she should give me up because her own life was in danger, but she went through with it. Kazuhisa, you stole the goat to come and see me, so I have to tell you the truth about myself, too. People like you are rare these days."

Kazuhisa said nothing.

"It was small, but I used to have a pretty nice club in Naha. Then the person I thought was my number-one supporter, an aunt on my mother's side, almost fifty at the time—this person walks off with three million yen I needed to keep the business going. My husband and I, we both looked for her for days, but we couldn't find her anywhere. I had trouble keeping the place running, so I had to let two of the hostesses go. My sister wasn't a hostess yet; she was only a junior high school student then. I was good to them and gave them separation money, but the two hostesses I let go cheated me and collected money from customers who owed on their accounts and then, boom, gone without a trace."

"That's terrible. Unbelievable."

Rie emptied her glass in one gulp and continued her story. As he listened, Kazuhisa prepared another drink for her.

"My husband got hysterical, ranting and raving about how my people didn't behave like real relatives. I didn't know what all he was saying, but I could sense—and I stayed pretty calm and cool about it—that I was probably going to lose him. I told myself that if it's something I'm going to lose anyhow, then when the time comes I just have to let it go. There'll be something to take its place later."

"What happened to the child?"

"I took it . . . but then it died. My husband was a good man; when he laughed you could see he didn't have any of his front teeth—mind you, it wasn't me who knocked them out." Rie laughed. Her teeth were straight and white.

"My sister quarreled with her husband every day from the time her belly started getting big. I think that's why the child is so sickly. I'm always telling her it would be better for the baby, too, for her to get a divorce."

"Happiness isn't a question of being divorced or married." Kazuhisa was beginning to feel the liquor quite a bit now, too.

"Have you come here because there's something you wanted to tell me, something maybe that's got you down? If you set your mind to it, what you want to say will come out by itself. You took that goat and hauled it all the way over here in the boat. This is a place where you talk about things locked up inside you. My sister and I come here to talk about things locked inside. That's how we can be hostesses."

Kazuhisa made no response.

"I wonder if I've ever seen a fellow with quite as much fight in him as you have—stealing the goat and bringing it over here. This deserves service straight from the heart, all I've got. It's really something, what you did—stealing a goat and bringing it all the way over here from T— Island."

Still Kazuhisa made no response.

"You're a gentleman is what you are. You drink and you don't get drunk, don't change a bit.

"I'm adopted."

"Adopted?"

"I'm an adopted husband."

"Adopted. That means the family that adopted you must have money. So how come you go around stealing people's goats?"

Kazuhisa began telling his story, how his wife had control of the money, how each day he was given a small amount to make the day's purchases, how he had to keep a record of the expenditures in a household account book. As he spoke, he complained more and more that not a single thing was in his name. On and on he went about not being suited to the family business, which was fishing, and how all the time he was made to feel inadequate and unimportant.

"But you're adopted into the family now, which means one day everything's going to be yours. That's why they adopted you—to inherit everything. You just have to bide your time. You can't seem too grasping, the way everyone thinks adopted people are."

Being called an adopted husband was distasteful to Kazuhisa. It made him feel he was not taken seriously.

"There are so few adopted husbands that it has to mean something to be one. In time you'll come to see that—what it means to be an adopted husband."

"What it means?"

"Yeah, I'd say an adopted husband is like going off as a bride—to a rich house, that is. There are any number of women who do that. For these women, too, the money eventually just falls into their laps. The greater vessels take time to fill, as the saying goes."

Kazuhisa was disappointed. By what it "means," he assumed she had something more profound in mind. Greater vessels taking time to fill also seemed a little off.

"My adopting family," he said, confused as to what else to say, "has a huge amount of military rental land."

"Then it really is a case of larger vessels taking time to fill. Are you going to start up a business or something later?"

Kazuhisa thought a business would be too much of a bother. Once the land became his, he intended to sell it to a real estate company and put the money in the bank. He could live well enough off the interest. Instead of work, he wanted to fish and learn how to play the *sanshin* or something.

"I guess I can close up now, since you've confided what's in your heart to me."

It had been over two hours and not one customer had come into the club. No one had even stuck a head in the door to take a peek. It didn't seem to make much difference if she left the club open or not.

Rie closed up. Kazuhisa suspected she would now start in on details about the land leased to the U.S. military and the family's other possessions. He assumed she was going to take him to her place for sex, then follow him, and show up a few days later at his house on T– Island. Once he saw this possibility, he could no longer sit by quietly. He had to refuse if she tried to detain him and then get the *sabani* launched and make his way over the dark waters. It was neap tide today, so it would be about now that the tide was out. There would be danger of running aground on the reefs. He was tipsy from all the liquor he had been drinking, but his head churned as he imagined one possibility and another.

"Are you drunk? You look a little pale."

"The boat gets to me. I'm still a little seasick from when I brought over the goat."

"I guess I'll have to look after you tonight. You can sleep with me." Kazuhisa made no reply.

"Just kidding. We'll have to be with each other a little more before we sleep together. Don't be calling out in the middle of the night for your new bride. She's over on T– Island. I'll be going back to my apartment; it's close by. If you can't put up with being all alone, give me a call. I'll come right back. You can sleep here on this couch. I'll take the goat with me. Be sure to lock the door from the inside. I'll be back in the morning at ten. Good night."

"Good night."

Kazuhisa admired how nicely she made her exit.

. 9 .

KAZUHISA FELL ASLEEP as the sun was coming up. At 9:30, Rie woke him up.

He cringed at the thought of going with her and was on the verge of asking if it was really necessary. But to say this seemed altogether too unmanly. Showing his fear yesterday and again today would convince Rie he lacked any nerve. If he started acting as unreasonably now as he had the night before, she'd just tell him to have it his way and go on back to his island and that she'd kill the goat by herself. Kazuhisa wondered why he hadn't slipped away during the night.

For someone going off to kill a goat, Rie was as heavily made up as she was when entertaining her customers. Her face had white powder and her lips were caked with red lipstick. Her naturally thick eyelashes and double eyelids gave her eyes prominent definition; but this hadn't stopped her from applying excessive amounts of eyeliner.

Rie opened some beer. After the two glassfuls they each drank, Kazuhisa had gotten hold of himself. They went out and got into the light van parked out front.

Rie drove. Directly behind Kazuhisa in the passenger seat was the goat. It stuck its head over the glass partition and poked its nose against the back of Kazuhisa's neck. Beyond the village they drove through farm fields and then entered a road through the trees. The sun was strong and a dim light filled his eyes, reflected off the crushed white limestone road pavement and the leaves of the several kinds of trees there. They saw no one else and no other vehicles. Rie, perhaps under the strain of the work ahead of her, had changed completely from the day before. She said hardly a word. The contours of her breasts were clearly visible through her polo shirt; they moved with each hard breath she took.

She parked the van in the weeds by the road, and she and Kazuhisa unloaded the goat. Rie took hold of the rope tied around the goat's neck and led it after her. It followed without resistance, seemingly unconcerned who its master might be. It stopped along the way to nibble on grass and tree leaves. They made their way along an ill-defined path through the trees leading to the beach. Within minutes, they came to the screw pines. The goat required attention almost immediately. Many of the trees had roots running parallel to the ground. Kazuhisa and Rie straddled these easily, but the goat came to a dead stop. Rie very skillfully shepherded the alarmed animal along, at times stopping when it did, at other times coaxing or forcing it ahead. Glimpses of the blue water began to show through the spaces between the trunks and leaves of the trees. A steady sea breeze also came through these openings.

They emerged from the screw pines. The pure white sand, the blue expanse of the sea, and the great columns of clouds riding the horizon leapt into Kazuhisa's eyes, which blinked and blinked in the bright light. They went down to the beach. To both the right and left were large rocks defining the ends of the beach. There was no need to worry that anyone would see them. A plastic bucket, a wooden storm door, and some straw had been placed on the sand within the pitch-black shadow cast by the large rocks. Inside the small bucket there was a kitchen knife, a razor, and a few other things.

"Let's get right to it. If we spend too much time with the goat, we'll let our feelings get involved with it. Are you going to do it?" she asked.

Kazuhisa shook his head firmly from side to side. His legs were shaking slightly.

"Then do exactly as I say."

Kazuhisa assented with a deep nod.

"This goat will taste good," she said. "Its eyes are full of life, it's fur has a nice shine to it, and best of all is how nicely proportioned it is. You really found a good one." She spoke jokingly, in an apparent effort to settle herself down. "I'll give you eighty thousand yen for it." She took out her wallet from the hip pocket of her jeans.

"Not now," Kazuhisa said firmly. If he got the money after the butchering, then he could think he had sold her goat meat rather than the goat itself. His sense of wrongdoing would lessen somewhat. Rie offered no resistance and put the wallet back in her pocket.

Then in a purposeful and firm tone she issued brisk instructions to Kazuhisa. They bundled the forelegs and then the hind legs of the goat, which until then had been licking salt or something from a vine. After a great struggle, they managed to suspend the goat upside down from the branch of a *kuwadiisaa* tree. Rie told Kazuhisa to stand close and hold the bucket under the goat's head. Kazuhisa did as directed, wondering what she was going to do.

"Will you cut the throat?" she asked, holding the razor out to him. Overcome with a sick feeling, Kazuhisa managed finally to shake his head firmly from side to side.

"This is the one part I hate doing, too. But if you don't, I have to do it."

Kazuhisa kept shaking his head. Rie nervously brought the razor forward and shaved the goat's neck. When she finished, she turned toward the horizon, sat down in the formal style with legs folded under her, brought her hands together in prayer, and bowed her head as she earnestly intoned some words. Kazuhisa just stood there, holding the bucket out in front of him. With vacant eyes and mouth wide open, the goat hung calmly, unaware of the fate in store for it.

Rie's eyes and mouth, in profile, were set stiffly. She clasped the long razor firmly in her right hand, in token of her resolve, it seemed, and approached the goat.

"I borrowed this razor from the barbershop. I'm sure they never dreamed I'd be using it to cut open the throat of a goat." She started to smile at Kazuhisa, but then her lips quickly took on a contorted look.

"Are you ready? At first, the blood comes gushing out, so bring it— yes, the bucket—close under the head. What are you doing? You have to hold it tightly. The blood is very valuable. It makes very good soup stock."

Kazuhisa wanted to throw the bucket down and run away. The *kuwadiisaa* tree moved, and a discolored leaf fell into the bucket. The blood gushing out caught Kazuhisa's eye for only a second. He looked away quickly. The goat squealed wildly. Kazuhisa felt sick to his stomach, wanted to throw up, but he held the bucket firmly under the goat's throat. Rie was reciting something that sounded like an incantation, and as she did she took firm hold of the goat's horns and was now using all her strength to control its violent struggle. The squealing gradually subsided into short fits and starts; the blood dropping into the bucket, likewise, had the pitter-patter sound of falling raindrops. The squealing came to an abrupt end. Kazuhisa kept his eyes closed tight.

"It's over," Rie said, a serious tone to her voice. "Let it down."

Kazuhisa placed the bucket on the ground under the tree, undid the netting holding the goat, and let it down. His legs were shaking, but he had regained some control over himself.

"Carry it over there and put it on the rock," she directed him.

Kazuhisa took the goat up in his arms, its head dangling loosely, and apologized to it as he walked. "I'm going to turn over a new leaf and change all my thinking. I'll do everything. And I won't let being an adopted husband bother me," he said to himself as he lay the goat out on the smooth, shiny surface of the rock.

"We have to burn off the hair," Rie said, "so bring all the straw over here. After we burn the fur off, then we carve the animal up. In the ocean, that is. We clean everything, including the intestines, which we turn inside out, so I'll need you to help. Everything will stink and won't taste good if you don't clean it right."

Kazuhisa ran back and forth several times transporting the straw. Rie picked up a handful. "There's a lighter in my pocket," she told him. "Pull it out and light this for me."

He felt for the lighter in the front pocket of her polo shirt and pulled it out. The soft sensation of her breast spread through his fingers.

. 10 .

RIE HAD SAID the day before that she planned to celebrate the first anniversary of her club by treating a number of her regular customers to goat soup. But here it was, 7:00 that evening, and the only ones in the Garden by the Sea Hibiscus were Rie, Kazuhisa, and Junko.

"Take a seat, Kazuhisa," Rie called out from the behind the counter. "It'll be ready in a minute."

Atop a small, portable gas cooker sat a large pot, the top of which was rattling from the boiling goat meat within. A peculiar odor filled the club.

The two women were doing the cooking. Kazuhisa was musing over the scene that morning: they laid the burnt-black goat on the old storm shutter, which they had set afloat in the shallows; Rie cut a long slit in the goat's belly and then skillfully detached the darkened internal organs; these she then removed from the carcass and soaked clean in the sea water; finally, she placed the organs in a second large bucket Kazuhisa held dangling out in front of him. He meant to keep his eyes averted, but at one point, for just an instant, he caught sight of the goat's liver. It was branded in his memory. The dull heaviness of the thing sent shivers through his entire body.

In an effort to forget, Kazuhisa took a drink of *awamori*. A moment later, Junko placed on the table in front of him a tray with bowls of goat soup on it.

"Hold on just a minute. We'll have a toast before we eat."

Kazuhisa stared at the goat soup. His body trembled. He would have to eat it; there was no escaping the goat after they'd killed it. It was just like any of life's problems: the more you tried to run from it, the more of a problem it became. He'd feel better once he ate some. It would make it worth taking the life.

Kazuhisa found it inconceivable that a woman as attractive, as subtly seductive, as Rie had it in her to kill a goat. Seeing her gut and fillet the *taman* that night hadn't made him realize it. After all, there were women on T— Island who could do that easily enough. But a woman who could kill a goat—well, you weren't likely to find any of those on T— Island. He wanted to get back there. He used to feel disappointment that Misako could not gut and fillet a fish, but what did it matter, really? And even if he were an adopted husband, it was the family, after all, that was the most important thing. There was no need for him to be fretting over every little thing.

Junko brought goat soup, rice, and pickles over on a large tray. Everything was laid out for the three of them, and Rie, now seated, poured *awamori* into their glasses. "Bottoms up," Junko said, and they all touched glasses.

"Are we celebrating the first anniversary of the club?" Kazuhisa asked after he had a mouthful of the *awamori*.

"That was the plan, but when I called the regulars, they all said they had other things they had to do—a meeting of a mutual loan group, anniversary of somebody or other's death, a child at home with a fever—something. True or not, who knows. It got to be a hassle, so I gave it up and didn't even call the rest of them. Actually, the anniversary isn't for another two months. So today it's just the three of us celebrating. I wonder what we should be celebrating—there must be something. What do you think?"

"Let's eat first," Junko said. They all began.

"Is this the meat from the whole goat?" asked Kazuhisa, blowing on his soup to cool it.

"This is just the part for us," Rie answered between quick bites on her food. "I sold the rest. I'll be paying you eighty thousand yen, you know. Don't forget to take out the money for the drinks. Eat up, eat up. We could eat ten bowls of the stuff and there'd still be plenty left over. Put in all the *fuuchi-baa* (mugwort leaves) you want, too."

Rie and Junko were both heavily made up for something as ordinary as eating some goat.

"It's really bad if you drink water," Junko said. She stopped eating her soup long enough to drink down some *awamori* as she spoke.

"Fat from the goat hardens inside your arteries. One of our uncles had a stroke from it and he died. He ate goat soup at the celebration when he was elected to the village council and then he drank water because it was so salty. Water's no good, right, Rie?"

"Don't worry. Kazuhisa's drinking *awamori*." Rie poured some into his glass. "If you drink *awamori*, then it won't kill you no matter how much goat soup you eat."

Kazuhisa drank a lot. As the women said, it tasted good with the goat soup. The smell of the *awamori* and the smell of the goat seemed to cancel each other out, making both of them smoother and mild. His portion of soup filled a large *ramen* bowl, but even so he wanted seconds. It was the first time he had ever had such a large amount of the soup. In his college days, he went once with a classmate who was fond of the soup to a goat restaurant near campus, but he didn't like it much. He felt now that the goat fat risen to his head had dissolved in the *awamori* he was drinking and washed through his whole body.

The two women were just as enthusiastically blowing on their soup to cool it. They looked up at Kazuhisa over their bowls as they took sips, exclaiming how delicious the soup was. The Okinawan folk song *"Tōsen dōoi"* (It's here, the ship from China) came over the radio. The song told of Okinawans dancing in celebration along the edges of the harbor as they awaited the approach of a ship back from China laden with goods. Kazuhisa knew little about Okinawan folk music, but it was a familiar song, played often to the free-form dancing called *kachaashii* that the bride and groom, as well as relatives and guests, give themselves over to at the end of a wedding banquet. The cheerful rhythm of the song seemed to quicken the tempo of their eating.

"Kazuhisa, you're eating quite a lot." It was Rie who spoke. "You'll be without sickness the whole year. Us, too. No colds, either."

"The oppression of the summer heat leaves you, too." Junko added.

Still eating, Kazuhisa listened to the almost lisping quality of Junko's voice. A smell likely to provoke nausea in anyone who didn't like the soup poured from the mouths of the two sisters. As they chewed the meat, large drops of sweat formed on their faces and on the backs of their necks.

"Is the air conditioner broken?" Kazuhisa changed the subject.

"No, it's off on purpose," Junko answered. "You should sip the soup boiling hot and in a place where it's as hot as possible. Then all the bad things in your body come out and you feel really good. It even makes you want to have sex. If that happens to you, let me know."

Kazuhisa didn't quite know how he should respond. He gulped down his soup. It set his throat on fire, so he quickly drank some *awamori*.

"Fine, but let's leave sex out of it," Rie said. "Kazuhisa, what size shoe do you wear?"

"Nine and a half."

"My, that's big. I'm going to give you a pair of white shoes as a present. They'll look great on you."

"And you, Kazuhisa," Junko told him, "you have to buy Rie a gold necklace that'll look great on her."

"You shouldn't say he has to. But if you want to give me something, Kazuhisa, I'll be happy to have it. It doesn't have to be a gold necklace, of course."

"Kazuhisa's good at night fishing. Why not a fish or something?"

"I don't want to think about fish when I'm eating goat."

"My sister, you see," Junko began, turning to Kazuhisa, "has gone six years now since her husband ran off, and she hasn't had sex all that time. Strange, I'd say."

Kazuhisa looked at Rie. Her face revealed nothing.

"Junko, go take a look at the stove," Rie addressed her. "If the soup is low, don't turn the heat off; just add a little more water."

Junko, offering no protest, got up immediately and went around behind the counter.

"Check the taste, too. Make sure it's just right," Rie called out in a loud voice toward the counter.

"It's really, really hot, you know," Junko called out from across the room.

"It has to be to clean out all the dirt in your body."

"I'd rather take a shower," Junko called back.

"It cleans out all the dirt that builds up in your body. Junko is young, so she doesn't have as much built up in her as I do. But even so, a whole lot'll come out, I'm sure of it. It cleans out the dirt left from guys, too."

Junko returned from behind the counter and took her seat again. "I'm not like my sister; I don't have any dirt from guys."

"A while back you had trouble when things weren't going so well with your boyfriend. That trouble ends up as dirt in your body."

"Trouble ends up as dirt?"

"As you go on living, one year after the other, the dirt keeps building up. For as long as you live in this world. You don't have to worry, though. If, that is, every now and then you have goat soup like we're doing now and clean it all out."

"Such a useful food!"

"We have Kazuhisa to thank for it. Usually we forget about the dirt in our bodies, and we never think to go to a goat restaurant, even though there's one close by. How many years has it been, I wonder, since I've had goat meat as fresh as this? All the dirt I've accumulated over the years will be cleaned away this night. Thanks, Kazuhisa," Rie said, taking his hand. "I really appreciate it."

It made Kazuhisa feel sorry for the goat, but he nodded his head in response. The two women had set their chopsticks down for a few minutes, but now they threw themselves back into eating, apparently intent on removing every last bit of dirt in their bodies. A stolen goat it may have been, but it was now benefiting others. Kazuhisa could see that his deed was bringing them pleasure.

He drank more. At home, he rarely drank after dinner and didn't care for the taste. It struck him as strange that he was able to drink so much now. His fears hadn't changed, though. Even as the drink took hold of him, he imagined what must be happening by now—people all over the island searching for his father-in-law's *sabani*.

"Have you got any dirt yourself, Kazuhisa?" Junko asked. "You've only just graduated from college, right? I wouldn't think others have left any dirt in you yet."

"Kazuhisa is an adopted husband," Rie said, choosing not to beat around the bush. "There's dirt that just naturally goes with that. Inheriting the estate isn't all an adopted husband does. There are times they're wholly at the mercy of the adopting family."

"Adopted husbands aren't the only ones wholly at the mercy of someone. I have to do what you tell me."

"And sometimes you don't have to," retorted Kazuhisa.

"Same is true for adopted husbands. It's the same for an adopted husband and for us."

"What's so bad about being an adopted husband, anyway?" Rie asked. "I used to have a kid. It's dead now, but . . . but, when it was alive, I had my mother look after it for me. This gave her a certain advantage over me, since she was the one taking care of the baby. Whenever I didn't give her all the money I was supposed to, she'd get angry and tell me how she wasn't going to look after such an ill-behaved kid anymore, you know, trying to put me in an impossible position. That's what she'd do to me all the time. So I'd say okay, I'll put the kid in a public nursery, and I took the kid from her, but then the next day, first thing, she'd come over and want the kid back again. Because of the money, you see. Even though it was all complete strangers, a public nursery was all right with me. I didn't care. But my mother, for some reason, didn't have any money coming to her from the government, although she was quite on in years. All she had was the money I was giving her to take care of the kid. She was living on just about nothing. I couldn't just abandon her."

"You didn't have her come live with you? Your mother, that is." Kazuhisa asked. He didn't seem concerned that he might be prying.

"Rie just then was in the process of getting a new boyfriend. It was a delicate time," Junko answered. "Things didn't work out. Come to think of it, Rie's always in a delicate time."

After what seemed a very long time, the three of them finished eating. The two women had acquired obvious bulges in their bellies. On legs now unsteady from the *awamori*, they carried the dishes and other things back to the counter.

"Kazuhisa, give us a hand," Junko called out from across the room. "If you don't use up some of that energy of yours, you'll get a nosebleed later when you're asleep."

Just as unsteady on his legs, Kazuhisa came around behind the counter. The bowls were nearly empty, but he transferred the bones and leftover soup into a plastic bucket as Junko had asked him.

"Be sure to put the lid on," she said. "The mice and cockroaches will come to it during the night."

Kazuhisa looked for the lid but couldn't find it. "The lid?"

"Not there? It should be—take another look."

Kazuhisa, squatting on his heels, moved around, looking. He didn't see it anywhere. "It's not here."

"Maybe it's in the van. We'll be leaving now, so why don't you come to the van with us. Rie wants the stuff to give her dead child."

Rie was packing the soup into an airtight container. "Little Yuki loved goat soup, so I'm going to give him some at the family altar," Rie said. She seemed oblivious to how Kazuhisa might react.

"He'll be happy," Junko said.

"How old was little Yuki—when he died, that is?" Kazuhisa joined in nonchalantly.

"Four," Junko answered.

"Only four and he liked goat soup?" Kazuhisa's eyes were wide in amazement. The smell and taste of goat meat were so strong that even some adults stayed clear of it. A good number of people believed that after a bowl had goat soup in it, the smell never left, no matter how many times you cleaned it. These people never ate from a bowl that had had goat meat in it.

"It's hereditary with Yuki boy," Rie told him as she placed the airtight container in a plastic bag.

"Was it sickness?" Kazuhisa asked, unconcerned again that he might be prying. It occurred to him that goat soup might have been the cause of the boy's death.

"An accident," Junko answered. "He fell into the ocean riding his bicycle."

"He'll be happy today," Rie said. "Thanks to you, Kazuhisa."

"Will you be all right sleeping alone?" Junko asked, laughing softly.

"Come now," Rie broke in. "It's only your second time with us. You can't be sleeping with either of us yet. Even if you do find me appealing. You sleep here in this chair. We'll be going back to our apartment. Unlike Junko, I live alone. I'd like to have you stay with me, but we'll have to put that off till another time. I have my pride. I'm not the sort of woman who sleeps with a guy right off. So, let's shake."

Kazuhisa took in his the hand she extended. But then his legs went wobbly, and his attempts to steady himself made it seem he was taking her in embrace. Rie disengaged her hand and reproved him.

"Come on now, I just told you tonight's out."

"No, no, I didn't . . ."

"Everything in time. Just be patient." She gave him a wink, like people did in the old days.

It was a little past 11:00 at night. The three of them walked along the path running by the side of the club and came out into a small open area covered with weeds. The women got in the van. Both were tipsy, but Junko got in behind the wheel.

"Here it is—the lid." Junko handed him a circular blue plastic lid that had been left on the passenger seat in front.

"Don't forget to lock the door from inside," Rie told him, very carefully cradling the airtight container in her hands. "You don't have to clean up anything. We'll come in the morning and take care of it. Don't forget to lock, though; stray dogs'll pick up the scent and get in. And then tomorrow, go back home to your wife. Being adopted isn't as bad as you think it is."

"She's right," Junko said. "Go back and be with your wife."

Kazuhisa nodded vaguely.

The van lurched forward and then sped off, zigzagging down the road.

Kazuhisa stretched out on a sofa. As soon as he lay down, he realized that the air conditioner was on too strong. He stayed where he was. He had trouble getting to sleep. His stomach was bloated, and the *awamori* still had hold of his head. The smell from the goat soup was mixed in with his incessant belches. It filled the whole room—it was in the carpet, in the sofa, in the ornamental plants, in his hair, in his clothes. The events of the past two days swirled through his head. The cable radio was on, as was the wall light, but to Kazuhisa the room seemed a vast natural cavern.

There was a telephone on the counter. It was too much trouble for Kazuhisa to think up an excuse to tell his wife and father-in-law. Where in the world have you been, he could already hear her asking him. One after the other, images of the two women and of the goat appeared to him. A little more *awamori*, he thought, might help him sleep, so he took a drink directly from the bottle on the counter. He felt worse afterward and wanted to throw up. He fought it off.

He thought he was wide awake, but in fact he was having a dream. Outside a fenced enclosure where two goats were fighting, goat soup was boiling over in one of the immense pots called *shimmee-naabi* by Okinawans. There were a great number of men and women there; the backs of their T-shirts and blouses were soaking wet. Since no one turned to look at him, Kazuhisa could not tell who any of them were. They were all eating with their heads buried in large disposable plastic bowls from which steam was rising. Restaurants serving goat usually charge fifteen hundred yen per bowl, but these were sold by an organization promoting the consumption of goat meat, and so the price was only three hundred yen. Kazuhisa ate, too, and as he ate, he watched the fighting goats. The goat he had stolen was there waiting to get in. Then he realized he had already killed the goat with Rie. He woke up.

Kazuhisa dozed off again. Rie was bent forward, her white breast exposed through the unbuttoned polo shirt she had worn when they killed the goat. Suddenly, she raised her head and gazed at him. He averted his eyes. And then he was in the Garden by the Sea Hibiscus with the two women. Rie was asleep and Kazuhisa was about to leave. Junko was awake and said, "Let's you and I go to your hotel." Kazuhisa was going back to the *sabani*, not to a hotel. He declined the invitation.

They were standing in the middle of the street, but she began kissing him vigorously. He felt a tingling pain in his lips. Junko's mouth smelled of goat. Consciousness rapidly faded.

. 11 .

THE NIGHT KAZUHISA had stolen the goat and then the night they had eaten the goat were the first since his marriage that he had spent away from home.

When he awoke, he got up from the sofa, held his arm up as if to shield his eyes from the light on the wall, and looked at his watch. It was 9:30.

The goat isn't all I stole; I also took my father-in-law's sabani. For him, all I have to do is return the boat. We've already eaten the old man's goat, so I'll have to give him money. Should I borrow it from my own family? Or should I sell things I own and my wife owns? Catch fish at night and sell them? Didn't I already consider all of these things before I stole the goat?

Rie hadn't given him the money for the goat yet. How much, he wondered, would remain after she had taken out the money for the drinks? In any case, the fact was that he had committed a theft, and therefore, he concluded—as if considering the case of some other person—it was something the police were going to get involved in.

He turned on the spigot behind the counter, washed his face, and rinsed out his mouth. He still felt nauseous. It seemed to him unlikely that he could launch the *sabani*. The telephone was right there in front of him on the counter. He wondered if he should call Misako, who was now either at the village office or at home. What would be the point? Just causing a big fuss did no good; things would work themselves out somehow. He felt nauseous, but the vital power in the goat soup he had filled himself with the night before was slowly but surely spreading to every part of his body.

He opened the refrigerator and drank some orange juice. He heard a sound. He couldn't tell where it was coming from. He strained to hear. Someone was knocking on the door. *Must be Rie,* he thought as he turned toward it. Then he realized Rie had the key.

He opened the door. His father-in-law was standing there. He was wearing a white dress shirt and a tie. Kazuhisa had never seen his father-in-law in a tie before. He immediately tried to step outside, but his father-in-law pushed him back in. His father-in-law surveyed the room and then took a seat at the counter.

"If there's any *awamori*," he said, "I'll have a little."

Kazuhisa mixed him an *awamori* and water. "You came by ferry?" he asked.

"First one out in the morning."

"You sure had no trouble finding me."

"I asked at a few bars if they had noticed any place smelling of goat meat."

"The goat I stole is . . ."

"That goat, let me tell you . . ." The older man spoke much more freely than usual. He told Kazuhisa that that particular goat had a tendency to wander off by itself, so there was a boy there looking after it, a boy in fourth grade in elementary school who was good at tracking down stray livestock—a high-strung boy, with some sort of ability to see into the future. "That night he had a feeling the goat might run off, so he went over to the shed and saw you making off with it."

Kazuhisa was convinced no one was there at the time, so maybe the boy had made up the story.

"When I adopted you, it made me feel small. My wife wasn't the problem, you see; my own seed had been wanting. All I was good for was the birth of only the one child, Misako."

"Yes, but after your wife died, there were chances to remarry. You turned them all down. If you hadn't, you very well might have had a boy."

"If I had remarried, I'm sure I'd have ended up an alcoholic. But you stealing that goat, hauling it in the *sabani*, selling it, buying a woman—having the spirit to do all that, well, it brought peace to my heart. It showed that being an adopted husband hadn't robbed you of your backbone."

"I didn't buy a woman or anything like that."

"Fine, fine, don't worry—I won't say anything to Misako."

"The hostess of this club will be coming any minute now. Ask her; she'll tell you."

"We can't be staying here. Misako's waiting for us to come in the *sabani*."

"The *sabani* is . . ."

"I know where you left it."

It was after 10:00 and Rie and Junko still hadn't come. "Well, let's be off," Kazuhisa's father-in-law said, getting up from the seat. Kazuhisa asked him to wait for just a moment and tore off a sheet from the pad of receipt forms. "Thanks for all you did for me," he wrote on the back. "Please come to T— Island again. I'll catch you another *taman*, and I hope you'll show me your marvelous skill with the cutting knife again."

His father-in-law knew a shortcut to the beach; the town, he explained, had been his stomping grounds back when he was in his twenties. They pushed the *sabani* across the sand and into the water. His father-in-law put Kazuhisa at the helm. It was calm both in the bay and out on the open sea. The prow of the *sabani* cut cleanly through the water, and, borne by the water, it made smooth and easy progress. The older man didn't say anything, but Kazuhisa was now feeling exuberant.

Misako was standing at the spot where her father docked his boat. She greeted them. Kazuhisa turned off the engine, jumped into the shallow water, and pushed the boat up onto the sand.

"Are you all right?" Misako asked, eyeing Kazuhisa intently.

"Everything's fine," he answered. "Looks like I'll be able to be a fisherman now," he said to her as they ascended the incline of the beach. He felt a strange elation. His wife's face showed that she was perplexed.

"Did something happen?"

"No, not really. . . . Just ate some goat soup."

"You're over your seasickness now?"

"The fish you catch just naturally die on their own; a goat, though, you have to kill if you're going to eat it."

"You killed the goat? You did it?"

"Me and another person," he said nonchalantly.

"Only guys could do something like kill a goat."

He was about to tell her that a woman had killed it, but it didn't seem to make any difference, so he said nothing.

"You didn't go away to kill a goat, now, did you? I bet you went to see another woman."

"To drink, yeah."

"If you like drinking, you should do it with Father. I wouldn't want you becoming an alcoholic, though. Come to think of it, people do go all the way over to the main island to drink."

The three of them got into the pickup truck, which Misako had parked under a pine tree. As they drove along the road hugging the shore, Misako turned to her father sitting in the back.

"Does this mean we have to have a child, Father?"

"He has what it takes to steal a goat, so I'm sure you can have all the children you want."

"I tell you—men—you just can't take your eye off them for one minute."

"You've been listening to too much music."

"And you, Father, you drink too much."

He turned his face toward the window.

"Father," Misako turned around to look at him again. "You should stop playing the *sanshin* by yourself and teach Kazuhisa, too. Then the three of us could take a course in folk music at the community center."

"Forget the community center. Hurry up and give me a grandchild."

"Right. You're right—the grandchild comes first."

Their truck entered the main street of the village. At the central intersection, Misako turned off the engine and went into a butcher shop. She emerged from the shop moments later carrying a large plastic bag.

"Meat?" Kazuhisa asked when she got back in the truck.

"We'll take it to Uncle Saburō."

Uncle Saburo was the owner of the goat Kazuhisa had stolen.

"He likes beef a lot," Misako said.

"And the money for the goat?"

"Paid it already."

"How much?"

"Hundred thousand yen."

"All this beef is for Uncle Saburō?"

"All of it."

This was taking things too far, in Kazuhisa's view, however much they might want to win back the old man's favor. The old man was living alone, after all. Kazuhisa was surprised all the same to see that Misako had it in her to manage things as well as she did. He felt gladdened and, for reasons not clear to him, excited by this. It made him want to take a drive around the island.

Pieces of limestone as large as a person's head were piled up around the old man's house. At the ungated entranceway, Misako parked the truck and got out.

"You stay here," her father told her as he opened the door.

"But I want to apologize to Uncle Saburō, too."

"This is no time for a woman to be butting in."

"All right. I don't know exactly what happened anyway."

"No need for you to be bothering about it. It's over with. Let me take care of things from here on out."

Misako handed the package of beef to Kazuhisa and got back in the pickup. "Steady does it," she told him, and drove off.

"I don't want you to be getting ideas in your head about me," his father-in-law told Kazuhisa. "It's not like I became an alcoholic because I wanted to."

"I know that. I've known that for a long time."

They entered through the gate. It occurred to Kazuhisa that the old man might demand he give back the goat, but he walked along with his chest thrust out. The yard was a spacious one, but there were no trees or plants or flowers in it. Strong sea breezes had covered the ground with white sand, and upon this the stone walls surrounding the yard and the red roof tiles above cast sharply defined shadows.

The old man was stretched out on the verandah, his head resting on his right arm as he watched Kazuhisa and his father-in-law approach. He held a fan in his other hand. The father-in-law stepped up on the verandah and sat down cross-legged; Kazuhisa sat on the edge of the verandah. The old man slowly pulled himself up into a sitting position. He poured some tea into two cups, but little came out of the kettle. He went into the kitchen, then reappeared carrying a thermos. He poured a cup for each of them, afterward offering them some black sugar.

Kazuhisa presented the beef to the old man.

"Did you have a good time over there on the main island?" the old man asked him. Kazuhisa took a moment to consider if he had or not, and then nodded his assent.

"You're young, so of course you did. It wouldn't do not to," the old man said. He pulled out the bottle of *awamori* he had placed in the shadows behind the wooden storm shutter. "Consider the goat my present to you."

"I'm afraid he caused you a lot of trouble, Pop." Kazuhisa's father-in-law said this as he topped off his and the old man's cups with *awamori*.

"It was about time for the butcher from the main island to come and buy it, anyway. It's much better to sell it to somebody in the family."

"Isn't it great, though, Pop? What Kazuhisa did—stealing that tough old goat to get money for a woman. Quite impressive. Wouldn't have thought he had it in him, to tell you the truth."

They drained their cups and then took turns refilling each other's.

"We used to do that all the time back in the old days."

"Yeah, those were good times back then, Pop."

"I guess we'll never see the likes of 'em again."

"Yeah, you've got to take what you can while you're young."

"That was a thing of beauty you did, Kazuhisa," his father-in-law said, holding out the bottle of *awamori*. "Get rid of that tea and drink some of this."

Kazuhisa drank the remainder of his tea. He then tossed down the *awamori* his father-in-law poured for him.

"Before he couldn't even get the *sabani* out there on his own," his father-in-law continued. "Really quite remarkable, wouldn't you say, Pop? And all the way to the main island, too. Really quite impressive."

Kazuhisa wondered if it really had been such a thing of beauty. Out in the spacious yard, two gray-colored birds, lovers perhaps, or husband and wife, flitted about. There were no berries or nuts in the yard, so, Kazuhisa guessed, little insects must have drawn them there.

TRANSLATED BY DAVID FAHY

TRANSLATORS

Davinder Bhowmik earned her Ph.D. in modern Japanese literature at the University of Washington, where she concentrated on regional fiction. Her research focuses on questions of history, memory, and representation in atomic bomb fiction, and issues of language, identity, and culture in Okinawan fiction.

David Fahy for many years lived in Okinawa, where he taught at the University of the Ryukyus. He now teaches Japanese at the University of California–Davis and is translating a collection of writings by Matayoshi Eiki.

Norma Field teaches in the Department of East Asian Languages and Civilizations at the University of Chicago. Her most recent book is *From My Grandmother's Bedside: Sketches of Postwar Tokyo* (1997). She is interested in literature, the translation of poetry, and the mechanisms of capitalism.

Hosea Hirata is assistant professor of Japanese at Tufts University. He is the author of several works, including *The Poetry and Poetics of Nishiwaki Junzaburo: Modernism in Translation* (1993).

Kimiko Miyagi is lecturer of comparative literature and English at Meio University and author of "Orikuchi Shinobu: Toward a Holistic Reading of Ancient Texts" (1994) and of regular articles on language and culture in Okinawa's newspapers and magazines.

Michael Molasky is associate professor of Japanese at Connecticut College and is the author of *The American Occupation of Japan and Okinawa: Literature and Memory* (1999). He has recently begun work on a book about jazz and Japanese culture.

Yukie Ohta received her B.A. from the University of Chicago and is now working at Weatherhill Publishers.

Steve Rabson is associate professor of Japanese at Brown University. He is the translator of *Okinawa: Two Postwar Novellas* (1989; reprinted 1996) and the author of *Righteous Cause or Tragic Folly: Changing Views of War in Modern Japanese Poetry* (1998).

Ann Sherif teaches at Oberlin College and is the author of *Mirror: The Fiction and Essays of Kōda Aya* (1999) and a number of translations of modern Japanese fiction and essays.

Rie Takagi received her B.A. in East Asian Languages and Civilizations from the University of Chicago. Her interests include literary translations and postwar Japanese literature.

William J. Tyler teaches modern Japanese literature at Ohio State University. His translations include *The Bodhisattva* and *The Legend of Gold and Other Stories* by Ishikawa Jun. Currently, he is preparing an anthology of Japanese modernist prose from the 1930s.

Melissa Wender teaches about Japan and Korea in the Department of German, Russian, and East Asian Languages and Literatures at Bates College. She is currently writing a book on the literature and social movements of the Korean community in Japan.

SOURCES FOR ORIGINAL TEXTS

———◦◦◦———

LISTED BELOW ARE the most readily available sources today for original Japanese texts of all translations in this anthology, in the order in which they appear.

The editors have made every effort to obtain permission from the authors holding the copyrights to the works appearing in English translation in this anthology. In two instances, these efforts have not been successful. The editor and publisher offer their apologies to the authors or their heirs, recognizing that every endeavor was made to trace them. Copyright remains with the original copyright holder of each work.

POETRY

A verse from "Translations of Old Okinawan Poems" (ca. 1922) by Serei Kunio: Okinawa bungaku zenshu henshu iinkai, eds., *Okinawa bungaku zenshū,* vol. 1 (Tokyo: Kokusho kankōkai, 1991), 94–95. This source will be cited hereafter as *OBZ,*

"My Last Letter" (1927) by Nakamura Kare: *OBZ,* vol. 1, 194.

Two poems by Tsukayama Issui: "Entering the Harbor of a Southern Island" (1931): *OBZ,* vol. 1, 209; and "Dead Body" (1931): *OBZ,* vol. 1, 219.

Two poems by Yamanokuchi Baku: "A Conversation" (1935): *OBZ,* vol. 1, 156–157; prefaced by the poet's reminiscences (1963): *Yamanokuchi Baku zenshū,* vol. 3 (Tokyo: Shichōsha, 1975), 305–316; and "Shell-shocked Island" (1964): *Yamanokuchi Baku zenshū,* vol. 1 (Tokyo: Shinchōsha, 1975), 169.

"Dream Revelations" (1984) by Takara Ben: *Misaki* (Naha: Kaifusha, 1984), 18–23.

FICTION

"Officer Ukuma" (1922) by Ikemiyagi Sekihō: *OBZ*, vol. 6, 51–62.

"Memoirs of a Declining Ryukyuan Woman" (1932) by Kushi Fusako: *OBZ*, vol. 6, 96–102; followed by the author's published rebuttal to her critics, "In Defense of 'Memoirs of a Declining Ryukyuan Woman'": *OBZ*, vol. 6, 102–103.

"Mr. Saitō of Heaven Building" (1938) by Yamanokuchi Baku: *OBZ*, vol. 6, 309–319.

"Dark Flowers" (1955) by Kishaba Jun: *OBZ*, vol. 7, 109–119.

"Turtleback Tombs" (1966) by Ōshiro Tatsuhiro: *OBZ*, , vol. 7, 221–256.

"Bones" (1973) by Shima Tsuyoshi: *OBZ*, vol. 8, 6–14.

"The Silver Motorcycle" (1977) by Nakahara Shin: *OBZ*, vol. 8, 142–158.

"Love Letter from L.A." (1978) by Shimokawa Hiroshi: *OBZ*, vol. 8, 159–173.

"Love Suicide at Kamaara" (1984) by Yoshida Sueko: *OBZ*, , vol. 9, 161–177.

"Will o' the Wisp" (1985) by Yamanoha Nobuko: OBZ, vol. 9, 116–131.

"Droplets" (1997) by Medoruma Shun: *Suiteki* (Tokyo: Bungei Shunjū, 1997), 5–50.

"Fortunes by the Sea" (1998) by Matayoshi Eiki: *Kahō wa umi kara* (Tokyo: Bungei Shunjū, 1998), 5–91.